QUALITY CONTROL FOR
MANAGERS AND ENGINEERS

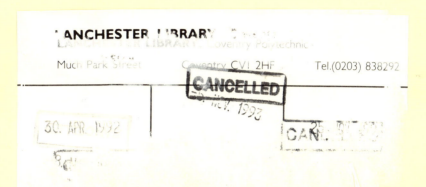

Quality Control for Managers and Engineers

E. G. KIRKPATRICK

PURDUE UNIVERSITY

John Wiley & Sons, Inc.,

NEW YORK · LONDON · SYDNEY · TORONTO

To My Wife Florence

Preface

Quality control in the principal industries has matured in the past ten years to the point where it has become a balanced and effective functional element of the production system. Early emphasis on inspecting quality into the product, subsequent overemphasis of statistical tools, and other "growing pain" considerations have been supplanted by a total administrative and engineering systems approach to the problem of satisfying the quality needs of the consumer.

The complex nature of many modern products has placed greater demands on accuracies, stress measurements, and exotic performance requirements in general. This, in turn, has resulted in an increasing complexity of quality activities—inspection and test, defect identification, causal analysis, and defect prevention. Thus, quality control has become a highly technical function dependent, to a great extent, on a cooperative and supporting relationship between the design engineering and quality-control departments.

In the preparation of this book, I have pursued the general objective of acquainting the student with the entire quality system, emphasizing in detail only those facets of the system which are comprehensible to the average student who lacks on-the-job industrial experience. Essentially the book explores, from a management and an engineering basis, the physical and economic factors involved in quality control from the product-design stage to manufacturing planning to quality assurance. The purpose is primarily to structure the various quality objectives and constraints into a logical and complete pattern. Chapter 2 indicates a systems approach to the quality problem and the balance of the book examines the quality subsystems in some detail. Chapter 3 structures the economics of quality and is preparatory for all cost-of-quality considerations that follow in subsequent chapters. Since all management and engineering students take one or more statistics courses very early in their college programs, a formal presentation of statistical methods is not given in this textbook.

The core of quality control is the technical specifications. The purpose of Chapters 4 through 6 is to develop for the student a simple digest of specifications nomenclature, elementary tolerance systems procedures, and an appreciation of the conflicting objectives and requirements in specifying for quality. Chapter 7 presents an organized treatment of statistical tolerances within the framework of interchangeability alternatives. This material is applications oriented and involves implementation detail as well as theory. A brief summary of production tolerances is given in Chapter 8. The purpose here is to expose measurement and control factors relevant to the quality effort and to integrate these into the quality system. Detailed production tolerance applications problems have been avoided since the average management student lacks the necessary experience with processes and process operations to cope with specific problems in this area.

This is not a statistical methods textbook. Emphasis is primarily on the quality system and the economics of quality. However, the usual statistical tools used in process control and sampling inspection are covered in Chapters 9 and 10. Each quality-control topic involving a statistical method is preceded by a review summary of the required statistical concept. Graphical explanations are utilized extensively in the review summaries and applications examples as an aid to management and engineering students who have been previously exposed to only one or two basic statistics courses.

Chapters 11 and 12 present topics that are a necessary part of a modern quality-control textbook directed at the quality system. The gaging hardware discussion in Chapter 11 is general and may even be omitted from a strictly management-oriented quality-control course. However, the measurement error analysis section of Chapter 11 is vital to a systems approach to quality control. Chapter 12 is an up-to-date summary of computer applications to quality control and includes an analysis of current and future quality-control trends together with a discussion of the relationship of reliability to quality control.

This book is designed for a quality-control course given in an engineering, management, or business school. In deference to the management student, mechanical designs used in examples are carefully abstracted to the point where only schematic drawings involving simple geometries are presented. My experience has indicated that management students have a great deal of enthusiasm for applications problems if they are presented from an appreciations basis, without involving complex engineering detail for which they are not prepared. This approach (and, in fact, the textbook material) has been used for a number of years in a quality-control course given to a mixed management and engineering group of students at Purdue University.

Elwood G. Kirkpatrick

West Lafayette, Indiana
July 6, 1969

Contents

xi

QUALITY CONTROL FOR
MANAGERS AND ENGINEERS

1

Elements of Quality

IMPORTANCE OF QUALITY

The American genius for production punches out everything from baby toys to hardware for space vehicles. It can send submarines under ice caps, make automobiles and airplanes that destroy space, and replenish the ever-changing storehouse of home appliances that take the work out of work. However, despite the variety and quantity of power-assisted products that are manufactured and used, increasing numbers of people have become irritated and disenchanted about things that fail. A fleet of airplanes is grounded because of trouble with a hydraulic valve; millions of automobiles are recalled because of potential defects relating to safety; thousands of TV sets have to be modified after the discovery of potential danger of radiation leaks; and so on. Few products are free from customer complaints and early servicing to correct troubles due to defectiveness.

A great deal of time is uselessly or wastefully spent because of product failure. A new automobile may require the equivalent of a whole week of working time to get it into satisfactory condition. Injuries resulting from defects can and do prove to be expensive to the manufacturers and sellers of products. Newspapers report significantly large compensatory judgments affirmed by the courts for suits brought by consumers against manufacturers and distributors of defective products. The measurement of defectiveness in meaningful economic terms is difficult. Yet, there are clues to its dimensions. The Office of the Secretary of Defense reports procurements of such things as hardware, food, and clothing (items that are typical of what the consumer buys) costing $25 billion a year. The rejection rate is approximately 5%, or about $1.25 billion in rejects. Assuming a similar rejection rate for consumer products, 5% of the gross national product amounts to about $40 billion per year. Another possible index of defectiveness is the frequency of repair. The Defense Department spends $17 billion a year for maintenance. It is difficult to project this expenditure to estimate maintenance costs of consumer products nationally. However, the enormity of these costs indicates the importance of quality.

QUALITY AND THE PRODUCTION SYSTEM

The development of product quality comprises the entire production system, from product design to manufacturing engineering to manufacturing operations, inspection, and test; to shipment, sales, and distribution of the product; and finally to installation and service in the field. The assurance of product quality involves a great deal more than the mere inspection of the product. It is dependent upon more than the use of statistical formulae by the control staff, or the use of sampling tables by the inspector. Quality is the responsibility of everyone in the enterprise.

Whether the manufacturing operation is manual or machine, the production worker is the one who can most effectively control quality or make information available for remedial action to assure quality. The person who exercises the most influence over the worker is the first line supervisor or foreman. The foreman is the coordinator for quality. He instructs, assists, and controls the production worker. He receives technical assistance from quality control, process engineering, and product-design engineering. Thus, product-quality activity is an integral part of every level of the production system. The student of quality control should, as a first step, become generally familiar with

2

the production system. A production system for a typical mechanical-industries product is described by the schematic diagram in Figure 1.1.

The production cycle starts with the customer. The sales department conducts market-research analyses to determine customer needs and receptions of proposed new products and modifications of existing products. Sales forecasts are prepared and submitted to management. The financial department, cooperating with the production department, prepares a production budget and estimates annual product-quantity requirements. Product-design engineering prepares drawings, parts lists, and specifications. The production budget is then adjusted accordingly. Instructions are issued to manufacturing engineering specifying product quantities, delivery schedules, and so forth. The technical information obtained from the product-design drawings, parts lists, specifications, and standards is made available to manufacturing engineering.

Inventory levels, schedules for materials and standard-parts procurement, production schedules, and general plant utilization are determined. Manufacturing engineering develops machine and equipment specifications, and requests for tools. The tool design section prepares design drawings and specifications for the jigs, fixtures, gages, and accessory tools that will be required. Purchasing chooses, contracts with, and retains vendors for materials, parts, machines, tools, and equipment. Complete detailed instructions are prepared regarding process operations and methods, machine loading and utilization, and production schedules. Shop orders are issued and manufacturing is authorized to start production.

Manufacturing operations together with inspection and test activities result in a product that is shipped to distributors and delivered to customers. Consumers use the product, and the experience of use becomes the basis for product redesign which, in part, starts the production cycle all over again. Installation, maintenance, and servicing field data generate engineering changes in product specifications, which may affect any or all of the elements of the production system.

CONTROL OF QUALITY

The control of product quality is a function of two related activities of the production system: (1) development of the general and technical specifications for the product, and (2) assurance of product conformance

3

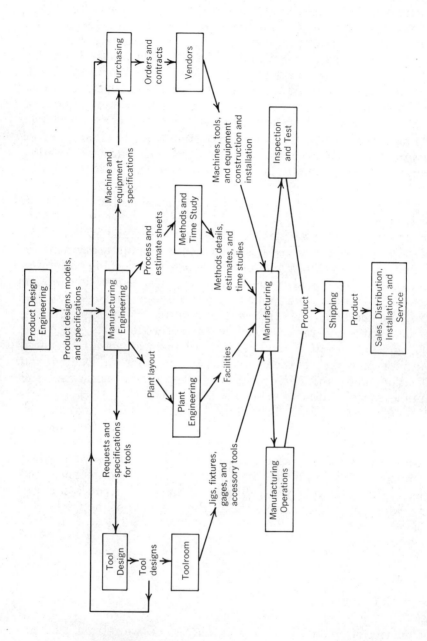

Figure 1.1. Production system.

to the technical specifications. Figure 1.2 illustrates this relationship.

General specifications for the product are mainly determined by the needs and desires of consumers. A given section of the consumer market may indicate a preference for a front-wheel-drive automobile with good directional stability and drive traction (e.g., general specifications). Designing an automobile to satisfy these consumer wants may involve new front-axle, universal-joint, and front-suspension designs. The technical specifications for these designs depend on the functional requirements of the design components and, in part, on the availability and cost of processes and materials.

The assurance of product conformance to the technical specifications depends on process capability, process control, and inspection. Determining process capability is usually considered to be a quality-control function. Decisions concerning process capability feed back to the design process and influence the technical specifications for the product. The procedures for process control are the joint responsibility of quality control and manufacturing supervision. Inspection is concerned with determining the degree to which production output conforms to the established specifications. It should be clear that even though product parts are manufactured to the same specification, the degree of conformance to the specification varies from one part to another. Inspection procedures for assessing conformance range from a simple comparison of measurements of a unit of production output to the specifications, to life-testing a sample of output under actual operating conditions.

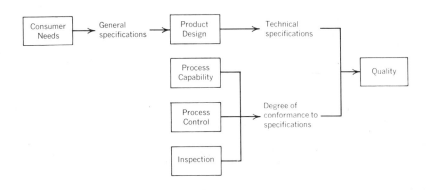

Figure 1.2. Specifications and quality.

Elements of Quality

The *quality* of a product is a composite of many quality character-istics. A *quality characteristic* is a property (e.g., a dimension, a temperature, a pressure, etc.) used to define the nature of a product. Figure 1.3 illustrates some dimensional-quality characteristics for a very simple component part.

The cylindrical pin has *size* quality characteristics of length, diameter, and chamfer, and *form* characteristics of roundness and straightness. Other quality characteristics might be material re-quirements, surface finish, or hardness. A major part of the quality-control problem is due to the fact that even simple products involve hundreds or thousands of quality characteristics and the facts re-garding the quality of these characteristics are widely scattered throughout the production organization.

Each quality characteristic is defined by a specification. For example (see Figure 1.3), the length is to be 2.000 ± 0.010 in., the diameter 0.500 ± 0.002 in., and the chamfer $\frac{1}{32}$ in. $\times$ 45°. The pin is to be round within 0.001 in. on a diameter and straight within 0.005 in.

The word *quality* means different things to different people, par-ticularly at the level of the marketplace. Relative to the production system, however, a distinction must be made between quality due to design and quality as a result of conformance to specifications.

Quality of design refers to a difference in specification for the same functional use. Given two identical component parts, P_1 and P_2, P_1 has a dimensional specification of 0.500 ± 0.001 in. The corresponding dimensional specification for P_2 is 0.500 ± 0.005 in. P_1 is considered to have a better quality of design. Generally, the greater the require-ment for operation, styling, life, and interchangeability of a product item, the better will be the quality of design.

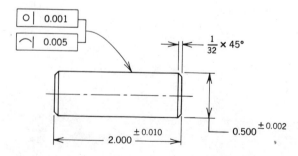

Figure 1.3.   Quality characteristics.

Quality of conformance is the degree to which the manufactured product conforms to the specification. A component quality characteristic has a specification of 0.500 ± 0.001 in. One unit of manufactured output, P_1, measures 0.501 in. Another unit, P_2, measures 0.502 in. P_1 has a better quality of conformance.

Cost and Value of Quality of Design

Even though one design may be superior to another in terms of its quality of design, it may not have increased value in the marketplace. The consumer may not feel justified in paying for this increased technical excellence in an amount commensurate with the increased costs incurred in its production. Usually there exists an optimum to quality of design. Above this optimum, the cost increase due to achieving a greater quality of design is larger than the increase in market value of the design. Below this optimum, the reduction in cost of achieving quality of design is less than the corresponding decrease in market value due to the quality degradation.

Figure 1.4 illustrates this concept. Moving from quality level 1 to quality level 2, an increase in cost c is incurred, together with an increase in value c'; c' is greater than c. However, moving to the right on the quality-of-design axis, a quality level k is reached such that an increase to quality level $k + 1$ generates c and c' values, where c' is less than c. This follows from the fact that as quality of design is increased, costs increase at an increasing rate while value increases at a decreasing rate.

In establishing technical specifications, the quality of design is, at least in concept, an economic decision. Certainly there exists a quality level k (see Figure 1.4) at which marginal value equals marginal cost. However, determining the quality level k involves a complex set of problems. The value curve may be very difficult to determine precisely. In addition, the problem of determining the optimum quality of design is complicated by supply-and-demand considerations. Higher costs due to the greater quality of design must be recovered in increased revenues. But, higher prices tend to lead to lower total revenues depending, of course, on the product-demand curve. Field summarizes the problem very well as follows:[1]

"Economists usually treat variations in quality in terms of 'product differentiation' and set up separate supply and demand schedules for each of the differentiated products. Perhaps a more realistic way of looking at variations

---

[1]Field, D. L. (October, 1966), "Thoughts on the Economics of Quality," *Industrial Quality Control*, Vol. 23, No. 4, pp. 178-184.

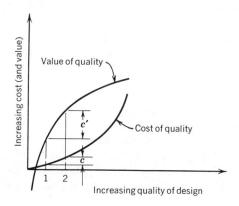

Figure 1.4.   Cost and value of quality.

in the quality of product would be to consider quality as a continuous variable and treat it as a third dimension in the supply and demand curves.

Figure 1.5 shows what happens to a simple demand curve when quality is added as a third dimension to the price-quantity relationship. Note that at any given price level the quantity demanded is greatest for the highest quality – demand increases directly with quality.

Figure 1.6 is a typical supply surface showing one way in which quantities

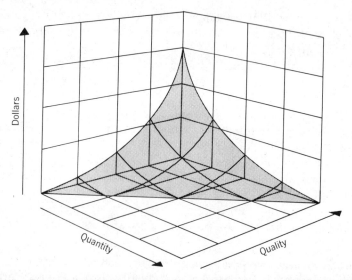

Figure 1.5.   Demand surface. From David L. Field (October, 1966), "Thoughts on the Economics of Quality," *Industrial Quality Control,* Vol. 23, No. 4, p. 180, Figure 3.

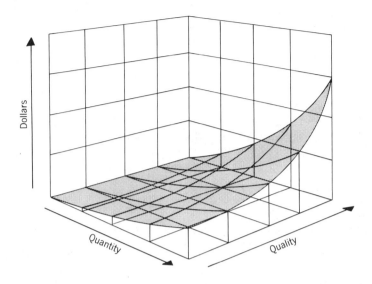

Figure 1.6. Supply surface. From David L. Field (October, 1966), "Thoughts on the Economics of Quality," *Industrial Quality Control,* Vol. 23, No. 4, p. 180, Figure 4.

may vary with price and quality. Note that supply is highest when price is highest and quality requirements are lowest. At any given price level the supply varies inversely with quality.

Obviously, with supply and demand surfaces as shown in Figures 1.5 and 1.6 there can be no equilibrium point. The intersection of supply and demand becomes a curve. In analyzing the supply and demand relationship, we should recognize the tendency for quality substitution. On the supply side, any lower quality will be offered in lieu of higher quality; and on the demand side, any higher quality will be accepted in place of lower quality at the same price. The curved surface concept of supply and demand functions provides some insight into the problems of procurement. Buyer's markets exist when supply exceeds demand, and seller's markets when demand exceeds supply. Quite probably both situations prevail at the same time if quality is considered as the third dimension. High quality is usually pretty much a seller's market, and low quality is almost surely traded in a buyer's market. This follows from the fact that buyers are always eager to substitute product of higher quality and sellers are usually willing to offer product of lower quality. One other important deduction that can be made from these supply and demand surfaces is the fact that suppliers of high quality product have access to the entire market, but suppliers of low quality product have access to a very limited portion of the market.

Economics of Quality of Conformance

Quality control is primarily concerned with product-output conformance to the technical-design specifications. Two interrelated functions are involved: (1) determining the capability of processes to meet specifications, and (2) monitoring processes to assure conformance to specifications. Generally, a greater degree of conformance can be obtained by utilizing more costly processes which have better capabilities. The use of a more capable process usually results in decreasing quality losses at a decreasing rate as shown in Figure 1.7. This suggests the possibility of there being an optimum to quality of conformance corresponding to a minimum point on the total cost curve. Total cost is considered to be the sum of the process-cost and quality-cost components, where quality cost refers to scrap, rework, and rectifying inspection.

Rectifying inspection is defined to be a 100% inspection of product output to assure product conformance to the design specifications. It is a necessary inspection operation, since the process is not capable of attaining the quality level specified by design. It is possible to use processes that are too good. A process obtainable at a lower cost may result in a higher rate of defective output (i.e., lower quality of conformance). However, the cost of the rectifying inspection required to bring output to an acceptable quality level may be considerably less than the decrease in process cost. Thus the process with the lesser conformance may, in fact, be more economic.

On the other hand, it may be economical to use a process which is too good for a given specification, when the alternative is a capital investment all out of proportion to the potential gain. Also, the cost of an owned process, plus the cost of a rectifying-inspection operation, may be more economic than a capital investment to obtain a new process with adequate capability of meeting specifications.

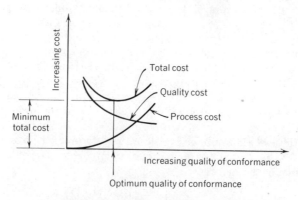

Figure 1.7.   Quality of conformance.

The goal of any quality-control program is quality assurance. The problem of assuring quality involves two distinct design phases: (1) the design of a product whose quality is economic in terms of its end use, and (2) the design of a set of processes which will, at economic levels, assure the attainment of the defined quality. The first phase deals with the *quality of design*, whereas the second is concerned with *quality of conformance*. It should be clear that quality does not have the popular meaning of "best" in any absolute sense. To industry, it means best for certain customer conditions.

For example,[2] a manufacturer is faced with two alternatives in the manufacture of a simple component part involving one punch-press operation. He may use a stock die and scrap materials to produce the part at a unit cost of $0.02. The quality of this part cannot be guaranteed for conditions of excess load or temperature. Or, he may use a special die and special materials to produce the part at a unit cost of $0.08, and he can guarantee the part for high load and temperature conditions. The customer has an application where load and temperature conditions are of no consequence but where cost is most important. The decision is to manufacture the part using a stock die and scrap materials. Thus the choice of quality is determined on the basis of the actual application and cost conditions specified by the customer.

Quality Control

The word *control* means to exercise a restraining or directing influence over something. Production control, inventory control, and cost control are examples of influencing or directing certain facets of the production system. Regardless of the element that is being directed, control consists of four basic procedures: (1) setting standards, (2) measuring variances from the standards, (3) taking corrective action to minimize the variances, and (4) planning for improvements in the standards and in conformance to the standards.

Quality control is a staff function whose objective is to coordinate the production facilities to produce a product at the quality level defined by the design specifications. The quality-control department should not attempt to assume the individual quality responsibilities that are integral parts of the day-to-day work of the line, staff, and functional groups which hold them. The marketing man can best evaluate the customer's quality needs. The design engineer can most effectively establish the technical specifications for quality. The line supervisor is the one who can best concentrate on building quality.

Quality control is a coordinating and integrating function. The

---

[2]This example is taken from Feigenbaum, A. V. (1961), *Total Quality Control*, McGraw-Hill, New York, p. 13.

quality-control group exists to lend support to manufacturing, and to report to management regarding the quality status of the company's products. Its principal job is to coordinate and integrate the various quality responsibilities to assure product conformance to the quality levels specified by design engineering. The basic problem confronting the quality-control group is one of communication. The modern production system is a complex organization. It is so large that the product designer, process engineer, production worker, and inspector are different persons in widely separated organizational groups. Furthermore, for any typical consumer product there are hundreds and even thousands of quality characteristics involved, and the facts relative to these quality characteristics are widely scattered throughout the organization.

STANDARDS FOR QUALITY

The technical specifications for the product are the core of quality control. All quality activities stem from the specifications. The specifications' effectiveness in controlling quality is dependent on a *standard* for interpretation and a method of measuring the quality characteristic that is consistent with the standard. For example, in Figure 1.3, the specification for roundness reads "round within 0.001 in. on a diameter." In this instance, the geometric interpretation is that the form of the product part may vary only within a true cylindrical zone whose thickness is 0.0005 in. as shown in Figure 1.8.

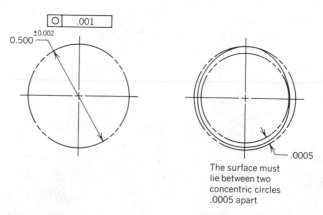

Methods of specifying roundness on drawings

The surface must lie between two concentric circles .0005 apart

Figure 1.8. From MIL-STD-8B (November 16, 1959), Superintendent of Documents, U. S. Government Printing Office, Washington, D. C., p. 50.

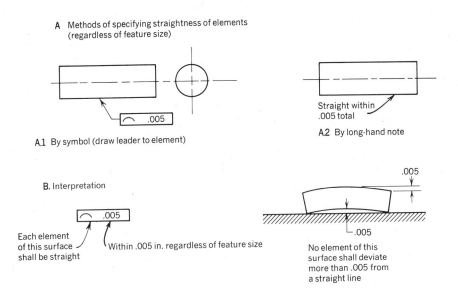

Figure 1.9. From MIL-STD-8B (November 16, 1959), Superintendent of Documents, U. S. Government Printing Office, Washington, D. C., p. 41.

The specification for straightness, "straight within 0.005 in.," views a cylinder as being composed of an infinite number of straight-line elements each parallel to and equidistant from a center line. The specification means that no element of the cylindrical surface may deviate more than 0.005 in. from being a straight line as shown in Figure 1.9.

The specification and a standard interpretation of the specification lead to a standard method of making a physical measurement of a product unit to assess its conformance to the design requirement. The specification will control the variability of the quality characteristic in question only if the specification (1) leads to a standard interpretation of the quality requirement, and (2) is translatable into a standard measurement method for assuring conformance.

Because of their extensive procurement activities, the defense agencies have had a great influence on the use of quality-control techniques. The Department of Defense is largely responsible for the development of many of the quality standards used today. A list of the sources of these quality standards, and others in common use, follows.

Department of Defense Standards:
Available from Information Officer,
Department of Defense, Pentagon Building,
Washington, D. C., 20311

Military Standards:
Available from Superintendent of Documents,
U. S. Government Printing Office,
Washington, D. C., 20402
Also available from U. S. Naval Supply Depot,
5801 Tabor Avenue
Philadelphia, Pennsylvania, 19120

American Standards:
Available from American Standards Association,
10 East 40th Street,
New York, New York, 10016

International Standards:
Available from American Standards Association.

British Standards:
Available from British Standards Institution,
2 Park Street,
London W. 1, England

Canadian Standards:
Available from Canadian Standards Association,
235 Montreal Road,
Ottawa 7, Canada

American Society for Quality Control
161 West Wisconsin Avenue
Milwaukee 3, Wisconsin

SUMMARY

Figure 1.10 summarizes the elements of quality control. The *quality* of a product is a composite of quality due to design and quality as a result of conformance to specifications. *Quality of design* depends on the function, styling, life, and interchangeability requirements of the product, and the availability and costs of processes and materials. Quality of design is in concept an economic decision. Cost and value analysis is required to determine optimum quality-of-design levels. *Quality of conformance* involves three principal quality activities: (1) process capability, (2) process control, and (3) inspection. The degree of conformance that is desirable is an economic decision in-

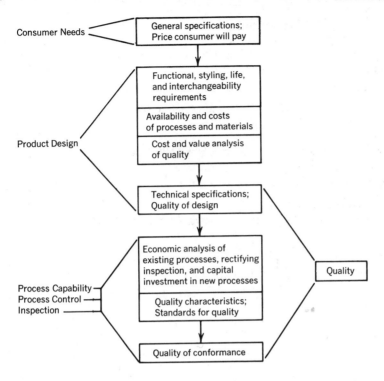

Figure 1.10. Quality-control elements.

volving alternative combinations of existing processes, rectifying inspection, and capital investments in new processes.

A *quality characteristic* is the elemental building block with which quality is constructed. Each quality characteristic is defined by a *specification*. The specification is the core of quality control. To be effective, as a control device, the specification must be related to a *standard* for interpretation and be translatable into a specific available method of physical measurement.

REFERENCES

Feigenbaum, A. V. (1961), *Total Quality Control,* McGraw-Hill, New York, p. 13.

Field, D. L. (October, 1966), "Thoughts on the Economics of Quality," *Industrial Quality Control,* Vol. 23, No. 4, pp. 178-184.

Hansen, B. L. (1963), *Quality Control,* Prentice-Hall, Engelwood Cliffs, New Jersey, Chapter 1.

Juran, J. M. (1962)., *Quality Control Handbook,* McGraw-Hill, New York, Chapter 1.

Military Standard MIL-STD-8B (1959), "Dimensioning and Tolerancing," Superintendent of Documents, U. S. Government Printing Office, Washington, D. C.

REVIEW QUESTIONS

1. State the two basic activities of the production system which are involved in the control of product quality.

2. What determines the general specifications for a given product?

3. What department of the manufacturing organization is responsible for determining the technical specifications (see Figures 1.1 and 1.2)?

4. State the two main factors that determine the technical specifications.

5. The assurance of product conformance to the technical specifications depends on three basic production elements. State these elements.

6. Define the term quality characteristic.

7. Define quality of design and quality of conformance.

8. A designer considers two possible specifications for a quality characteristic: (a) 0.750 ± 0.001 in., and (b) 0.750 ± 0.005 in. Which specification represents the better quality of design?

9. Assuming the specification 0.750 ± 0.005 in. is adopted and two manufactured parts have actual sizes of 0.755 in. and 0.752 in., which part has the better quality of conformance?

10. The cost and value of quality curves (Figure 1.4) indicate that, for quality-of-design levels close to the origin, increases in quality of design result in costs c and c' where $c' > c$, whereas moving to the right on the quality-of-design axis results in $c > c'$. State the reason for the inequality being reversed.

11. Discuss the possible existence of an optimum quality of conformance (see Figure 1.7).

12. The statement has been made that "it is possible to use processes which are too good." Consider two possible processes A and B for a given production job, where the operating cost for A is \$10,000 and for B is \$6000. Process A is superior. A rectifying inspection is required to bring the output-quality level for B up to that for A. For what range of rectifying inspection cost is it more economic to utilize process B for the production job? (Assume that the cost of the extra scrap product generated by process B is \$1500.)

13. State the four basic procedures involved in control of any element of the production system.

14. State two constraints that generate the basic communications problem confronting the quality-control department.

15. What two conditions are necessary for a specification to be effective as a control device?

2

The Quality System

THE QUALITY-CONTROL FUNCTION

The quality-control function is actually a collection of activities within the production system. Sales, purchasing, product design, process development, manufacturing, inspection, and so forth, are all different functions within the production system. Yet, each of these activities includes a sub-activity devoted to quality. The sales department conducts market-research analyses which are concerned with (among other things) the evaluation of consumer-quality needs. One of the many product-design tasks is to establish technical specifications to control functional product characteristics within certain quality boundaries. And so on, each production function includes quality as one of its considerations. A fundamental question is whether or not quality control is really only a label for a set of diverse activities. Or, is there some unifying physical or conceptual framework that makes quality control a separate function in its own right? In this connection, an interesting analogy can be drawn between financial control and quality control.

Financial-control problems existed even for eighteenth- and nineteenth-century industries. The industries were small and primitive. Usually they were of the single-proprietorship form, where the owner operated and controlled the business enterprise. The owner also handled the financial aspects of the business and the problem of balancing incomes and expenses was relatively simple. However, this situation changed rapidly in the twentieth century. Industries grew in size and complexity. Giant corporations with many plants and vendor suppliers became commonplace. Within a single plant, many departments received income in the form of money, materials, and machines. All departments incurred expenses in various forms. The problem of balancing incomes and expenses for such large business enterprises became very complicated.

A solution to the problem was the development of a unified approach to the many financial activities of the business. All incomes and all expenses, wherever incurred, would be identified and evaluated. A common *accounting* language was invented to facilitate identification and evaluation. Techniques were developed to summarize assets and liabilities, incomes and expenses, and profits and losses. Other techniques, such as depreciation and accruals, were developed to facilitate handling the more complex income and expense variables. Tools, such as budgets and standard costs, were devised to establish standards of performance.

The unified approach to the financial activities of the business made it possible to (1) set broad financial policies, (2) define specific financial objectives, (3) assign financial responsibilities, and (4) develop a financial control system involving standards of performance, measures of variances from the standards, and requisite actions to eliminate or at least minimize the variances.

Returning to the quality-control function, one observes some parallels to the financial-control function. The life of a business enterprise depends on maintaining a balance between incomes and expenses (i.e., financial control). The quality-control function is also vital. A company can remain in business only so long as the quality of its product is acceptable to the consumer. Incomes and expenses occur in every department of the business. Similarly, every department in the company influences the quality of the company's product. The concept of financial control is based on the identification and evaluation of all incomes and expenses. A corresponding conceptual approach to quality control is that all efforts for achieving quality and all benefits derived from achieving quality be identified and evaluated. Efforts and benefits, in this connection, correspond to expenses and incomes (i.e., costs of achieving quality and cost reductions due to the achievement of quality). Various quantitative tools have been invented for financial-control purposes. Quantitative tools have also been developed for quality control (e.g., process capability, control charts, sampling-inspection plans, and other statistical measures).

Finally, the benefits accruing from a unified quality-control effort are analogous to the returns expected from a unified financial-control effort: (1) setting of over-all company quality policies, (2) defining specific quality objectives, (3) assigning quality responsibilities, and (4) developing a quality-control system whereby quality standards are defined and variances from the standards trigger corrective quality actions.

SYSTEM CONCEPT

A *system* is a physical or conceptual entity comprised of interdependent parts that interact within boundaries established to achieve some common goal or goals. The electrical engineer works with electrical systems, the mechanical engineer with mechanical systems, and the production engineer with production systems. Figure 2.1 illustrates a production system. Materials, labor, and other components constitute the *input* to the system. Goods and/or services are the *output* from the system.

Most systems incorporate some kind of a control mechanism. In a mechanical or electrical system this control is accomplished by some kind of automatic *feedback*. The feedback device senses an imbalance between actual output and desired output and varies the input to correct the variance. Thus, feedback provides a *closed loop* from the output to the input. Figure 2.2 shows a production system with a control mechanism. The information lines represent both communication inputs and feedback information regarding actual outputs. Technical specifications, procedure manuals, production orders, time

Figure 2.1.   Production system.

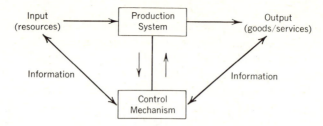

Figure 2.2. Controlled production system.

standards, and quality standards are a few examples of communication inputs to a production system. Feedback can take the form of such items as time cards, machine-downtime reports, and quality reports.

The systems-engineering approach to problems makes it possible to solve problems in one field by forming an analogy with another field. The mechanical engineer may solve a mechanical problem by forming an analogy with an electrical system; the electrical engineer may solve an electrical problem by forming an analogy with a mechanical system. Analogies between mechanical, electrical, and fluids systems facilitate the solution of engineering problems. One very useful aspect of the analogy is that it makes possible construction of models of systems which are much smaller and cheaper than full-scale designs.

Models may be physical, schematic, or mathematical. Using the model to simulate the real system, input variations' effects on output can be observed and useful predictions can be made regarding the system. It seems possible that the analogy technique may become an important means of solving production problems. However, the dynamic nature of a production system makes it very difficult to form an analogy with a physical system and thereby construct a useful model. Not only are the inputs to a production system changed in response to feedback information, but the system itself may undergo changes. Furthermore, the output changes not only in quantity, but also in quality and configuration of the product. Thus, the problem becomes one of controlling a very dynamic system and this system, since it is partly composed of people, changes from one moment to the next.

The principal characteristic of a systems approach to a problem is that it involves an orderly way of assessing and meeting a requirement. The system designer starts at the highest echelon of the system and reaches a decision regarding the optimal manner of achieving the desired output with the available inputs (or modifications of inputs). Usually systems are comprised of subsystems and subsubsystems which can be designed and evaluated in the same manner as the main system. The designer progresses deeper into the total system in a layerlike manner, in increasing levels of detail, proceeding from functional requirements to solid implementation. Thus gradual analysis of the system is achieved as shown in Figure 2.3.

An important principle in system design is that the subsystem contributions are not necessarily maximized; the goal is the optimization of the main system. Synthesis of the subsystems into the main system may indicate that one or more subsystems must operate at other than optimum levels to achieve over-all optimization of the main system.

The interdependent parts of the system are called subsystems. These subsystems are frequently referred to as systems. In this sense, the following paragraphs will refer to the *quality-control system*. Actually, quality control is a subsystem of the production system.

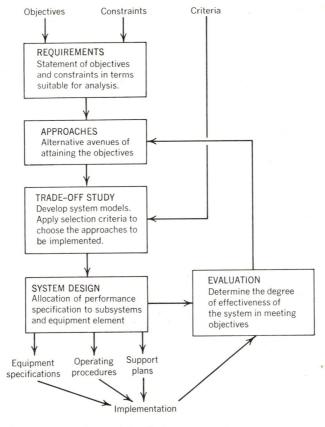

Figure 2.3.   Systems approach.

QUALITY SYSTEM

The quality system is the network of administrative and technical operations required to manufacture a product of specified quality standards. Such a system is shown in Figure 2.4.

Subsystem S_1 is regarded as a communication system closed on the consumer's quality requirements. In this concept of the quality system, consumer needs and desires are assessed by the business organization. Products, processes, and distribution methods are planned to effectively meet these needs and desires. The planning information flows to manufacturing operations where the plans are carried out and the product is manufactured. Finally, the product is distributed to the consumer and the needs and desires of the consumer are filled.

This closed-loop communications system should operate continuously. Changes in consumer needs and desires should be detected as quickly as possible so plans can be promptly revised and operations changed accordingly. Thus, the consumer's revised needs and desires are best served. The concept of the business organization as a dynamic feedback system constantly "tuned in" to the consumer's needs clearly implies that the organization should be market oriented. The organization continues in existence if it fills needs and desires of consumers, not if it produces products that are unattractive to the consumer.

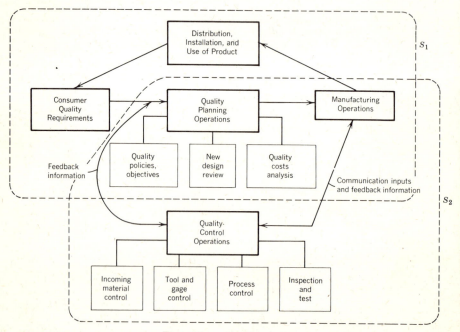

Figure 2.4.   Quality system.

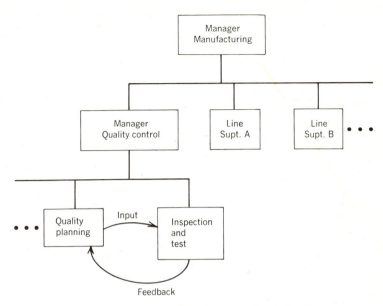

Figure 2.5.   Centralized quality-control organization.

Subsystem S_2 is a communication system closed on the quality-planning function. From the standpoint of quality decision making, S_2 is really a network of feedback systems. The communications inputs to the quality-control operations are those from quality planning, manufacturing operations, and installations and servicing data from the field. These feedback systems must be well designed from the standpoint of (1) prompt feedback so corrective action can be quickly applied, and (2) continuing feedback, that is, the feedback network should not break down. Design of the feedback network should incorporate the concept of self-correction. Responsible managers must be made aware of any breakdown in the feedback network, and hopefully the breakdown will be quickly corrected.

Quality control is primarily a planning and control, or feedback function. Too much division of responsibility interferes with the basic purpose of the function. For example, if the inspection and test operations were separated from quality control and assigned under manufacturing supervision, the basic purpose of the quality-control function might be nullified. Figures 2.5 and 2.6[1] indicate the difficulties that could develop.

---

[1]For an excellent discussion of quality organizations for a variety of manufacturing industries, see A. V. Feigenbaum, *Total Quality Control*, McGraw-Hill, New York, 1961, Chapter 4.

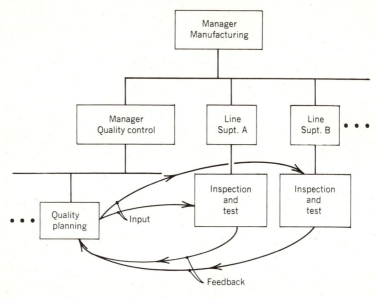

Figure 2.6.   Divided quality-control organization.

Figure 2.5 shows the short and direct feedback loops found in a centralized quality-control organization. Prompt feedback of quality information and early corrective quality action are to be expected from such a feedback system. Figure 2.6 illustrates the longer loops and additional loops for feedback of quality information in a decentralized quality-control organization. The usual result of such a feedback system is slow response in quality information feedback and corrective quality action. Further, such a system frequently leads to "buck passing" when product of poor quality is produced. Manufacturing supervision and quality control are each reluctant to accept responsibility for the poor quality product.

QUALITY PLANNING

The *quality planning* subsystem (see Figure 2.4) includes three principal quality activities: (1) setting over-all quality policies and objectives for the business, (2) conducting new design reviews, and (3) carrying out quality-cost analyses.

Quality Policies and Objectives

Some distinction should be made between the problem of establishing the company's broad objective of meeting the quality needs of its customers, and the much narrower technical objective of meeting the quality specifications. Setting company policies and establishing quality objectives is primarily a business problem. This broad planning for quality involves the business, economic, and management activities associated with quality. Reliable estimates must be made regarding what constitutes "market quality," what quality level is required to compete in the market, and whether or not this quality level will be affected by changes in competitors' quality levels or changes in customer preferences. These are really quality-of-design considerations and, as pointed out in Chapter 1, cost and value analyses are essential to establish optimum quality-of-design levels and assure a satisfactory return on the quality investment.

Factors of quality reputation and customer goodwill are also involved. Should the company aim for quality leadership, a respectable quality grade, or merely marginal quality? Will it be economic to strive for a positive quality reputation and use this as a weapon in advertising? Should emphasis be placed on product guarantees to minimize losses to customers? All of these considerations are business and economic in nature. How they are handled will vary considerably from one company to another, and with market conditions which change from one time period to another. The principal managerial activities pervasive to these considerations are (1) setting over-all quality policies, (2) establishing specific quality objectives, (3) defining quality responsibilities, (4) evaluating quality results, and (5) acting on quality deficiencies.

New-Design Reviews

A *new-design review* is a formal, documented, and systematic study of a new product design by specialists from every department of the production system. An effective design-review procedure accelerates the maturing of all elements of a design—function, reliability, value, and appearance. Since many design changes occur routinely in the development of any new product, the costs of making changes may be a significant part of the total cost of producing and marketing a new product. Figure 2.7 gives typical comparative costs of making design changes with and without design reviews.

25

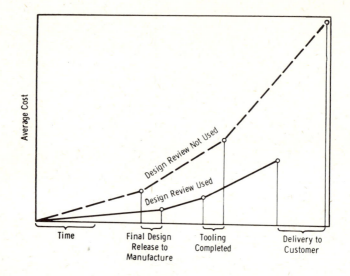

Figure 2.7. Relative average cost of making design changes with design reviews versus without design reviews. From R. M. Jacobs (February, 1967), "Implementing Formal Design Review, *Industrial Quality Control*, Vol. 23, No. 8, p. 404, Figure 4.

It is usually desirable to have design reviews at more than one point in the design and development cycle of a new product. Figure 2.8 indicates the points in the product's life cycle where design reviews are most productive.

There are three basic types of design review: (1) preliminary, (2) intermediate, and (3) final. Preliminary design reviews are conducted to establish early communication among the marketing, engineering, purchasing, and manufacturing departments. The purpose of the pre-

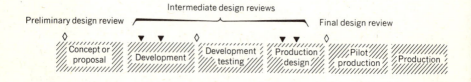

Figure 2.8. Product life cycle and design review schedule. From R. M. Jacobs (February, 1967), "Implementing Formal Design Review," *Industrial Quality Control*, Vol. 23, No. 8, p. 400, Figure 1.

liminary review is to confirm the product design as being representative of the customer's requirements and to expose divergent requirements and/or interpretations.

Intermediate design reviews take place during the development, testing, and production-design stages of the new product design. These reviews provide a recheck of product-conformance requirements in the light of development and design experience, and take into account any problems that may develop with long lead-time components.

Final design reviews occur when material lists and drawing specifications are completed and when pre-production product models are tested and analyzed. This is the last opportunity for design changes without seriously affecting production schedules. The cost of design revisions at this point is considerably less than the cost of accomplishing the same changes later by field revisions or model changes. The final review concentrates on final-performance requirements, critical cumulative tolerances, and servicing-in-the-field considerations. This review disposes of all questions before the design is released to production.

The examples given in the following figures indicate the general nature of design reviews. Figure 2.9 shows the participants in a representative design-review committee and their respective responsibilities. Figure 2.10 presents a part of a typical design-review checklist.

Quality control is, of course, only one of the participants in the design-review procedure. The principal aspects of the design review which are relevant to the quality effort can now be summarized. During the review procedures, an analysis is made of all product functional, life, and interchangeability requirements and their associated technical specifications. This analysis leads to classification of all quality characteristics and definition of specific quality levels required and standards for checking product conformance to these levels. The classification of characteristics concept (denoted "C of C") is especially important in quality-control work.

Quality characteristics are classified according to their relative importance. For example, a twofold classification system rates each quality characteristic as "Significant" or "Minor." A Significant characteristic is one that is to be controlled with special emphasis. A Minor characteristic is one that, if defective, does not materially reduce the usability of the product for its intended purpose. Another C of C example is a classification prescribed by *Military Standard* MIL-W-9411A wherein all characteristics are rated as "Critical," "Major," or "Minor." Several benefits are derived from a classification system. The system is a means of placing emphasis on product charac-

Group Member	Responsibilities	Type of Design Review		
		PDR	IDR	FDR
Chairman	Calls, conducts meetings of group and issues interim and final reports.	X	X	X
Design engineer (s) (of product)	Prepares and presents design and substantiates decisions with data from tests or calculations.	X	X	X
Reliability manager or engineer	Evaluates design for optimum reliability consistent with goals.	X	X	X
Quality-control manager or engineer	Ensures that the functions of inspection, control, and test can be efficiently carried out.		X	X
Manufacturing engineer	Ensures that the design is productible at minimum cost and schedule.		X	X
Field engineer	Ensures that installation, maintenance, and operator considerations were included in the design.		X	X
Procurement representative	Assures that acceptable parts and materials are available to meet cost and delivery schedules.		X	
Materials engineer	Ensures that materials selected will perform as required.		X	
Tooling engineer	Evaluates design in terms of the tooling costs required to satisfy tolerance and functional requirements.		X	
Packaging and shipping engineer	Assures that the product is capable of being handled without damage, etc.		X	X
Marketing representative	Assures that requirements of customers are realistic and fully understood by all parties.	X		

Group Member	Responsibilities	Type of Design Review		
		PDR	IDR	FDR
Design engineers (not associated with unit under review)	Constructively reviews adequacy of design to meet all requirements of customer	X	X	X
Consultants, specialists on components, value, human factors, etc., (as required)	Evaluates design for compliance with goals of performance, cost and schedule.	X	X	X
Customer representative (optional)	Generally voices opinion as to acceptability of design and may request further investigation on specific items.			X

Figure 2.9. Design-review group responsibilities. From R. M. Jacobs (February, 1967), "Implementing Formal Design Review," *Industrial Quality Control*, Vol. 23, No. 8, p. 399, Table 1.

teristics according to their relative importance to end-product requirements. This facilitates the development of inspection and test plans, and makes possible directed allocation of limited resources—inspection and test equipment, inspectors, quality-control staff, and so on. Also, a classification system aids in the standardization of product-acceptance criteria.

The next design-review procedure that is pertinent to the quality effort is an appraisal of the technical specifications for all quality characteristics (which have now been classified) relative to the process capabilities, both in-plant and vendor. Problems are identified for both process-control and inspection activities. Decisions are made concerning specific gaging methods to be used and gaging hardware that is required for checking the conformance of each quality characteristic to its technical specification. The objective is to identify and prepare for all possible quality troubles before the start of formal production. If the review analysis discloses serious variances between the technical specifications and the process capabilities, the tolerances in question will be reconsidered from the standpoint of interchangeability objectives. Interchangeability alternatives and their effects upon production tolerances and costs are discussed in some detail in Chapter 7.

	Yes	No	Not Applicable

1. Does the design *specification* include all customer requirements?
2. Does the design meet all functional requirements?
   a. Are maximum stresses within limits through full range of travel, load, voltage, etc.?
   b. Is derating utilized, wherever possible, to increase reliability?
   c. Does design represent optimum in simplicity?
   d. Have failure modes of critical elements been considered?
   e. Are proper locking devices utilized?
3. Is the design satisfactory for all environmental conditions?
   a. Temperature (operating, transportation, and storage)?
   b. Humidity (operating, transportation, and storage)?
   c. Vibration (operating and transportation)?
   d. Shock (operating and transportation)?
   e. Corrosive ambients (salt air, sea water, acids, etc.)?
   f. Foreign materials (dirt, oil, sand, grit, etc.)?
   g. Immersion (water, oil, inerteen, etc.)?
   h. Pressure and/or vacuum?
   i. Magnetic fields?
   j. Sound ambients?
   k. Weather?
   l. Radio interference?
   m. Nuclear radiation?
4. Has available data on similar designs been reviewed, including:
   a. Factory test malfunction reports?
   b. Field service trouble and failure reports?
   c. Customer complaints?
5. Have standard, time-tried parts been used wherever possible?
6. Are drawing and specification tolerances achievable in production?
7. Does the design minimize installation problems?
8. Does the design minimize maintenance problems?
9. Has a thorough value engineering or MATS analysis been made?
10. Have all provisions for personnel safety been included?
11. Has a study of product appearance been made?

Figure 2.10. Typical design-review check list. From R. M. Jacobs (February, 1967), "Implementing Formal Design Review," *Industrial Quality Control*, Vol. 23, No. 8, p. 402, Table 3.

Quality-Cost Analysis

In studying economic factors in quality management, there are two principal areas to be examined — the broad business and management considerations associated with quality planning and the more detailed area of economic optimization in connection with specific operating quality costs. The former is concerned with quality-of-design alternatives, market quality considerations, return on the quality investment, quality budgets, and quality-cost control. The latter area includes all specific quality costs stemming from operations and decisions at the manufacturing-operations level. What are the costs of rectifying inspection for specific manufacturing operations? What are the alternative costs associated with various sampling-inspection plans? How are failure costs affected by increases in defect-prevention expenditures? There are many specific quality-cost situations of this sort at the operating level of a manufacturing enterprise.

In the late 1950's, General Electric Company developed a classification of quality costs for accounting purposes which has since become widely accepted. Comparison bases were devised to measure quality costs, in much the same way that burden or overhead is accounted for in connection with production costs. These techniques have been refined to the point where today the uses to which quality-costs data are put have, in principle, become reasonably standardized. These quality-cost considerations will be discussed in Chapter 3 in connection with the development of a quality-costs structure.

QUALITY CONTROL

The quality control subsystem (see Figure 2.4) includes the quality activities: (1) incoming material control, (2) tool and gage control, (3) process control, and (4) inspection and test.

Incoming-Material Control

Incoming-material control includes all of the quality activities associated with the receiving and stocking of raw materials and finished product component parts and assemblies from sources outside of the manufacturing plant. The outside sources may be other plants and divisions of the same company, or vendor suppliers.

Modern incoming-material control procedures emphasize control of material at its source. Close product-quality relationships are developed and maintained between the vendor and the purchaser companies. Receiving inspection by the purchaser company is only a part of the incoming-material control routine. Further, statistical sampling inspection plans are used as widely as possible to reduce the inspection time, labor, and cost.

In planning and organizing for incoming-material control, the quality-control department works closely with the production-control and purchasing departments and the laboratory testing facilities of the manufacturing plant. Requests for materials and parts usually originate with production control at the time production schedules are established. Purchasing prepares purchase inquiries which may be sent to several vendors. Appraisals are made of the vendors' facilities, quality systems, and quality capabilities. Orders are placed and contacts are maintained with the vendor during production of materials and parts. This contact activity may also include the approval of pre-production samples. The material is delivered to the purchaser plant and may then be examined for conformance to specifications. Appropriate records are kept and feedback information is supplied to the purchaser plant's technical and purchasing people, and perhaps also to the vendor company.

Incoming-material inspection is generally more extensive and rigid on first product lots shipped by a vendor on a new order. To establish

VENDOR'S RECORD

Part No. _113,562_   Part Name   _Contact_   Vendor   _xx Co._

Receiving Report Data			Inspection Results				Percent Defective Chart					
Date of Receipt	Receiving Rpt. No.	Total Quantity	Quantity		Percent Defective	Disposal of Lot	1	2	3	4	5	6
			Inspected	Rejected								
12/7	27651	5,000	225	3	1.33	Accept						
12/15	27892	8,300	300	6	2.00	Accept						
12/22	27999	6,700	225	2	0.89	Accept						
12/31	28308	5,000	225	4	1.78	Accept						
1/21	29010	10,140	300	4	1.33	Accept						
2/13	29786	4,650	225	6	2.67	Sort						
3/3	30453	7,490	225	13	5.77	Return						
3/25	31224	9,025	300	5	1.67	Accept						
Totals												

Figure 2.11.   Record of supplier's quality. From G. B. Carson (1958), *Production Handbook,* The Ronald Press Company, New York, p. 8.15.

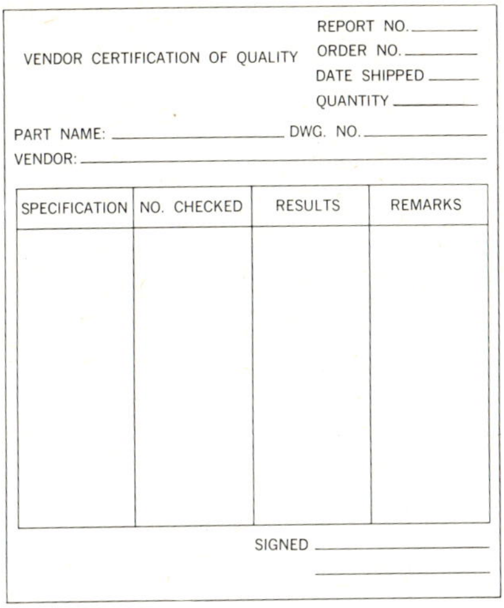

VENDOR CERTIFICATION OF QUALITY

REPORT NO. ______
ORDER NO. ______
DATE SHIPPED ______
QUANTITY ______

PART NAME: ______ DWG. NO. ______
VENDOR: ______

SPECIFICATION	NO. CHECKED	RESULTS	REMARKS

SIGNED ______

Figure 2.12. Vendor certification of quality form.

the vendor's production-quality level, 100% inspection may be necessary on the first lots. If the quality level is satisfactory, subsequent lots will be examined on a sampling-inspection basis. Further, the sampling-inspection plan will probably provide for reduced inspection if the vendor's acceptable-quality level continues with subsequent shipments of material. The purchaser plant continues to maintain appropriate statistical data on the vendor's shipments so that the vendor can be rated on his quality performance (see Figure 2.11). *Vendor-rating plans* are useful in connection with future purchases of materials and parts on other products the company will manufacture.

Finally, even the reduced-sampling inspection will be replaced by *vendor certification.* A vendor-certification procedure eliminates the need for all or a major part of receiving inspection on the part of the purchaser company. The reputable vendor "certifies" that, on the basis of his process control and final-inspection results, the shipped material is of satisfactory quality. The certificates take various forms. One may be a certified statement of the chemical and physical composition of a shipment of raw material. Another may require the vendor to complete a form as shown in Figure 2.12. Or, the certificate may simply be a frequency-distribution tally as shown in Figure 2.13. In any event, the purchaser company conducts acceptance-sampling inspection checks only occasionally on certified lots unless quality difficulties develop with these materials on production lines.

				110-5	
				A 76212	
				4/10/68	
				1000	

Locater Pin   F- 7624 - 1

ABC Company

Sample Size: 50		Specification	Remarks
0.5010	I	+ 0.002	
0.5008	II	0.500 − 0.001	
0.5006	II	O. D.	
0.5004	++++		
0.5002	++++ I		
0.5000	++++ III		
0.4998	++++ IIII		
0.4996	++++ ++++ I		
0.4994	IIII		
0.4992	II		

E. Smith

Figure 2.13.   Vendor certification of quality form.

Tool-and-Gage Control

Product quality depends, to a large extent, on the quality of the tools and gages used in the manufacturing and inspection operations. The term *tool* in the manufacturing industries refers to any device that is capable of working a material into a desired shape, holding the material while it is being worked on, or measuring the material when the work has been completed. Common tools are machine tools, cutting tools, jigs, fixtures, press dies, and gages (although gages will be treated separately in this discussion). A jig is a device for holding the material being machined while an operation is performed, at the same time guiding the tool that performs the operation. A fixture is a device for holding the material while an operation is performed. A gage is a device for measuring a quality characteristic to check its conformance to the technical specification.

Tools and gages provide the physical means of attaining volume production and interchangeability of component parts. Tools and gages are subject to constant wear and deterioration. Thus, it is essential that a system of tool-and-gage control be established to maintain the quality of the tools and gages. Another reason for strict tool control is that frequently tools are designed and used to control the dimensional-quality characteristics of the product without the benefit of inspection. Quality control of the product is indirect—that is, the tool controls the product characteristic and scheduled inspections of the tool replace product-parts inspection.

There are three general classes of gages—working gages, inspection gages, and master gages. The classification is based on the use of the gage. Working gages are used by process operators and process-setup people. Inspection gages are used by inspectors, and master gages are references for checking working and inspection gages. Considerable analysis and control detail is involved not only to assure that the gages function properly to guarantee product quality but also to avoid conflict-in-measurement problems between the different classes of gages in use. These considerations are discussed in Chapter 11. For now, it is sufficient to note the need for an effective control system to maintain gage accuracies and to guarantee that the gages will, in fact, assess production parts properly in relation to the technical specifications for the product.

A gage-control system is adequate if it can supply answers to two fundamental questions: (1) where is the gage now? (2) how accurate is the gage? There are other considerations, of course. However, just getting the answers to these two questions raises further detailed questions dealing with the issue, use, calibration, condition, and location of each gage. These questions and the required answers indicate the type and scope of record system needed for gage control in a given plant.

There are certain minimum ingredients for effective tool-and-gage control procedures. A system of positive identification for each individual tool and gage is required. The identification should reflect such information as tool number, name, inspection and approval date. The numbering system should relate the tool or gage to the product part number, the quality characteristic, the technical specification for the characteristic, the process equipment, and the process operation requiring the use of the tool or gage. New tools and gages must be inspected and "proved" relative to product specification requirements. That is, product meeting the specifications should be accepted by the gages and product not meeting the specifications should be rejected by the gages. The control system should provide for periodic recall of tools and gages from the production floor for reinspection and calibration. Tool and gage records should be maintained, giving the history and location of each tool and gage. Historical information will consist mainly of issue date, type and amount of usage, inspections and cali-

John Doe Manufacturing Co.
Measuring and Calibrating Frequency Chart

Type	Minimum Frequency[a]	Calibration Method
Gage block sets	All sets cleaned and visually inspected every 6 months; all sets calibrated every year	Calibrated against master set traceable to National Standard (by approved source)
Hand micrometer	On request or every 3 months	Gage blocks, ball bearings (optical flats, if necessary)
Inside micrometer	On request or every 6 months	Gage blocks and attachments
Depth micrometer	On request or every 6 months	Straight edge and gage blocks
Vernier calipers	On request or every 2 months	Gage blocks and attachments
Height gages	Once a year	Gage blocks and functional check
Comparator	Every 6 months	Gage blocks
Torque wrenches	Once a year	Weights and arms
Standard plug gages	On request or once a year	Gage blocks and amplifying comparator
Air gage spindles	Once a month	Micrometer and functional check
Air gage master rings	Once only	By approved source
Parallels	Once a year	Surface plate
Thread wires and thread triangles	Once a year	By approved source
Thread ring gages	On request or once a year	Setting plugs
Thread plug gages	On request or once a year	Reference micrometer, thread wires, and triangles
Thread ring setting plugs	Once only	By approved source
Surface plates	Every 2 years	By approved source
Dial indicators	On request	Gage blocks, functional test
V-Blocks	Once a year	Comparator limit height gages, plug gages

Figure 2.14. Measuring and calibrating frequency chart for inspection equipment. From C. P. Covino and A. W. Meghni, *Quality Assurance Manual*, Industrial Press, New York, 1962, p. 6b, Figure 2-2A.

brations, servicing and repairs, and dates for each of these maintenance activities.

Record-documentation procedures vary from one manufacturing plant to another. The following figures are intended to be only suggestive of what is typical. Figure 2.14 shows an inspection and calibration schedule for gages. Figure 2.15 is an example of an issue record for tools and gages. Figure 2.16 indicates a typical gage-control record card.

[a]All users are required to return for recalibration and inspection any measuring device subjected to unusually heavy use or known to have been dropped or otherwise damaged.

ABC MANUFACTURING CO.
Tool and Gage Issue Record

Issue date	Signature	Gage number	Inspection operation	Inspected prior to use		Date Ret.	Date Re-insp.	Remarks
				Yes	No			

Figure 2.15.   Issue record of tools and gages outstanding.

GAGE INSPECTION CARD

Type of Gage	Serial No.	Location:
Date Received	Style	Make

DATE	INSP.	REMARKS	DATE	INSP.	REMARKS

Figure 2.16.   Gage-control record card.

Process Control

The primary objective of *process control* is to provide quality information and assistance to the production worker and his first-line supervisor so that product parts can be manufactured correctly. The purpose is not to be continually engaged in inspecting and sorting out defective product, but to prevent the occurrence of defective product. Whenever a manufacturing system attains an operative level of producing quality product parts a high percentage of the time, inspectors and quality-control staff can be released from corrective-action activities and put to work on the more positive prevention-of-defects

37

activities of quality control. Instead of operating as the policeman of manufacturing operations, inspection can become a real component of the process-control function.

Process control is concerned with the determination of (1) process capabilities, (2) degree of product conformance to technical specifications, (3) sources of variation, (4) causes of nonconformance to specifications, and (5) corrective actions required to eliminate or at least minimize variation effects that cause nonconformance.

Modern process-control practices have been greatly influenced by quantitative methods, particularly the statistical methods utilizing control charts, sampling theory, and analysis-of-variance. These techniques are examined in Chapter 9. The student should note, however, that although these techniques are important in quality-control work, they are simply quantitative tools. The nucleus of quality control is the technical specification. How well the specification accomplishes the design purpose (i.e., functional, styling, life, and interchangeability requirements) is a product-design matter. Furthermore, the feasibility of the specification in terms of manufacturing operations is a production-design matter. When quality troubles develop, quantitative tools represent an invaluable diagnostic aid in locating and identifying the quality-deficiency cause. Together with quality-control administrative procedures, the quantitative methods facilitate a definition of the quality problem. The problem solution, however, is engineering in nature and involves the technology of both product and process design.

Inspection and Test

Inspection is primarily concerned with determining the degree to which production output conforms to the established technical specifications for the product. The resulting inspection information is used for two purposes: (1) to control manufacturing operations and product-quality characteristics, and (2) to prepare quality audits to generate feedback information to the quality-planning operations and upper-level management sections.

The inspection operation may be classified in two categories based on the method of measurement-variables inspection and attributes inspection. *Variables* inspection includes any inspection operation where the gage indicates, on a continuous scale, deviations from the technical specification. For example, a dimensional specification may be 0.500 ± 0.001 in., and inspection of manufactured product may yield values 0.501, 0.502, 0.503, etc. (or, 0.499, 0.498, etc.). With *attributes* inspection, the gage merely classifies the product into discrete categories. For example, the gage may classify product as being effective or defective. Another common classification is undersize, oversize, and within the specification limits. The categories into which the product is separated are discrete and usually few in number.

The inspection operation may also be classified in terms of the proportion of production output which is actually inspected. A 100% inspection operation involves the examination of every product item in the production *lot* or batch. This type of inspection is called *screening* or *detailing*. It should be clear that the cost of 100% inspection is high, and sometimes prohibitively so. For example, if every quality characteristic on the thousands of component parts of an automobile were 100% inspected, the sales price of the automobile would be out of reach for the average consumer. *Sampling inspection* refers to the inspection of only *n* items of a product lot composed of *N* product items, where *n* is less than *N*. Statistical sampling-inspection plans are designed to facilitate decision-making regarding the production lot. Decisions are based on the limited information available from a relatively small random sample taken from the lot. Sampling inspection is used when (1) the inspection operation destroys the product item being inspected; (2) the cost of 100% inspection is prohibitive; or (3) production delay due to the inspection operation is not feasible.

Inspection may also be classified as to its purpose. *Acceptance-sampling* inspection distinguishes acceptable production lots from nonacceptable lots. Acceptance sampling is used for (1) incoming or vendor inspection, where raw materials or finished product is moving from the vendor company to the purchaser company; (2) process inspection, where product parts are moving from one production department to another production department for further processing operations; and (3) final inspection, where the product is moving from the producer to the distributor and to the customer.

Control-sampling inspection obtains measurement data for the purpose of exercising control over the process, operator, or inspector. Any grading or sorting of product on the basis of the inspection results is incidental to the main purpose, which is control.

Based on the purpose of 100% inspection, we have operational sorting or corrective sorting of product. *Operational sorting* is viewed as a scheduled manufacturing operation and is regarded as an unavoidable manufacturing cost. It is a necessary sorting of effective and defective product. The inspection operation is unavoidable since the process is not adequate to meet the technical product specifications on a production basis. A decision has been made to use the existing process and a rectifying inspection to assure product conformance to the specifications. This situation was referred to in Chapter 1 in connection with the economics of quality of conformance involving various combinations of existing processes, rectifying inspection, and capital investments in new processes. *Corrective sorting* refers to a 100% inspection of product, the inspection being required since manufacturing difficulties needlessly created defective product. That is, even though the process is adequate to meet specifications, defective product has resulted because of process-control deficiencies. Although accounting practices will differ in this regard, the cost of corrective sorting should rightfully be charged as a quality cost (i.e., a loss due to quality failure).

Sorting is economical only when the expected cost of a defective is greater than the cost of inspection necessary to find the defective.

If c = cost of inspecting one unit of product, and p = fraction of the product lot which is defective, then c/p = cost of finding one defective unit.

For example, if $p = 0.05$, then it is necessary to inspect (on the average) $1/p = 20$ units of product to find one defective. Then, if $c = \$0.02$, the cost of finding one defective is $(\$0.02)(20) = \$0.40$, or $(c)(1/p)$.

Now, if k represents the cost generated from failure to find the one defective, then it is economical to sort product only if c/p is less than k. Or, stated a bit differently, $p = c/k$ is the fraction defective value above which sorting is economical. Figure 2.17 summarizes these relationships.

The value c/k is frequently referred to as break-even quality. The loss k is easily estimated when the consumer is another manufacturing department of the producing plant. That is, k represents manufacturing costs (or losses) when the undetected defective part causes manufacturing difficulties involving unscheduled corrective operations

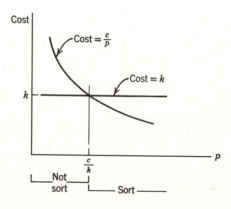

Figure 2.17. Economics of sorting.

40

or scrapped materials. This is the case when the defective part is scheduled to undergo further process operations or is going direct to assembly stations.

If the customer is the consumer, k may be difficult to estimate. In this case, we assume the unidentified defective part is assembled into a product unit and eventually reaches the customer and causes trouble. The resulting servicing-in-the-field costs and customer-claim-adjustment costs are difficult to determine in advance. Furthermore, the intangible losses caused by loss of customer goodwill and damage to the company's quality reputation are even more difficult to quantify.

SUMMARY

Quality control is a planning-and-control, or feedback function. The quality system is composed of two principal subsystems. One subsystem is viewed as a closed-communications system wherein consumer-quality requirements initiate quality-planning operations. Quality-planning information flows to manufacturing operations. Product is manufactured and distributed to the consumer, and the needs and desires of the consumer are satisfied. In theory, the system operates continuously, detecting changes in consumer preferences and altering plans and operations accordingly.

Another subsystem is regarded as a closed-communications system whereby quality-planning operations institute quality-control operations. The quality-planning operations subsystem includes determination of quality policies and objectives, new-design reviews, and quality-costs analyses. The quality-control operations subsystem is composed of incoming-material control, tool-and-gage control, process control, and inspection and test operations.

Several classifications of inspection are possible. One classification, based on the method of measurement, is *variables* and *attributes* inspections. Another classification, dependent on the number of product items examined, is 100% inspection (called *screening* or *detailing*) and *sampling inspection*.

Based on the purpose of the inspection operation, 100% inspection is either *operational sorting* or *corrective sorting*. Similarly, regarding purpose, sampling inspection is either *acceptance sampling* or *control sampling*. The question of whether or not to sort product is an economic problem involving an estimate of the cost generated by failure to detect defectives as they occur in the manufacturing system.

REFERENCES

Cook, L. E. (February, 1966), "The Quality Assurance Pre-Production Conference," *Industrial Quality Control*, Vol. 22, No. 8, pp. 408-410.

Covino, C. P., and Meghri, A. W. (1962), *Quality Assurance Manual*, Industrial Press, New York, Chapter 2.

Enrick, N. L. (1966), *Quality Control and Reliability*, Industrial Press, New York, Chapter 10.

Feigenbaum, A. V. (1961), *Total Quality Control*, McGraw-Hill, New York, Chapter 15.

Freund, R. A. (August, 1965), "Quality Control—A Decade of Progress," *Industrial Quality Control*, Vol. 22, No. 2, pp. 67-72.

Hansen, B. L. (1963), *Quality Control*, Prentice-Hall, Englewood Cliffs, N. J., Chapter 20.

Jacobs, R. M. (February, 1967), "Implementing Formal Design Review," *Industrial Quality Control*, Vol. 23, No. 8, pp. 398-404.

Jacobs, R. M., and Hulme, H. D. (May 3, 1965), "Commercial Design Review and Data Analysis Program," *ASQC Annual Convention Transactions*.

Juran, J. M. (November, 1964), "The Two Worlds of Quality Control," *Industrial Quality Control*, Vol. 21, No. 5, pp. 238-244.

REVIEW QUESTIONS

1. Discuss the analogy between financial control and quality control.
2. State four beneficial activities made possible by a unified quality-control effort.
3. Define the quality system. ✓
4. Describe the main elements of the quality-planning subsystem S_1.
5. What are two basic criteria for designing the feedback network of a quality-control system?
6. State the three principal quality activities of the quality planning subsystem.
7. What are the two main advantages of a new-design review?
8. Discuss the aspects of the new-design review which are directly relevant to the quality-control effort.
9. Describe the main elements of the quality-control subsystem S_2.
10. What is the principal advantage of the vendor certification procedure?
11. State two reasons why a tool-and-gage control system is necessary.
12. Define working gage, inspection gage, and master gage.
13. What are the two fundamental questions which concern a gage-control system?

14. Identify the five principal activity areas of process control.

15. Distinguish between variables and attributes inspection.

16. When is sampling inspection feasible?

17. If a defective product unit is not detected by an inspection operation, a production loss of $10 is incurred. Unit-inspection cost is $0.15. The expected fraction defective is 0.02. (a) What is the average cost of finding one defective product unit? (b) Is a 100% inspection operation economic? (c) Sketch the cost curves involved (see Figure 2.17) and determine the break-even quality level identifying the quality level at which there is no gain or loss from a 100% inspection operation.

3

Quality Costs

From an economic standpoint, all efforts to improve product quality are either income-expansion or cost-reduction expenditures. Increasing income through quality improvement involves quality-of-design analysis whereas reducing costs by quality improvement deals with quality of conformance.

INCOME-EXPANSION EXPENDITURES

Converting higher quality of design into higher revenues for the product is complicated by supply-and-demand considerations and the difficulty of accurately determining a value curve (see Figure 1.4), Nevertheless, as pointed out in Chapter 1, the marketability of a product depends greatly on its quality. A high-quality product generally commands a higher share of the market and, under certain supply-and-demand conditions, sells at a premium price.

There have been some dramatic examples of increasing revenues considerably by increasing expenditures for better quality of design. For example, an automobile manufacturer increased the reliability of one of its models and in several years doubled the company's share of the market for that type automobile. The company's profit increase represented a much larger return from the quality expenditure than that which could have been obtained by an equivalent expenditure to reduce manufacturing scrap and rework costs. Examples of this kind strengthen the belief that the economic effect of increasing income through better quality of design can be far greater than the economic effect of reducing costs by improving quality of conformance.

The problem of exploiting quality of design is, however, a subtle one. An increase in the technical excellence of the product usually means an increase in sales price commensurate with the increased manufacturing costs. It is difficult to determine just how much a customer will pay for increased technical excellence. The effect of quality of design on share of the market, income margins, and so forth, is highly uncertain.

In addition to the uncertainties involved in estimating the market response to alternative quality-of-design levels, there is also the problem of influencing the consumer regarding economic quality levels. It is difficult to educate the consumer to pay an extra $50 for a $300 appliance so he can save $300 or more in service charges over the life of the appliance. In many modern product situations, the customer purchases or leases hardware to obtain services of some kind. Yet, the cost of keeping the hardware in service during its normal lifespan exceeds considerably the original cost of the hardware. This follows from the fact that the manufacturer of the hardware is concerned with minimizing his costs in order to make the sales price of his product competitive. Indeed, he may even be looking to the replacement-parts business for necessary income to make a profit. Ideally, the customer should be interested in minimizing his total costs. If he knew the facts, he would probably prefer to use his entire expenditure (i.e., purchase cost plus a portion of the anticipated service costs) to purchase failure-free hardware in the first place.

All of this is, of course, a business problem arising from the organization of our economy. Simply stated, the alternatives are to either optimize the manufacturer's economics or optimize the customer's total-cost situation. It seems that there is a trend developing in the direction of selling the service rather than the hardware. The telephone business was the first outstanding example. Automobile batteries, tires, and even engine parts are now being sold under guaranteed life and service provisions. Many appliances are being advertised from the same guarantee basis. It is likely that the expensive data-processing hardware will eventually be marketed on this same basis. If the trend continues, many consumer items will be sold on the basis of so many hours of service life.

COST-REDUCTION EXPENDITURES

A previous reference has been made to the degree of product conformance to specifications which is feasible for a given process operation, assuming that more costly and capable processes are available (see Figure 1.7). The basic problem here is one of minimizing the sum of two essentially opposing sets of costs (in this case, process costs and quality costs). Many economic decisions of this sort are required at the operations level of a manufacturing plant. Is it more economic to use an existing process plus a rectifying inspection, or make a capital investment in a more capable process? Is the cost of monitoring a process justified, or would a rectifying inspection cost less than the control effort? Is it more economical to rework or to scrap rejected product? Is one sampling inspection plan more economic than another proposed plan? Selected questions of this type will be examined in the following paragraphs. The presentation is not intended to be exhaustive. Some of the economic optimization questions have been reserved for later chapters, particularly those dealing with process control and sampling inspection.

Review of Manufacturing Costs

The various manufacturing costs are usually regarded as being either capital costs or operating costs. This cost classification is outlined in Figure 3.1.

The terminology used to identify the cost elements is reasonably standard. However, a brief definitional review of the production costs shown in Figure 3.1 is presented here.

Direct labor cost represents the wages paid to the production worker for labor performed directly on the product. Direct labor costs for specific job orders are determined from time or job tickets prepared daily by the production worker or his foreman.

Direct material cost is the cost of the material actually consumed in the manufacture of the product and refers only to the material from which the product part has been made. Direct material costs for specific job orders are determined from invoices and requisitions for purchased materials.

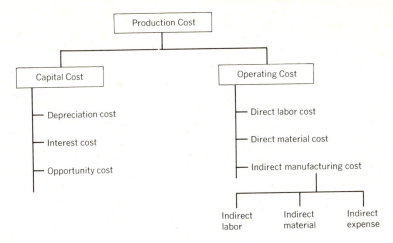

Figure 3.1.   Basic production costs.

Indirect manufacturing cost refers to all costs not directly identifiable with specific job orders but, nevertheless, costs that are incurred by the general operation of the manufacturing plant. These costs are frequently called *overhead* or *burden*. Three principal categories of indirect manufacturing costs are indirect labor, indirect material, and indirect expense.

Indirect labor cost is the cost of labor not directly applied to the manufacture of the product. Examples of indirect labor are line supervisors, stores-keepers, toolroom personnel, and in-plant transportation workers. *Indirect material* cost is the cost of material used during the manufacture of the product but which does not become a part of the finished product. Examples of indirect materials are cutting oils, lubricants, and most manufacturing supplies. *Indirect expense* refers to all other costs not included in the foregoing classifications, costs that are associated with the general operation of the manufacturing plant. Certain indirect expenses do not vary with changes in manufacturing output. Within limits they are independent of manufacturing activity and utilization of equipment. These are considered to be *fixed* expenses. Examples are property taxes, insurance on buildings, and building rental. Other indirect expenses vary with changes in manufacturing output and are considered to be *variable* expenses. Examples are heat, light, power, worker's compensation insurance premiums, and machine and process maintenance. Costs cannot be classified as permanently fixed or variable because, in general, any cost can be altered by strong administrative action or, on the other hand, remain constant as the result of a failure to act. However, it is convenient to regard indirect expense as being composed of fixed and variable cost components.

Cost accounting distributes indirect manufacturing costs to manufacturing departments and thence to work centers within departments in such a way that each product is charged its fair share of these general and indirect expenses. The problem, of course, is that indirect manufacturing costs are not directly identifiable with specific job orders and processing operations required to fill these orders. Any indirect method of associating these general costs with specific job orders should (1) allocate the costs fairly, (2) be simple to administrate, and (3) not involve excessive accounting costs. The usual method of allocating indirect manufacturing costs to job orders is by use of a ratio or percentage coupled to a measurable base.

Example

Job charges for a specific process operation are $100 of direct labor and $50 of direct material.

Indirect manufacturing cost for the job is computed to be 150% of the direct labor cost, or $150.

Total charge for the process operation is $100 + $50 + $150 = $300.

In the preceding example, 150% is called the burden or overhead *rate*. Direct labor is the *base*. The assumption underlying this method is that each base expenditure generates, or is linked with, a directly proportionate amount of indirect manufacturing cost. In other words, the assumption is one of proportionality or linearity as indicated in Figure 3.2.

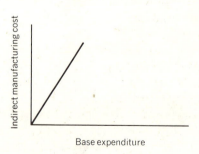

Figure 3.2.   Overhead allocation.

The accuracy of any indirect method of overhead allocation depends on the selection of an appropriate base for the particular manufacturing and cost conditions that are involved.

Operating Quality Costs

Quality costs can be classified in much the same way as were production costs (see Figure 3.1). Figure 3.3 shows such a classification.

Prevention-quality costs are expenditures made in an effort to prevent poor quality. Typical cost elements included in this category are for the following quality activities: quality planning, engineering, and administrative staff work; design and development of quality-measuring equipment; quality training and preparation of instructional materials; and staff time involved in vendor surveys.

Appraisal-quality costs are costs of measuring quality characteristics to assure conformance to the technical specifications. Appraisal costs include expenditures for all inspection labor and supervision and any indirect labor required, such as that used in receiving inspection of bulk raw materials. Also included are indirect labor charges for gage calibration and maintenance, indirect material charges for inspection and test supplies, laboratory-test charges, and costs of outside certifications.

Failure-quality costs are expenses generated by product not meeting the quality requirements. *Internal failure* costs include all production losses. These losses include labor, material, and overhead charges on

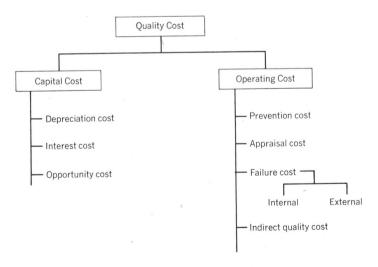

Figure 3.3. Quality costs.

scrapped product, that is, expenses accumulated for a product item up to the time that nonconformance is detected. Other production losses are labor, material, and overhead charges for rework operations, and labor charges due to downtime in the production line caused by quality deficiencies. Internal failure costs also include any engineering or quality-control staff time required for corrective action to solve immediate quality problems that develop on the manufacturing floor. *External failure* costs include all expenditures for handling customer complaints and performing field service required because of quality deficiencies.

Capital costs attributable to the quality effort are mainly expenditures for new gaging hardware and data-processing equipment. Accounting methods vary in this connection. These costs may be basic production charges. However, to evaluate specific quality efforts, the necessary quality costs can be extracted from the conventional accounting summaries. *Indirect quality* costs are the vendor's quality costs, which are reflected in the purchase price of the materials and thus represent a quality cost to the purchaser company.

Typically, prevention costs are approximately 10% of the total quality cost. Appraisal costs are about 25% and failure costs 50 to 75% of the total quality cost. Budgeting for quality follows the basic strategy of searching for an optimum balance between these three sets of costs. Figure 3.4 illustrates the strategy.

Increases in prevention costs usually result in better quality of conformance. With better quality of conformance, appraisal costs are likely to decrease, that is, less routine inspection is required since there are fewer defectives in each manufacturing lot. Also, failure costs are expected to decrease. Moving to the right on the quality-of-conformance axis, nominal increases in prevention expenditures are accompanied by significant reductions in both failure and appraisal costs, resulting in a net decrease in total quality cost (which is regarded here to be the sum of the prevention, appraisal, and failure costs). Clearly, there exists some optimum quality-of-conformance level, q, such that total quality cost is minimized.

For certain manufacturing and cost conditions the argument will vary slightly. Expenditure increases may be for appraisal only, with the expected return being significant decreases in failure costs. Or, the expenditure increases may be for both prevention and appraisal.

If we consider nominal prevention and/or appraisal expenditures as the input to the quality-cost system, the output is significant reductions in failure costs. However, the output may also reflect reductions in basic production costs. It may be difficult to extract a quantitative measure of this return for the quality effort from the con-

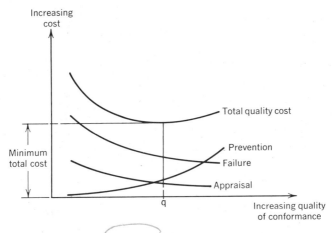

Figure 3.4. Prevention, appraisal, and failure costs.

ventional accounting summaries. Nevertheless, the potential for such a return on the quality investment certainly does exist. In the following paragraphs, some specific examples of this will be examined.

An important production-cost reduction resulting from good quality of conformance is the possible elimination of process operations. A simple example is a brass part requiring a cold form plus two polishing operations. Improving the uniformity of the cold-form operation (i.e., quality of conformance) eliminates the need for one of the polishing operations.

Another possible reduction in production costs made possible by better quality of conformance is a decrease in indirect labor and material costs associated with tooling. For example, consider a component part that requires several consecutive manufacturing operations. Better control of a dimensional quality characteristic at one operation may reduce the complexity of the tooling required for a subsequent process operation. In fact, some tooling may be eliminated entirely, particularly jigs and fixtures used for locational purposes.

Increased quality of conformance may also reduce the overhead due to excess production capacity required because of a high percentage of defective manufacturing output. This is the familiar situation of producing, for example, 500 product units a day to get 350 good units. The portion of plant capacity required for the extra 150 units of production output per day involves overhead that must be charged to something. Although this is a controversial issue with accountants, if we are interested in evaluating specific quality efforts, we must

51

conclude that this overhead cost is assignable to the presence of defectives. Thus it is a fair charge against poor quality of conformance.

Measurement Bases for Operating Quality Costs

Quality-planning operations are based on quality-costs data. Essentially there are four general uses to which this data is put: (1) measuring over-all quality activities, (2) identifying high manufacturing-loss areas, (3) programming available quality-control staff for corrective action, and (4) budgeting quality expenditures to balance prevention, appraisal, and failure costs.

Regarding the measurement of over-all quality activities, management is concerned with comparing quality cost for one time period with that for another time period. Usually this is done on a monthly or quarterly basis. Since the total manufacturing activity varies for different time periods, it is impossible to compare quality costs in terms of absolute dollar amounts. Comparisons can be made, however, if the quality cost for each period is first related to a base which measures the degree of manufacturing activity for that period. This is somewhat analogous to the indirect method of allocating overhead by using a percentage coupled to a measurable base. For example, suppose that expenditures for direct labor are proportional to the volume of manufacturing activity. That is, 100 units of direct labor are used for 1000 units of manufacturing activity, 200 units of direct labor for 2000 units of manufacturing activity, and so forth. Using direct labor as a base, quality cost can be expressed as a percent of direct labor. This procedure will delete the volume-of-manufacturing-activity effect on the quality cost measure. (Clearly, if all variables remain constant except volume of manufacturing activity, which increases, then quality cost is also expected to increase. Thus, any comparison of quality cost from one time period to another would be meaningless, if quality cost were expressed in absolute dollar amounts.) Figure 3.5 shows a comparison plot of quality costs by quarters, where each quality cost is expressed as a percent of direct labor cost for the quarter.

Quality-cost comparisons are valid only if the base accurately reflects the degree of manufacturing activity. The base should be sensitive to changes in volume of manufacturing activity and should not be influenced by extraneous factors. For example, for each of two quarters quality cost and manufacturing activity are identical, $100 of quality cost for 100,000 units of manufacturing activity. Assume that direct labor is the base and $10,000 direct labor cost is incurred in the first quarter. Mechanization of processes reduces the amount

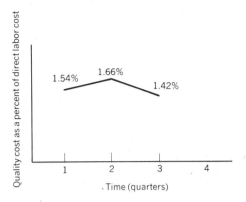

Figure 3.5. Quality cost comparison, expressing quality cost as a percent of direct labor cost.

of labor required and $5,000 direct labor cost is incurred in the second quarter. Volume of manufacturing activity is the same for each quarter; quality cost is the same. Yet, using percent of direct labor as a measure, quality cost for the first quarter is (100) ($100/$10,000) or 1%, and for the second quarter is (100) ($100/$5,000) or 2%. The extraneous factor (i.e., mechanization) has distorted the quality cost measure.

Now, the student may question why the 100,000 units of manufacturing activity was not used as a base. The fact is these units are not known. Are the units dollars or number of product items completed? The student of accounting will recall that, at the end of each accounting period, manufacturing activity for the period has resulted in not only finished product but unfinished product as well (i.e., work-in-process). To further complicate the matter, a product mix may be involved. The company may be producing simultaneously product A, product B, and so on.

Quality-cost measures have been developed using a number of different bases.[1] Categories of bases commonly used are labor bases, manufacturing-cost bases, sales bases, and unit bases. The choice of base to be used varies with different manufacturing and cost conditions. A conservative approach is indicated by Figure 3.6. Three bases are used. Only one base from each of the four general categories of bases is used. Quality-cost measures used here are (1) quality cost expressed as a percent of direct labor cost, (2) quality cost per equiva-

[1]Detailed examples are given in Feigenbaum, A. V. (1961), *Total Quality Control*, McGraw-Hill, New York, Chapter 5.

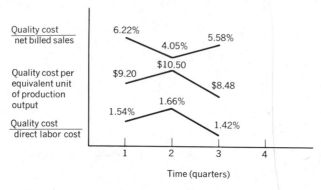

Figure 3.6. Quality cost comparison, using three different base measures.

lent unit of production output, and (3) quality cost expressed as a percent of net billed sales. If all three bases give approximately the same trends, it is likely that the three measures are accurately reflecting quality costs for the respective time periods (unless, of course, all three are being distorted by the same extraneous factor). If the trend lines are not parallel, an investigation of possible causes of nonparallelism may lead to a correct choice of a base for the given manufacturing and cost conditions.

One of the bases used in Figure 3.6 is quality cost per equivalent unit of production output. This base is frequently used in product-mix situations. An example of this quality-cost measure is given in Tables 3.1 and 3.2. Table 3.1 gives the cost data for three products—A, B, and C. The products are ordered in the table, from high to low, on the basis of net billed sales. Table 3.2 summarizes the computation. Contributed value is net-billed sales minus direct material cost. Unit-contributed value is contributed value divided by production volume. The factor value for each product is arrived at by dividing its unit-contributed value by the unit-contributed value for product A. Equivalent-production output is computed by multiplying production volume by the factor value. Now, suppose the quality cost for the time period was $50,581. Dividing this cost by the total of the equivalent-production output yields $3.55 quality cost per equivalent unit of production output.

This quality-cost measure is suitable for product-mix situations. Direct material cost has been subtracted from the measure, since this cost reflects the supplier's operating cost and not the purchaser company's cost. As the product mix changes from one time period to

Table 3.1. Quality Cost Per Equivalent Unit of Production
Output

Product	Net Billed Sales	Direct Material	Volume of Production
A	$500,000	$80,000	10,000
B	200,000	50,000	5,000
C	50,000	8,000	7,000

Table 3.2. Quality Cost per Equivalent Unit of Production
Output

Product	Contributed Value	Unit-Contributed Value	Factor	Equivalent-Production Output
A	$420,000	$42.00	1.00	10,000
B	150,000	30.00	0.71	3,550
C	42,000	6.00	0.14	980
				14,530

another, the base changes accordingly. That is, the equivalent-unit-of-product-output base is sensitive to the product-mix change and thus closely follows manufacturing activity.

An Illustrative Application[2]

An excellent summary example of quality-cost auditing reported by Charles A. Bicking is abstracted here by courtesy of the Carborundum Company.

The most frequently analyzed element of quality cost is losses due to rejection of product material and parts. The collection of information on rejects is essential to any program of defect prevention. A typical loss ticket for recording such information is shown in Figure 3.7. Using the standard value of production of the rejected items, the information from loss tickets can be translated into dollar value of losses in the plant. This information can be conveniently collected and tabulated on an electronic computer. A typical section of a computerized loss report is given in Table 3.3. Reports from individual plants are summarized for management as shown in Table 3.4.

[2]Bicking, C. A. (December, 1967), "Cost and Value Aspects of Quality Control," *Industrial Quality Control*, Vol. 24, No. 6, pp. 306-308.

SALVAGE INSTRUCTIONS						DISTRIBUTION: WHITE—IBM 32–3

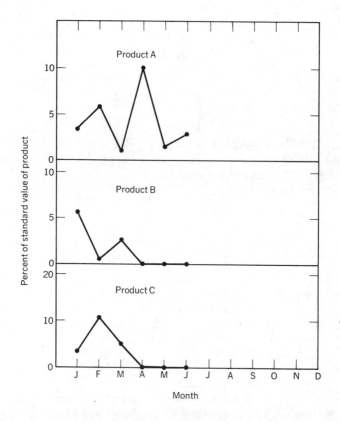

Figure 3.7. Sample of loss ticket. From C. A. Bicking (December, 1967), "Cost and Value Aspects of Quality Control," *Industrial Quality Control,* Vol. 24, No. 6, p. 307, Figure 1.

Figure 3.8. External failure costs by product lines. From C. A. Bicking (December, 1967), "Cost and Value Aspects of Quality Control," *Industrial Quality Control*, Vol. 24, No. 6, p. 308, Figure 4.

Table 3.3. Weekly Loss Report

Defect Code	Defect Designation	Pieces Rejected	Percent of Rejection	Standard Value	Percent of Total
117	Broken or cracked	408	25.0	$ 335	22.6
135	Boiled	59	3.5	58	3.8
231	Too hard or soft	664	40.2	731	48.6
350	Out of dimension	36	2.1	48	3.1
417	Appearance	406	24.8	235	15.8
900	Miscellaneous	73	4.4	92	6.1
Total		1646	100.0	$1499	100.0

From Bicking, C. A. (December, 1967), "Cost and Value Aspects of Quality Control," *Industrial Quality Control*, Vol. 24, No. 6, p. 307, Table 1.

Table 3.4. Weekly Loss Report Summary

Plant	Standard Value of Production	Losses Standard ($)	Percent of Standard Value	Volume of Production	Losses Pieces	Percent of Production
A	$ 31,348	$ 1,499	4.8	28,879	1646	5.7
B	198,355	22,734	11.4	31,497	3579	11.3
C	123,098	8,273	6.7	3,005	117	3.9
D	85,888	4,630	5.4	44,152	2009	4.6
E	52,065	1,031	2.0	25,989	222	0.9
F	72,083	747	1.0	21,677	244	1.1

From Bicking, C. A. (December, 1967), "Cost and Value Aspects of Quality Control," *Industrial Quality Control*, Vol. 24, No. 6, p. 307, Table 2.

Table 3.5. Complaints and Credits Report for Defective Product

Plant	Total Number of Complaints	Cause of Complaint Grade	Dimensions	Breakage	Misc.	Sales Credits
A	11	3	0	1	7	$ 1,211
B	26	7	5	5	9	2,308
C	22	5	6	4	7	4,279
D	1	0	0	0	1	375
E	9	2	1	3	3	1,790
F	30	9	5	7	9	4,808
Totals	99	26	17	20	36	$14,771

From Bicking, C. A. (December, 1967), "Cost and Value Aspects of Quality Control," *Industrial Quality Control,* Vol. 24, No. 6, p. 307, Table 3.

Another source of losses usually tabulated for analysis is the number of complaints and the dollar value of credits issued for defective product which is returned by the customer. This information may be collected as shown in Table 3.5. Also, it is useful to plot the information as shown in Figure 3.8.

An important monthly report usually issued by the quality-control department summarizes total quality costs by product lines (see Figure 3.9) and gives a detailed breakdown of quality costs as percentages of standard value of production (see Figure 3.10). The cost data is derived from standard financial statements issued monthly by the accounting department.

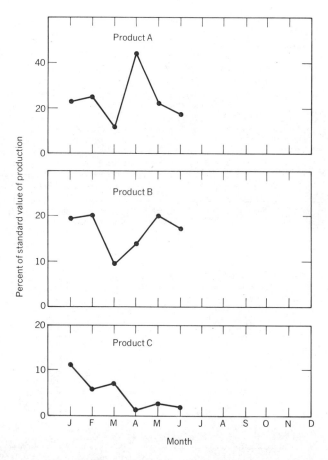

Figure 3.9. Total quality costs by product lines. From C. A. Bicking (December, 1967), "Cost and Value Aspects of Quality Control," *Industrial Quality Control*, Vol. 24, No. 6, p. 308, Figure 3.

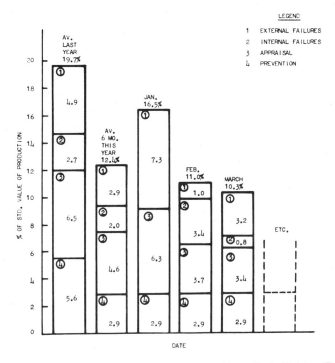

Figure 3.10.   Breakdown of quality costs by elements. From C. A. Bicking (December, 1967), "Cost and Value Aspects of Quality Control," *Industrial Quality Control,* Vol. 24, No. 6, p. 307, Figure 2.

Budgeting and Control of Quality Costs

It is presumed that the student has been exposed to the principles and methods of cost control and is familiar with the various types of budgets employed in a manufacturing enterprise. These topics will not be discussed here except as they relate to the quality effort.

A comprehensive budgeting system consists of three types of budgets: (1) an *operating* budget, showing plans for operations for the following time period, (2) a *cash* budget, showing the anticipated sources and uses of cash, and (3) a *capital* budget showing planned changes in fixed assets. The quality-control manager is principally concerned with preparing an operating budget.

Figure 3.11[3] is an example of a budget work sheet. Based on the estimated monthly sales for the budget period, estimates are made of monthly purchases of raw materials, finished components, and direct

[3]Squires, F. A. (November, 1966), "On the Quality Scene," *Quality Assurance,* Vol. 5, No. 11, p. 14.

Figure 3.11. Budget work sheet. From F. A. Squires (November, 1966), "On The Quality Scene," *Quality Assurance,* Vol. 5, No. 11, p. 14.

Metalunar Corporation
Quality Assurance Budget: Year beginning January 1, 1967.
All figures are estimated monthly averages.

Area and amount to be billed or expended	Inspection				Direct Supervision	Quality Engineering	Administration
	Rate in $/$1000	Total $	Inspector's Rate $	Number of Inspectors	No. $		
Purchased materials, $	$	$	$	No.	No. $	$	$
Machine shop, $ of direct labor	$	$	$	No.	No. $	$	$
Assembly,$ of direct labor	$	$	$	No.	No. $	$	$
Functional test, billing in $	$	$	$	No.	No. $	$	$

Figure 3.12. Operating quality budget. From F. A. Squires (November, 1966), "On The Quality Scene," *Quality Assurance,* Vol. 5, No. 11, p. 14.

Metalunar Corporation
Estimated cost of Quality Assurance Program for the year
beginning January 1, 1967.

Costs are estimated averages per month for the 12 months.

1. Inspecting purchased material	$2400
2. Machine shop inspection	5000
3. Assembly inspection	4000
4. Functional test	2000
5. Cost of supplier control	600
6. Cost of direct supervision	1340
7. Cost of administration and quality engineering	2080

labor costs for the fabrication and assembly areas. Matching entries on the work sheet are for average inspection costs estimated from past records. Examples are: average inspection cost in dollars per $1000 of purchased materials, and average inspection cost per $1000 of direct labor for fabrication. Similar estimates are made of average inspection cost per $1000 of assembly direct labor and average inspection and test cost per $1000 of shipped products. Using standard wage rates for inspection labor, the quality-control manager estimates inspection and test costs for specified manufacturing areas. Corresponding estimates are made for direct supervision in the inspection areas, and for quality engineering and administration. Work sheet computations are preliminary to the preparation of a formal operating budget. A typical operating budget is shown in Figure 3.12.

The method of estimating the budget elements, as indicated in Figures 3.11 and 3.12, is a common practice. However, it should not be accepted without examination. The use of a ratio of quality-control man-hours to direct labor man-hours rests on the same assumption that underlies the allocation of overhead charges to the product— namely, that the two variables are linearly related. An expenditure for one variable is assumed to be directly proportional to the expected expenditure for the other variable. In the case of quality-control man-hours being related to direct labor man-hours, this relationship (if it exists!) will change from one time period to another simply because the amount of direct labor hours required is sensitive to the installation of automated process equipment. Also, the use of historical data to determine the ratio is suspect. The inspection man-hours required in previous production situations may have been, in part, for sorting-of-product purposes rather than for quality control. Perhaps a more reliable procedure would be to determine if the man-hour variables are correlated. For a given manufacturing and cost situation, a regression analysis[4] can be made, linking a number of proposed dependent variables with the independent variable-number of quality-control man-hours required. The resulting predictor equation may be a more accurate device for estimating the elements of the operating quality budget.

Some Optimization Problems

Reference has been made to the question of degree of product conformance to the specifications which is feasible for a given process operation, assuming that more costly and capable processes are available (see Figure 1.7). This is an economic problem involving alternative combinations of existing processes, rectifying inspection, and

---

[4] An application example is given in Hansen, B. L. (1963), *Quality Control,* Prentice-Hall, Englewood Cliffs, New Jersey, p. 322.

capital investments in new processes. A simplified example is presented here to indicate the nature of the problem.

Example

Alternatives for performing a given process operation are an existing machine A and a machine B which can be purchased in the used-equipment market. Machine A does not have good capability and requires a rectifying inspection operation to bring output to an acceptable quality level. The output from machine B will meet specifications and no inspection is required, other than that for monitoring the process. Annual operating costs for A are a direct labor cost of $900 plus a rectifying-inspection cost of $500. Total annual operating cost for B is $1300, a figure that reflects a higher direct labor cost (i.e., a more skilled machine operator is required) and a nominal cost for process control inspection. The present value of machine A is $1000 and the investment cost of machine B is $1600. Estimated remaining service life for A is 5 years and for B is 8 years. To simplify the example, salvage values are considered to be zero.

It is convenient to summarize the cost data on time scales as shown in Figure 3.13. In terms of operating costs only, machine B has an annual advantage of $100. The question of whether or not to make the capital investment is pertinent. That is, what is the expected return on the quality investment? Using the rate-of-return criterion, the computations are as follows.

Equating annual costs

$$(1000) \, (_{i-5}crf) + 1400 = (1600) \, (_{i-8}crf) + 1300$$

A first trial, using $i = 0\%$

$$(1000) \left(\frac{1}{5}\right) + 1400 \stackrel{\wedge}{=} (1600) \left(\frac{1}{8}\right) + 1300$$

$$1600 \stackrel{\wedge}{=} 1500$$

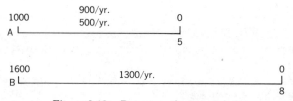

Figure 3.13.   Return on the investment.

Therefore, at $i = 0$, annual cost of A $>$ annual cost of B by $100 and i is at least $= (100/600)100) = 16.7\%$.

A second trial,[5] using $i = 20\%$

$$(1000) \, (_{.20-5}crf) + 1400 \overset{\wedge}{=} (1600) \, (_{.20-8}crf) + 1300$$

$$1734 \overset{\wedge}{=} 1718$$

Therefore, at $i = 20\%$, annual cost of A $>$ annual cost of B by $16 and i is at least $20 + (16/600)100) = 22.7\%$.

A third trial, at $i = 25\%$

$$(1000) \, (_{.25-5}crf) + 1400 \overset{\wedge}{=} (1600) \, (_{.25-8}crf) + 1300$$

$$1772 \overset{\wedge}{=} 1781$$

Therefore, using $i = 25\%$, annual cost of A $<$ annual cost of B by $9. Interpolation yields:

$$i = 20 + \frac{16}{25} \, (5) = 23.7\%.$$

If the minimum required rate of return for projects of this sort is not greater than 23.7%, then it is economic to make the capital investment required for alternative B.

Example

The cost and value analysis of quality of design (see Figure 1.4) is an optimization problem. Interest here is in determining an optimum quality level, where marginal cost is equal to marginal value. This optimization refers to unit cost and value. A broader optimization problem related to quality of design is suggested in the section of Chapter 3 that deals with income expansion expenditures. The objective here is to maximize total revenue by using higher quality of design to capture a commanding share of the market.

Example

The strategy of increasing prevention and/or appraisal expenditures (see Figure 3.4) involves searching for an optimum balance between

[5] There are many sources of tables for the rate-of-return factors used in this example (i.e., the *crf* or capital recovery factor used here). An excellent reference for the student is Taylor, G. A. (1964), *Managerial and Engineering Economy,* Van Nostrand, Princeton, N.J.

the three sets of operating-quality costs. The purpose is to minimize total operating-quality cost, where this cost refers to the sum of prevention, appraisal, and failure costs.

Example

Another optimization problem involves a decision of whether to salvage rejected product through rework operations or to scrap the rejected product. Simply stated, the problem is to determine which cost is smaller—the cost of the rework operations or the cost of the rejected product item up to and including the last process operation when nonconformance was detected.

Although the decision seems to be a straightforward one, it hinges on primary data which may be difficult to obtain. Only by means of a good scrap and rework-reporting system (see Figure 3.7) can this data be readily secured. Furthermore, there are other costs to consider when product parts are reworked. There are additional burdens of material review, reordering of material and supplies, machine setups, unscheduled labor, production delays, reinspection, follow-up record keeping, and perhaps loss of customer goodwill for reasons of late shipment and delivery of product.

Example

A number of alternatives exist in connection with determining the degree of interchangeability which is feasible on a production basis. A high degree of interchangeability is accompanied by high process costs due to restrictive technical specifications governing the matching quality characteristics of mating component parts. On the other hand, a low degree of interchangeability, resulting from more liberal technical specifications, involves lower process costs. Typical optimization problems deal with opposing sets of costs with interest centered on minimization of the sum of the costs. The problems involve both quality-of-design and quality-of-conformance considerations. This topic is covered in detail in Chapter 7.

Example

One of the major responsibilities of machine operators, setup men, and line supervisors is to control processes in order to manufacture quality-product parts. Production personnel are continually and routinely engaged in the technology of process control. Their efforts constitute an unavoidable manufacturing cost.

Formal process-control assistance by quality-control staff and inspectors is frequently required to assure acceptable quality of production output. This extra control effort involves expenses (avoidable costs) that must be weighed against the expected benefits from the expanded control activity. Too little control can result in significant quality losses. Too much control may not be economically justified. More than one company has "controlled itself" out of existence. The question of how much control is feasible is certainly an economic matter. A simple optimization example concerns a single process operation. Is it more economic to use formal quality-control procedures? Or, is it less costly to dispense with the control procedures, accept a process output with inferior quality of conformance, and use a rectifying-inspection operation to bring the output to a satisfactory quality level?

Formal quality-control procedures use quantitative methods such as process-capability evaluations and control charts. Specific economic problems develop with the use of these methods. For example, the effectiveness of a control plan using a statistical control chart depends on the ability of the chart to detect assignable causes of variation. A control chart procedure is basically a test of a hypothesis. Two types of decision errors are possible—rejecting the hypothesis when it is true, and accepting the hypothesis when it is false. These decision errors lead to production expenses associated with looking for trouble that does not exist and failing to look for trouble that does exist. Certain optimization problems in this connection will be examined in Chapter 9.

Example

The concept of sampling inspection was introduced in Chapter 2. A number of optimization problems occur in relation to sampling-inspection applications. A basic problem is the selection of an economic sampling-inspection plan to minimize total inspection.

Decision errors are possible, which are similar to those attendant to control chart applications. Using a sampling-inspection plan, it is possible to reject a lot of acceptable quality product. Also, it is possible to accept a lot of unacceptable quality product. Any attempt to minimize the total cost of sampling inspection must consider the cost of the consequences of these decision errors. These questions will be considered in Chapter 10.

SUMMARY

Efforts to improve product quality are either income-expansion or cost-reduction expenditures. One quality objective is to maximize total revenue by using higher quality of design to capture a commanding share of the market. Another quality objective is to reduce manufacturing costs by improving quality of conformance. Operating-quality costs are classified as *prevention, appraisal,* or *failure* costs. Budgeting for the quality effort is based on the concept of nominal increases in prevention and/or appraisal expenditures generating significant reductions in failure costs and thereby minimizing total operating quality cost. Another expected return from these quality expenditures is reductions in basic manufacturing costs.

Quality activity and cost comparisons for different accounting periods are made possible by relating quality costs to a measurable base which reflects the degree of manufacturing activity for the period. Quality-cost measures utilize labor, manufacturing cost, sales, and unit bases.

The collection of information on quality costs due to rejected product is essential to any program of defect prevention. Reliable quality-costs information on rejected product can be obtained only by means of a good scrap and rework-reporting system.

Many economic optimization problems occur at the operations level of a manufacturing plant. Some typical examples involving the quality effort have been described at the conclusion of this chapter. Problem details have been deferred for later chapters and will be presented in connection with the topics to which they pertain.

REFERENCES

Barabee, J. M. (January, 1965), "The Development of a Scrap Cost Program," *Industrial Quality Control,* Vol. 21, No. 7, pp. 342-345.

Bicking, C. A. (December, 1967), "Cost and Value Aspects of Quality Control," *Industrial Quality Control,* Vol. 24, No. 6, pp. 306-308.

Feigenbaum, A. V. (1961), *Total Quality Control,* McGraw-Hill, New York, Chapter 5.

Field, D. L. (October, 1966), "Thoughts on the Economics of Quality," *Industrial Quality Control,* Vol. 23, No. 4, pp. 178-184.

Hansen, B. L. (1963), *Quality Control,* Prentice-Hall, Englewood Cliffs, N. J., Chapter 21.

Holguin, R. (January, 1968), "What Cost Reduction Can Do For You," *Industrial Quality Control,* Vol. 1, No. 1, pp. 22-24.

Juran, J. M. (August, 1965), "Whose Quality Costs," *Industrial Quality Control,* Vol. 22, No. 2, pp. 82-83.

McMullen, J. W. (May, 1965), "Quality Budget Control," *Industrial Quality Control,* Vol. 21, No. 11, pp. 558-559.

Squires, F. A. (November, 1966), "On the Quality Scene," *Quality Assurance,* Vol. 5, No. 11, p. 14.

REVIEW QUESTIONS

1. All efforts to improve product quality can be classified as being either income-expansion or cost-reduction expenditures. Discuss the economics of increasing income through better quality of design as compared to reducing costs by improving quality of conformance.

2. Define prevention, appraisal, and failure quality costs.

3. Distinguish between internal and external failure quality costs.

4. What are indirect quality costs?

5. Increases in prevention expenditures are usually expected to reduce failure costs. Explain why an increase in prevention expenditure may also result in decreased appraisal cost.

6. Discuss the possible existence of an optimum quality of conformance level such that total quality cost is minimized (see Figure 3.4).

7. Some examples were given illustrating the effects of expenditures for quality generating reductions in basic production costs. Explain how overhead cost may be reduced in this manner.

8. State four general applications of quality costs data.

9. Why are quality cost comparisons (for various time periods) of little value if expressed in absolute dollar amounts?

10. Explain the practice of using simultaneously a number of measurement bases for comparisons of operating quality costs.

11. In the computation of quality cost per equivalent unit of production output, the contributed value is obtained by subtracting direct material cost from net billed sales. What is the rationale underlying this procedure?

12. What is the most frequently analyzed element of quality cost (see Figure 3.7)? State another related quality cost element that is usually tabulated for analysis.

13. In budgeting for quality control, a ratio of quality-control man-hours to direct labor man-hours is frequently used. What is the underlying assumption to justify this procedure? Demonstrate by an example that this assumption may be invalid.

14. State the two main costs involved in the decision to scrap or salvage rejected product.

15. What is the economic alternative to formal process-control procedures?

4

The Technical
Specifications

The nucleus of quality control is the technical specification. The control of product quality revolves around two principal activities: (1) development of the technical specifications for the product, and (2) assurance of product conformance to the technical specifications. The first activity deals with quality of design, the second with quality of conformance.

The technical specification consists of two specifying elements—nominal size and tolerance. *Nominal* size is a designation used for general identification. For example, a cylindrical pin may be referred to as a $\frac{1}{2}$ in. pin, although the actual size may be 0.4985 in. In this case, the nominal size is $\frac{1}{2}$ in. *Tolerance* is the total permissible variation of the quality characteristic. For example, a specification of 0.500 $\pm$ 0.002 in. (see Figure 1.3) states that the size quality characteristic may vary from 0.498 in. to 0.502 in. The tolerance is 0.004 in. Control of quality characteristics is largely a matter of controlling variation. Thus, interest will be primarily on the tolerance component of the technical specification.

THE TOLERANCE PROBLEM

A principal objective in designing for production is to establish tolerances compatible with probable process variations. In theory, the problem is a simple one. The product designer need only specify the largest tolerance consistent with product operation and life requirements, and manufacturing should then provide ways and means to attain that tolerance. However, in practice there are many factors to consider and the problem becomes complex and difficult to solve.

Conflicting Requirements and Factors

Essentially, a proper manufacturing tolerance is a compromise between alternative actions and cost consequences. Small tolerances, which tend to increase manufacturing costs, are necessary to permit interchangeable assembly and to control quality, performance, and life of the product. Large tolerances avoid restriction of output, waste of material and effort, and generally tend to reduce manufacturing costs. In designing products, engineers have responsibilities which may be summarized to include function, durability, appearance, and cost. The constant challenge is to force the first three and the last one apart, that is, to either maintain quality at lower cost or to improve quality at fixed cost. Some conflicting requirements affecting this objective are given below.

Factors Operating to Reduce Tolerances

1. Product function, durability, and appearance requirements (accomplished by maintaining correct fit, alignment, and clearance of component parts, proper material characteristics, surface finishes, etc.).
2. Maintenance of in-plant interchangeability with a minimum of fitting or adjustment at assembly.
3. Interchangeability-in-the-field demands.
4. Need for a tolerance reserve or factor of safety to cover engineering uncertainty regarding maximum variation compatible with satisfactory product performance.
5. In-process interchangeability requirements to establish intermediate tooling locations.
6. Other special manufacturing requirements.

Factors Operating to Enlarge Tolerances

Unnecessarily restrictive tolerances generate serious increases in time and cost absorbed in some or all of the following production factors:

69

1. Production planning, tool design, and tool fabrication.
2. Tool and process setup.
3. Tool adjustment and regrinding.
4. Tool maintenance and replacement.
5. Extra manufacturing operations.
6. Process yield.
7. Inspection and gage supply, control, and maintenance.
8. Scrap and salvage operations.
9. Direct labor and associated line supervision.
10. Proportion of indirect to direct labor.

Physical Factors Affecting Tolerance Decisions

Modern tolerancing systems and procedures recognize four basic product conditions to be controlled by tolerances: (1) size, (2) form, (3) location, and (4) conditions of assembly, operation, or function. Figure 4.1 indicates examples of these conditions. Parts A and B are mating components; the shaded portion of B fits into the slot in A. The difference, size A minus size B, is called *clearance* and is a simple example of an assembly condition.

Size conditions, particularly those of elementary surfaces, are relatively simple to specify and control. Form and location conditions are more complex, especially where composite surfaces and cumulative tolerances are involved. Few industrial tolerancing systems attempt to comprehensively provide for form and location definition and specification. Reliance is usually placed on the jigs and fixtures, and much of the quality assurance responsibility is shifted to the tool-design function. Conditions of assembly, operation, and function frequently produce cumulative tolerance situations wherein dependent conditions of size, form, and location are involved for a set of related surfaces. The total resultant variation of the assembly or functional characteristic may be the critical factor whereas the individual feature variations are independently of little importance. It is difficult and costly to control all of the contributing quality characteristics to small tolerances. The most direct and effective quality-assurance procedure is to provide for a test specification on the critical assembly or functional characteristic and use a functional gage to assure conformance.

A physical factor, which makes it difficult to define and control product-quality characteristics, is the lack of geometric perfection. Shapes or forms into which material is fabricated may be defined by geometric terms. The geometric definition assumes a perfect form. However, since perfect forms cannot be produced, variations must be restricted if a specific quality is to be maintained. These geometric

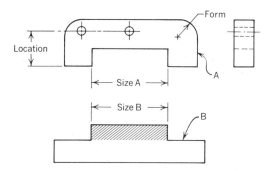

Figure 4.1.   Product conditions.

variations, often referred to as *macro* errors (as opposed to *micro* or surface finish deviations) are straightness, flatness, parallelism, squareness, angular displacement, symmetry, concentricity, roundness, and eccentricity. When a product feature is affected by macro errors, size conditions may be altered. In fact, size may not even be uniquely defined as, for example, in the case of an out-of-round cylindrical form where diameter is not defined. Furthermore, product function may and frequently does depend on the combined effect of actual sizes and macro errors.

Closely related to the problem of lack of true geometric form is the lack of perfect rigidity. Production materials stretch, spring, warp, and bruise. Departures from perfect rigidity affect geometric form, size, and location conditions. Extensive engineering analysis is required to determine the resulting effects upon product-function variation. Frequently, these effects are determinable only through experiment and test activity.

Measurement Factors Affecting Tolerance Decisions

In Chapter 1 the point was made that the effectiveness of the specification in controlling quality is dependent on a standard for interpretation (see Figures 1.8 and 1.9) and a method of measuring the quality characteristic consistent with the standard. It is necessary to translate the product dimensional specifications into inspection gage specifications, and to assure that product satisfying the prescribed inspection will be entirely adequate relative to the product specifications. Consideration must be given to the conditions the gages will and will not control. Permissible product variations must be analyzed in light of those conditions that will be acceptable to the gage. It is to be noted

71

that when a master gage has been verified and accepted, its actual size and form supersedes all corresponding product-specification information. This is also true for the inspection gage. Once production has begun, product is manufactured to suit the gages and corrective adjustments to tooling and setups are made only as indicated by the gages. All manufacturing will follow the gages, even though there may seem to be technical violations of geometric interpretations of the product specifications. Hence, translatability of product specification to gage specification is a basic criterion affecting tolerance decisions.

Many problems, both technological and economic, are encountered in the selection and design of gaging equipment to assure conformance of today's high-quality products. Production-accuracy requirements are frequently of the order of a tenth of a thousandth of an inch. Production jobs calling for accuracy in millionths of an inch are no longer rare. The tradition under which the product designer, machine-tool designer, and gage designer have all occupied separate worlds — meeting only occasionally in case of trouble — is no longer workable. For example, gage designers and quality-control personnel must now possess (1) an engineering familiarity with the many physical properties and associated specifications for their company's products, (2) an analytical understanding of the manufacturing processes and an appreciation of process variations and likely effects upon product requirements, and (3) a working knowledge of all the refinements that scientists and researchers have wrought in today's measuring instruments. It is not enough to know where gaging hardware is to be procured and how it is to be operated. Knowledge is also required of such physical concepts as compression, deflection, and surface deformation (both elastic and permanent), of temperature effects, and of heat transfer behavior of the product object being measured and of the gage itself. Analysis of error sources and action to minimize error effects is essential. In many cases, the combination of error effects will involve statistical analyses.

Economic Factors Affecting Tolerance Decisions

In the section of this chapter dealing with conflicting requirements and factors, some ten production factors were identified as incurring serious cost increases as a result of unnecessarily restrictive tolerances. It is common knowledge that product design determines manufacturing costs, and choices do exist between design elements which can either increase or decrease product costs. Few of the many factors involved can exercise a more powerful control over product costs than the manufacturing tolerances adopted, and it would be difficult to over-emphasize the cumulative effect of tolerances on product costs.

Over-all quality of product is very closely linked with manufacturing precision. Improvements in quality are allied with higher production precision and too often result in increased product cost. Conversely, lower production precision and lower cost result in lesser quality. These factors have a natural tendency to behave as directly proportionate variables. Although the order of importance varies from one product to another, cost is always a prime consideration.

With any product, it is the design engineer's task to attain as nearly as possible a balance between product function, durability, and appearance requirements and cost. In attempting to reach an economic balance between these factors, the design engineer in many organizations finds himself handicapped by lack of cost information to guide his selection of quality level compatible with reasonable cost boundaries. His only alternatives are time-consuming research or postponement of cost considerations. In the latter case, when cost information becomes available through actual production experience, positive corrective action becomes possible. Meanwhile, serious production expenses may have been incurred. Further, engineering time and development costs are involved in whatever corrective actions are deemed necessary.

Several facts are worth noting: (1) Many quality characteristics can be resolved into definable increments lending themselves to measurement; (2) cost behavior patterns tend to become buried in industrial engineering data designed for use in plant operational control; (3) such cost data is in a language adapted specifically for plant control purposes; (4) this data is extractable and translatable into information needed by the average design engineer.

In most cases, it is possible to utilize the above mentioned data to tabulate time and cost differentials for all standardized quality differentials. Any such tabulation will reveal that cost varies with varying quality specifications, and that the degree of change is predictable. A number of examples are shown in Figures 4.2 through 4.8.

NOMENCLATURE OF SPECIFICATIONS

For the purpose of developing standard tolerance language and definitions, examples will be restricted to simple size conditions and the assembly condition of clearance between matching quality charac-

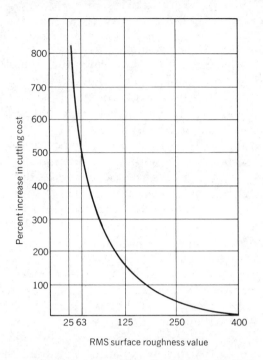

Figure 4.2. Cost comparison chart in which cost is plotted with respect to surface quality standards. From L. J. Bayer (August, 1956), "Manufacturing Cost as Related to Product Design," *Tooling and Production*, Vol. 22, No. 5, pp. 73-76.

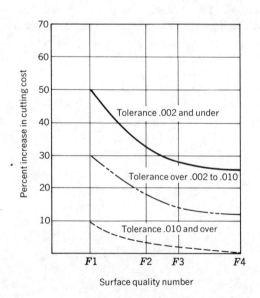

Figure 4.3. Cost comparison showing the effect of two quality variables—surface quality and dimensional tolerance. From L. J. Bayer (August, 1956), "Manufacturing Cost as Related to Product Design," *Tooling and Production*, Vol. 22, No. 5, pp. 73-76.

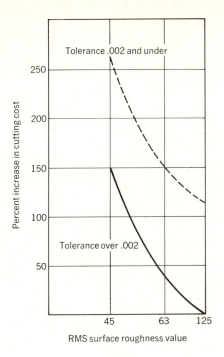

Figure 4.4.   Comparing surface quality and dimensional tolerance in face milling. From
L. J. Bayer (August, 1956), "Manufacturing Cost as Related to Product Design," *Tooling
and Production,* Vol. 22, No. 5, pp. 73-76.

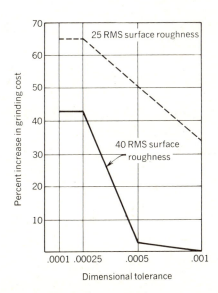

Figure 4.5.   Comparing surface quality and tolerance in cylindrical grinding. From
L. J. Bayer (August, 1956), "Manufacturing Cost as Related to Product Design," *Tooling
and Production,* Vol. 22, No. 5, pp. 73-76.

teristics. The definitions and quantitative procedures involved agree with accepted standards for the mechanical industries.

Tolerance

A *tolerance* is a specified permissible magnitude of error and generally refers to a single quality characteristic. Tolerance specifications are denoted in two fundamental forms. One form states the design size and tolerance. An example is 0.500 ± 0.002 in. where the design size is 0.500 in. and the tolerance is 0.004 in. The notational form is bilateral, that is, tolerance or variability is measured in both directions from the design size. Examples of other bilateral notations are: 0.501 + 0.001 − 0.003 in. and 0.499 + 0.003 − 0.001 in. All three examples refer to the same numerical specification, namely, that product size may vary from 0.502 in. to 0.498 in. The latter two examples represent a psychological attempt on the part of product design to influence manufacturing as to which limit is to be favored. Such a practice is

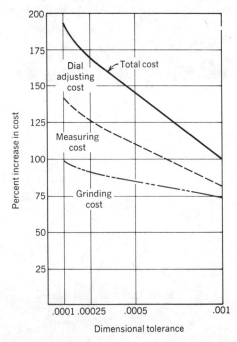

Figure 4.6. Comparing varying tolerances in internal grinding. From L. J. Bayer (August, 1956), "Manufacturing Cost as Related to Product Design," *Tooling and Production,* Vol. 22, No. 5, pp. 73-76.

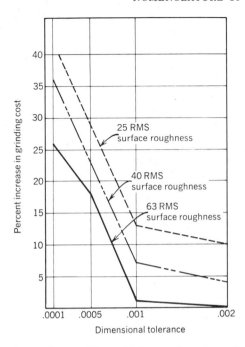

Figure 4.7. Comparing surface quality and tolerance in reciprocating surface grinding. From L. J. Bayer (August, 1956), "Manufacturing Cost as Related to Product Design," *Tooling and Production,* Vol. 22, No. 5, pp. 73-76.

questionable since manufacturing will usually favor the maximum material limit (i.e., the limit associated with the most material remaining on the quality characteristic after processing).

Bilateral representation has the disadvantages of possible arithmetic error (manufacturing personnel perform the addition and subtraction from the design size) and visual error (the ± notation may become illegible on shop prints). A possible advantage of bilateral notation—equal variability in both directions from the design size—is to emphasize the middle value design size. This is important where statistical process-control charts are being used.

Another notational form of the tolerance specification is to state the two limits. An example is 0.502/0.498 in. All examples to this point refer to the same numerical specification: *maximum limit* is 0.502 in. *minimum limit* is 0.498 in. These are frequently referred to as upper and lower limits. Another term requiring definition at this point is *nominal.* There are actually two definitions of this term depending on the area of use. For identification purposes in purchasing activities, nominal refers to the closest fractional value with the smallest increment being $\frac{1}{64}$ in. The nominal size in the above example is $\frac{1}{2}$ in. In

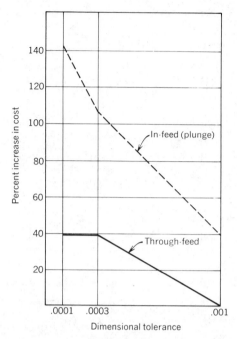

Figure 4.8. Comparing tolerance and design in centerless grinding. From L. J. Bayer (August, 1956), "Manufacturing Cost as Related to Product Design," *Tooling and Production,* Vol. 22, No. 5, pp. 73-76.

manufacturing language, however, nominal usually refers to the mean average of the two limits (i.e., 0.500 in the above example). The latter interpretation will be assumed in the following chapters.

Clearance and Fit

A common assembly condition involving cumulative tolerances is indicated in Figure 4.9. Parts A, B, C, and D are assembled in that order into the assembly space (in this case, the slot in E). Concern is with whether or not D will actually assemble, that is, there may be an interference condition. Or, if assembly is possible, interest is on the magnitude of the *clearance* between D and E.

The most simple case of clearance between fitting parts is illustrated by Figure 4.10. The matching quality characteristics here are the outside diameter of A and the inside diameter of E. The quality characteristic of interest is the clearance between these two diameters.

Specified clearance refers to the difference between the limits of two matching quality-characteristic specifications. Maximum specified clearance is the maximum limit of the interior quality characteristic

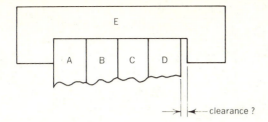

Figure 4.9.   Clearance condition.

(i.e., hole diameter, slot width, etc.) minus the minimum limit of the matching exterior characteristic (i.e., shaft diameter, width of a square pin, etc.). Minimum clearance is the minimum limit of the interior quality characteristic minus the maximum limit of the exterior characteristic. Clearances may be positive or negative, depending on whether or not there exists actual physical clearance. For example, in press or shrink fits clearances may be negative. Assembly is performed by means of considerable pressure and/or temperature changes to alter the sizes of the mating quality characteristics during assembly.

Allowance

Allowance is minimum specified clearance. Allowance describes the condition of tightest possible fit between the matching quality characteristics under the prescribed tolerances. Allowance is usually defined in terms of *maximum material limit* (MML), which refers to the limit associated with the most material remaining on the quality characteristic after processing. The MML of a shaft diameter is the maximum limit; the MML of a hole diameter is the minimum limit.

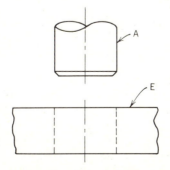

Figure 4.10.   Clearance condition.

79

Thus, allowance is the difference between the MML's of the two mating quality characteristics. Traditional engineering practice involves designing from a basis of allowance values. It is suggested that this practice be modified somewhat in light of the statistical arguments presented in the following chapters.

A Summary Example

The following specifications refer to Figure 4.10. The specification for A is 0.5010/0.5006 in. outside diameter, and for E it is 0.5000/0.5010 in. inside diameter. It is convenient to summarize tolerance and clearance information as shown in Figure 4.11.

The student should verify the numerical values listed below:

Nominal: $\frac{1}{2}$ in.
Tolerance: part A, 0.0004; part E, 0.001
MML: part A, 0.5010; part E, 0.5000
Allowance: −0.0010
Maximum clearance: +0.0004
Mean clearance: −0.0003

In design language, fits are described as "varying from −0.001 tight to +0.0004 loose." *Note:* Notational form of the specification:

(Interior q.c.)   (Exterior q.c.)

Design Size   Design Size
Min. Material Limit   Min. Material Limit

Systems of Fits

There are a variety of systems for the definition of standard fits. The American Standards Association ASA Y14.5, the British Standard BS.1916, and the International Standards Organization Bulletin 25 are but a few. All systems are developed by varying the allowance values for fixed range of nominal sizes. The resulting fits are separated into a certain number of classes, each class being identified with common design requirements.

The purpose here is not to explore tables of standards in detail, but to develop the language common to standards. *Fit* refers to the range of tightness which may result from the application of a specific combination of allowance and tolerances in the design of mating components. Differentiation of fit is by class and grade. *Class* of fit is a classification based on allowance values. Standard systems generate

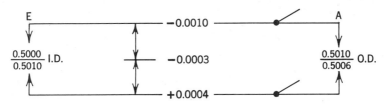

Figure 4.11.   Tolerances and clearances.

three general classes of fit: *clearance* fits where both maximum and minimum clearances are positive; *interference* fits where both maximum and minimum clearances are negative; and *transition* fits having minimum clearance negative and maximum clearance positive. *Grade of fit* is a classification indicating the range of possible fits for fixed tolerance combinations. In the preceding example, the class of fit was transitional and the range, -0.001 to $+0.0004 = 0.0014$, referred to the grade of fit.

All tolerancing standards use the terms basic size and design size. *Basic size* is the theoretical size, a reference or point of departure for the application of tolerance and allowance. If design requirements indicate a nominal size of $\frac{1}{2}$ in., then basic size is simply 0.5000 in. (i.e., theoretical size in that no error is specified). *Design size* is a theoretical size used as a point of departure for the application of tolerance only.

Basic Hole and Basic Shaft Procedures

Basic hole and basic shaft tolerancing practices can be defined in several ways. The definitions that follow are in terms of specification-determination procedure. In *basic hole* procedure, the design size of the hole is identical to the basic size. The design size of the hole, coupled with the allowance value, establishes the design size of the shaft. The *basic shaft* procedure is just the opposite: the design size of the shaft corresponds to basic size and the application of the allowance determines the design size of the hole.

The same fits may be obtained by either basic hole or basic shaft procedure. However, the basic hole method is most commonly used. The main reason it is preferred is that the physical hole size cannot be varied conveniently because of fixed sizes of standard drills, reamers, broaches, plug gages, and so forth, whereas the shaft size is generally controlled with adjustable tools or grinding wheels. The basic-shaft method is preferred in some branches of industry that use a large volume of cold finished shafting in their product. This

81

permits the use of stock without machining it, and the mounting of several component parts with different fits on the same shaft without stepping it.

Unilateral and Bilateral Procedures

The following discussion is concerned with specification determination and not specification notation. As far as notation is concerned, any given specification may be represented either unilaterally or bilaterally simply by changing the design size. For example, 0.500 ± 0.002 in. and $0.498 + 0.004 - 0.000$ in. both yield the same limits, 0.502 in. and 0.498 in. In specification determination, *unilateral* procedure means that the tolerance will be applied in one direction only from the design size, a plus direction for the hole and a minus direction for the shaft. *Bilateral* procedure involves applying the tolerance in both directions from the design size. (Note: in unilateral procedure, design size is identical to maximum material limit, MML.)

Both procedures are encountered in design departments. However, all modern standard systems of fits are based on unilateral procedure. There are two principal advantages to the adoption of unilateral procedures. First, the tolerance specifications determined in this manner will be compatible with the sizes of commercial fixed-type cutting tools and gages for producing holes. Second, if tolerances are relaxed as they usually are when manufacturing difficulties arise, component parts produced after the tolerance change are interchangeable with product made before the change. This is not necessarily true under bilateral procedure.

DETERMINING THE SPECIFICATIONS

The procedures that follow are primarily for a condition of fit and usually for shaft-hole combinations.

Example

Given the nominal size, allowance, and tolerance values, determine the specifications for two mating quality characteristics (for example, a shaft-hole combination). Design requirements indicate the nominal size to be $\frac{1}{2}$ in. Functional requirements determine the allowance to be $+0.0002$ in. Functional plus manufacturing requirements establish the tolerances to be 0.0005 in. on each component quality characteristic. (This is not realistic since more tolerance is usually allocated to

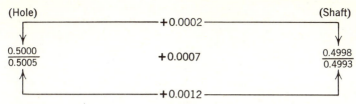

Figure 4.12.   Specifications and clearances.

the interior characteristic; however, the equal tolerance condition is intentional to simplify the example.)

The specifications and resulting clearances are summarized in Figure 4.12. Basic size is 0.5000 in. Assume basic hole procedure; this establishes the design size of the hole to be 0.5000 in. Application of the +0.0002 in. allowance determines the design size of the shaft to be 0.4998 in. Application of the 0.0005 in. tolerance to each design size determines the maximum hole size to be 0.5005 in. and the minimum shaft size to be 0.4993 in.

Fits will vary from +0.0002 tight to +0.0012 loose, with a specified mean clearance of +0.0007.

The student should note that tolerance determination may proceed along a slightly different route. Design requirements may fix nominal size, minimum clearance, and maximum clearance. An infinite number of tolerance specifications are then possible. The designer selects a solution that will yield enough tolerance to satisfy manufacturing requirements on the interior quality characteristic and leave a reasonable tolerance for the exterior characteristic. Usually more tolerance is allocated to the interior characteristic, which is usually more difficult to process to close tolerances on a production basis.

Example

Using the same numerical values from the preceding example, the requirements now are (1) basic size to be 0.5000 in., and (2) clearances are to vary from +0.0002 in. to +0.0012 in. From this information only the maximum material limits can be determined as shown in Figure 4.13. An infinite number of pairs of minimum material limits exist which would result in a maximum clearance of +0.0012.

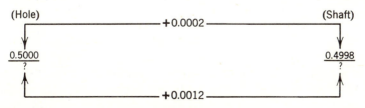

Figure 4.13.   An incomplete solution.

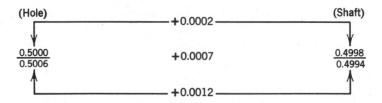

Figure 4.14. Unequal tolerance allocation.

In practice, the designer may allocate more tolerance to the inside diameter characteristic. Figure 4.14 indicates such a solution. The hole specification has a tolerance of 0.0006 in., the shaft specification a tolerance of 0.0004 in.

In examples in subsequent chapters, the tolerances will frequently be allocated equally to each component (in this example, the specifications would then become identical to those of Figure 4.12). The student should appreciate the fact that, though this may not be practical, it is done to simplify examples and, in particular, to yield unique solutions.

Another method of tolerance determination is to use the design information regarding nominal size and standard class of fit required, then enter a table of standard fits and read the specification limits directly. This practice may be satisfactory for an apprentice designer, but it usually leads to tolerance specifications that are much too restrictive. Such tables should only be used as guides.

SUMMARY

The technical specification consists of two specifying elements—*nominal* size and *tolerance*. Control of quality characteristics is largely a matter of controlling variation. Thus, interest is primarily on the tolerance component of the technical specification.

The proper choice of a tolerance is the result of a compromise between alternative factors and cost consequences. To satisfy certain product-design objectives, tolerances may have to be reduced. On the other hand, there exist production factors which require that tolerances be increased.

In the mechanical industries, product conditions controlled by tolerances are size, form, location, and conditions of assembly, operation, or function. There are many physical factors affecting tolerance decisions. For example, lack of geometric perfection and perfect rigidity makes it difficult to formulate tolerances that control size, form, and location characteristics. Likewise, there are many measurement and economic factors which also affect tolerance decisions.

A basic nomenclature of specifications has been presented to acquaint the management student with the technical language of specifications. Such terms as tolerance, clearance, allowance, design size, and maximum material size are fundamental to tolerance discussion. Furthermore, in subsequent chapters, it will be necessary for the student to determine simple specifications in order to deal with tolerances computed from a probability basis.

REFERENCES

American Standard ASA Y14.5 (1957), American Standards Association, 10 East 40 st., New York.

Bayer, L. J. (August, 1956), "Manufacturing Costs Related to Product Design," *Tooling and Production*, pp. 73-76.

British Standard BS. 1916 (1953), British Standards Institution, 2 Park St., London W.I., England.

Buckingham, E. (1954), *Dimensions and Tolerances for Mass Production*, Industrial Press, New York.

Conway, H. G. (1966), *Engineering Tolerances,* Pitman, London, pp. 125-238.

Mechanical Engineering Drawing Standards B78 (1954), Canadian Standards Association, 235 Montreal Road, Ottawa 7, Canada.

Military Standard MIL-STD-8B (1959), "Dimensioning and Tolerancing," U. S. Government Printing Office, Washington, D. C.

REVIEW QUESTIONS

1. State the two basic specifying elements of the technical specification.

2. What is a principal objective in designing for production?

3. Briefly discuss small tolerances and large tolerances in terms of purpose, production effects, and manufacturing costs.

4. Identify four general product conditions that are controlled by tolerances.

5. State two physical factors that make it difficult to define and control product-quality characteristics.

6. The statement has been made that product costs depend greatly on the manufacturing tolerances that are adopted. Consider an internal grinding

operation for which the specification tolerance has been reduced from 0.001 in. to 0.0001 in. (see Figure 4.6). What is the percent increase in total cost for the operation?

7. Define tolerance, clearance, and allowance.

8. Give two definitions of nominal size and identify the activity area to which each definition pertains.

9. Define clearance, interference, and transition fits.

10. Distinguish between basic size and design size.

PROBLEMS

1. A specification tolerance is 0.500 ± 0.005 in. outside diameter. State the numerical values of (a) nominal size, (b) tolerance, (c) maximum limit, and (d) minimum limit.

2. The following specification information is for the two matching product parts shown in Figure 4.10: nominal size, ¾ in.; allowance, +0.0003 in.; and tolerance, 0.0006 in. for each part diameter (i.e., outside diameter of A and inside diameter of the matching hole in E). Using basic hole and unilateral tolerancing procedures, determine (a) the specifications for A and E, (b) minimum and maximum clearances, and (c) mean clearance.

3. Identify for each product part in problem 2 (a) maximum material limit and (b) design size.

4. Assume that in problem 2 the specification information is nominal size, ¾ in.; and clearances, +0.0004 in. to +0.0012 in. Using basic hole and unilateral tolerancing procedures (a) determine the specifications for A and E allocating tolerance equally to each part, (b) revise the specifications, assuming that 0.0006 in. tolerance is required for E.

5. Figure 4.9 describes a slot (part E) into which is fitted four parts A, B, C, and D. The nominal width size of each of the four parts is ½ in. The specification for the width of the slot in E is 2.004 ± 0.002 in. Assume the required clearance is to be +0.002 in. to +0.010 in. Determine the specifications for the widths of A, B, C, and D, assuming equal tolerance allocation to each.

5

Some Design Considerations

Product quality is dependent on the development of proper technical specifications for the product and the assurance of conformance to these specifications. Assuring conformance to specifications is, in part, a production design matter. Determining specifications is a product-design matter. Both activities are engineering in nature and involve the technology of the product and the processes. Ideally, the quality-planning operations should be staffed by engineers. This may not be necessary for the quality-control operations. However, even at the control level, the average quality-control man must be knowledgeable regarding the technology of his company's products and the process operations required for their manufacture. Although not a design engineer, he nevertheless should be acquainted with design objectives, constraints, and procedures which determine the technical specifications. The purpose of this chapter is to summarize some of the elementary design factors that are pertinent to the quality effort.

CREATING A NEW PRODUCT

Figure 5.1 indicates the cycle of design and development activities required to create a new product. Sketches, drawings, and research lead to an experimental design (also called *experimental* model). The

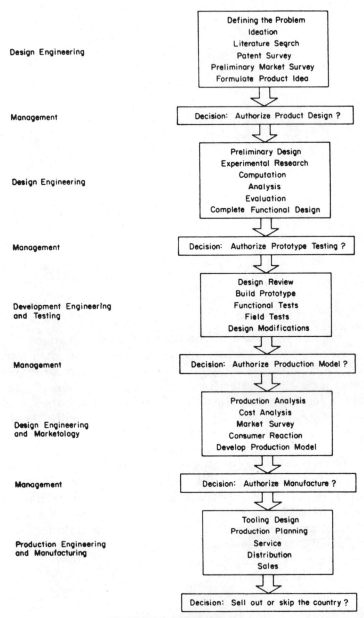

PRODUCT DEVELOPMENT

Decisions! Decisions! Decisions!

Figure 5.1. Creating a new product. From L. Harrisberger, (1966), *Engineermanship—A Philosophy of Design*, Brooks/Cole, Belmont, Calif., p. 83.

technical specifications required for manufacture receive little attention during this development phase. The major effort at this point is to confirm a design that will be representative of the customer's requirements.

Approval of the experimental model initiates redesign activity to facilitate manufacture. Decisions are made either to change existing manufacturing equipment to suit the product-design requirements, or to alter product-design details to satisfy the limitations of existing processes and equipment. The result of this redesign effort is a new design called the production design (or *production model*).

Final design reviews (see New Design Review, Chapter 2) reveal manufacturing difficulties requiring further redesign of product parts. Tool and gage design and development expose still other manufacturing problems that may affect the production design. And, even after formal production is initiated, manufacturing troubles develop, necessitating further redesign of the product.

Clearly, all of these corrective actions have an effect on the technical specifications. Many specifications will be reviewed and altered. The effects of specifications changes on quality requirements will then have to be determined. This may involve extensive experiment and test activity. Many companies make several *manufacturing models* of the product to the first production-design specifications. These models are used for experiment and test and may be retained as functional gages to prove the first tool-made parts of the production run.

Engineering Drawing Specifications

There are three classes of engineering-drawing specifications: layouts, assembly drawings, and detail drawings. Layouts represent the first step in defining design concepts on paper. A *layout* consists chiefly of outlines of assemblies and defines all of the major design and many of the relationships between the respective assemblies. Few dimensional specifications emerge at this point.

Assembly drawings are similar to layouts but are much more complete and show far more detail. An example of an *assembly* drawing is shown in Figure 5.2. Considerable redesign activity occurs between the layout and the assembly drawing stages to utilize standard purchased parts wherever possible and to facilitate manufacture of component parts in general. The assembly drawing defines the kind and number of component parts required and establishes the relationships between the component parts. Some functional specifications may also be established.

A *detail* drawing is prepared for each component part. The detail drawing defines the component part and completely supplies all neces-

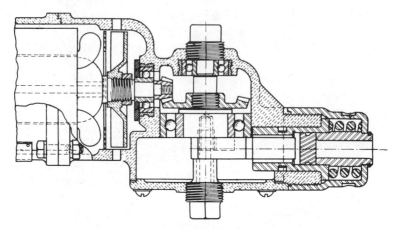

Figure 5.2.   Assembly drawing.

sary specifications so the part can be fabricated without reference to any other drawing specification. Figure 5.3 shows a typical detail drawing. When vendor-manufacturing units are involved, the detail drawing serves as the legal basis of contract between the purchaser and the manufacturer.

All of the foregoing pertains to product-design specification drawings. The student should note that there also are production drawing specifications. For example, frequent use is made of forging and casting drawings that give only forging and casting dimensional specifications. Further, if a product component is especially complex, separate production drawings may be prepared giving intermediate processing specifications such as rough, semi-finish, and finish turning, grinding, and other operations. Also, separate drawings and specifications are established for the design and procurement of tools, jigs, fixtures, and gages.

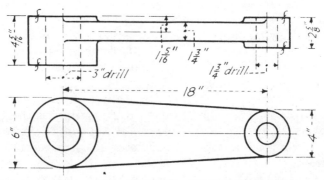

Figure 5.3.   Detail drawing.

Dimensions and Tolerances

Determining the engineering-drawing specifications is a job that challenges the best design and production talent in the organization. There is probably no other place in the organization where so much money can be saved by attention to detail, and there is certainly no other place where so much money can be wasted by carelessness and ignorance. Dimensioning and tolerancing an engineering drawing is the stage at which the designer's theoretical concepts are translated to practical production concepts. The designer's concept of a product component is one of a number of theoretical centers and exact geometries with a suitable amount of surrounding metal. Production, however, is usually supplied with a piece of material which already possesses a shape of some description. Inside the confines of this shape, it is production's job to locate the centers and generate reasonable approximations to the exact geometries. Furthermore, whereas a drawing dimension is a fixed value, the introduction of tolerances makes the dimension a variable quantity. This generates serious problems concerning error effects, error relationships, cumulative errors, and so forth, along with disturbing inadequacies, ambiguities, and redundancies inherent to the dimensional language of the drawing specification. A comprehensive treatment of this topic is beyond the scope and purpose of this textbook. However, since the matter of cumulative tolerances is so important in quality control, this topic is briefly discussed in the remainder of this chapter.

CUMULATIVE TOLERANCES

Knowledge of the exact function of each product part is necessary to formulate correct definitive specifications. Functional and nonfunctional specifications must be clearly separated. A nonfunctional specification is one which may have a comparatively larger tolerance without affecting the function of the part. Functional specifications govern operation, life, and interchangeability requirements of the product. It is important that functional specifications be expressed in direct terms. Indirect expression of functional specifications tends to obscure the function requirements and is a serious handicap to the inspection department. Moreover, indirect expression invariably leads to more restrictive production tolerances.

Figure 5.4 illustrates an indirect specification of a functional requirement leading to reduced production tolerances. The functional requirement F is location of the surfaces a and a' of the rectangular hole A with respect to the reference center line b of the reamed holes B. Direct locational specification of a and a' yields tolerances of 0.008 in. each. If a size dimension S is preferred for A, to achieve the same functional control of F $\pm$ 0.004 in., it becomes necessary to halve the tolerances for locating a and a'.

Two important tolerancing principles are illustrated by this example. First, indirect control of functional characteristics requires more dimensional specifications (two dimensions are required to locate a' indirectly, where only one would locate it directly). Second, if more dimensions are required to control an assembly characteristic, their respective tolerances will necessarily be smaller (from 0.008 in. to 0.004 in. in this example).

Another example is indicated by Figure 5.5. One design alternative concerns three components — A, B, and C — fitting into an assembly space E. If a design requirement necessitates four components — A, B, C, and D — fitting into the same space, the 0.012 in. available tolerance distributed over four components will restrict each component tolerance to an average of $\pm$ 0.0015 in.

The preceding examples have been simplified considerably — only size conditions and elementary geometries being involved. Typical product-assembly conditions are generated by dozens of component-dimensional characteristics dealing with composite conditions of size, form, and location.

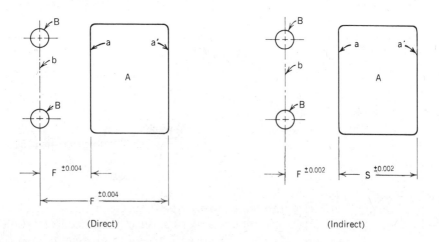

Figure 5.4.   Direct and indirect specification of functional requirement F.

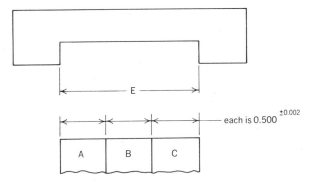

Figure 5.5.   Direct and indirect specification.

Dimensional Datums

In developing technical specifications, the product designer establishes datums from which the component-part features are located. A *datum* is a line or plane reference from which location requirements are established. (In Figure 5.4, *b* was the design datum.) Design datums are used for product-feature locations. Production datums are required by manufacturing for product-part location in chuck, jig, or fixture for the various process operations. Inspection datums are used for measurement purposes in the inspection of quality characteristics.

The difficulty in datum selection is that design datums may not be convenient for use as production datums and neither may be suitable as inspection datums. If different datums are used for the same quality characteristic by design, production, and inspection, this will constitute indirect control of the characteristic and will necessarily restrict tolerances for the same reasons advanced in the example of Figure 5.4. The ideal situation is when all three datums are identical. This will make possible the largest production tolerances compatible with product-functional requirements.

Generally, the product designer does not attempt to forecast the exact method of production for each product part. The production method will depend on the available manufacturing facilities and may also depend on the quantity of product parts to be produced. For these reasons it is not feasible for product design to establish production datums. However, direct expression of functional specifications on the engineering drawings will tend to assure the correct selection of production datums.

As we have observed, increasing the number of dimensions required

93

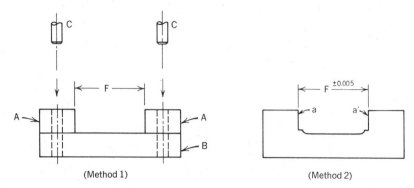

Figure 5.6. Use of a casting to minimize the number of location dimensions required.

to control a functional or assembly characteristic reduces the available tolerance for the individual dimensions. A simple example of this is given in Figure 5.6. The functional dimension F is to be controlled within ± 0.005 in. Fabrication method 1 shows parts A and B located at assembly by pins C. The diameters of the pins and pinholes are subject to size errors. Further, the pinhole locations may vary. To control F, the available 0.010 in. tolerance will have to be distributed over nine dimensions, restricting each one to a very small tolerance. Fabrication method 2 uses a casting with surfaces a and a' being machined directly to the specification F. The entire 0.010 in. tolerance is available for this process operation.

In developing product specifications, there are as many groups of locational dimensions (and a datum for each group) as there are separate functional or assembly requirements. Design alternatives to minimize the number of locational groups of dimensions (and thus the number of datums) are (1) the use of weldments or castings, and (2) a redesign to combine critical surfaces compactly in a unit subassembly that can be assembled and tested independently. Economic considerations affect the first alternative. Use of castings is feasible only if the quantity of parts to be produced is a sufficiently large base over which the cost of the patterns and castings can be distributed. The second alternative is affected by field-service requirements; for example, it may become necessary to replace the entire subassembly rather than just the worn or malfunctioning component part.

Stack-ups

A *stack-up* refers to an evaluation of the cumulative effect of the separate product-part tolerances on the functional or assembly quality characteristic. In Figure 5.5, the maximum sum of the sizes of

A, B, and C is 1.506 in., and the minimum sum is 1.494 in. If the specification for E is 1.508 ± 0.002 in., the stack-up indicates possible clearances from zero to 0.016 in.

Table 5.1 is an example of a stackup for an aerospace industry product. Eighteen dimensions from five component parts accumulate to determine an assembly condition of clearance. The nominal values are accumulated in the left-hand column. Addition or subtraction depends on the geometric relations involved. Tolerances are accumulated in the right-hand column and are always added.

It is interesting to observe that the cumulative tolerance (± 0.1035 in.) exceeds the cumulative nominal size (± 0.0878 in.) This indicates that if manufacturing errors are always the maximum permitted by the specifications (and in the same direction, either plus or minus), a condition of negative clearance or interference will result.

Stack-ups are formally generated as a matter of record at the drawing-approval stage called the checking function. Senior designers or checkers carry out appropriate dimensional analyses to assess choice of datums and corresponding dimensional groups, cumulative tolerances, possible redundant specifications, and so forth.

Table 1. **Stack-up example**

An interference exists on Assembly 138474 between the terminal board located in the cover and the nut retaining the magnet holder in the gimbal. The *dimensional stack-up* is as follows.

    Base: 138669
1.   0.0600 ± .0050 Ledge thickness
2. +0.4625 ± .0075 Inside ledge to trunnion support
3. +2.3725 ± .0075 Trunnion support to trunnion support
4. +0.2500 ± .0150 Trunnion support thickness
     3.1450 ± .0350
    −0.0400 ± .0010 Bearing C' bore depth
     3.1050 ± .0360
   Bearing: 138696
6.   3.1050 ± .0360 Carry down from above
   +0.0415 ± .005   Bearing flange
     3.1465 ± .0365
7. −0.1557 ± .0005 Bearing width
     2.9908 ± .0370
   Gimbal: 138670
8.   2.9908 ± .0370 Carry down from above
  −2.2350 ± .0050 Bearing surface to bearing surface
     0.7558 ± .0420

Table 1. (cont'd)

---

9. 0.0300 ± .0150 Bearing surface to start dimension
10. 0.9800 ± .0100 Start to of radius
11. <u>0.7250 ± .0050</u> Radius F
     2.4908 ± .0720
12. <u>−0.0500   max.</u> Balance weights 138474 (F1291)
     2.4408 ± .0720
13. <u>−0.1080 ± .0060</u> Nut thickness MS 35649 or AN 340
     2.3328 ± .0780

Cover: 138815
1. 2.1000 ± .0080 Inside cover to tapped hole
2. <u>−1.4750 ± .0025</u> Term board hole to coordinate
    0.6250 ± .0105
3. <u>+1.6100 ± .0150</u> Coordinate to board end
    2.2350 ± .0255
Term Board: 138795
4. 0.1285 ± .0035 Term board hole diameter
5. <u>−0.1120   max.</u> Screw major diameter
    0.0100   max. Hole screw mis-match
    <u>+2.2350 ± .0255</u> Carry down from above
    2.2450 ± .0255
Result:
    2.3328 ± .0780
    <u>2.2450 ± .0255</u>
    .0878 ± .1035

From Kirkpatrick, E. G. (1962), **Engineering Report No. GR-1488**, Lear Siegler, Inc., Grand Rapids, Michigan.

Preceding examples have illustrated *product-tolerance stack-ups*. Another type of stack-up, to be considered in Chapter 11, is a *product-gage error stack-up* which indicates the allocation of product tolerance to gaging error and production error. Figure 5.7 is an example of a product-gage error stack-up. Permissible manufacturing error is restricted to 0.0004 in.

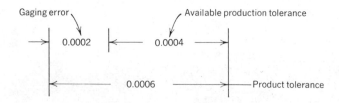

Figure 5.7.   Product-gage error stackup.

Additive and Overlapping Tolerances

Additive tolerancing refers to the traditional product-design practice of making the sum of the contributing part tolerances in the stack-up equal to the specified functional or assembly tolerance. The purpose is to make it impossible for defective functional or assembly conditions to occur, if the product parts are manufactured to their respective specifications.

Overlapping tolerancing is a design practice of allowing the sum of the contributing part tolerances in the stack-up to be slightly greater than the functional or assembly tolerance. Overlapping tolerancing was used in the example described by Table 5.1. Obviously, this practice makes possible larger production tolerances for the product part quality characteristics. The designer is simply "taking a chance" that no production-assembly difficulties will develop. A surprising number of products are successfully manufactured from this basis.

SUMMARY

The cycle of design and development activities for creating a new product results in *experimental, production,* and *manufacturing* models. Considerable redesign occurs in the development of the production model. Many product specifications are reviewed and altered to comply with limitations of manufacturing facilities.

Functional and nonfunctional specifications are separated to facilitate manufacture. Direct expression of functional specifications aids inspection operations and makes possible larger production tolerances. Design, production, and inspection *datums* are necessary to control dimensional-quality characteristics. The ideal situation is that all three datums be identical. However, production and inspection constraints frequently make this impossible.

Stack-up analysis is necessary to avoid production and inspection difficulties. Two principal stack-ups are considered: (1) *product tolerance stack-up,* and (2) *product-gage error stack-up.*

Additive and *overlapping* tolerancing procedures are used in industry. The latter practice is based on probability considerations and will be examined in Chapter 7.

REFERENCES

American Society of Tool and Manufacturing Engineers (1963), *Manufacturing and Estimating Handbook*, McGraw-Hill, New York, pp. 15-25 to 15-40.

Buckingham, E. (1954), *Dimensions and Tolerances for Mass Production*, Industrial Press, New York.

Harrisberger, L. (1966), *Engineermanship—A Philosophy of Design*, Brooks/Cole, Belmont, California, Chapter 5.

Kirkpatrick, E. G. (1962), *Engineering Report No. GR-1408*, Lear Siegler, Inc., Instrument Division, Grand Rapids, Michigan.

Military Standard MIL-STD-8B (1959), "Dimensioning and Tolerancing," U. S. Government Printing Office, Washington, D. C.

Wakefield, L. P. (1964), *Dimensioning for Interchangeability*, MacMillan, New York, Chapter 1.

REVIEW QUESTIONS

1. Distinguish between experimental model and production model in terms of purpose and attention given to the technical specifications.

2. State three classes of engineering-drawing specifications. Which type of drawing may serve as the legal basis of contract between the purchaser company and the manufacturer company?

3. Compare functional and nonfunctional specifications.

4. What are the disadvantages of indirect expression of functional specifications?

5. Define the term dimensional datum.

6. State three types of datums used to control product-feature locations.

7. Describe the ideal situation regarding the datum types referred to in question 6.

8. Define the term dimensional stack-up and state two general types of stack-ups involved in production situations.

9. Compare additive and overlapping tolerancing.

10. What is the purpose of additive tolerances?

6

Process Capability

There are three sources of variation in any process: the operator, the material, and the process machine. The variation from the first two can be reduced to a minimum by using a skilled operator and homogeneous material. A measure of the remaining variation can be viewed as the *capability* of the process. This measure is especially useful in assigning production jobs to specific machines. For many years, production foremen and process engineers have used their knowledge of process capability to select machines and equipment for processing operations. This knowledge has been gained from years of experience with success or failure of machines on various jobs.

Processing problems caused by specifications with small tolerances have stimulated special studies of process capabilities. An increasing interest has been shown in developing quantitative measures of capability. To have an intuitive opinion that a machine can work to ± 0.0005 in. for a particular operation is not enough. It is useful to also know the percentage of the time that the machine will attain ± 0.0005 in. accuracy for the operation.

The term *process capability* (or *natural tolerance*) means the best effort of the process in the sense that assignable causes of variation have been eliminated or at least minimized. Assignable causes are sources of variation which can be recognized and corrected – process operator, product material, process setup, process adjustment, etc.

In arriving at a measure of process capability, it is necessary to

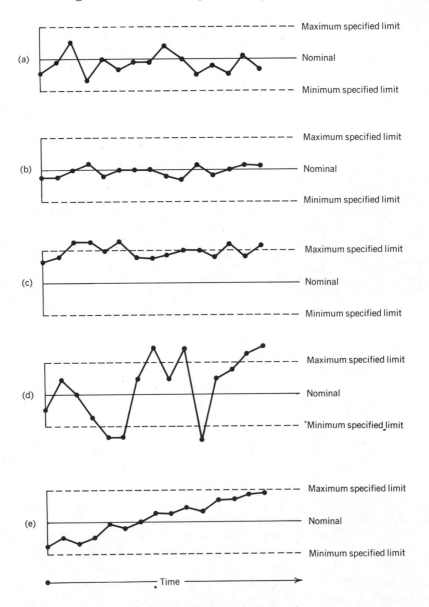

Figure 6.1. A process capability plot.

first establish control of the process. Quantitative measures of control are developed in Chapter 9. Logically, a study of process control should precede an examination of process capability measures. However, the process capability topic is presented here as a preliminary to certain statistical concepts required in the following chapter dealing with interchangeability alternatives.

Frequency Distribution

A good first impression of the process capability for a given operation can be obtained by plotting individual measurements as indicated in Figure 6.1. Plot (a) indicates adequate capability, (b) very good capability, and (c) good capability but a misdirected process setup. Plot (d) shows poor capability, and (e) adequate capability but a rapid tool-wear trend.

When making a capability study, it is important to minimize the effects of factors extraneous to the study. Such factors are unusual material variations, process adjustments, and process deterioration due to tool wear. A log should be kept of changes in tool settings, material lots, operators, machine feeds and speeds, temperature, and so on. This will facilitate the identification of data points associated with possible assignable causes of variation. The individual measurements should be in the order of manufacture. Measurements should preferably be made with laboratory gaging equipment.

It is more convenient to represent capability data as shown in Figure 6.2. The ordinate axis measures frequency of occurrence of the observed measurement values. The plot is a frequency distribution.

A formal definition of a frequency distribution is summarized here. A sample is composed of $x_1, x_2, \ldots, x_i, \ldots, x_n$ where some of the x_i's may have the same numerical value. It is convenient to represent the sample by a *frequency distribution*

$$x_1, x_2, \ldots, x_j, \ldots, x_k$$
$$f_1, f_2, \ldots, f_j, \ldots, f_k \qquad \sum_{j=1}^{k} f_j = n$$

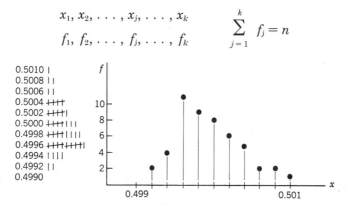

Figure 6.2. Frequency plot.

101

x_j	f_j
0.507	1
0.508	1
0.509	2
0.510	3
0.511	2
0.512	1
	$n = 10$

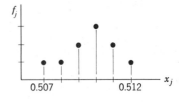

Figure 6.3. Frequency distribution.

where f_j is the number of times x_j occurred in the sample. The observations $x_1, \ldots, x_k$ are usually arranged in numerical order. An example of a frequency distribution table and plot is given in Figure 6.3.

SOME STATISTICAL CONCEPTS

The data sets in Figures 6.1 through 6.3 are considered to be samples from populations. A *population* is a conceptual term meaning the totality of items under consideration. A population may be finite or infinite. The size of a population is denoted by N (finite case) or ∞ (infinite case).

Example

A manufacturing lot is composed of $N = 1000$ product parts. The population is finite.

Example

Given an experiment which may be repeated. Each repetition results in an outcome. An infinite number of replications of the experiment are possible. In this sense, the population of outcomes is infinite.

A *sample* is a part of a population. The size of the sample is denoted by n. A *random sample* is a sample selected in such a way that each population item has an equal chance of being selected. The statistical objective is to obtain a sample that is representative of the population.

Example

A population consists of the numbers 1, 1, 1, 2, 2, 2, 3, 3, 3. An ideally representative sample is 1, 2, 3.

A *model* is a representation of a system under study. A mathematical model is one in which the system is represented by symbols that can be manipulated by mathematical rules.

Example

Manufacturing overhead is incurred at a rate that is directly proportional to expenditures for direct labor. The model is $f(x) = A_0 + A_1 x$. The independent variable x represents expenditure for direct labor. The function $f(x)$ represents manufacturing overhead. The values A_0 and A_1 are *parameters* in the model.

Population and Sample Description

A population is described by a mathematical model. The parameters of the model are usually denoted by Greek letters. An example is shown in Figure 6.4. The model is a function of x, ϕ_1, and ϕ_2 and is denoted by $f(x, \phi_1, \phi_2)$. The sample is described by a frequency distribution and certain parameters called sample *statistics*. These parameters are denoted by Latin letters.

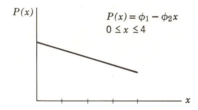

Figure 6.4. A simple mathematical model.

Any function $g(x_1, \ldots, x_n)$ of the n observations is called a sample *statistic*. Common statistics used to describe samples are arithmetic mean, variance, and range.

Let x_i denote the independent variable of interest. In the process capability data, Figures 6.1 and 6.2, x_i denotes the product-measurement values. For ungrouped x_i values the *arithmetic mean* is

$$\bar{x} = \frac{1}{n} \sum_{i=1}^{n} x_i \qquad i = 1, 2, \ldots, n$$

Example

Sample x_i values are 4, 6, 6, 5, 2, 2, 3, 5, 5, 5,

$$\bar{x} = \tfrac{1}{10}(4, + 6 + 6 + \ldots + 5) = 4.3$$

103

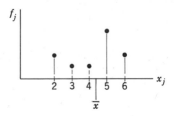

Figure 6.5.   Arithmetic mean.

The frequency distribution plot is given in Figure 6.5. The arithmetic mean is a representative or typical x-value locating the data set on the x-axis.

Since

$$\sum_{i=1}^{n} x_i = \sum_{j=1}^{k} f_j\, x_j$$

the arithmetic mean for grouped x_i values may be expressed as

$$\bar{x} = \frac{1}{n} \sum_{j=1}^{k} f_j\, x_j \qquad j = 1, 2, \ldots, k$$

where k refers to the number of different numerical values of x. An example is shown in Figure 6.6. The x_i values from the preceding example are collected in a frequency table.

x_j	f_j	$f_j\, x_j$	
2	2	4	
3	1	3	
4	1	4	$\bar{x} = \frac{1}{10}(43) = 4.3$
5	4	20	
6	2	12	
$\sum_{j=1}^{k}$	$n = 10$	43	

Figure 6.6.   Frequency distribution table.

A descriptive measure of variation within the sample is the variance denoted by s_x^2. For ungrouped x_i values, the *variance* is given by

$$s_x^2 = \frac{1}{n} \sum_{i=1}^{n} (x_i - \bar{x})^2$$

The square root of the variance is called the *standard deviation*. For grouped x_i values, the variance is

$$s_x^2 = \frac{1}{n} \sum_{j=1}^{k} f_j (x_j - \bar{x})^2$$

Another commonly used measure of variation is the sample *range*, R given by the algebraic difference

$$R = (\text{largest } x_i) - (\text{smallest } x_i)$$

Statistical methods are mainly concerned with decision making based on the limited information available from a random sample. An important decision-making area deals with estimating population parameters or testing hypotheses involving population parameters. Some notational distinction should be made regarding sample parameters (i.e., *statistics*) and corresponding population parameters. The mean and the variance for the population are denoted

$$\mu = \frac{1}{N} \sum_{i=1}^{N} x_i \qquad \text{(arithmetic mean, ungrouped } x_i)$$

$$\mu = \frac{1}{N} \sum_{j=1}^{K} f_j x_j \qquad \text{(arithmetic mean, grouped } x_i)$$

$$\sigma_x^2 = \frac{1}{N} \sum_{i=1}^{N} (x_i - \mu)^2 \qquad \text{(variance, ungrouped } x_i)$$

$$\sigma_x^2 = \frac{1}{N} \sum_{j=1}^{K} f_j (x_j - \mu)^2 \qquad \text{(variance, grouped } x_i)$$

Sample parameter notations are mean average $\bar{x}$ and variance s_x^2. The notation used here is reasonably standard in statistics textbooks. The

105

American Society for Quality Control uses primed symbols to denote population parameters and unprimed symbols for sample parameters. For example, the range of the sample x_i is denoted R, and the corresponding population value is R'.

Computing Sample Parameters

Longhand computation of $\bar{x}$ and $s_x{}^2$ is conveniently performed in tabular form as shown in Table 6.1. Computation may be simplified by coding the data. This is accomplished by a transformation on x. Let

$$u_j = \frac{x_j - x_0}{c}$$

where x_0 is an x_j-value near the middle of the frequency distribution (e.g., $x_j = 0.510$, Table 6.2).[1]

It is assumed that the x-values are equally spaced, otherwise the transformation will have to be

$$u_j = x_j - x_0.$$

Table 6.1. **Computation Table in x-Units.**

x_j	f_j	$f_j x_j$	$x_j - \bar{x}$	$(x_j - \bar{x})^2$	$f_j(x_j - \bar{x})^2$
0.507	1	0.507	-0.0027	0.00000729	0.00000729
0.508	1	0.508	-0.0017	0.00000289	0.00000289
0.509	2	1.018	-0.0007	0.00000049	0.00000098
0.510	3	1.530	$+0.0003$	0.00000009	0.00000027
0.511	2	1.022	$+0.0013$	0.00000169	0.00000338
0.512	1	0.512	$+0.0023$	0.00000529	0.00000529
$\sum_{j=1}^{k}$	$n = 10$	5.097			0.00002010
$\dfrac{1}{n}\sum_{j=1}^{k}$		0.5097			0.00000201

$\bar{x} = 0.5097$ $\qquad$ $s_x{}^2 = 0.00000201$ $\qquad$ $s_x = 0.001418$

[1] A choice of x_0 near the middle of the frequency distribution results in small number u-values. If an office calculator is used, a convenient choice for x_0 is the smallest x_j value, thus making all u-values positive numbers.

106

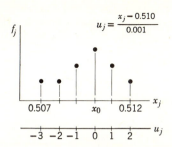

Figure 6.7. A u-transformation on x.

The effect of the transformation is simply a change of origin (from 0 to x_0) and a change of scale as shown in Figure 6.7, producing a frequency distribution of u_j. The table computation in u-units for the data of the preceding example is given in Table 6.2.

Table 6.2. Computation Table in u-Units.

u_j	x_j	f_j	$f_j u_j$	$u_j - \overline{u}$	$(u_j - \overline{u})^2$	$f_j (u_j - \overline{u})^2$
-3	0.507	1	-3	-2.7	7.29	7.29
-2	0.508	1	-2	-1.7	2.89	2.89
-1	0.509	2	-2	-0.7	0.49	0.98
0	0.510	3	0	$+0.3$	0.09	0.27
$+1$	0.511	2	$+2$	$+1.3$	1.69	3.38
$+2$	0.512	1	$+2$	$+2.3$	5.29	5.29
$\sum\limits_{j=1}^{k}$		$n = 10$	-3			20.10
$1/n \sum\limits_{j=1}^{k}$			-0.3			2.01

$\overline{u} = -0.3 \qquad s_u^2 = 2.01$

To transform u and s_u to $\overline{x}$ and s_x, respectively

$$\overline{x} = c\,\overline{u} + x_0$$
$$= (0.001)\,(-0.3) + 0.510$$
$$= 0.5097$$

$$s_x = c\,s_u$$
$$= 0.001\,\sqrt{2.01}$$
$$= 0.001418$$

To obtain the transformation equations for $\bar{u}$ and s_u, we need only substitute for x in the definitional formulas for $\bar{x}$ and s_x^2.
From

$$u_j = \frac{x_j - x_0}{c}, \qquad x_j = c\,u_j + x_0$$

Then

$$\bar{x} = \frac{1}{n} \sum_{j=1}^{k} f_j\,x_j = \frac{1}{n} \sum_{j=1}^{k} f_j\,(c\,u_j + x_0)$$

$$= \frac{1}{n} \sum_{j=1}^{k} f_j\,c\,u_j + \frac{1}{n} \sum_{j=1}^{k} f_j\,x_0$$

$$= c\,\bar{u} + x_0$$

Also

$$s_x^2 = \frac{1}{n} \sum_{j=1}^{k} f_j\,(x_j - \bar{x})^2$$

$$= \frac{1}{n} \sum_{j=1}^{k} f_j\,(c\,u_j + x_0 - c\,\bar{u} - x_0)^2$$

$$= \frac{1}{n} \sum_{j=1}^{k} f_j\,[c(u_j - \bar{u})]^2$$

$$= c^2\,s_u^2$$

If computation of s_x^2 is done using a desk calculator, a table is not necessary. Convenient computational formulas are

$$s_x^2 = \frac{1}{n} \left[\sum_{i=1}^{n} x_i^2 - \frac{1}{n} \left(\sum_{i=1}^{n} x_i \right)^2 \right]$$

or

$$s_x^2 = \frac{1}{n} \left[\sum_{i=1}^{n} x_i^2 - n\,\bar{x}^2 \right]$$

Z-Transformation

A *Z*-transformation is used frequently in statistical problems. Generally speaking, the *Z*-transformation is defined

$$Z = \frac{\text{variable} - \text{mean of the variable}}{\text{standard deviation of the variable}}$$

An example of a *Z*-transformation is shown in Figure 6.8.

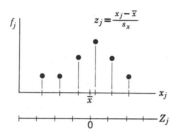

Figure 6.8. A *Z*-transformation on x. *Z*-axis is calibrated in multiples of s_r.

Distribution Functions

A simple example of a *frequency function* is indicated in Figure 6.9. The random variable x can assume only the discrete values $1, 2, \ldots, 5$ with respective probabilities denoted by $f(x)$. The corresponding *probability function*,[2] denoted $F(x)$, is given in Figure 6.10. It is a step function constant over every interval not containing any of the x-

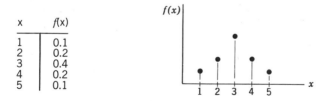

x	f(x)
1	0.1
2	0.2
3	0.4
4	0.2
5	0.1

Figure 6.9. Frequency function for a discrete variable x.

---

[2]The term probability function may be used for either $f(x)$ or $F(x)$, the exact meaning being derived from the context. Many textbooks call the frequency function a probability-density function.

values. This function describes the respective probabilities for $x \leq b$ where $b = 1, 2, \ldots, 5$. Note that if the probability of $a < x \leq b$ is desired, this is $F(b) - F(a)$. For example,

$$P(2 < x \leq 4) = F(4) - F(2) = 0.6$$

Any function $F(x) = P(x \leq b)$ is a probability function if

$$F(-\infty) = 0 \qquad F(+\infty) = 1$$

$F(x)$ is a nondecreasing function

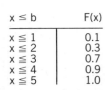
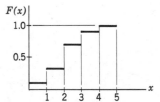

$x \leq b$	$F(x)$
$x \leq 1$	0.1
$x \leq 2$	0.3
$x \leq 3$	0.7
$x \leq 4$	0.9
$x \leq 5$	1.0

Figure 6.10. Probability function for a discrete variable x.

The concept of frequency and probability functions for a continuous variable x is analogous to that for a discrete variable. An example is shown in Figure 6.11. The frequency function is

$$f(x) = \frac{1}{c - a} \qquad a \leq x \leq c$$

The probability function is

$$F(x) = P(x \leq b) = \int_{a}^{b} \frac{1}{c - a}\, dx$$

The shaded area under $F(x)$ represents the $P(x \leq b)$. Again, as in the discrete variable case, the probability of x being in any interior interval can be obtained by subtraction. Thus, in Figure 6.11, if the interval (a,c) is $(2,6)$ then

$$f(x) = \frac{1}{6 - 2} = \frac{1}{4}$$

110

and if x being in the interval $(3,5)$ is of interest

$$P(3 < x \leq 5) = F(5) - F(3)$$

$$= \int_2^5 \frac{1}{4}\, dx - \int_2^3 \frac{1}{4}\, dx$$

$$= \frac{3}{4} - \frac{1}{4} = \frac{1}{2}$$

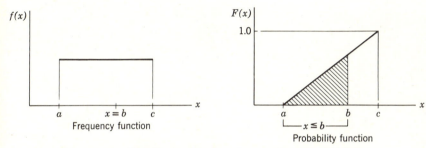

Figure 6.11. Distribution functions for a continuous variable x.

For a function $f(x)$ to be a frequency function, it must satisfy

$$f(x) \geq 0 \qquad \int_{-\infty}^{+\infty} f(x)\, dx = 1$$

This is analogous to the discrete variable case where

$$\sum_x f(x) = 1$$

The Normal Distribution

Many quality characteristics have frequency functions that follow the normal distribution model reasonably well. The frequency function for this model is

$$f(x) = \frac{1}{\sigma_x \sqrt{2\pi}} e^{-\frac{(x - \mu)^2}{2\sigma_x^2}}$$

which is a function of the independent variable x and the parameters μ and σ_x. A Z-transformation on x yields

$$f(Z) = \frac{1}{\sqrt{2\pi}}\, e^{-\frac{Z^2}{2}}$$

The probability function is

$$F(x) = P(x \leq b) \;=\; \int_{-\infty}^{b} f(x)\ dx$$

$$= P(Z \leq Z_b) = \int_{-\infty}^{Z_b} f(Z)\ dZ$$

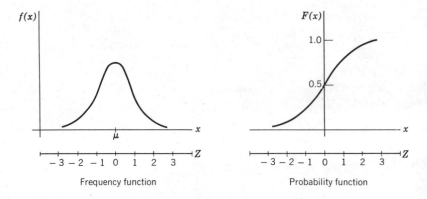

Figure 6.12. Normal distribution function.

Figure 6.12 shows the frequency and probability functions. The frequency function cannot be integrated directly. However, values of $F(Z)$ can be obtained from the table in Appendix A. This table gives values for

$$0.5 - \int_{0}^{Z} f(Z)\ dZ$$

Mathematical Expectation

Assume there is associated with the random variable x some value $g(x)$ depending on x. The function $g(x)$ is also a random variable. If the following sums or integrals exist, the mathematical *expectation* of the random variable $g(x)$ is defined by

$$E\,[g(x)] = \begin{cases} \sum_{x} g(x) \cdot f(x) \text{ (discrete case)} \\[2em] \int_{-\infty}^{+\infty} g(x) \cdot f(x)\, dx \text{ (continuous case)} \end{cases}$$

The expected values of certain functions $g(x)$ are of particular interest in describing the properties of distributions. For example,

$$E(x) = \begin{cases} \sum_{x} x \cdot f(x) \\[2em] \int_{-\infty}^{+\infty} x \cdot f(x)\, dx \end{cases} = \mu_x$$

$$E\,[(x-\mu)^2] = \begin{cases} \sum_{x} (x-\mu)^2 \cdot f(x) \\[2em] \int_{-\infty}^{+\infty} (x-\mu)^2 \cdot f(x)\, dx \end{cases} = \sigma_x^2$$

PROCESS CAPABILITY MEASURES

A frequently used measure of process capability is $6\sigma_x$. This is a measure of the variability of the process operation under study. The value $6\sigma_x$ represents the best effort of the process. Thus, the study should be made under controlled conditions obtainable in a production environment. Specifically, this means that assignable causes of process variation have been minimized. The product-quality characteristic is denoted by x. The distribution of x represents the output from the process operation. The value $6\sigma_x$ measures the range of x-values oc-

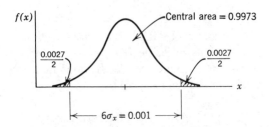

Figure 6.13. Process capability for a normally distributed quality characteristic.

curring a high percentage of the time. For example, if x follows a normal distribution model, $6\sigma_x$ defines the range of quality-characteristic values being generated by the process operation 99.73% of the time. Figure 6.13 illustrates a normally distributed quality characteristic where the process operation generating the characteristic has a capability of 0.001 in. (or, $\pm$ 0.0005 in.).

Estimating the Capability Value

The standard deviation σ_x is a population parameter. Thus, $6\sigma_x$ is viewed as the true capability of the process operation. An estimate of σ_x, based on the observed x-values from the capability study, is required to establish the process-capability value. The sample standard deviation s_x may be used as an estimate of σ_x. Or, an estimate of σ_x may be obtained using the range values of successive samples as a basis for computation. The problem of obtaining "good" estimates of unknown population parameters is treated in any standard statistics textbook. Only a brief summary of the estimation concept is presented here.

The general problem of estimation involves a random variable x with distribution function $f(x,\theta)$ where θ is an unknown parameter. For example, θ may be the mean μ, or the standard deviation σ_x. Some function $g(x_1, \ldots, x_n)$ of the sample values must be found that approximates θ. This function is called $\hat{\theta}$, that is,

$$\hat{\theta} = g(x_1, \ldots, x_n)$$

Examples of $\hat{\theta}$ estimates of θ are $\bar{x}$ to estimate μ, and s_x to estimate σ_x. Clearly, $\bar{x}$ and s_x are each functions of the x-values of the sample.

114

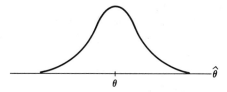

Figure 6.14.   Unbiased estimator $\hat{\theta}$.

Two principal criteria for judging estimators are unbiasedness and efficiency. An estimator $\hat{\theta}$ is an *unbiased* estimator of θ if

$$E(\hat{\theta}) = \theta$$

This condition is illustrated in Figure 6.14. Unbiasedness is a desirable property for an estimator. It is reassuring to know that the $\hat{\theta}$-values (from sample to sample) distribute about θ as a mean. Efficiency refers to the variability of the estimator. An *efficient* estimator has a minimum variance, that is, the $E\left[(\theta - \hat{\theta})^2\right]$ is smaller than the variance for any other statistic that might be used to estimate θ. An example of this concept is illustrated by Figure 6.15. The estimator $\hat{\theta}_1$ is a more efficient estimator than $\hat{\theta}_2$ since the variability of $\hat{\theta}_1$ is smaller than that for $\hat{\theta}_2$. This may be inferred simply from a comparison of the ranges, R_1 being less than R_2.

An unbiased estimate of the population variance σ_x^2 is given by

$$\hat{s}_x^2 = \frac{1}{n-1} \sum_{i=1}^{n} (x_i - \bar{x})^2$$

This is the same as the definitional form of the sample variance (given earlier in this chapter and denoted s_x^2) except that division is

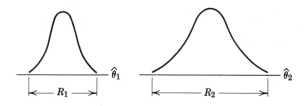

Figure 6.15.   The efficiency criterion.

115

by $n-1$ instead of n. The estimate s_x^2 is a biased estimate of σ_x^2 (i.e., s_x^2 is usually smaller than σ_x^2 from sample to sample).

We may also obtain an estimate of σ_x using range values from consecutive samples. Let R_j denote the range of the jth sample. then, for k samples

$$\overline{R} = \frac{1}{k} \sum_{j=1}^{k} R_j \quad j = 1, 2, \ldots, k$$

A quantity d_2, dependent on sample size n, can be determined such that

$$E\left(\frac{R}{\sigma_x}\right) = d_2$$

or

$$E\left(\frac{R}{d_2}\right) = \sigma_x$$

and, replacing $E(R)$ by its estimate $\overline{R}$, an estimate of σ_x is given by

$$\sigma_x = \frac{\overline{R}}{d_2}$$

Values of d_2 corresponding to various n-values are given in Appendix B.

Thus, in estimating σ_x, we compute $\overline{R}$ from the sample observations and divide by d_2. The value of d_2 for a sample size of five is 2.326. For smaller samples, d_2 will be smaller and for larger samples, d_2 will be larger.

An Illustrative Application

Process-capability computation is illustrated here using the data from Figure 6.2. Two methods are shown. The process capability value $6\sigma_x$ is estimated first by $6\hat{s}_x$ and then by $6(\overline{R}/d_2)$.

A transformation

$$u_j = \frac{x_j - 0.5000}{0.0002}$$

transforms the x_j to u_j, with origin $u = 0$ corresponding to $x = 0.5000$. Computation is shown in Table 6.3.

116

Table 6.3. **Computation for** s_x

u_j	x_j	f_j	$f_j u_j$	u_j^2	$f_j u_j^2$
−5	.4990	0			
−4	.4992	2	− 8	16	32
−3	.4994	4	−12	9	36
−2	.4996	11	−22	4	44
−1	.4998	9	− 9	1	9
0	.5000	8	0	0	0
+1	.5002	6	+ 6	1	6
+2	.5004	5	+10	4	20
+3	.5006	2	+ 6	9	18
+4	.5008	2	+ 8	16	32
+5	.5010	1	+ 5	25	25
Σ		50	−16		222

$$\hat{s}_u{}^2 = \frac{1}{n-1}\left[\sum_{u=-5}^{+5} f_j u_j^2 - \frac{1}{n}\left(\sum_{u=-5}^{+5} f_j u_j\right)^2\right]$$

$$= \frac{1}{49}\left[222 - 5.12\right] = 4.426$$

$$\hat{s}_u = 2.104$$

Converting to x-units

$$\hat{s}_x = (0.0002)\, s_u$$

$$= 0.00042$$

An unbiased estimate of the population $6\sigma_x$ value is

$$6\hat{s}_x = 6(0.00042) = 0.0025$$

Table 6.4 presents the same data recorded in the order of production. Sample size is five. Ten samples have been examined.

Table 6.4 **Computation of** $\overline{R}/d_2$.

Sample Number	1	2	3	4	5	6	7	8	9	10
u_1	0	0	−1	−1	0	−2	0	−1	+1	−4
u_2	+1	−3	−2	+2	+1	0	+1	+3	−2	−1
u_3	−2	−2	−3	+2	−2	+5	−2	0	+2	−1
u_4	+3	−1	+2	−1	−4	+4	0	−2	−2	+1
u_5	−2	0	−2	−3	+2	+1	−3	−1	−1	+4
Maximum u	+3	0	+2	+2	+2	+5	+1	+3	+2	+4
Minimum u	−2	−3	−3	−3	−4	−2	−3	−2	−2	−4
R_j	5	3	5	5	6	7	4	5	4	8

Computing the mean range

$$\overline{R} = \frac{1}{k} \sum_{j=1}^{k} R_j$$

$$= \frac{1}{10} (52) = 5.2$$

Estimating σ_u

$$\sigma_u = \frac{\overline{R}}{d_2} = \frac{5.2}{2.326} = 2.2356$$

Converting to x-units

$$\sigma_x = (0.0002) \sigma_u$$

$$= 0.00045$$

An unbiased estimate of the population $6\sigma_x$ value is

$$6\sigma_x = 6(0.00045) = 0.0027$$

The average-range method of estimating process capability has two principal advantages. It is easier to compute, and trends or other abnormal conditions occurring in the capability study can be detected more readily.

Physical Interpretation of Capability

Process capability or natural tolerance refers to a specific process operation for a given quality-characteristic geometry. It follows that for any process there are many capability values, each being associated with a given operation and product-part geometry. Also, as a process machine ages, the variability of the machine will increase, thus changing the capability values.

It has been stated that process control is a prerequisite condition for a process-capability study. Clearly, the quality-characteristic distribution must be repeatable if the distribution range is to be used as a capability measure. Process control implies that assignable causes of process variation have been minimized, leaving for the most part only random causes of variation. If such be the case, repeatable distributions are possible.

A remaining question is what physical interpretation can be placed on random causes of process variation. A process machine is a mechanical device composed of many mating component parts. The clearances, end-plays, and other error effects due to the fits of mating parts determine the variability of the machine. Each error effect is small in magnitude. Many error effects are involved. The error effects combine in a random manner to determine the over-all machine variability. In this sense, a controlled process is composed mainly of random causes of variation. Furthermore, as a machine ages, deterioration will cause the error effects to increase in magnitude. Even though they combine and accumulate randomly, the resultant over-all machine variability will increase.

SUMMARY

Process capability or *natural tolerance* describes the best effort of a process in the sense that assignable causes of process variation have been minimized. The remaining variation is, for the most part, due only to random causes inherent to the process.

A common statistical measure of capability is the distribution range for the quality characteristic involved in the particular process operation. This range is usually taken to be $6\sigma_x$. Thus, the capability measure indicates expected limits of variation which will be exceeded only a small percentage of the time, if the process is controlled. The population standard deviation σ_x can be estimated from the sample standard deviation $\hat{s}_x$ or from the ratio $\overline{R}/d_2$ where d_2 values for various sample sizes are given in Appendix B.

Process capability refers to a specific process operation for a given quality-characteristic geometry. For any process there are many capability values, each being associated with a given operation and product-part geometry. Capability values vary with the age of the process machine. As a machine ages, deterioration increases the process variability and the capability values change accordingly.

Many companies find it useful to tabulate process capabilities for typical process operations involved in the manufacture of their products. This capability data is a manufacturing aid in assigning production jobs to specific machines. It is also useful to product designers in arriving at technical specifications that will be attainable on a production basis.

119

REFERENCES

Bowker, A. H., and Lieberman, G. J. (1959), *Engineering Statistics,* Prentice-Hall, Englewood Cliffs, N. J.

Feigenbaum, A. V. (1961), *Total Quality Control,* McGraw-Hill, New York, pp. 557-576.

Hansen, B. L. (1963), *Quality Control,* Prentice-Hall, Englewood Cliffs, N. J., Chapter 7.

Juran, J. M. (1962), *Quality Control Handbook,* McGraw-Hill, New York, pp. 257-260.

Seder, L. A. and Cowan, D. (1956), *Span Plan Method of Process Capability Analysis,* American Society for Quality Control, Milwaukee, Wisconsin.

REVIEW QUESTIONS

1. What are the three principal sources of variation in any process?

2. Define the term process capability. State another name for process capability.

3. The standard deviation for a quality characteristic that is generated by a particular process operation is 0.0015 in. State the process capability value and explain what this value means in terms of expected variation.

4. Define two unbiased estimators of σ_x used to determine process capability values.

5. State two advantages of estimating process capability by the average range method (i.e., using $\overline{R}/d_2$ as an estimator).

PROBLEMS

1. Compute $\overline{x}$ and s_x for the following data: 2, 2, 4, 6, 8, 6, 2, 4, 4, 2 (see Table 6.1).

2. Compute $\overline{u}$ and s_u for the data given in problem 1. Choose the origin at $x_0 = 2$ (see Table 6.2).

3. Convert the $\overline{u}$ and s_u values in problem 2 to $\overline{x}$ and s_x.

4. Compute s_u^2 for the data given in problem 1 using the computational formula:

$$s_u^2 = \frac{1}{n} \sum_{j=1}^{k} f_j\, u_j^2 - \overline{u}^2 .$$

5. Prepare a frequency distribution plot for the data given in problem 1. Show x_j, u_j, and Z_j scales (see Figures 6.5, 6.7, and 6.8).

6. An experiment involves the toss of a single fair die with interest being on the value of the upturned face. Each of the faces (and thus each of the numerical values 1, 2, ..., 6) is equally likely to be the upturned face. Prepare frequency function and probability function tables and plots (see Figures 6.9 and 6.10). If x refers to the number on the upturned face, what is the probability $P(3 < x \leq 5)$?

7. A frequency function is given by $f(x) = 1/4$, $1 \leq x \leq 5$ (see Figure 6.11). (a) Prepare frequency and probability function plots. (b) What is the probability $P(2 < x \leq 3)$?

8. A random variable x is normally distributed with mean 10 and variance 16. Compute the following probabilities: (a) $P(x \geq 18)$, (b) $P(x \leq 3)$ and (c) $P(3 \leq x \leq 18)$.

9. Compute the expected value of x for the die toss experiment of problem 6. For the same experiment, suppose the random variable is $Y = x^2 - 4x + 3$. Compute the expected value of Y.

10. Ten samples of five measurements each are recorded in the following table. Estimate the population process capability value $6\sigma_x$ by two methods: (a) using $\hat{s}_x$ as an estimator, and (b) using $\overline{R}/d_2$ as an estimator.

1	2	3	4	5	6	7	8	9	10
.205	.213	.206	.209	.210	.208	.206	.211	.209	.206
.208	.207	.204	.208	.206	.210	.206	.208	.209	.211
.207	.205	.212	.209	.206	.213	.208	.207	.208	.207
.211	.210	.211	.209	.207	.203	.210	.207	.207	.209
.211	.210	.210	.207	.208	.206	.208	.207	.209	.207

7

Interchangeability
Alternatives

Considerable compromise is involved in establishing proper technical specifications for the product. The tolerances must be small enough to control quality, performance, and life characteristics of the product and, on the other hand, be large enough to be compatible with probable process variations. Small tolerances increase manufacturing costs. Large tolerances increase production output, minimize waste of materials and productive effort, and generally are responsible for significant reduction of manufacturing costs. The economics of tolerance determination is mainly a matter of establishing the degree of interchangeability which is feasible on a production basis. A number of interchangeability alternatives will be examined in this chapter.

In-Plant Interchangeability

A limited interchangeability accomplished by matching the tooling is called *in-plant interchangeability*. Only a small percentage of

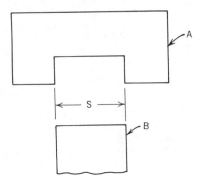

Figure 7.1.   In-plant interchangeability.

modern products are manufactured in this manner. Applications of this interchangeability method are restricted to custom products and small-volume production, where servicing in the field is not a major requirement. A simplified example is given in Figure 7.1. Part B fits into the slot in part A. The size dimension S for each component is stated in terms of nominal size and type of fit required, with no tolerance specified; for example, "$\frac{1}{2}$ in., slip fit." Assume the production lot of part A is completed first. The actual distribution of part A sizes is a basis for processing the production lot of part B. That is, the tooling for part B is matched against the actual results of the processing of A. Clearly, this interchangeability method avoids restrictive tolerancing. Thus the influence of tolerances on production costs is negligible.

Full Interchangeability

The manufacturing situation that results in all mating product parts being interchangeable from plant to plant and with spare parts in the field is called *full interchangeability*. This is accomplished by *additive* tolerancing (see Chapter 5). The influence of tolerances on production costs is significant. Frequently the restrictive tolerances involved result in production costs which are prohibitively high.

Modified Full Interchangeability

The *modified full interchangeability* method is applicable where full interchangeability tolerances are difficult or impossible to attain on a production basis. In this case, *overlapping* tolerances (see Chapter 5) are permitted and manufacturing operates on either a selective assembly or random assembly basis. With *selective assembly*, component parts are graded at inspection stations and selectively fitted at the assembly operation (e.g., parts are graded +0.001, +0.002, etc. oversize and −0.001, −0.002, etc. undersize). The selection and fitting procedure is such that oversize component deviations cancel undersize deviations of mating components and established assembly tolerances are satisfied. For example, in Figure 5.5, if part A is 0.504 in., part B is 0.504 in., and part C is 0.498 in., the assembly specification of 1.500 ± 0.006 in. (i.e., for the three components) will still be achieved.

The same cancellation effect can be obtained by *random assembly*. In the preceding example, random selection of parts A, B, and C from quantities of each will rarely result in choices such that A, B, and C, for one assembly, will all be extremely oversize (or extremely undersize). When reliance is placed on random-assembly procedure, tolerances are statistically determined to restrict defective assemblies to a small and acceptable percentage level.

The choice, selective or random assembly, is an economic one. Selective assembly involves extra production costs. Selecting and fitting parts increases the direct labor cost of assembly. Sorting and grading parts increases inspection cost. Inventory cost increases due to extra expenses incurred in stocking graded parts. On the other hand, random assembly involves discovery and correction costs at assembly and test stations for a small percentage of defective assemblies.

Figure 7.2 is an example in which the economic choice was modified full interchangeability implemented by random assembly.

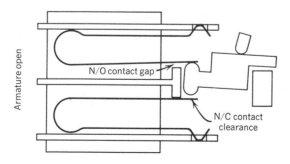

Figure 7.2. Modified full interchangeability. By courtesy of International Business Machines Corporation, General Products Division, Endicott, N.Y.

Tolerances for P-M Relay

	Gap	Statistical Tolerance	Limit Tolerance	Clearance	Statistical Tolerance	Limit Tolerance
Normally open	0.012	±0.0029	±0.008	0.005	±0.0021	±0.005
Normally closed	0.011	±0.0021	±0.005	0.006	±0.0029	±0.008

Permissive-make relay contact system.

A relay—known as the "permissive-make relay"—is the first complete assembly produced by IBM in quantity through the probability concept of tolerance accumulation. IBM has assembled more than one million of these relays and over 95% of them have met performance specifications without adjustment.

Significant is the fact that initial analysis of the device indicated that it could not be produced economically under the restrictions of limit dimensioning.

Gaps and clearances at the contacts are the critical mechanical areas. To obtain the speed desired the normally open gap should average 0.012 in. and the normally closed gap 0.011 in. with a minimum of 0.002 in. for the clearances. Nine dimensions have tolerances which influence the workability of the normally open gap in the relay.

Tolerances were computed on a probability basis, giving a total of 0.0058 in. variation, while the arithmetic sum of these same tolerances would have been 0.016 in., or nearly three times the acceptable variation.

Tolerance Analysis of Gap Variation

Component Dimension	Tolerances (in.)
Actuator backstop	0.003
Actuator wire lifter	0.003
Wire lifter parallelism	0.001
Base pad flatness and parallelism	0.001
Yoke thickness	0.002
Yoke flatness	0.002
Armature flatness	0.001
Contact alignment	0.001
Contact wire alignment	0.002
Total gap variation (statistically dimensioned)	0.0058
Total gap variation (if limit dimensioned)	0.016

MATHEMATICS FOR STATISTICAL TOLERANCES

If economic considerations indicate a modified full-interchangeability approach using overlapping tolerances and random assembly procedure, then tolerances should be statistically determined to control defective assemblies to a small and acceptable percentage level. Essentially, statistical determination of tolerances will indicate the magnitude of tolerance increase that is possible, based on an acceptable risk of incurring a small percentage of defective assemblies.

Combinations of Independent Random Variables

Computation of statistical tolerances is based on the following theorem.

If $x_1, x_2, \ldots, x_j, \ldots, x_K$ are independent random variables with respective means

$$\mu_1, \mu_2, \ldots, \mu_j, \ldots, \mu_K$$

and variances

$$\sigma_1^2, \sigma_2^2, \ldots, \sigma_j^2, \ldots, \sigma_K^2$$

and if $a_1, a_2, \ldots, a_j, \ldots, a_K$ are constants and Y is a linear combination of the x_j, that is

$$Y = a_1 x_1 \pm \ldots \pm a_j x_j \pm \ldots \pm a_K x_K$$

then Y is a random variable having the following properties:

(1) $\mu_Y = a_1 \mu_1 \pm a_2 \mu_2 \pm \ldots \pm a_K \mu_K$

(2) $\sigma_Y^2 = a_1^2 \sigma_1^2 + a_2^2 \sigma_2^2 + \ldots + a_K^2 \sigma_K^2$

(3) If $x_1, x_2, \ldots, x_K$ are each normally distributed, then Y is normally distributed.

If the x_j are not all normally distributed and if the variances σ_j^2 are approximately homogeneous, then from the Central Limit Theorem of statistics, as K increases, the Y distribution rapidly approaches the normal distribution.

Each x-distribution range measures the variability of the x-variable. The Y-distribution range measures the variability of the linear com-

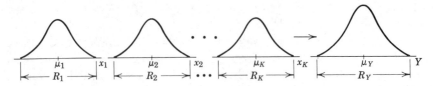

Figure 7.3. Distribution ranges and tolerances.

bination of the x_j. In most product-tolerance situations, the tolerance for the assembly quality characteristic is a linear combination of the tolerances for the respective component quality characteristics. Thus, in tolerance applications, each x-distribution range corresponds to the tolerance for the component quality characteristic. The Y-distribution range corresponds to the tolerance for the assembly quality characteristic. This correspondence is summarized in Figure 7-3.

The ranges R_1, R_2, . . . , R_K represent the respective component quality-characteristic tolerances. Range R_Y represents the assembly quality-characteristic tolerance. Mean values μ, μ_2, . . . , μ_K correspond to the nominal specification values for the respective components, and μ_Y denotes the nominal specification value for the assembly characteristic. The standard deviation σ_Y will be used as a measure of R_Y (for example, let $6\sigma_Y = R_Y$). In the same manner σ_1, σ_2, . . . , σ_K will measure R_1, R_2, . . . , R_K, respectively. The number of component quality characteristics generating the assembly characteristic is denoted by K. Thus, there are K component distributions involved.

The examples in the following paragraphs assume mathematical conditions to be reasonably satisfied on the manufacturing floor. Essentially this will mean that component dimensions are approximately normally distributed independent random variables. Then, after the student has become familiar with the computation methods, the mathematical conditions will be reviewed. Conservative implementation procedures will be developed to handle practical situations where the mathematical conditions are not fully satisfied.

STATISTICAL TOLERANCE APPLICATIONS

Regarding design purpose, application problems can be separated into two classes. (1) The assembly tolerance is fixed by functional requirements. The problem is to statistically determine the overlapping tolerances for the components. (2) Component tolerances are fixed, either because of process limitations or the fact that the components are standard purchased parts. The problem is to estimate probable cumulative-error effect on the assembly quality characteristic. In both cases, computation will be based on an acceptable risk of incurring defective assemblies. The risk value, denoted by λ, is the probability of occurrence of a defective assembly. The value of λ is dependent on economic considerations and will vary from one production situation to another.

The applications examples which follow are restricted to product conditions of size, location, and an assembly condition of clearance. For the most part, complex mechanical designs have been avoided. Schematic drawings are presented which involve only elementary surfaces and simple geometries. The tolerance functions that occur are

$$Y = x_1 + x_2 + \ldots + x_K \qquad \text{(size condition)}$$

$$Y = x_1 \pm x_2 \pm \ldots \pm x_K \qquad \text{(location condition)}$$

$$Y = x_1 - x_2 \qquad \text{(clearance condition)}$$

Example

Four components assemble adjacent to each other as indicated in Figure 7.4. Their respective sizes are denoted by x_1, x_2, x_3, and x_4. The additive component tolerances shown in the figure generate the assembly value $Y = 2.510 \pm 0.008$ in. The Y-specification is fixed by functional requirements and the problem is to enlarge the tolerances for the x-specifications. The risk of incurring defective assemblies is $\lambda = 0.003$ (i.e., 0.3%). To simplify the example, perfect form geometries and identical component tolerances will be assumed. The latter con-

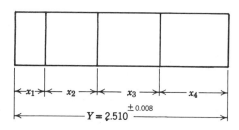

Figure 7.4. Additive tolerances. Component specifications: $x_1 = 0.370 \pm 0.002$; $x_2 = 0.625 \pm 0.002$; $x_3 = 0.750 \pm 002$; $x_4 = 0.765 \pm 0.002$.

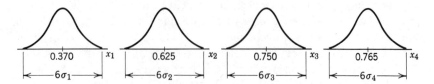

Figure 7.5. Component distributions.

dition is not a necessary one and will be relaxed in succeeding examples. Figure 7.5 shows the four component distributions.[1] Mean averages correspond to nominal specification values. Distribution ranges are measured by $6\sigma_x$. The assembly distribution is given in Figure 7.6. The distribution mean corresponds to the nominal assembly specification value. The fixed assembly tolerance determines the limit dimensions for Y to be 2.502 and 2.518 in. The risk value $\lambda/2$ is represented by the shaded tail areas, which correspond to the probability of incurring defective assemblies.

Since $\lambda = 0.003$, the Y-distribution range is $6\sigma_y$. The student should verify this by reference to Appendix A. Corresponding to a Z-value of 3.0, the tail area is 0.00135. Thus, for $\pm 3Z$ or ± 3 standard deviations, the sum of the tail areas is 0.0027 or approximately 0.003.

Considerable judgment is involved in deciding when statistical tolerances can be used. On the other hand, the computations are very simple.

Using property (2) of the theorem for combinations of independent random variables,

$$\sigma_Y^2 = \sigma_1^2 + \sigma_2^2 + \sigma_3^2 + \sigma_4^2$$

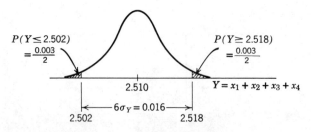

Figure 7.6. Assembly distribution.

[1]All distribution figures are schematic. No attempt is made to show distribution ranges to scale.

If the component tolerances are identical,

$$\sigma_Y{}^2 = 4\sigma_x{}^2$$

where $\sigma_x = \sigma_1 = \sigma_2 = \sigma_3 = \sigma_4$.

Since $6\,\sigma_Y = 0.016$ (see Figure 7.6),

$$\left(\frac{0.016}{6}\right)^2 = 4\sigma_x{}^2$$

and

$$\sigma_x = 0.00133$$

Since the component distribution ranges correspond to the respective component tolerances,

$$6\sigma_x = 6\,(0.00133)$$

$$= 0.008$$

$$= \pm\,0.004 = \text{component tolerance.}$$

Thus, the additive component tolerance of $\pm\,0.002$ in. can be replaced by an overlapping tolerance of $\pm\,0.004$ in. This advantage is gained by relaxing from 100% to 99.73% the percentage of assemblies expected to meet the fixed size requirement of 2.510 ± 0.008 in. This assumes, of course, that the component size dimensions are independent random variables, each normally distributed with mean average corresponding to the nominal specification value, and that component selection (at assembly work stations) is on a random basis.

Component distribution ranges are always set at $6\sigma_x$. Equating the component tolerance to $6\sigma_x$ is equivalent to requiring that most of the components (theoretically 99.7%) be manufactured to the overlapping tolerance specifications. If this is not the case, the percentage of defective assemblies may actually be greater than 100λ. The assembly distribution range is $C\sigma_Y$, C being a constant associated with the magnitude of λ. In the preceding example, $C = 2Z_\alpha$ where Z_α from Appendix A was 3.0 for $\alpha = 0.00135$.

Risk of Incurring Defective Assemblies

The risk of incurring defective assemblies, λ, was arbitrarily taken to be 0.003 in the preceding example. In practice, λ depends on economic considerations. Two sets of costs are involved: (1) cost of producing components to restrictive additive tolerances, and (2) discovery and correction costs at assembly and test work stations, these costs being due to the occurrence of a small percentage of defective assemblies. The anticipated advantage is an increase of component tolerances and thus, a considerable reduction in the cost of processing components to specifications. At the same time, nominal increases in assembly and test costs are incurred.

The magnitude of tolerance increase depends on λ and K. To illustrate the effect of varying λ, assume that λ was taken to be 0.0456 in the preceding example. Reference to Appendix A indicates that normal distribution tail areas of 0.0456/2 are associated with a four-standard deviation range (see Figure 7.7).

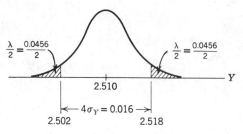

Figure 7.7.   Varying the risk, λ.

Then

$$4\sigma_Y = 0.016$$
$$\sigma_Y = 0.004$$

and

$$\sigma_Y^2 = 4\sigma_x^2$$
$$(0.004)^2 = 4\sigma_x^2$$
$$\sigma_x = 0.002$$

Component tolerance is

$$6\sigma_x = 6(0.002)$$

$$= 0.012$$

$$= \pm 0.006$$

Thus, by increasing λ, larger tolerance increases are made possible.

Larger component tolerances also result from larger K-values. In the preceding examples $K = 4$. However, for typical mechanical assemblies, K is usually much larger. (For example, in Table 5.1 the stackup was generated by eighteen component dimensions.) Figure 7.8 indicates tolerance increases for $K = 2, 4, \ldots, 14$. The graph has been prepared for fixed assembly tolerances of $K(0.002)$ in., $\lambda = 0.003$, and equal component tolerances. If $K = 4$, component tolerance is increased from 0.002 in. to 0.004 in. If $K = 14$, component tolerance is increased from 0.002 in. to 0.0075 in.

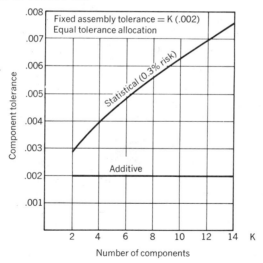

Figure 7.8. Tolerance increases for various K-values.

Two general design purposes have been stated. The preceding examples have been approached from the design viewpoint of the assembly tolerance being fixed by functional requirements. Before proceeding further, the same data for these examples will be used to illustrate a problem solution based on component tolerances being fixed. The problem now will be to compute probable variation of the assembly quality characteristic.

Example

Figure 7.9 gives essentially the same tolerance distributions as those of Figures 7.5 and 7.6. The only difference is that now the fixed component tolerances determine the respective limit dimensions shown on the component distributions, whereas the limiting values of the assembly distribution range are unknown.

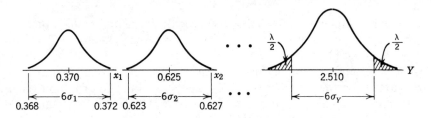

Figure 7.9.   Component tolerances fixed.

Again, using property (2) of the theorem,

$$\sigma_Y^2 = \sigma_1^2 + \sigma_2^2 + \sigma_3^2 + \sigma_4^2$$

If the component tolerances are identical,

$$\sigma_Y^2 = 4\sigma_x^2 \qquad \sigma_x = \sigma_1 = \sigma_2 = \sigma_3 = \sigma_4$$

Since $6\sigma_x = 0.004$ (see Figure 7.9),

$$\sigma_Y^2 = 4\left(\frac{0.004}{6}\right)^2$$

and

$$\sigma_Y = \frac{0.004}{3}$$

Thus, probable assembly variation is

$$6\sigma_Y = 6\left(\frac{0.004}{3}\right)$$

$$= 0.008$$

$$= \pm 0.004$$

The conclusion is that, if component size dimensions are independent random variables, each normally distributed with mean average identical to the nominal specification value, then the probable assembly variation (i.e., 99.7% of the time) is ±0.004 in.

Unequal Tolerance Allocation

The preceding examples assumed equal component tolerances. This condition simplified the computation considerably, only one unknown quantity being involved in the variances equation. If unequal tolerance allocation is required, careful consideration must be given to property (3) of the theorem for combinations of independent random variables. The Y-distribution must be reasonably normal for the probability considerations involving λ and the distribution ranges to be valid. If the x-distributions are not normal, K should be equal to or greater than 4 to increase the likelihood of the assembly distribution being approximately normal. Furthermore, some restriction should be placed on the magnitude of the tolerance differences. For example, one component tolerance should not be 5 to 10 times larger than another. Allocating tolerances unequally is equivalent to assuming unequal variances. Any combination of the following conditions may result in a λ-value larger than that assumed in the computations: (1) x-distributions not normal, (2) small K-value, and (3) x-distribution variances not homogeneous.

Fortunately, in converting additive to overlapping tolerances in practice, component tolerances under consideration will usually be of the same order of magnitude. Primary interest is in relaxing restrictive, small tolerances that are likely to cause production difficulties. There is no economic advantage in increasing large tolerances which are easily attained on a production basis.

The following example will indicate the computational procedure for unequal tolerance allocation. However, in all subsequent examples equal tolerance allocation will be assumed, to simplify the examples and, in connection with assembly clearance conditions, to yield unique solutions.

Example

Figure 7.10 gives additive size tolerances for three components assembling adjacent to each other. The tolerance distributions are shown in Figure 7.11. The Y-specification is fixed by assembly requirements.

The component tolerances can be increased unequally to obtain any desired numerical tolerance differences. For illustration, the

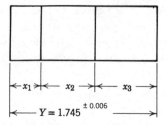

Figure 7.10. Additive tolerances. Component specifications: $x_1 = 0.370 \pm 0.001$; $x_2 = 0.625 \pm 0.002$; $x_3 = 0.750 \pm 0.003$.

component tolerances will be increased, preserving the ratio of 1:2:3 of the additive tolerances. Economic considerations indicate λ should be 0.0456.

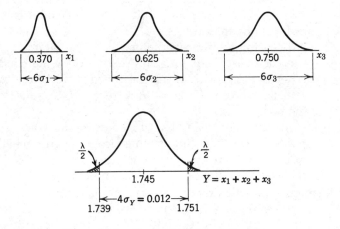

Figure 7.11. Unequal tolerance allocation.

Since $\lambda = 0.0456$,

$$4\sigma_Y = 0.012$$

and

$$\sigma_Y = 0.003$$

The overlapping tolerances will follow a ratio of 1:2:3. Therefore, let

$$w = \sigma_1 \qquad 2w = \sigma_2 \qquad 3w = \sigma_3$$

Then,

$$\sigma_Y{}^2 = \sigma_1{}^2 + \sigma_2{}^2 + \sigma_3{}^2$$

$$(0.003)^2 = w^2 + (2w)^2 + (3w)^2$$

$$= 14w^2$$

and

$$w = \frac{0.003}{\sqrt{14}}$$

Overlapping component tolerances are

$$6\sigma_1 = 6w$$

$$= 6\left(\frac{0.003}{\sqrt{14}}\right)$$

$$= \frac{0.018}{\sqrt{14}} \qquad (x_1 \text{ tolerance})$$

$$6\sigma_2 = 12w$$

$$= 12\left(\frac{0.003}{\sqrt{14}}\right)$$

$$= \frac{0.036}{\sqrt{14}} \qquad (x_2 \text{ tolerance})$$

$$6\sigma_3 = 18w$$

$$= 18\left(\frac{0.003}{\sqrt{14}}\right)$$

$$= \frac{0.054}{\sqrt{14}} \qquad (x_3 \text{ tolerance})$$

Assembly Condition of Clearance

A common assembly condition involving cumulative tolerances is that of clearance between fitting parts. One or more exterior quality characteristics match with an interior quality characteristic. The resulting assembly condition is either clearance or interference. Specification tolerances control the magnitude of the clearance or interference condition (see Figures 4.9 through 4.11).

In the following example, an interior component quality characteristic x_1 and a matching exterior characteristic x_2 generate a clearance condition identical to that of Figure 4.10. The tolerance function is

$$Y = x_1 - x_2$$

where Y denotes clearance, and clearance values may be either positive or negative (i.e., a negative clearance is equivalent to interference). Since K is only two, it is essential that the component characteristic distributions be reasonably normal.

Example

Basic size is 0.500 in. Clearances may vary only between +0.0002 in. and +0.0012 in., with mean clearance of +0.0007 considered to be optimum. Economic considerations have established λ to be 0.0456. Equal tolerance allocation to components is assumed. Basic hole and unilateral tolerancing procedures are followed in determining specifications. The additive specifications are given in Figure 7.12. The problem is to enlarge component tolerances, under a risk λ, working from a fixed assembly requirement of clearances from +0.0002 in. to +0.0012 in. Figure 7.13 indicates the tolerance distributions.

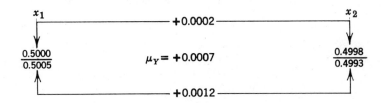

Figure 7.12.   Additive specifications.

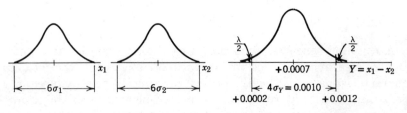

Figure 7.13.   Clearance condition.

138

$$\sigma_Y^2 = \sigma_1^2 + \sigma_2^2$$

If the component tolerances are identical,

$$\sigma_Y^2 = 2\sigma_x^2 \qquad \sigma_x = \sigma_1 = \sigma_2$$

Since $4\sigma_Y = 0.0010$,

$$\left(\frac{0.001}{4}\right)^2 = 2\sigma_x^2$$

and

$$\sigma_x = 0.000177$$

Component tolerance is

$$6\sigma_x = 6(0.000177)$$

$$= 0.001$$

$$= \pm0.0005$$

Thus, if x_1 and x_2 are normally distributed independent random variables, with mean averages corresponding to their respective nominal specification values, additive tolerances may be converted to overlapping tolerances. For each component, the tolerance can be increased from 0.0005 in. to 0.0010 in.

Converting an additive specification to an overlapping specification involves two distinct operations: (1) computing the overlapping tolerance, and (2) formulating the overlapping specification. The second operation depends on the following design decisions. The tolerancing procedure is a first consideration. Basic hole and unilateral tolerancing procedures are assumed in all examples. As pointed out in Chapter 4, this is a generally accepted specification practice. Secondly, the matter of equal or unequal tolerance allocation must

139

be settled. A previous example indicated the computation procedure for unequal tolerances. Subsequent examples in this chapter assume equal tolerance allocation to simplify the computation and, in some instances, to yield unique solutions. Finally, a design decision is required as to which is more critical: defective assemblies due to fits that are too tight, or defective assemblies where the fits are too loose.

Example

The data from the preceding example is used to illustrate specification determination. Additive specifications are given in Figure 7.12. Based on a risk $\lambda = 0.0456$, computation has yielded an overlapping tolerance of 0.0010 in.

Tight fits and loose fits are assumed to be equally critical. Thus

$$\frac{\lambda}{2} = P(Y \leq + 0.0002) = P(Y \geq + 0.0012)$$

The overlapping specifications are given in Figure 7.14. Basic hole practice establishes the 0.5000 limit, and the overlapping tolerances of 0.0010 determines the 0.5010 limit for the x_1 specification. An infinite number of specifications having a 0.0010 in. tolerance are possible for x_2. Only one specification will preserve the + 0.0007 in. mean clearance that was considered optimum. This specification is easily determined by computing minimum and maximum clearances as follows

$$+ 0.0007 - 0.0010 = - 0.0003$$

$$+ 0.0007 + 0.0010 = + 0.0017$$

Minimum clearance is − 0.0003 in. Applying this value to the 0.5000 limit of x_1, determines the 0.5003 limit for the x_2 specification. In like manner, the maximum clearance of + 0.0017 in. establishes the 0.4993 limit for the x_2 specification.

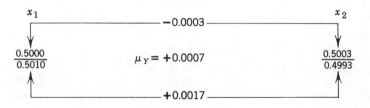

Figure 7.14. Overlapping specifications.

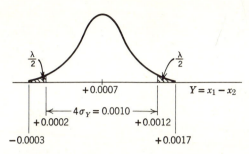

Figure 7.15. Additive and overlapping clearances.

Figure 7.15 summarizes the additive and overlapping tolerance considerations; 95.5% of the assembly clearances are expected to be between + 0.0002 in. and + 0.0012 in.; 100% of the clearances will be between − 0.0003 in. and + 0.0017 in., assuming that manufacturing and inspection operations follow the specifications.

Many designers intuitively manipulate the specification limits to favor either minimum or maximum clearance for product functional reasons. This is a reasonable approach but a bit suspect since the associated probability considerations have been ignored. The following example considers the possible consequences of this design procedure.

Example

The data from Figure 7.12 is again used as an illustration. A clearance less than + 0.0002 in. is considered to be functionally more critical than a clearance greater than + 0.0012 in. Overlapping component tolerance is 0.0010 in.

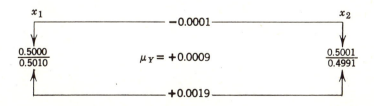

Figure 7.16. Overlapping specifications to minimize tight fits.

141

The designer decides to arbitrarily manipulate the x_2 specification limits to decrease the possibility of tight fits. The resulting overlapping specifications are given in Figure 7.16. The designer's arbitrary selection of x_2 specification limits has altered the mean clearance ($\mu_Y = +0.0009$), and this affects the λ-value. Figure 7.17 summarizes the assembly distribution information. The x_1 and x_2 distributions are assumed to be normal, resulting in a normal Y-distribution. The Z-values shown follow from the transformations:

$$Z_{+0.0002} = \frac{(+0.0002)-(+0.0009)}{0.001/4}$$

$$= -2.8$$

$$Z_{+0.0012} = \frac{(+0.0012) - (+0.0009)}{0.001/4}$$

$$= +1.2$$

The probabilities of nonconforming fits are:

$$P(Y \leq +0.0002) = P(Z \leq -2.8) = \int_{-\infty}^{-2.8} f(Z)\, dZ$$

$$P(Y \geq +0.0012) = P(Z \geq +1.2) = \int_{+1.2}^{+\infty} f(Z)\, dZ$$

These probabilities, read from Appendix A, are 0.00256 and 0.1151 respectively. If the manufacturing setups are aimed at the nominal specification values for x_1 and x_2, assembly clearances will distribute about a mean of $+0.0009$ in. There will be a 0.25% chance of fits which are too tight. (The designer accomplishes his objective!) However, there is a 11.51% chance of fits which are too loose. The risk λ is actually 0.1176.

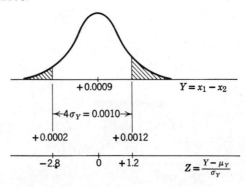

Figure 7.17.   Risk value λ is changed.

A direct approach, splitting λ into unequal components, is recommended in determining overlapping specifications when tight fits and loose fits are not equally critical. For example, λ could be partitioned for the preceding example conditions as follows:

$$P(Y \leq +0.0002) = 0.00135$$

$$P(Y \geq +0.0012) = 0.04365$$

$$\lambda = 0.00135 + 0.04365 = 0.045$$

Using the same problem conditions from the preceding example, and the probabilities above, another solution to the same example is presented.

Example

Figure 7.18 summarizes the assembly distribution information. The x_1 and x_2 distributions are assumed to be normal, resulting in a normal Y distribution.

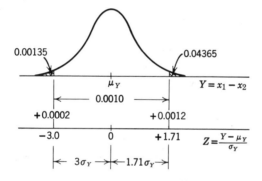

Figure 7.18.   Risk value λ is divided unequally.

$$\sigma_Y^2 = \sigma_1^2 + \sigma_2^2$$

If the component tolerances are identical,

$$\sigma_Y^2 = 2\sigma_x^2 \qquad \sigma_x = \sigma_1 = \sigma_2$$

Since $4.71 \; \sigma_Y = 0.0010$

$$\left(\frac{0.001}{4.71}\right)^2 = 2\sigma_x^2$$

and

$$\sigma_x = 0.00015$$

143

Component tolerance is

$$6\sigma_x = 6(0.00015)$$

$$= 0.0009$$

Computing new mean clearance,

$$\mu_Y = (+0.0002) + \left(\frac{3}{4.71}\right)(0.0010)$$

$$= +0.00083$$

New overlapping specifications based on a mean clearance of $+0.0008$ in. and an overlapping tolerance of $+0.0009$ in. are given in Figure 7.19.

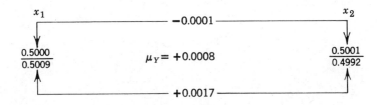

Figure 7.19. Overlapping specifications to minimize tight fits.

At the beginning of the discussion of overlapping tolerances applied to assembly-clearance situations, the statement was made that since K was only 2, it was essential that component quality characteristic distributions be reasonably normal. The tolerance function, $Y = x_1 - x_2$, applies to any two matching quality characteristics generating an assembly condition of clearance. For some of these matching part situations, the quality characteristics involved will tend to be normally distributed. For others, the characteristics may not be normally distributed. Clearly, overlapping tolerances are economic and should be used when the mathematical conditions underlying their use are reasonably satisfied under production conditions. However, even when overlapping tolerances are not justified, the computations illustrated by the examples are useful in establishing boundaries for tolerance increases. When manufacturing difficulties stimulate tolerance reviews, the overlapping tolerance computations establish maximum tolerance increases that are possible under the risk λ. This is extremely useful information to the product designer when he relaxes tolerances to facilitate manufacture.

In practice, there are many product-clearance conditions where K is greater than 2. The following simplified example is presented to illustrate a number of questions regarding clearance problems in general.

Example

Four components A, B, C, and D assemble adjacent to each other in the slot in E as shown in Figure 7.20. The x_1 specification is attainable on a production basis and will not be converted to an overlapping specification. The fixed assembly requirement is that clearances are to vary between +0.002 in. and +0.010 in. The risk λ is 0.0456. The additive specifications and tolerance distributions are given in Figure 7.21.

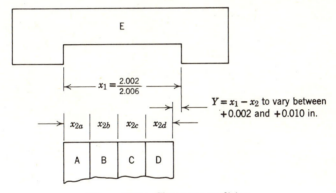

Figure 7.20. Clearance condition.

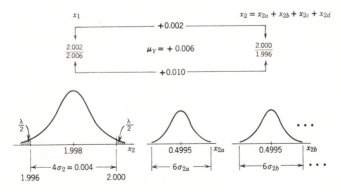

Figure 7.21. Additive specifications and tolerance distributions, x_1-specification is fixed. The additive specification is 0.500/0.499 in. for each $-x_{2a}$, x_{2b}, x_{2c}, and x_{2d}.

145

The clearance problem reduces to a size condition where

$$x_2 = x_{2a} + x_{2b} + x_{2c} + x_{2d}$$

and

$$\sigma_2{}^2 = \sigma_{2a}{}^2 + \sigma_{2b}{}^2 + \sigma_{2c}{}^2 + \sigma_{2d}{}^2$$

If the component tolerances are identical,

$$\sigma_2{}^2 = 4\sigma_x{}^2 \qquad \sigma_x = \sigma_{2a} = \sigma_{2b} = \sigma_{2c} = \sigma_{2d}$$

Since $4\sigma_2 = 0.004$

$$\left(\frac{0.004}{4}\right)^2 = 4\sigma_x{}^2$$

and

$$\sigma_x = 0.0005$$

component tolerance is

$$6\sigma_x = 6(0.0005)$$

$$= 0.003$$

The tolerance for each of the x_2 components can be increased from 0.001 in. to 0.003 in. The overlapping specification for each x_2 component is 0.501/0.498 in.

If the respective x_2 specifications and also the x_1 specification were to be converted from additive to overlapping tolerances, the tolerance function would be

$$Y = x_1 - x_2$$

$$= x_1 - (x_{2a} + x_{2b} + x_{2c} + x_{2d})$$

and

$$\sigma_Y{}^2 = \sigma_1{}^2 + \sigma_{2a}{}^2 + \sigma_{2b}{}^2 + \sigma_{2c}{}^2 + \sigma_{2d}{}^2$$

A solution of the variances equation (unequal tolerance allocation, preserving the original 4:1 ratio of the additive tolerances) would yield maximum overlapping tolerances of 0.0107 in. for x_1 and 0.0027 in. for each of the x_2 components. This solution is not recommended because the variances are not homogeneous, σ_1 being four times as large as σ_{2a}, σ_{2b}, σ_{2c}, and σ_{2d}. (See Problem 7, Review Questions and Problems.)

However, the solution does indicate that if it is necessary to increase the x_1 tolerance slightly for production reasons, meanwhile holding the x_2 tolerances to approximately 0.003 in. each, only a small percentage of defective assemblies would probably result.

Of course, x_1 and x_2 could be converted from additive to overlapping tolerances and the x_2 overlapping tolerance could be distributed additively among the four x_2 components. Under a $\lambda = 0.0456$ risk, this would yield a maximum overlapping tolerance of 0.008 in. for x_1 and 0.002 in. for each of the x_2 components. This result supports the previous conclusion.

An important implementation procedure is illustrated by the preceding example. One can partition stack-ups, assigning additive tolerances to some quality characteristics, and overlapping tolerances to others. The total stack-up in the preceding example was

$$Y = x_1 - (x_{2a} + x_{2b} + x_{2c} + x_{2d})$$

However, in the first solution, the x_1 specification involved an additive tolerance and the overlapping tolerances for the x_2 components were computed from the substack-up

$$x_2 = x_{2a} + x_{2b} + x_{2c} + x_{2d}$$

Non-linear Combinations of Quality Characteristics

In the theorem for combinations of independent random variables, the linearity requirement was

$$Y = a_1x_1 \pm a_2x_2 \pm \ldots \pm a_Kx_K$$

For the preceding mechanical assembly examples, the tolerance functions have been of the form

$$Y = x_1 \pm x_2 \pm \ldots \pm x_K \qquad a_j = 1$$

An example[2] is presented to illustrate a procedure for obtaining a linear approximation for Y when Y is a non-linear function.

[2]This example has been abstracted from Johnson, R. H. (January, 1953), "How To Evaluate Assembly Tolerances, *Product Engineering*, pp. 179-181.

Example

Figure 7.22 indicates the component specifications and assembly requirement for a voltage-transformer-amplifier combination. The student will recognize this example as a design situation (see Figure 7.9) of working from fixed component specifications and estimating probable cumulative component error effect on the assembly quality characteristic. The risk λ is 0.003.

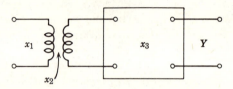

Figure 7.22. Nonlinear combination of tolerances. Component specifications: input voltage, $x_1 = 40 \pm 0.5$ volts; transformer, $x_2 = 2$ to $1 \pm 1\%$; amplifier, $x_3 = 3 \pm 2\%$. Assembly specifications: output voltage, $Y = 60$ volts $\pm 3\%$.

The tolerance function is

$$Y = x_1 \cdot x_2 \cdot x_3$$

The initial problem is to obtain a linear approximation to Y. A Taylor's series expansion is used for this purpose, expanding the original function about the means μ_1, μ_2, μ_3, neglecting higher order terms.

$$Y \overset{\wedge}{=} \mu_1\mu_2\mu_3 + (x_1 - \mu_1)\frac{\delta Y}{\delta x_1}\Big|_{\mu_1,\mu_2,\mu_3} + (x_2 - \mu_2)\frac{\delta Y}{\delta x_2}\Big|_{\mu_1,\mu_2,\mu_3}$$

$$+ (x_3 - \mu_3)\frac{\delta Y}{\delta x_3}\Big|_{\mu_1,\mu_2,\mu_3} + \cdots$$

$$Y \overset{\wedge}{=} \mu_1\mu_2\mu_3 + (x_1 - \mu_1)\mu_2\mu_3 + (x_2 - \mu_2)\mu_1\mu_3 + (x_3 - \mu_3)\mu_1\mu_2 + \cdots$$

$$Y - \mu_1\mu_2\mu_3 = (x_1 - \mu_1)\,\mu_2\mu_3 + (x_2 - \mu_2)\,\mu_1\mu_3 + (x_3 - \mu_3)\,\mu_1\mu_2 + \cdots$$

Neglecting higher order terms, this is a function of the form

$$Y = a_1X_1 + a_2X_2 + a_3X_3$$

and the coefficients $\mu_2\mu_3$, $\mu_1\mu_3$, $\mu_1\mu_2$ correspond to a_1, a_2, a_3 respectively in

$$\sigma_Y{}^2 = a_1{}^2\ \sigma_1{}^2 + a_2{}^2\sigma_2{}^2 + a_3{}^2\sigma_3{}^2$$

The tolerance distributions are shown in Figure 7.23. Percent error has been translated to absolute error for the x_2 and x_3 distributions.

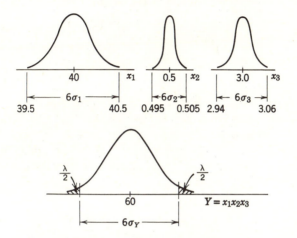

Figure 7.23.   Nonlinear combination of tolerances.

The specification limits for the x_2 distribution are

$$\mu_2 \pm 0.01\ \mu_2$$

and for the x_3 distribution are

$$\mu_3 \pm 0.02\ \mu_3$$

$$\mu_Y = \mu_1\mu_2\mu_3$$

$$= (40)\ (0.5)\ (3.0)\ \equiv 60\ \text{volts}$$

$$\sigma_Y{}^2 \stackrel{\wedge}{=} (\mu_2\mu_3)^2\sigma_1{}^2 + (\mu_1\mu_3)^2\sigma_2{}^2 + (\mu_1\mu_2)^2\sigma_3{}^2$$

$$\stackrel{\wedge}{=} [(0.5)(3.0)]^2 \left(\frac{1}{6}\right)^2 + [(40)(3.0)]^2 \left(\frac{0.01}{6}\right)^2 + [(40)(0.5)]^2 \left(\frac{0.12}{6}\right)^2$$

$$\sigma_Y \stackrel{\wedge}{=} \frac{1}{6}(3.074)$$

149

and

$$6\sigma_Y = 3.074$$

Thus, probable assembly variation is

$$60 \pm \frac{1}{2}(3.074) \text{ volts}$$

or $\qquad 60 \pm 1.537$ volts

or $\qquad 60$ volts $\pm 2.56\%$ error.

The conclusion is, if component quality characteristics are independent random variables, each normally distributed with mean average identical to the nominal specification value, then the probable assembly variation (i.e., 99.7% of the time) is 60 volts $\pm 2.56\%$ error. Thus, it seems that, under the established tolerances for the purchased components x_1, x_2, and x_3, the output voltage requirement of 60 volts $\pm 3\%$ error will be satisfied.

Composite Condition of Size and Location

The following example[3] is presented to illustrate stack-up and tolerance analysis for an actual design problem.

Example

Assume that 25 component size and location specifications interrelate to determine clearance (or interference) between two small capacitors. The tolerance function is

$$Y = x_1 \pm x_2 \pm \ldots \pm x_{25}$$

A design check-print showing principal components is given in Figure 7.24. A geometric abstraction of the tolerance problem is shown in Figure 7.25.

The algebraic sum of the nominal size and location specifications for the contributing component quality characteristics determines

[3]This example is taken from Kirkpatrick, E. G. (1962), *Engineering Report No. GR-1408*, Lear Siegler, Inc., Instrument Division, Grand Rapids, Michigan.

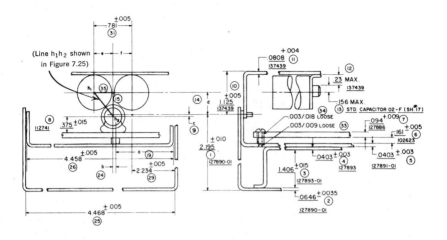

Figure 7.24. Composite condition of size and location. From E. G. Kirkpatrick (1962), *Engineering Report No. GR-1408*, Lear Siegler, Inc., Instrument Division, Grand Rapids, Michigan.

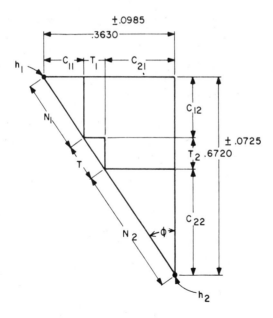

Figure 7.25. Error geometry. From E. G. Kirkpatrick (1962), *Engineering Report No. GR-1408*, Lear Siegler, Inc., Instrument Division, Grand Rapids, Michigan.

151

Table 7.1. **Additive tolerance stack-up.**

x	Part Number	$\bar{x}$	Tolerance
x_1	127890-01	+ 2.195	± .010*
x_2	127890-01	− .0646	± .0035
x_3	127893-01	− 1.406	± .015*
x_4	127893	− .0403	± .003
x_5	127891-01	− .0403	± .003
x_6	102623	− .161	± .005*
x_7	127886	− .094	+ .009
x_8	112741	− .375	+ .015
$x_9 =$	$x_1 - (x_2 + \ldots + x_8)$	.0138	$\Sigma = \pm .0635$
x_{10}	137439	+ 1.125	± .005*
x_{11}	137439	− .0808	± .004
x_{12}	137439	− .23	Maximum
x_{13}	02-F	− .156	Maximum
$x_{14} =$	$x_{10} - (x_{11} + x_{12} + x_{13})$	.6582	$\Sigma = \pm .009$
$x_{15} =$	$x_9 + x_{14}$	.6720	$\Sigma = T_2 = \pm .0725$
x_{16}	127891	+ .469	± .015*
x_{17}	127891	+ 1.362	± .005*
x_{18}	127891	+ .797	± .005*
$x_{19} =$	$x_{16} + x_{17} + x_{18}$	2.628	$\Sigma = \pm .025$
x_{20}	127886	+ 1.250	± .015*
x_{21}	127886	− .223	± .010*
x_{22}	127886	− .797	± .005*
x_{23}	127886	− .216	± .010*
$x_{24} =$	$x_{20} - (x_{21} + x_{22} + x_{23})$	.014	$\Sigma = \pm .040$
x_{25}		+ 4.468	± .005*
x_{26}		− 4.458	± .005*
$x_{27} =$	$x_{25} - x_{26}$	.010	$\Sigma = \pm .010$
$x_{28} =$	$x_{19} + x_{24} + x_{27}$	+ 2.652	$\Sigma = \pm .075$
x_{29}		− 2.234	± .005*
$x_{30} =$	$x_{28} - x_{29}$	.418	$\Sigma = \pm .080$
x_{31}		.781	± .005*
$x_{32} =$	$x_{31} - x_{30}$	.363	$\Sigma = \pm .085$
x_{33}	.0045 Loose		± .0045
x_{34}	.009 Loose		± .009
x_{35}		.363	$\Sigma = T_1 = \pm .0985$

$N_1 + N_2$ = nominal distance between centers, h_1 and h_2.

Based on design considerations, the assembly tolerance or specified maximum error, denoted by T, is

$$T = (\text{maximum clearance} - \text{zero clearance})$$

N_1, N_2, and T are represented by coordinate print specifications:

$$N_1 + N_2 + T = \sqrt{(c_{11} + c_{21} + T_1)^2 + (c_{12} + c_{22} + T_2)^2}$$

T_1 depends on the tolerances for all specifications contributing to c_{11} and c_{21}. T_2 depends on the tolerances for all specifications contributing to c_{12} and c_{22}.

The additive tolerance stack-up is shown in Table 7.1. It seems likely that the process operations for 15 specifications will generate quality characteristic distributions that satisfy the mathematical conditions for combination of independent random variables. Thus, these 15 specifications (denoted by asterisks in Table 7.1) can be converted from additive to overlapping specifications.

Two distinct stack-ups, x_{15} and x_{35}, are involved (see Figure 7.25):

$$c_{11} + T_1 + c_{21} = 0.3630 \pm 0.0985$$
$$c_{12} + T_2 + c_{22} = 0.6720 \pm 0.0725$$

Thus,

$$T_1 = 2(0.0985)$$

$$= 0.1970$$

---

*will be statistically toleranced.
If D_{C1} = diameter of capacitor #1
  D_{C2} = diameter of capacitor #2
  E_1 = eccentricity of C_1
  E_2 = eccentricity of C_2
then $(.6720 - .0725)^2 + (.3630 - .0985)^2 > [1/2 \, (D_{C1} + D_{C2}) - (E_1 + E_2)]^2$ to assure a clearance condition > 0.

From Kirkpatrick, E. G. (1962), *Engineering Report No. GR-1408*, Lear Siegler, Inc., Instrument Division, Grand Rapids, Michigan.

and

$$T_2 = 2(0.0725)$$
$$= 0.1450$$

Treating each stack-up separately,

$$T_1 = 0.1970 = \Sigma \text{ tolerances for } x_{16}, x_{17}, \ldots, x_{34}.$$

Since x_{33} and x_{34} receive additive tolerances, these tolerances are subtracted from T_1 to establish the fixed assembly distribution range associated with the risk λ. Assume $\lambda = 0.003$, then

$$6\sigma_Y = 0.1970 - (0.009 + 0.018)$$
$$= 0.170$$

and

$$\left(\frac{0.170}{6}\right)^2 = \sigma_{16}{}^2 + \sigma_{17}{}^2 + \ldots + \sigma_{31}{}^2$$

where $+ \ldots +$ refers to the specification tolerances denoted by asterisks in Table 7.1.

Since unequal component tolerances are involved, a solution of the variances equation proceeds as indicated (for unequal tolerance allocation) earlier in this chapter.

Similarly, for stack-up T_2

$$T_2 = 0.1450 = \Sigma \text{ tolerances for } x_1, x_2, \ldots x_{11}$$

Subtracting the additive tolerances from T_2,

$$6\sigma_Y = 0.1450 - 0.0750$$
$$= 0.070$$

and

$$\left(\frac{0.070}{6}\right)^2 = \sigma_1{}^2 + \sigma_3{}^2 + \sigma_6{}^2 + \sigma_{10}{}^2$$

STATISTICAL TOLERANCE IMPLEMENTATION

Examples in this chapter are based on the theorem for combination of independent random variables. Practical implications of this theorem will now be examined.

Independence Requirements

Under production conditions, x_1, x_2, ..., x_K are seldom completely independent. The practice of using the same production datum for product-part location in chuck, jig, or fixture for multiple-process operations introduces a strong tendency in the direction of relationship. If the x_j are not independent, an additional correction term involving the correlation coefficient may be introduced into the variances equation. For example,[4] in the simple case of $Y = x_1 \pm x_2$,

$$\sigma_Y^2 = \left(\frac{\delta Y}{\delta x_1}\right)^2 \sigma_1^2 + \left(\frac{\delta Y}{\delta x_2}\right)^2 \sigma_2^2 + 2\left(\frac{\delta Y}{\delta x_1}\right)\left(\frac{\delta Y}{\delta x_2}\right) \rho_{x_1,x_2} \sigma_1 \sigma_2$$

where $Y = f(x_1,x_2)$ and the partial derivatives are evaluated at the means μ_1 and μ_2. In practice, however, establishing the correlation-coefficient value ρ is impractical. A simple practical approach to the question of independence follows. (1) Operations sheets analysis of process operations and tooling methods will quickly identify the specifications that clearly are not independent. Use additive tolerances for these specifications. This procedure was followed in the preceding example. (2) Assure random-assembly conditions at assembly-work stations. Mix components before delivery to stock or assembly stations to prevent possible assembly in the order of production.

Random Variable Requirement

The physical implication of the random variable requirement is that processes which generate the component quality characteristics x_j must be "controlled." This can be accomplished by statistical control methods or by effective practical methods. In either case, assignable causes of variation in the process should be minimized. Quality-characteristic distributions must be repeatable and not influenced by large variations due to assignable causes. Procedure (2) in the preceding paragraph will facilitate random conditions. Also, procedure (1) in the same paragraph may be followed to eliminate nonrandom varia-

---

[4]See *An Introduction to the Statistical Treatment of Measurement Data*, U.S. Department of Commerce, National Bureau of Standards, Washington, D.C., NBS Report 8677 (April 19, 1965), p. 23.

bles from consideration. For example, quality-characteristic dimensions generated by presswork operations should not receive statistical tolerances. Dies are designed to initially produce components at one specification limit and are used until die wear is such that production output is concentrated at the other specification limit. Short production runs may result in production output being concentrated at one limit or the other.

Processes Aimed at Nominal Specifications

The constraint of aiming processes at nominal specifications follows from the correspondence of the distribution mean μ to the nominal specification value for both assembly and component quality characteristics. Only with the cooperation of manufacturing can this condition be satisfied. Generally, production people prefer to aim processes at maximum material limits. This practice maximizes permissible process drift due to tool wear, and thus increases machine cycle time (i.e., time the machine runs without interruption for changing or regrinding tools).

To obtain the necessary manufacturing cooperation in aiming processes at nominal specification values, it is necessary to educate production people to the fact that they are not actually being restricted in the matter of process settings. Figures 7.26 and 7.27 illustrate the argument. Overlapping tolerances are not recommended for the tolerance situation given in Figure 7.26. There is no economic advantage in increasing additive tolerances that are easily attained on a production basis. Therefore, in this situation, the additive tolerances will be retained and manufacturing can aim processes at maximum material limits.

In the tolerance case described by Figure 7.27, even with an additive

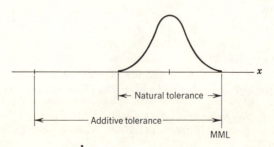

Figure 7.26.   Process can be aimed at the maximum material limit.

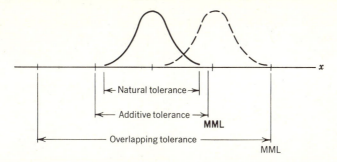

Figure 7.27.   Process must be aimed at the nominal specification value.

tolerance, manufacturing must aim the process-setting at the nominal specification value, since only a slight process drift or inaccurate first piece process-setting will generate a large percentage of defective product. Thus, if the additive tolerance is converted to an overlapping tolerance, the requirement of aiming the process at the nominal specification value is a manufacturing constraint that would have been acceptable under the more restrictive additive specification. The point, however, is that manufacturing is not permitted to aim the process at the maximum material limit for the overlapping specification (as shown by the dashed line distribution in Figure 7.27). The following example indicates the consequence of not aiming processes at nominal component specification values.

Example

The data from Figure 7.12 is again used as an illustration. The nominal overlapping specification values (see Figure 7.14) are 0.5005 in. for x_1 and 0.4998 in. for x_2. Actual manufacturing distributions are shown in Figure 7.28.

The x_2 distribution is satisfactory. The x_1 distribution, however, has a mean of 0.5006 in. Thus, the mean clearance, which ideally should be + 0.0007 in. is

$$\mu_Y = \mu_1 - \mu_2$$

$$= 0.5006 - 0.4998$$

$$= + 0.0008$$

The result is an excessive number of assemblies having fits which are too loose.

157

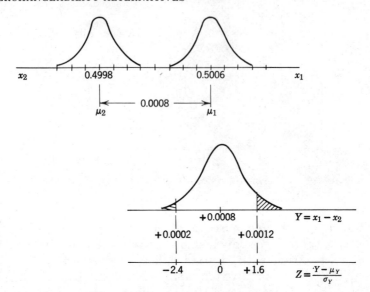

Figure 7.28. x_1-distribution mean not identical to the nominal specification value.

$$P(Y \leq + 0.0002) = \int_{-\infty}^{-2.4} f(Z)\, dZ = 0.0082$$

$$P(Y \geq + 0.0012) = \int_{+1.6}^{+\infty} f(Z)\, dZ = 0.0548$$

On the average, 0.82% of the fits have clearances less than + 0.0002 in., and 5.48% clearances greater than + 0.0012 in. And

$$\lambda = 0.0082 + 0.0548$$

$$= 0.0630$$

Normal Assembly Distribution Requirement

There is the famous remark[5] that "everybody believes in the law of errors (normal distribution), the experimenters because they think it is a mathematical theorem, the mathematicians because they think it

[5]From Cramer, H. (1946), Mathematical Methods of Statistics, Princeton University Press, Princeton, N. J., p. 232.

is an experimental fact." Actually, although there are manufacturing distributions that are decidedly non-normal, many are approximately normal.

Since the risk λ is based on the normal probability function model, the assembly distribution must be at least approximately normal. If the component distributions are normal, then the assembly distribution is normal. If the component distributions are not normal, and if their distribution ranges are approximately homogeneous, then as K increases, the assembly distribution rapidly approaches the normal distribution. This reassuring fact is illustrated by Figure 7.29. Assume that component quality characteristics are distributed rectangularly. A rectangular distribution is perhaps the worst type of distribution encountered in manufacturing. It usually is due to a significant cause of erratic process variation which, for economic reasons, cannot be corrected. Figure 7.29 indicates assembly distributions for $K = 2, 3,$ and 4 rectangular component distributions.

If K is large, then perhaps even nonhomogeneous component distribution ranges, as well as non-normal component distributions, may be accepted. To examine the nature of the resulting assembly distribution it is necessary to simulate the combination of component quality characteristics. If process capability data is available, with only a small additional effort, simulation procedures can usefully classify overlapping tolerancing situations for typical process operations and product geometries where the mathematical conditions seem to be violated. A simplified example is presented here.

Example

The following data represent the distributions of size quality characteristics x_1, x_2, x_3, and x_4. For simplicity of illustration, assume the x variables are identically distributed. Then

x	f
0.500	1
0.501	2
0.502	6
0.503	17
0.504	24
0.505	24
0.506	17
0.507	6
0.508	2
0.509	1

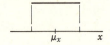

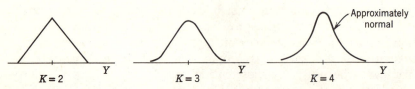

Figure 7.29. Combination of rectangularly distributed component quality characteristics.

Four sets of two-digit random numbers are assigned to four identical sets of data points. Each set of data points consists of 100 numbers. Each number in each set of random numbers occurs once and only once. The random numbers and corresponding data points are punched on I.B.M. cards, one pair of numbers to a card. These cards are sorted so that every consecutive four cards contains a data point from each of the four sets. These cards are processed to give the results shown in Table 7.2.

Table 7.2. **Computer simulation of the assembly distribution.**

Computer Printout:

2.008	2.016	2.017	2.019	2.021
2.009	2.016	2.017	2.019	2.021
2.011	2.016	2.017	2.019	2.021
2.011	2.016	2.018	2.019	2.021
2.012	2.016	2.018	2.019	2.021
2.013	2.016	2.018	2.019	2.021
2.014	2.016	2.018	2.019	2.021
2.014	2.016	2.018	2.019	2.021
2.014	2.016	2.018	2.019	2.021
2.014	2.017	2.018	2.019	2.021
2.015	2.017	2.018	2.019	2.022
2.015	2.017	2.018	2.020	2.022
2.015	2.017	2.018	2.020	2.022
2.015	2.017	2.018	2.020	2.022
2.015	2.017	2.018	2.020	2.023
2.015	2.017	2.018	2.020	2.024
2.015	2.017	2.018	2.020	2.024
2.015	2.017	2.019	2.020	2.025
2.015	2.017	2.019	2.020	2.027
2.015	2.017	2.019	2.020	2.029

Assume the overlapping assembly specification is 2.018 ± 0.007 in. Table 7.2 indicates four assembly dimension values not conforming to the specification. The probability of incurring defective assemblies is taken to be

$$\lambda = \frac{4}{100} = 0.04$$

Note that the simplified procedure used in the example involved selecting without replacement from the component quantities. A program could be developed for random selection with replacement to generate assembly distributions based on larger population size N.

If the assembly distribution is not normal, the risk λ may actually be larger than that assumed when the designer established the overlapping tolerance. Many designers compute an overlapping tolerance based on fixed assembly requirements and an assumed λ value, and then consider the overlapping tolerance to be the maximum boundary for relaxing the additive tolerance. Various compromise techniques have been adopted, all of which are equivalent to determining the specification tolerance to be somewhere between the additive tolerance as a minimum and the computed overlapping tolerance as a maximum.

Many process operations naturally generate normal distributions, particularly if the processes are controlled. Also, many operations result in distributions which are decidedly non-normal. In general, manually operated processes generate different distributions than those obtained from automatic processes. It is difficult to assure a normal distribution with mean average equal to the nominal specification value when fixed tool setups are involved. Examples of this are sintered metal, plastic molding, and punch and die operations. Another example is heat treatment operations. A part may be cut by a broach and then heat treated. Or the part may be roughed, milled, and then hardened. In both cases, heat treatment effects will cause a shift in the mean dimension and an increase in the distribution range. Often it is necessary to initially cut the part so it is out of tolerance and then depend on the heat treatment operation to pull it within tolerance limits.

Implementation for Statistical Tolerances

Effective use of overlapping tolerances requires a closely coordinated program involving design, manufacturing, and quality control, with design necessarily accepting the major part of what is essentially a joint responsibility. If economic considerations indicate the need for a modified full interchangeability approach, some additive tolerances will be converted to overlapping tolerances. The conversion method enables the product designer to determine maximum tolerance increases under the risk λ. The method also establishes some production responsibilities and control procedures to restrict the expected percentage of defective assemblies to 100λ or less. If implementation procedures are carried out properly, the tolerance increases will reduce process costs considerably.

Statistical Tolerance Specification Implications

For purposes of comparing additive and overlapping tolerances, consider an additive tolerance example: 0.500 ± 0.002 in. This specification merely states that product may not exceed 0.502 or be less than 0.498. It does not specify or restrict the distribution of product sizes. In fact all, or a majority, of the product may be concentrated at one or the other specification limit, causing actual assembly fits never intended by the product designer. Quality may thus be only marginal.

The statistical concept of a tolerance specification implies a great deal more. Usually some identification symbol is used to denote a statistical specification, such as 0.500 ± 0.002 (STAT). This specification also identifies maximum and minimum acceptable sizes. An implicit consequence of the specification, however, is that the average product size is to be 0.500, and the distribution of product sizes about 0.500 is delineated. Optimum fits, as conceived by the product designer, actually correspond to the average fit being manufactured. Quality is generally good.

Statistical specifications place some extra control responsibilities on manufacturing and quality assurance. In return, manufacturing receives an additional degree of freedom in the form of increased production tolerances.

Implementation Responsibilities

Product-design engineering determines the overlapping specifications and accepts responsibility for all statistical considerations pertaining to the possibility of assembly and test difficulties. Manufacturing has three principal obligations: (1) to assure that processes are in control, (2) to aim processes at nominal specification values, and (3) to provide a physical plan assuring random assembly. This

IBM

INTERNATIONAL BUSINESS MACHINES CORPORATION

VENDOR QUALITY SPECIFICATION

DATE April 17, 1958

PART NO.	MACHINE	PART NAME	DEPT. NO	DATE	ENG CHANGE NO
444222	407	Bushing	68Q		
OPERATION NUMBER		MACHINE NAME Printer	ANALYST 5		

1.	Shoulder thickness .295 S-D (See Note I) MAJOR AQL 1.0%		Mics.
2.	Shank dia. .500 S-D (See Note I) MINOR AQL 2.5%		Mics.
10	Hole dia. .312		Plug Gage

NOTE I – A lot of product is classified as acceptable for this dimension if not more than 15% of the parts fall outside ± .0015 (.295 dim.) ± .001 (.500 dim.) and if not more than 1.0% of the parts fall outside the print limits.

SPECIAL SAMPLING PLAN – Sample Size 100 pcs.

Dimension	Narrow Limit	Acceptance No.	Print Limits	Acceptance No.
.295	± .0015	20	± .003	2
.500	± .001	20	± .002	2

Figure 7.30. Vendor quality specifications. (By courtesy of International Business Machines Corporation, General Products Division, Endicott, N. Y.).

is a joint responsibility of setup men, process operators, and patrol inspectors.

Quality control assures that product is manufactured under controlled conditions. Quality control also identifies product lots. Those lots that meet the statistical specification without 100% sorting of product are delivered to stock or to assembly stations. Lots meeting statistical specifications, but with excessive sorting involved to do so, are separated for a 100% inspection to tighter additive tolerance specifications.

Vendor Instructions

If components are produced in vendor plants, control over the responsibilities discussed in the preceding paragraph will depend on special vendor quality specifications. One approach is indicated by Figure 7.30 (see Note I on the vendor specification). Conformance conditions are specified in terms of the percentages of parts that are to exist in various tolerance-range segments (Figure 7.31).

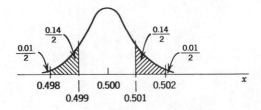

Figure 7.31. Distribution effect of vendor specification.

The shank diameter specification is 0.500 ± 0.002 (STAT). Acceptance occurs if a maximum of 14% of the submitted product occurs in the tolerance ranges 0.498 to 0.499 and 0.501 to 0.502, and a maximum of 1% of the product is less than 0.498 or greater than 0.502, as

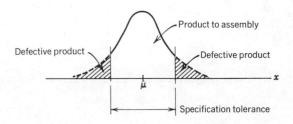

Figure 7.32. Sorting of product to meet specifications.

shown in Figure 7.31. This specification procedure tends to force a normal distribution of the component quality characteristic. In particular, this specification procedure has the specific purpose of imposing on the vendor the constraint that overlapping specifications are not to be attained by means of a severe rectifying inspection (i.e., a high percentage of the vendor's production output must meet the overlapping specification without the aid of a 100% inspection). As shown in Figure 7.32, if a rectifying inspection is necessarily imposed on the process output, then the component tolerance distribution of parts going to assembly (shown by the continuous line in Figure 7.32) is approximating a rectangular distribution. If component distribution tails are eliminated, then the assembly distribution tails may be altered (particularly if $K = 2,3$) and the risk λ may be increased considerably.

SUMMARY

The economics of tolerance determination is mainly concerned with establishing the degree of interchangeability which is feasible on a production basis. Principal alternatives are *in-plant, full,* and *modified full interchangeability.* Full interchangeability is accomplished by additive tolerancing, usually resulting in restrictive and costly product tolerances. Modified full interchangeability involves overlapping tolerances, and implementation alternatives are *selective assembly* or *random assembly.* If the modified full interchangeability method with random-assembly procedure is utilized, statistical techniques are used to compute the maximum tolerance increase that is possible, based on an acceptable risk of incurring defective assemblies.

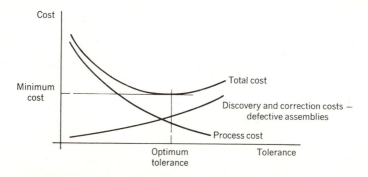

Figure 7.33. Economics of overlapping tolerances.

Figure 7.33 indicates the economic argument for tolerance increases. Use of overlapping tolerances will result in a small percentage of production-assembly difficulties. Either parts will not assemble, or if they do assemble, the assembly may be defective for reasons of improper fits. Thus, discovery and correction costs are incurred at assembly and test work stations (i.e., costs due to the necessary replacement of defective components in the assemblies). With tolerance increases, nominal increases in discovery and correction costs are expected, together with very significant reductions in process costs. The result is an expected net decrease in total cost. (In this situation, total cost is viewed as the sum of process costs and discovery and correction costs.) For each quality characteristic and its associated process operation, there exists an optimum tolerance that minimizes total cost.

REFERENCES

Acton, F. S. and Olds, E. G., (November, 1948), "Tolerances — Additive or Pythagorean," *Industrial Quality Control*, Vol. 5, No. 3, pp. 6-12.

Barrows, M. D., (November, 1949), "Probability Methods for Establishing Tolerances," *Product Engineering*, pp. 106-110.

Bowker, A. H. and Lieberman, (1961), *Engineering Statistics*, Prentice-Hall, Englewood Cliffs, N. J., pp. 51-66.

Burr, I. W., (1953), *Engineering Statistics and Quality Control*, McGraw-Hill, New York.

Burr, I. W., (September, 1958), "Tolerances for Mating Parts," *Industrial Quality Control*, Vol. 15, No. 3, pp. 18-22.

Burr, I. W., (September, 1961), "Distribution of Products and Quotients for Random Variables," *Industrial Quality Control*, Vol. 18, No. 3, pp. 16-18.

Duncan, A. J., (1959), *Quality Control and Industrial Statistics*, Richard D. Irwin, Homewood, Illinois, pp. 72-74.

Grant, E. L., (1964), *Statistical Quality Control*, McGraw-Hill, New York, pp. 299-314.

IBM, (1959), *A Vendor Guide for Statistical Dimensions*, International Business Machines Corporation, Endicott, New York.

Johnson, R. H., (January, 1953), "How to Evaluate Assembly Tolerances," *Product Engineering*, Vol. 24, No. 1, pp. 179-181.

Juran, J. M., (1962), *Quality Control Handbook*, McGraw-Hill, New York.

Kirkpatrick, E. G. (1962), *Engineering Report No. GR-1408*, Lear Siegler, Inc., Instrument Division, Grand Rapids, Michigan.

Kirkpatrick, E. G., (March, 1964), "Statistical Tolerancing," *Production*, pp. 76-79.

Kirkpatrick, E. G., (September, 1963 — November, 1963), "The Case for Statistical Tolerancing," *Modern Machine Shop*, Vol. 36, Nos. 4, 5, 6.

NBS Report 8677, (April 19, 1965), *An Introduction to the Statistical Treatment of Measurement Data*, U. S. Department of Commerce, National Bureau of Standards, Washington, D. C., p. 23.

Wilks, S. S., (March, 1941), "Determination of Sample Size for Setting Tolerance Limits," *Annals of Mathematical Statistics*, Vol. 12, pp. 91-96.

Wilks, S. S., (December, 1942), "Statistical Prediction with Reference to Tolerance Limits," *Annals of Mathematical Statistics*, Vol. 13, pp. 400-409.

REVIEW QUESTIONS

1. State three principal types of interchangeability and identify the tolerancing procedure for each (i.e., no tolerance, overlapping, or additive tolerances).

2. Identify the two assembly alternatives for modified full interchangeability and describe the associated costs.

3. Describe the two general types of statistical tolerance application problems (i.e., based on design purpose).

4. Discuss the economics of overlapping tolerances (see Figure 7.33). What is the purpose of statistical tolerancing?

5. The point has been made that unequal tolerance allocation (for overlapping tolerances) requires careful consideration of property (3) of the theorem for combinations of independent random variables. What conditions may result in a λ-value larger than that assumed in the statistical tolerance computations?

6. In connection with the conditions mentioned in question 5, what is a conservative general procedure?

7. It is important that the Y-distribution be approximately normal, if statistical tolerances are to be utilized. If the x-distribution ranges are reasonably homogeneous, what conditions assure normality of the Y-distribution?

8. What is the purpose of the Taylor's series expansion in the voltage-transformer-amplifier example (Figure 7.23)?

9. What is the physical implication of the random variable requirement in the theorem underlying statistical tolerance applications?

10. Processes must be aimed at nominal specification values if statistical tolerances are to be safely used. Why do production people generally object to this constraint?

11. Explain why the condition mentioned in question 10 is not actually a constraint.

12. What three departments of the manufacturing organization are involved in implementation of statistical tolerance applications? Which department accepts the major responsibility for this joint effort?

13. Briefly outline the specific implementation responsibilities of the respective departments mentioned in question 12.

PROBLEMS

1. Five independent, normally distributed, random variables $x_1, x_2, \ldots, x_5$

167

have respective means of 2, 3, 4, 5, 6 and standard deviations of 0.1, 0.1, 0.1, 0.2, 0.3, and the x_j are related by $Y = x_1 + x_2 + \ldots + x_5$. Compute the $P(Y \geq 20.06)$.

2. Three components assemble adjacent to each other in the manner shown in Figure 7.4. Their respective additive sizes are: $x_1 = 0.500 \pm 0.001$, $x_2 = 0.500 \pm 0.001$, and $x_3 = 0.500 \pm 0.001$ in. Assume that x_1, x_2, and x_3 are each normally distributed, independent, random variables. Prepare an additive tolerance stack-up to determine the additive assembly value Y. Considering the Y-specification to be fixed, assuming a λ-risk value of 0.01242, and allocating component tolerance equally, determine statistically the overlapping component-tolerance specifications.

3. What given condition in problem 2 justifies making the respective standard deviations identical (i.e., $\sigma_x = \sigma_1 = \sigma_2 = \sigma_3$)?

4. State precisely the conditions for using the overlapping-tolerance specifications computed in problem 2 and briefly describe the expected production results.

5. Assume that the x_j additive specifications in problem 2 involve extremely difficult and costly process operations and the economics of the situation indicate that the λ-risk value could be as large as 0.3174. Compute the overlapping-tolerance specifications.

6. Assume that the design situation in problem 2 is one of component tolerances being fixed (i.e., each is 0.500 ± 0.001 in.). Compute the probable variation of the assembly value Y (i.e., 99.73% of the time).

7. Two matching component parts A and B (see Figure 7.1) involve clearance requirements for the size condition S, which is a normally distributed, independent, random variable. Nominal size is 5/8 in. Clearances may vary between +0.0003 in. and +0.0019 in. Economic considerations yield a λ-risk value of 0.0456. Assume equal tolerance allocation to components. Use basic hole and unilateral tolerance procedures. Compute: (a) additive specifications for the S dimension for A and B, and (b) overlapping tolerance for each component dimension (do not try to write the overlapping specifications). Answer to part (b): 0.0017 in.

8. Write the overlapping specifications for problem 7. Assume that tight fits and loose fits are equally critical and that mean clearance is to be identical to that for the additive tolerance case.

9. Suppose in problem 8 that tight fits are more critical than loose fits and the designer arbitrarily establishes the overlapping specifications to be: (A) 0.6250/0.6267 in., (B) 0.6250/0.6233 in. Compute the λ-risk value.

10. Additive specifications for component parts A and B (see Figure 7.1) are: (A) 0.5002 ± 0.0002 in., (B) 0.4993 ± 0.0002 in. Assume that clearance Y is normally distributed. Loose fits are more critical than tight fits and thus

the following probabilities have been established: P(fits too tight) = 0.0548, P(fits too loose) = 0.0107. Compute the overlapping specifications for A and B.

11. If the respective x_2-specifications and also the x_1-specification in the Example (see Figures 7.20 and 7.21) are to be converted from additive to overlapping tolerances, the overlapping tolerance for x_1 is 0.0107 in. and for each of the x_2-components is 0.0027 in. Verify this by performing the computations, preserving the 4:1 ratio for the additive tolerances.

12. Assume the following costs for the Example (see Figure 7.4): process failure cost (i.e., defective components produced) is $1 per defective component, and assembly failure cost (i.e., discovery and correction costs for defective assemblies) is $10 per assembly unit. A production order is issued for 1000 assemblies. Assuming ideal conditions of normally distributed, independent, random variables x_j, processes aimed exactly at nominal specification values, and process capability for producing components being 0.008 in., compare the expected total failure costs for additive and overlapping tolerances.

13. Suppose in problem 12 that process capability for producing components is 0.012 in. Briefly discuss the effect of this condition on the cost comparison.

14. Two matching component parts A and B (see Figure 7.1) involve clearance requirements for the size condition S. Control studies indicate that the actual manufacturing distributions for the S-dimension for A and B are (A) normally distributed with mean 0.5120 in. and standard deviation 0.001 in., (B) normally distributed with mean 0.5005 in. and standard deviation 0.0015 in.

Clearance requirements are +0.004 to +0.015 in. with +0.0095 considered to be optimum. Clearly, the present process settings result in an excessive number of assemblies having fits that are too loose. Compute the probabilities P(fits too loose) and P(fits too tight).

15. How can the process settings be changed to correct the undesirable situation described in problem 14?

16. In the Example (see Figure 7.22), what is the probability of defective assemblies?

8

Production Tolerances

Obtaining proper technical specifications for the product is largely a matter of establishing correct tolerances. The first and prime consideration in determining tolerances is the control of quality, performance, and life characteristics of the product. The second consideration is the capability of the production system to manufacture the product to the specified tolerances at reasonable cost. The latter consideration is concerned with the production tolerances that are adopted.

PRODUCTION TOLERANCE

A *production tolerance* refers to the tolerance specified for a process operation. The production tolerance is related to the product-specification tolerance, but the two are not necessarily equal in magnitude. In

Figure 5.4, the product-specification tolerance for the location of a' from the design datum b was ± 0.004 in. However, if manufacturing preferred a as a production datum, the production tolerance for locating a' was ± 0.002 in.

Another example is shown in Figure 8.1. For the given product specifications, various production tolerances develop, depending on the choice of datum b, b', or b''. Production tolerances resulting from datum b'' are optimum. When design, production, and inspection datums do not coincide, an indirect control of quality characteristics is necessary, resulting in reduced production tolerances. Thus, datum selection is one factor that determines production tolerances.

Another factor that influences production tolerances is provision for stock removal when multiple-process operations are required to generate a quality characteristic. Figure 8.2 indicates a simple example. To produce the diameter quality characteristic to the specified size and surface finish, turn and grind operations are required. Suf-

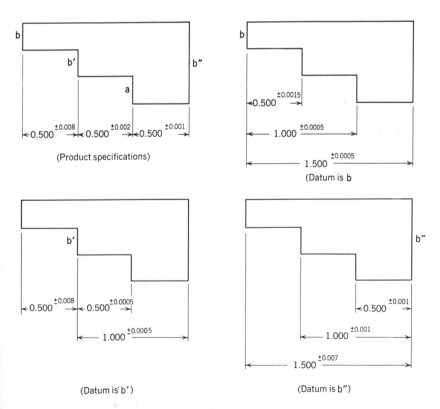

Figure 8.1. Datum transfer and production tolerances.

171

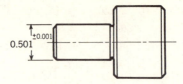

Figure 8.2.   Stock-removal and production tolerance.

ficient stock must be provided for the grind operation. Thus, the production tolerance is 0.511 ± 0.002 in. for the turn operation, leaving an average of 0.010 in. of stock to be removed by grinding. Economic considerations dictate a minimum stock removal compatible with the process-operation capability. On the other hand, enough stock removal allowance must be made to correct macro errors of straightness, squareness, parallelism, etc. Clearly, stock removal is another factor which determines production tolerances.

If the product specification tolerance is very small, the percentage of the available tolerance, which must be provided for measurement error, becomes significant. A *product-gage error stack-up* is shown in Figure 5.7. This stack-up is an evaluation of the cumulation of measurement error and production error. The available tolerance from the product specification is viewed as being partitioned into two components, a permissible tolerance for measurement error and a remaining tolerance for production error. Thus, production tolerance is equal to the product specification tolerance minus the tolerance provision for measurement error.

TOLERANCE CHARTS

A *tolerance chart* is a graphical and systematic method of presenting the process-operations specifications of a product part or assembly at all stages of its manufacture. Tolerance charts are used mainly for studying specification problems of individual component parts. However, in many cases, they are equally useful in processing assemblies. The chart provides an intermediate control system of checks and balances to insure that process-operations specifications will result in quality characteristics satisfying the product technical specifications.

The primary purpose of the tolerance chart is to facilitate manufacture and reduce production cost. The chart is an aid in establishing proper process-operations sequences and production tolerances for the operations. It enables the production engineer to determine, in advance of tooling provisions, whether or not the product part can be manufactured to the product technical specifications. Many product designs initially have specifications that are not adequate for manufacture (see experimental and production models—Chapter 5). The tolerance chart also assures sufficient stock removal provision for each process operation. When the process capability is known, the chart will indicate whether or not the required process operation is capable of meeting the particular product specifications. Finally, the tolerance chart is a rational instrument for negotiating with product design when the product specifications cannot be attained economically.

Figure 8.3 gives product specifications for a cylindrical shaft. Stock removal and process-operation considerations for the four diameter quality characteristics are relatively simple and a tolerance chart is not needed for these characteristics. The four linear quality characteristics require a tolerance chart analysis (see Figure 8.4). Columns (4) and (5) present nominal process operation specifications and production tolerances. For example, operation 10 affecting surface e has a nominal process specification of 5.180 in. and a production tolerance of 0.040 in. (i.e., ± 0.020 in.). Column (7) gives the nominal stock removal. Column (8) shows the stock-removal tolerance. This is the cumulative stock-removal tolerance due to all preceding process operations plus the production tolerance for the present operation. For example, if operation 10 (affecting surface e) produces a 5.200 in. length and operation 20 (affecting surface a) a 5.110 in. length, then 0.090 in.

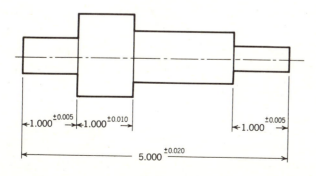

Figure 8.3.   Product specifications.

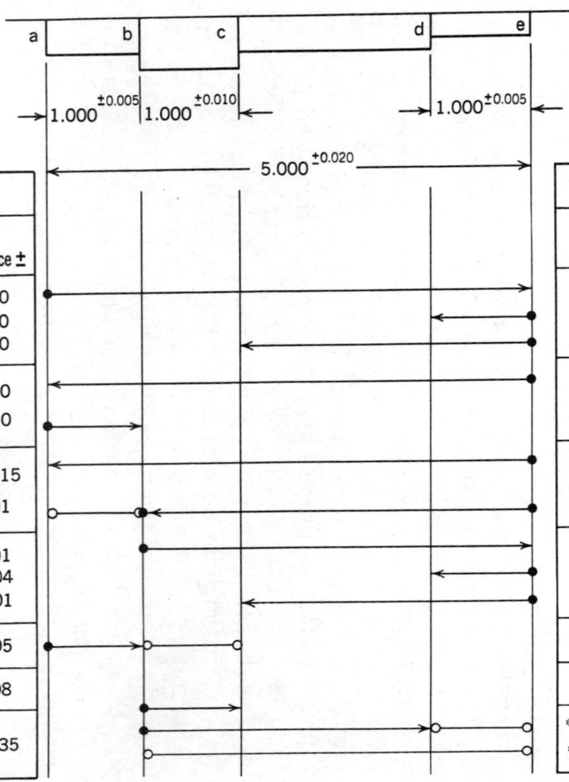

Operator number	Surface processed	Machine	Production Dimension	Production Tolerance ±
10	e d c	Bar machine	5.180 0.990 2.990	0.020 0.020 0.020
20	a b	Chucker	5.120 0.990	0.010 0.010
30	a b	Lathe	5.060 4.070	0.0015 0.001
40	e d c	Lathe	4.010 0.990 2.990	0.001 0.004 0.001
50	b	Grinder	*1.000	0.005
60	c	Grinder	*1.000	0.008
70	d	Grinder	3.000	0.0035

Resultant	Stock removal	Total tolerance ±
	Solid Solid Solid	
	0.060 Solid	0.030
0.990 ±0.0025	0.060 0.060	0.0015 0.021
1.010 ±0.0005	0.060 0.060 0.060	0.002 0.026 0.023
*1.000 ±0.0005	0.010	0.0025
*5.000 ±0.0035	0.010	0.0085
	0.010	0.009

Figure 8.4.   Tolerance chart.

of stock is removed. If operation 10 results in a 5.160 in. length and operation 20 a 5.130 in. length, then 0.030 in. of stock is removed. Thus, stock removal is 0.060 in. (column 7) ± 0.030 in. (column 8). Column (6) gives *resultant* dimensions. For example, operation 30 affecting surface *b*, generates the 4.070 ± 0.001 in. dimension and also the 0.990 ± 0.0025 resultant. The final product-part dimensions resulting from the process operations are each denoted by an asterisk.

Considerable technical skill is needed to prepare a tolerance chart. A knowledge of manufacturing operations and process capabilities is essential. Also, experience in tolerance chart computational routine is required. Stock removal is computed for the last operation, the next to the last operation, and so on, in that order, back to the first operation. Balancing techniques are used to enlarge restrictive tolerances and to make necessary changes to satisfy manufacturing constraints and product design engineering changes.

A number of systematic routines have been developed for preparing tolerance charts. These detailed procedures are considered to be beyond the scope and interest of this textbook. A computation summary chart is given in Figure 8.5. The student may trace through the stock-removal stack-up to observe how stock removal for a given operation is affected by production tolerances for preceding operations. The stack-up computation column of Figure 8.5 determines the stock removal stack-up, which is identical to columns (7) and (8) of the tolerance chart of Figure 8.4. The process operations stack-up column of Figure 8.5 determines the resultant dimensions shown on the tolerance chart.

SUMMARY

The structure of specification tolerances may now be summarized. Functional and interchangeability requirements, manufacturing constraints, and cost considerations at the product design level result in the following.

1. A separation of functional and nonfunctional specifications.

2. A choice between additive and overlapping tolerances and, in the case of the latter, a choice between selective and random assembly procedure.

3. Establishment of the design datums.

4. Formulation of the technical specifications for the product.

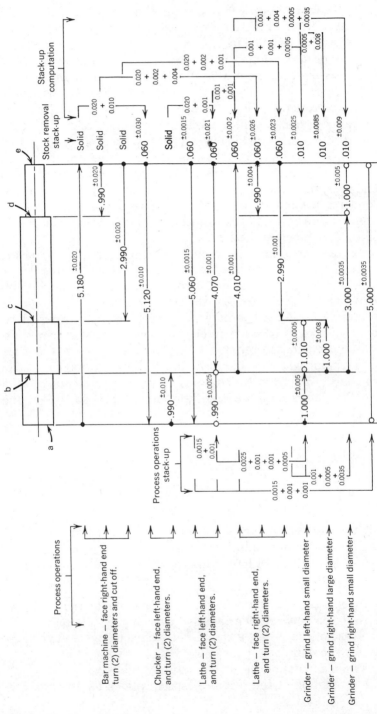

Figure 8.5.   Computation summary.

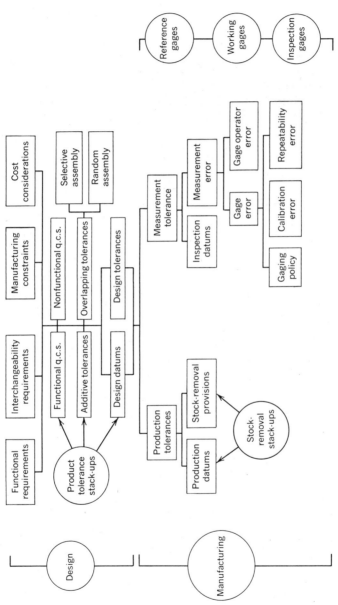

Figure 8.6.   Product and manufacturing tolerances structure.

The establishment of product technical specifications initiate certain decisions at the manufacturing planning level:

1. Determination of process operations and inspection operations to be required.
2. Establishment of production and inspection datums.
3. Consideration of measurement error and any requisite partitioning of product-specification tolerance into measurement and production-tolerance components.
4. Determination of process-operations sequences, stock-removal provisions, and production tolerances.

Figure 8.6 summarizes the decision elements. The segment of this figure that deals with measurement tolerances will be discussed in Chapter 10.

REFERENCES

American Society of Tool and Manufacturing Engineers (1963), *Manufacturing and Estimating Handbook*, McGraw-Hill, New York, Chapter 14.
Eary, D. F. and Johnson, G. E. (1962), *Process Engineering for Manufacturing*, Prentice-Hall, Engelwood Cliffs, N. J., Chapter 5.
Wade, O. R. (1967), *Tolerance Control in Design and Manufacturing*, Industrial Press, New York.

REVIEW QUESTIONS

1. Define the term production tolerance.

2. When the b-datum is used (see Figure 8.1), one specification is 0.500 ± 0.0015 in. Explain why the production tolerance of ±0.0015 in. is necessary.

3. State two principal factors that influence production tolerances.

4. What two conditions govern the magnitude of the stock-removal provision?

5. The product specification tolerance is viewed as being split into two variation components. Identify the two components.

6. What is the principal purpose of a tolerance chart?

9

Process Control

To maintain effective control of quality characteristics, it is necessary to obtain information on the capabilities of processes which generate the characteristics. Furthermore, this information should be such that it can be used to identify process instability and correct the process to its expected state. For many process situations, information of this type is not available. The process may be external to the production system (e.g., product received from vendor suppliers), or it may not be possible to preserve the process identity of manufacturing output. In many cases, however, control information is available and process control is the best means of assuring conformance of output to specifications.

For any process in which output is expected to conform to some measurable standard, variation in this output will occur. In each case, a decision must be made as to whether or not the observed variation between an output measurement and the expected standard is "acceptable." If the variation is not acceptable, this exception to acceptable performance should be a basis for corrective action on the process.

The question arises as to what is acceptable variation and what constitutes an exception to acceptable variation. Two problems develop in this connection: (1) defining an acceptable level of variation, and (2) devising quantitative means to measure deviations from this level. In the process-capability discussion of Chapter 6, a controlled process was viewed as one composed mainly of random causes of variation. A physical interpretation of random causes of variation was developed for a process machine. In summary, the variation due only to random causes reflected the inherent or natural variability of the process machine. Thus, it is reasonable to define acceptable variation as that which is due only to random causes. Exceptions indicating corrective action will be variations due primarily to assignable causes external to the machine. Generally, these causes are process operator, product material, process setup and adjustment, and environmental factors.

If random versus assignable causes of variation is accepted as a criterion for judging process control, the quality problem will be to detect assignable changes in any given process as reflected by output variation. A quantitative method of doing this is to test the hypothesis that the process is in control and, having once accepted it, continue monitoring the process by repeating the test at appropriate intervals.

A REVIEW OF HYPOTHESIS TESTING

A *statistical hypothesis* is an assumption regarding a population being sampled. Two types of hypotheses are of interest: (1) assume the population has a certain frequency function, and (2) assume a population parameter has a specified value. The second hypothesis type is pertinent to process control.

A *test* of a hypothesis is a decision rule by which a hypothesis is either accepted or rejected. The rule is usually based on the distribution of the sample *statistic* used to test the hypothesis. Since hypothesis testing is based on sample statistics computed from only n observations, decisions are subject to error. Two decision errors are possible: (1) rejecting the hypothesis when it is true, and (2) accepting the hypothesis when it is false. The first is called a *Type I error,* the second a *Type II error.* The probability of a Type I error is denoted by α, and the probability of a Type II error by β. One objective in hypotheses-testing is to design a test such that α and β are minimized. The usual procedure is to fix α at some predetermined level, and then formulate the decision rule in such a way that β is minimized. Practically, this means that β is established from a basis of possible cost consequences due to a Type II decision error, and sample size n is determined such that a $(1-\beta)$ protection against the Type II error is assured.

The assumption, which is of primary interest, is called the *null* hypothesis and is denoted by H_0. A quantitative consideration of the probability of a Type II decision error (i.e., β) requires the formulation of an alternative hypothesis, which is also of interest. This hypothesis is denoted by H_1. For example, the product specification for a quality characteristic is 0.500 ± 0.004 in. It is desired to test the hypothesis that the process setup is such that product output from the process will average 0.500 in. in size. The null hypothesis is that mean product size is 0.500 in. and is denoted

$$H_0: \mu = 0.500$$

Also of interest is the possibility that average product-output size may be as large as 0.503 in. (in which case, a large percentage of defective product will probably result!). The alternative hypothesis is that mean product size is 0.503 in. and is denoted

$$H_1: \mu = 0.503$$

In making the hypothesis test, primary interest is on the null hypothesis. Using the preceding example as illustration, the general procedure for testing hypotheses is as follows.

1. Formulate the null and alternative hypotheses, that is,

$$H_0: \mu = 0.500 \qquad H_1: \mu = 0.503$$

2. Obtain a mathematical model describing the probability of sample values for the parameter under consideration. In this case, the normal probability function describes the probabilities of various sample mean values $\bar{x}_j$.

3. Establish a decision rule based on the model. Essentially, this involves a consideration of α, β, and n.

4. Obtain a random sample of measurements of product output from the process. Make a decision (in accordance with the predetermined decision rule) to accept or reject the null hypothesis H_0.

181

Example

Consider a process operation generating output units which are characterized by measurements $x_1, x_2, \ldots, x_N$. The null and alternative hypotheses are

$$H_0: \mu = 0.500 \qquad H_1: \mu = 0.503$$

Assume the process variability is known and is measured by $\sigma_x = 0.004$ in. Let $\alpha = 0.05$, $\beta = 0.10$, and sample size $n = 16$.

The distribution models are summarized in Figure 9.1. If H_0 is true, the x_i-population of individual measurements is characterized by a mean $\mu = 0.500$ in. and standard deviation $\sigma_x = 0.004$ in. If H_1 is true, the x_i-population is characterized by a mean $\mu = 0.503$ in. and standard deviation $\sigma_x = 0.004$ in. All possible samples of size $n = 16$ from the x_i-populations generate $\bar{x}_j$-populations of mean values as shown. If H_0 is true, the $\bar{x}_j$-population has a mean $\mu = 0.500$ in. and standard deviation

$$\sigma_{\bar{x}} = \frac{\sigma_x}{\sqrt{n}} = \frac{0.004}{\sqrt{16}} = 0.001$$

If H_1 is true, the $\bar{x}_j$-population has a mean $\mu = 0.503$ in. and standard deviation $\sigma_{\bar{x}} = 0.001$ in.

The decision rule is based on the $\bar{x}_j$-populations. It is essential that the $\bar{x}_j$-distributions be normal. If x_i is normally distributed, then $\bar{x}_j$ is

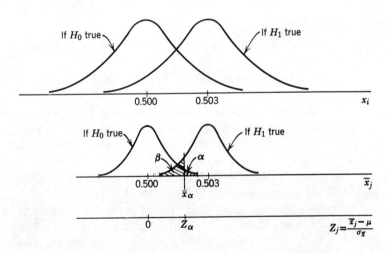

Figure 9.1. Test of a hypothesis regarding the mean μ.

also normally distributed. If x_i is not normally distributed, but sample size $n \geq 30$, then $\bar{x}_j$ is approximately normally distributed.

From the table in Appendix A, $Z_\alpha = 1.645$ for $\alpha = 0.05$. Therefore, the decision rule is

$$Z_{\text{data}} \geq Z_\alpha = 1.645, \text{ reject } H_0$$

$$Z_{\text{data}} < Z_\alpha = 1.645, \text{ accept } H_0$$

A random sample of $n = 16$ measurements of process output yields a mean average $\bar{x}_{\text{data}} = 0.502$ in.

Thus

$$Z_{\text{data}} = \frac{0.502 - 0.500}{0.001} = 2.0$$

and the hypothesis H_0 is rejected.

The preceding example was simplified by stating the sample size n. Usually, α and β are fixed, and then n is determined such that a $(1-\beta)$ protection against the Type II error is assured. That is, n is not arbitrary. Choice of α and β-values determines n.

A solution for n in the preceding example is summarized here. The Z_α-value of 1.645 followed from a Z-transformation on $\bar{x}_\alpha$, referring $\bar{x}_\alpha$ to the origin 0.500. However, referring $\bar{x}_\alpha$ to the origin 0.503 and performing a Z-transformation on $\bar{x}_\alpha$, the resulting Z-value (denoted Z_β) is

$$Z_\beta = \frac{\bar{x}_\alpha - 0.503}{\sigma_{\bar{x}}} \qquad \text{where } \sigma_{\bar{x}} = \frac{\sigma_x}{\sqrt{n}}$$

From the table in Appendix A, $Z_\beta = -1.282$. That is, for the tail area $\beta = 0.10$, the Z-value corresponding to $\bar{x}_\alpha$ is -1.282.

In summary

$$Z_\alpha = \frac{\bar{x}_\alpha - 0.500}{\sigma_x/\sqrt{n}}$$

$$Z_\beta = \frac{\bar{x}_\alpha - 0.503}{\sigma_x/\sqrt{n}}$$

Subtracting the second equation from the first

$$Z_\alpha - Z_\beta = \frac{(\bar{x}_\alpha - 0.500) - (\bar{x}_\alpha - 0.503)}{\sigma_x/\sqrt{n}}$$

Since σ_x was known to be 0.004 in.

$$Z_\alpha - Z_\beta = \frac{0.003}{0.004/\sqrt{n}}$$

or

$$(1.645) - (-1.282) = \frac{0.003 \sqrt{n}}{0.004}$$

and

$$n = \left[\frac{(2.927)(0.004)}{0.003}\right]^2 = 15.23$$

Being conservative, sample size n is taken to be 16.

Operating Characteristic Curves

Computation of sample size n can be avoided by reference to an appropriate operating characteristic curve. Standard statistics textbooks[1] usually present operating characteristic curves for the common hypothesis tests.

An *operating characteristic,* or *OC curve,* describes the probability of accepting H_0 for various alternative H_1-values, for fixed α and n. The definitional form of the OC curve for the preceding example is given in Figure 9.2.

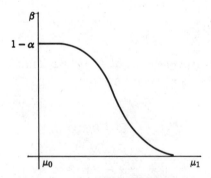

Figure 9.2.   OC curve in definitional form.

[1]A complete set of operating characteristic curves is presented in Bowker, A. H. and Lieberman, G. J. (1959), *Engineering Statistics,* Prentice-Hall, Engelwood Cliffs, N.J., Chapters 6 and 7.

A standard form of the OC curve can be obtained by means of a transformation

$$d = \frac{\mu_1 - \mu_0}{\sigma_x}$$

where μ_0 denotes the null hypothesis value and μ_1 the alternative hypothesis value. The resulting OC curve (see Figure 9.3) is the same as that of Figure 9.2 except for the origin, which is shifted to μ_0, and the abscissa scale, which is calibrated in multiples of σ_x.

A complete set of OC curves, for $\alpha = 0.05$, is presented in Figure 9.4. These OC curves are for the hypothesis test illustrated by the preceding example, that is, for

$$H_0: \mu = \mu_0 \quad \sigma_x \text{ known}$$

$$H_1: \mu = \mu_1 > \mu_0$$

To determine n for the preceding example

$$d = \frac{\mu_1 - \mu_0}{\sigma_x}$$

$$= \frac{0.503 - 0.500}{0.004} = 0.75$$

Entering the set of OC curves in Figure 9.4 with $d = 0.75$ and $\beta = 0.10$, sample size n is indicated to be approximately 15.

Operating characteristic curves have several applications to quality control. In Chapter 10, OC curves are used to describe the probability

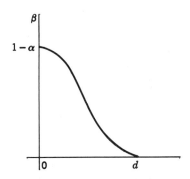

Figure 9.3.   OC curve in standard form.

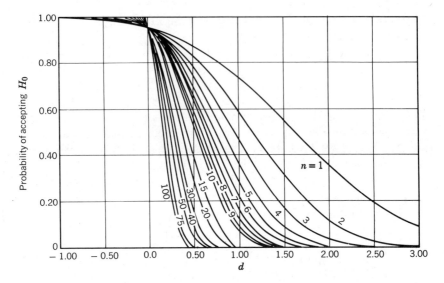

Figure 9.4. OC curves for a one-sided test on the mean of a normal distribution, for $\alpha = 0.05$. From R. H. Bowker and G. J. Lieberman (1959), *Engineering Statistics*, Prentice-Hall, Engelwood Cliffs, N. J., p. 118.

of accepting product lots, having specified quality levels, under different sampling inspection plans.

One-Sided and Two-Sided Tests

The preceding example is an upper one-sided hypothesis test. The alternative hypothesis is concerned only with a possible increase in the mean μ. A lower one-sided test would involve a possible decrease in μ. For the size specification 0.500 ± 0.004 in. of the preceding example, interest usually is on a possible increase or decrease in μ (i.e., a two-sided hypothesis test). Figure 9.5 indicates the distribution models for the hypotheses.

$$H_0: \mu = 0.500 \qquad \sigma_x = 0.004$$

$$H_1: \mu = 0.503 \text{ or } 0.497$$

$$\alpha = 0.05 \qquad \beta = 0.10$$

The risk α is partitioned into two components as shown. This alters the decision rule, which is now

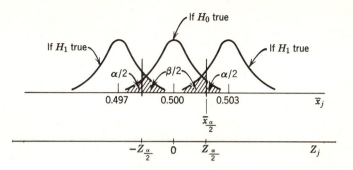

Figure 9.5. Two-sided test of a hypothesis regarding the mean μ.

$$\left| Z_{\text{data}} \right| \geq Z_{\frac{\alpha}{2}} = 1.960, \text{ reject } H_0.$$

$$\left| Z_{\text{data}} \right| < Z_{\frac{\alpha}{2}} = 1.960, \text{ accept } H_0.$$

Likewise, β is partitioned into two elements

$$\frac{\beta}{2} = P(\text{accepting } H_0, \text{ when } \mu = 0.503)$$

$$\frac{\beta}{2} = P(\text{accepting } H_0, \text{ when } \mu = 0.497)$$

The procedures presented here can be used to test many different hypotheses. Common tests are those regarding a single mean, two means with various assumptions about the corresponding variances, one variance, and two variances. A good discussion of various tests is given by Dixon and Massey.[2]

VARIABLES CONTROL CHARTS

A test of a hypothesis regarding a mean μ of a normal distribution is based on the following relationships.

[2]Dixon, W. J. and Massey, F. J. (1957), *An Introduction to Statistical Analysis*, McGraw-Hill, New York, pp. 88-138.

1. If H_0 is true, the x_i-population of individual measurements is distributed with mean μ_0 and variance σ_x^2.

2. All possible samples of size n from the x_i-population generate an $\bar{x}_j$-population of mean values where

$$\sigma_{\bar{x}}^2 = \frac{\sigma_x^2}{n}$$

3. Thus, if H_0 is true, the $\bar{x}_j$-population is distributed with mean μ_0 and variance $\sigma_{\bar{x}}^2$.

4. If the x_i-population is normal, the $\bar{x}_j$-population is normal. If the x_i-population is not normal, but sample size n is sufficiently large, the $\bar{x}_j$-population is approximately normal.

If x_i is a random variable, normally distributed with mean μ_0 and variance σ_x^2 (see Figure 9.6), then

$$P(\mu_0 - 3\sigma_x \leq x \leq \mu_0 + 3\sigma_x) = 0.9973$$

and

$$P(\mu_0 - 3\sigma_{\bar{x}} \leq \bar{x} \leq \mu_0 + 3\sigma_{\bar{x}}) = 0.9973$$

The second probability statement is the basis for the $\bar{x}$-control chart

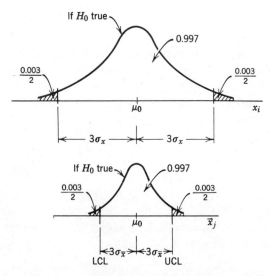

Figure 9.6. Normal populations under a hypothesis, H_0.

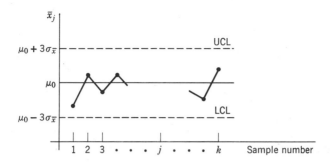

Figure 9.7. $\bar{x}$-control chart.

shown in Figure 9.7. The ordinate axis indicates $\bar{x}_j$-values. The abscissa axis identifies sample numbers 1, 2, ..., j, ..., k. The lower control limit (LCL) corresponds to $\mu_0 - 3\sigma_{\bar{x}}$, the upper control limit (UCL) to $\mu_0 + 3\sigma_{\bar{x}}$.

The $\bar{x}$-control chart is a hypothesis test where

H_0: process is in control at a quality level μ_0

$\alpha = P(\text{reject } H_0, H_0 \text{ true}) = 0.003$

The process operation, to which the $\bar{x}$-chart is applied, is monitored by repeating the hypothesis test at appropriate intervals (denoted by sample number 1, 2, ..., k). If, for each test, the sample mean occurs in the interval $\mu_0 \pm 3\sigma_{\bar{x}}$, the hypothesis is accepted and the process is considered to be in control. If, however, the sample mean occurs outside of the interval $\mu_0 \pm 3\sigma_{\bar{x}}$, the hypothesis is rejected and the process is considered to be out of control. This decision is a basis for corrective action relative to the process.

The decision to reject the hypothesis is equivalent to a refusal to accept only random causes as an explanation for the unusual event of a sample mean occurring outside the interval $\mu_0 \pm 3\sigma_{\bar{x}}$ (i.e., for a controlled process centered at μ_0, this event can occur, by chance alone, only 3 times in 1000). Accepting the hypothesis is equivalent to considering the sample mean value as being due only to random causes of variation.

Estimates of Population Parameters

In most practical applications, μ_0 and σ_x are not known. Thus,

189

estimates of these parameters must be obtained. It is desirable that these estimates be based on at least 25 samples of n observations. Of course, the larger the number of samples, the better the estimates will be, provided the process is in control over the time period in which the samples are taken.

The $\bar{x}$-control chart is a tool for detecting shifts in the process average and assumes that process variation remains essentially constant. If historical data on the process operation are available, an estimate of μ_0 is possible from physical and historical information. If data of this sort are lacking, an estimate of μ_0 is based on a set of observations over some initial production period. Preferably, physical efforts should be made to minimize assignable causes of variation during this observation period. If it can be assumed that the process centering is unchanged during this period, the sample means available from k sets of observations are all estimates of the same population value μ_0. An unbiased estimate of μ_0 is given by

$$\bar{\bar{x}} = \frac{1}{k} \sum_{j=1}^{k} \bar{x}_j$$

Each sample mean is a random event and the standard deviation of these means is

$$\sigma_{\bar{x}} = \frac{\sigma_x}{\sqrt{n}}$$

Thus, the problem of estimating $\sigma_{\bar{x}}$ is one of estimating σ_x. If σ_x is estimated in the usual way by pooling all observations, and if the hypothesis that the process average is unchanged during the initial observation period is not true, then the opportunity to test for this has been lost. However, k independent estimates of σ_x are possible and even if the process average has changed, the sample standard deviations provide estimates of the process variation over a short enough period that their reliability should be high.

Computation of a standard deviation for each of k samples yields

$$\hat{s}_1, \hat{s}_2, \ldots, \hat{s}_j, \ldots, \hat{s}_k$$

and

$$\bar{s} = \frac{1}{k} \sum_{j=1}^{k} \hat{s}_j$$

A quantity c_2, dependent on sample size n, can be determined such that

$$E\left(\frac{\hat{s}}{\sigma_x}\right) = c_2$$

or

$$\frac{E(\hat{s})}{c_2} = \sigma_x$$

and replacing $E(\hat{s})$ by its estimate $\bar{s}$

$$\frac{\bar{s}}{c_2} = \sigma_x$$

Values of c_2 for various sample sizes n are given in Appendix B.

In most industrial applications, the difficulty of computing a standard deviation for each sample makes the use of $\bar{s}/c_2$ as an estimator of σ_x somewhat impractical. For small samples, another measure of variation, the range R, is sufficiently stable to be useful. The relationship between the mean range $\bar{R}$ and the standard deviation σ_x was established in Chapter 6. A quantity d_2, dependent on sample size n, can be determined such that

$$E\left(\frac{R}{\sigma_x}\right) = d_2$$

or

$$\frac{E(R)}{d_2} = \sigma_x$$

and replacing $E(R)$ by its estimate $\bar{R}$

$$\frac{\bar{R}}{d_2} = \sigma_x$$

Values of d_2 for various sample sizes n are given in Appendix B.

Computing Control Limits

Tabled coefficients greatly simplify the computation of control limits. The appropriate coefficients for the $\bar{x}$-chart are summarized here. There are three cases.

1. If historical data are available for a given process operation and the variability is known, σ_x is known. Thus, the control limits are

$$E(\overline{x}) \pm 3\sigma_{\overline{x}} \quad \text{where } E(\overline{x}) = \mu_0$$

Replacing μ_0 by its estimate $\overline{\overline{x}}$ and $\sigma_{\overline{x}}$ by its equivalent $\sigma_x/\sqrt{n}$, the limits are

$$\overline{\overline{x}} \pm 3\left(\frac{\sigma_x}{\sqrt{n}}\right)$$

The coefficient $3/\sqrt{n}$ is denoted by A and, for various n-values, is given in Appendix B. Control limits are computed by

$$\overline{\overline{x}} \pm A\sigma_x$$

2. If σ_x is unknown and is estimated by $\overline{s}/c_2$, the control limits are

$$E(\overline{x}) \pm 3\sigma_{\overline{x}}$$

or

$$\overline{\overline{x}} \pm 3\left(\frac{\sigma_x}{\sqrt{n}}\right)$$

Replacing σ_x by its estimate $\overline{s}/c_2$, the limits are

$$\overline{\overline{x}} \pm \frac{3\overline{s}}{c_2\sqrt{n}}$$

The coefficient $3/c_2\sqrt{n}$ is denoted by A_1 and, for various n-values, is given in Appendix B. Control limits are computed by

$$\overline{\overline{x}} \pm A_1\overline{s}$$

3. If σ_x is unknown and is estimated by $\overline{R}/d_2$, the control limits are

$$E(\overline{x}) \pm 3\sigma_{\overline{x}}$$

or

$$\overline{\overline{x}} \pm 3\left(\frac{\sigma_x}{\sqrt{n}}\right)$$

Replacing σ_x by its estimate $\overline{R}/d_2$, the limits are

$$\overline{\overline{x}} \pm \frac{3\overline{R}}{d_2\sqrt{n}}$$

The coefficient $3/d_2\sqrt{n}$ is denoted by A_2 and for various n-values is given in Appendix B. Control limits are computed by

$$\overline{\overline{x}} \pm A_2\overline{R}$$

If control limits are being established by observations over an initial production period, A_2 and $\overline{R}$ are used to compute the limits. If, as more data is accumulated on the process operation, a more efficient estimate is desired, A_1 and $\overline{s}$ can be used to compute a revised set of limits.

Example

Seven samples of 5 observations each yield individual measurements, means, and ranges as indicated in Table 9.1.

Table 9.1. $\overline{x}$ and R table computation.

Sample Number	1	2	3	4	5	6	7
x_1	0.503	0.502	0.503	0.503	0.503	0.505	0.507
x_2	0.505	0.501	0.499	0.504	0.503	0.505	0.504
x_3	0.501	0.503	0.503	0.505	0.503	0.504	0.505
x_4	0.502	0.505	0.503	0.505	0.504	0.504	0.501
x_5	0.500	0.502	0.502	0.504	0.503	0.505	0.504
Sum of x	2.511	2.513	2.510	2.521	2.516	2.523	2.521
$\overline{x}$	0.5022	0.5026	0.5020	0.5042	0.5032	0.5046	0.5042
R	0.005	0.004	0.004	0.002	0.001	0.001	0.006

An estimate of μ_0 is given by

$$\overline{\overline{x}} = \frac{1}{k}\sum_{j=1}^{k}\overline{x}_j$$

$$= \frac{1}{7}(3.523) = 0.5033$$

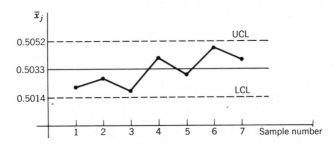

Figure 9.8. $\bar{x}$-control chart.

The mean range value is

$$\overline{R} = \frac{1}{k} \sum_{j=1}^{k} R_j$$

$$= \frac{1}{7} (0.023) = 0.0033$$

The table, Appendix B gives $A_2 = 0.577$ for $n = 5$. The control limits are

$$\bar{\bar{x}} \pm A_2 \overline{R}$$

$$= 0.5033 \pm (0.577)\,(0.0033)$$

$$= 0.5052 \,,\, 0.5014$$

The resulting control chart is given in Figure 9.8.

$\bar{x}$ and R Charts Combination

The $\bar{x}$-control chart is designed to detect shifts in the process average. If the process average changes from μ_0 to μ_1 as shown in Figure 9.9, the shaded tail area represents the probability λ that the change will be detected by the next sample following the change. The probability that the shift will be detected in M successive samples following the shift is $1 - (1-\lambda)^M$.

Changes in process variation are not effectively detected by the $\bar{x}$-chart. For example, variation changes, as shown in Figure 9.10, are concealed by the $\bar{x}$-chart. Sample means from each of the three populations shown will be nearly identical, and each will be well within

194

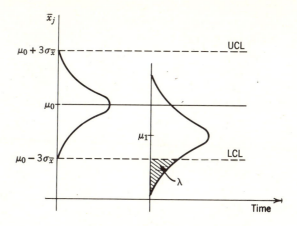

Figure 9.9.   Change in process mean.

the control limits. (Of course, there is a chance that a sample mean from the right-hand population in the figure will be outside the control limits interval, but this chance is small and this is not an efficient means of identifying a variation change.) Thus, in order to exercise effective control over the process, it is necessary to have a chart that will reveal changes in process variation.

An *R-chart* is usually used to supplement an $\bar{x}$-chart. Whereas the $\bar{x}$-chart operates to disclose between-sample variation, the *R*-chart acts to detect within-sample variation. Stated differently, the $\bar{x}$-chart tends to detect consistent sources of assignable variation (e.g., tool

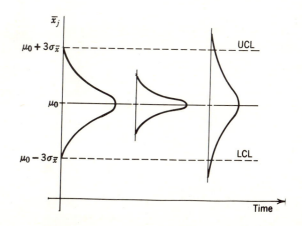

Figure 9.10.   Change in process variation.

195

wear, stock change, etc.—variation causes affecting the process average). On the other hand, the R-chart discloses erratic sources of assignable variation (e.g., a loose tool block, chuck, bearing, etc.— causes of within-sample variation).

Again, tabled coefficients simplify computation of control limits. There are two cases: (1) σ_x known, and (2) σ_x unknown and estimated by $\overline{R}/d_2$.

1. If σ_x is known from physical knowledge or historical data on the process operation, it is necessary only to establish a relationship between R and σ_x. The distribution of R is approximately related to the chi-square distribution, and $99 + \%$ of the R_j occur in the interval

$$E(R) \pm 3\sigma_R.$$

Assuming the process is in control (within samples), the distribution of the ratio R_j/σ_x can be used again. That is,

$$E\left(\frac{R}{\sigma_x}\right) = d_2$$

or

$$E(R) = d_2\sigma_x$$

Also, the standard deviation of R_j/σ_x may be determined. This is denoted d_3 and is given in Appendix B for various n-values. Thus,

$$\sigma_R = d_3\sigma_x$$

The control limits are

$$E(R) \pm 3\sigma_R$$

or

$$d_2\sigma_x \pm 3d_3\sigma_x$$
$$= \sigma_x (d_2 \pm 3d_3)$$

The coefficients $(d_2 + 3d_3)$ and $(d_2 - 3d_3)$ are denoted by D_2 $_{and}$ D_1 respectively and for various n-values are given in Appendix B. Control limits are computed by

$$D_2 \sigma_x \text{ and } D_1 \sigma_x$$

2. If σ_x is unknown and is estimated by $\overline{R}/d_2$, the control limits are

$$E(R) \pm 3\sigma_R$$

Replacing $E(R)$ by its estimate $\overline{R}$ and σ_R by $d_3\sigma_x$, the limits are

$$\overline{R} \pm 3d_3\sigma_x$$

Replacing σ_x by its estimate $\overline{R}/d_2$, the limits are

$$\overline{R} \pm \frac{3d_3\overline{R}}{d_2}$$

or

$$\overline{R}\left(1 \pm \frac{3d_3}{d_2}\right)$$

The coefficients $1 + (3d_3/d_2)$ and $1 - (3d_3/d_2)$ are denoted by D_4 and D_3 respectively and for various n-values are given in Appendix B. Control limits are computed by

$$D_4\overline{R} \text{ and } D_3\overline{R}$$

Example

For the preceding example of Table 9.1, control limits for $\overline{R}$ are

$$D_4\overline{R} = (2.115)\,(0.0033)$$

$$= 0.0070$$

$$D_3\overline{R} = 0$$

The central chart line corresponds to $E(R)$ and is usually estimated by $\overline{R}$.

The $\overline{x}$ and R-control charts are usually used together, in a supplementary manner, as indicated in Figure 9.11.

Standard Deviation Chart

Another control chart for detecting within-sample variation is the s-chart. The s-chart uses $\overline{s}$ to estimate process variation. For sample

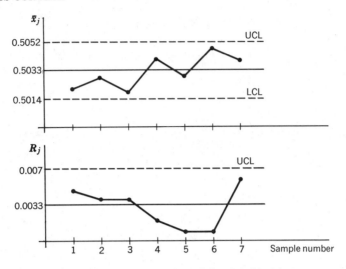

Figure 9.11. $\bar{x}$ and R-control chart combination.

sizes greater than 12, $\bar{s}/c_2$ yields a more efficient estimate of σ_x than does $\bar{R}/d_2$. The efficiency advantage does not, however, seem to compensate for the difficulty of computation (i.e., an $\hat{s}_x$ value is required for each sample). Thus, in most industrial applications, the R-chart is preferred. A brief summary of the s-chart is given here.

An example of an s-chart is given in Figure 9.12. There are two control limit cases: (1) σ_x is known, and (2) σ_x is unknown and is estimated by $\bar{s}/c_2$.

The distribution of $\hat{s}_x$ is related to a chi-square distribution, and 99+% of the $\hat{s}_j$ occur in the interval

$$E(\hat{s}_x) \pm 3\sigma_{\hat{s}}$$

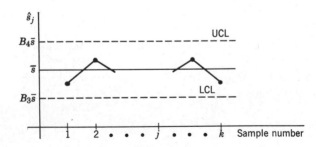

Figure 9.12. s-control chart.

1. If σ_x is known, the control limits are

$$E(\hat{s}_x) \pm 3\sigma_s$$

Relationships between $\hat{s}_x$, $\sigma_{\hat{s}}$, and σ_x are

$$E(\hat{s}_x) = c_2\sigma_x$$

and

$$\sigma_{\hat{s}} = \left[2(n-1) - 2nc_2^2 \right]^{\frac{1}{2}} \left(\frac{\sigma_x}{\sqrt{2n}} \right)$$

Thus, the control limits are

$$c_2\sigma_x \pm 3 \left[2(n-1) - 2nc_2^2 \right]^{\frac{1}{2}} \frac{\sigma_x}{\sqrt{2n}}$$

or

$$\sigma_x \left\{ c_2 \pm \frac{3}{\sqrt{2n}} \underline{\left[2(n-1) - 2nc_2^2 \right]^{\frac{1}{2}}} \right\}$$

The quantity c_2 plus the underlined part of the preceding expression is denoted by B_2, and c_2 minus the underlined part is denoted by B_1. For various n-values, B_2 and B_1 are given in Appendix B. Control limits are computed by

$$B_2\sigma_x \text{ and } B_1\sigma_x$$

2. If σ_x is unknown and estimated by $\bar{s}/c_2$, the control limits are

$$E(\hat{s}_x) \pm 3\sigma_{\hat{s}}$$

or

$$\sigma_x \left\{ c_2 \pm \frac{3}{\sqrt{2n}} \left[2(n-1) - 2nc_2^2 \right]^{\frac{1}{2}} \right\}$$

Replacing σ_x by its estimate $\bar{s}/c_2$, the limits are

$$\frac{\bar{s}}{c_2} \left\{ c_2 \pm \frac{3}{\sqrt{2n}} \left[2(n-1) - 2nc_2^2 \right]^{\frac{1}{2}} \right\}$$

or

$$\overline{s}\left\{ 1 \pm \frac{3}{c_2\sqrt{2n}}\left[2(n-1) - 2nc_2{}^2 \right]^{\frac{1}{2}} \right\}$$

The quantity 1 plus the underlined part of the preceding expression is denoted by B_4, and 1 minus the underlined part is denoted by B_3. For various n-values, B_4 and B_3 are given in Appendix B. Control limits are computed by

$$B_4\overline{s} \text{ and } B_3\overline{s}$$

The central chart line corresponds to $E(\hat{s}_x)$ and is usually estimated by $\overline{s}$.

Control Chart Application

The null hypothesis being tested by the $\overline{x}$-chart is that the process is in control at a quality level μ_0. The R-chart and s-chart also test for process control. The null hypothesis for the R-chart assumes a quality level R_0, and for the s-chart a quality level σ_0. An $\overline{x}$-chart is a tool for detecting process-average changes due to assignable causes. R and s-charts operate to detect variation changes. All charts provide a rational basis for determining when to take corrective action on the process. Essentially, the charts minimize two kinds of decision errors: (1) looking for trouble that does not exist, and (2) failing to look for trouble that does exist. The first error usually leads to overadjustments of processes, an action which tends to increase variability rather than decrease it. The second error results in defective product which could have been prevented.

The matter of rational subgrouping of process output into samples receives considerable attention in developing control-chart theory. This topic is treated in any standard statistics textbook. Briefly, rational subgrouping deals with preserving the process identity of the output samples and guarding against the possibility of a sample being composed of x_i from more than one population.

Preserving the process identity of the samples means sample identification over time (or, with the order of production). Identification of samples with process conditions (e.g., process adjustments, tool grinds, etc.) makes possible the recognition of assignable causes of variation. Taking samples in the order of production is also a statistical requisite. The success of the control chart method depends on grouping the x_i-observations into samples: (1) within which a stable system of random causes is operating, and (2) between which the output variations may be due to assignable causes of variation. Stated differently, the samples are selected in such a way to give (1) the maximum opportunity for the x_i in each sample to be alike, and (2) the maximum opportunity for the samples to differ one from another.

Regarding the possibility of the x_i for a given sample coming from more than one population, consider again Figure 9.9. If the process average changes from μ_0 to μ_1 during the initial production period during which the control limits are established, the computation of $\bar{\bar{x}}$ and the control limits based on $\bar{\bar{x}}$ is not valid. The computation of $\bar{\bar{x}}$ amounts to pooling observations from two populations, one with mean μ_0 and the other with mean μ_1, and $\bar{\bar{x}}$ is only a weighted average of the two process settings. This problem was mentioned earlier in this chapter. Strong technological control over the process was recommended for this initial production period, when control limits are being established. But, the same problem persists in formal production, after the control limits have been set. A sample mean may be an average of x_i values from more than one population. This is the point of the present discussion—to find out how to avoid pooling x_i-observations from more than one population when the chart is being used to control the process.

A solution to the problem would be to divide the process output according to the time when the process changed. However, this is impossible and also redundant. If a-priori knowledge regarding process changes was available, there would be no need for control charts. Nevertheless, a condition can be imposed which makes it likely that process changes will approximately coincide with division of output into samples. This condition is to make sample size small. If a process change is abrupt and of short duration, samples taken over as short a time period as possible increase the possibility of the process change occurring between samples rather than within a sample. If the process is subject to slow, continuous change, a small sample size will increase the possibility that the process variation within the sample will be small relative to that between samples. In any case, there is a strong argument in favor of small samples. One constraint exists, however, relative to minimum sample size. The sample size should be greater than or equal to 4, so that samples from a nonnormal x_i-population will, nevertheless, generate an approximately normal $\bar{x}_j$-population. For this reason, sample size is usually taken to be four or five.

Control charts are primarily used as an aid in controlling process operations. However, control charts also serve a number of other purposes. If overlapping tolerance specifications are used, it is important that processes be aimed at nominal specification values (see

Example, Figure 7.28). Assuring this condition involves monitoring the process average. The $\bar{x}$-chart is an appropriate tool for evaluating the process average over time.

Another control chart purpose is related to sampling inspection. The selection of a sampling inspection plan depends on a-priori estimates of product quality levels. Control chart procedures make possible good estimates of quality levels for the various quality characteristics.

In Chapter 6, the point was made that process control is a prerequisite for process capability measures. A process must first be brought into a controlled state before process capability limits are established. The $\bar{x}$ and R-charts are tools for assuring the requisite control conditions. In this connection, it is important to note that product specification limits cannot be directly compared with control limits. For example, the $\bar{x}$-chart is based on a distribution of mean averages of samples. The control limits are directed at averages of quality characteristic measurements. Product specification limits refer to individual quality-characteristic measurements, and can be compared only to process-capability limits. That is, specification limits can be compared to $\mu_0 \pm 3\sigma_x$ (see Figure 9.6), but cannot be compared to $\mu_0 \pm 3\sigma_{\bar{x}}$.

ATTRIBUTES CONTROL CHARTS

The $\bar{x}$, R, and s-charts are appropriate for variables measurement (see Inspection and Test, Chapter 2) of quality characteristics. However, quality measurements are frequently expressed in attributes terms (e.g., effective or defective, oversize or undersize, etc.). Two principal control charts used for attributes measurements are (1) *p-chart*, and (2) *c-chart*.

Fraction Defective Control Chart

The usual hypothesis test regarding a population proportion π involves testing whether π is at some satisfactory minimum level π_0, or whether it is as large as some nonacceptable value π_1. The hypothesis is

$$H_0 : \pi \leq \pi_0$$

$$H_1 : \pi = \pi_1 > \pi_0$$

Possible sample proportion values p are

$$\frac{0}{n}, \frac{1}{n}, \frac{2}{n}, \ldots, \frac{x}{n}, \ldots, \frac{n-1}{n}, \frac{n}{n}$$

and the probabilities of the respective x-values and also the respective proportion values are given by

$$\binom{n}{x} \pi_0^x (1 - \pi_0)^{n-x}$$

The above expression refers to a binomially distributed random variable x, and is valid under two assumptions: (1) population size N is very large relative to sample size n, assuring the probability of x to be approximately constant, and (2) H_0 is true.

The decision rule is $p_{\text{data}} \geq p = \frac{r}{n}$, reject H_0, where $x = r$ is selected such that the probability of a Type 1 decision error is

$$\alpha = \sum_{x=r}^{n} \binom{n}{x} \pi_0^x (1 - \pi_0)^{n-x}$$

$$p = \frac{0}{n}, \frac{1}{n}, \frac{2}{n}, \ldots, \frac{r}{n}, \ldots, \frac{n-1}{n}, \frac{n}{n}$$

In the control chart application, π and p correspond to population and sample fraction defective respectively. Since two control limits may be desired, a two-sided hypothesis test is required and α is partitioned such that

$$\frac{\alpha}{2} = \sum_{x=0}^{s} \binom{n}{x} \pi_0^x (1-\pi_0)^{n-x} = \sum_{x=r}^{n} \binom{n}{x} \pi_0^x (1 - \pi_0)^{n-x}$$

$$p = \frac{0}{n}, \frac{1}{n}, \ldots, \frac{s}{n}, \ldots, \frac{r}{n}, \ldots, \frac{n-1}{n}, \frac{n}{n}$$

To simplify control limit computation, limits are set at plus or minus three standard deviations from the expected fraction defective value. The random variable $\frac{x}{n}$ is distributed with mean π and standard deviation

$$\sigma_{\frac{x}{n}} = \frac{1}{n} \sigma_x = \frac{1}{n} \sqrt{n\pi (1 - \pi)} = \sqrt{\frac{\pi (1 - \pi)}{n}}$$

203

Thus, control chart limits are

$$\pi_0 \pm 3\sigma_{\frac{x}{n}}$$

or,

$$\pi_0 \pm 3 \sqrt{\frac{\pi_0 (1 - \pi_0)}{n}}$$

An estimate of the population fraction defective π is given by

$$\bar{p} = \frac{1}{k} \sum_{j=1}^{k} p_j \qquad j = 1, 2, \ldots, k$$

where k refers to the number of samples and the sample sizes are identical. If sample sizes are unequal,

$$\bar{p} = \frac{1}{N} \sum_{j=1}^{k} x_j \qquad N = \sum_{j=1}^{k} n_j$$

where x_j refers to the observed number of defectives in the jth sample. Replacing the population value π_0 by its estimate $\bar{p}$, control limits are

$$\bar{p} \pm 3 \sqrt{\frac{\bar{p} (1 - \bar{p})}{n}}$$

and the central control chart line corresponding to π_0 is usually based on the estimate $\bar{p}$.

Example

Fifteen samples of 50 observations each yield fraction defective values as shown in Table 9.2. An estimate of π_0 is given by

$$\bar{p} = \frac{1}{k} \sum_{j=1}^{k} p_j$$

$$= \frac{1}{15} (0.76) = 0.051$$

The control limits are

$$\bar{p} \pm 3 \sqrt{\frac{\bar{p}(1 - \bar{p})}{n}}$$

$$= 0.051 \pm 3 \sqrt{\frac{0.051 \ (0.949)}{50}}$$

$$= 0.144 \ , \ 0$$

The resulting control chart is shown in Figure 9.13.

Table 9.2. **Fraction defective data.**

Sample	n	x	p
1	50	4	0.08
2	50	2	0.04
3	50	1	0.02
4	50	4	0.08
5	50	5	0.10
6	50	1	0.02
7	50	1	0.02
8	50	2	0.04
9	50	3	0.06
10	50	3	0.06
11	50	1	0.02
12	50	4	0.08
13	50	2	0.04
14	50	2	0.04
15	50	3	0.06
Total	750	38	0.76

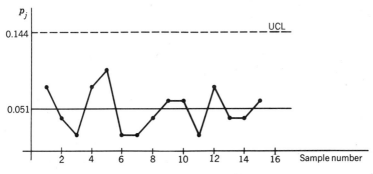

Figure 9.13. p-control chart.

The p-chart is not as sensitive a tool for detecting process change as is the $\bar{x}$- and R-chart combination. However, the cost of running a p-chart analysis is usually small. A p-chart can be used to monitor several quality characteristics simultaneously. On the other hand, one $\bar{x}$- and/or R-chart is required for each quality characteristic. Also, inspection activities usually generate fraction-defective data routinely, whether or not control charts are being used. Thus, the existing data-generating activity can be incorporated into control procedures. For control purposes only, an economic procedure is to utilize p-charts in patrol inspection to discover troublesome process operations, and then apply $\bar{x}$- and R-charts for a more comprehensive study of these operations.

For manufacturing and inspection reasons, sample size n will frequently vary. Possible solutions to this problem are the following. (1) Compute control limits for every sample and show these fluctuating limits on the p-chart. (2) Compute one set of control limits based on average sample size. (3) Initially construct several control limit sets on the p-chart corresponding to different sample sizes. Methods (2) and (3) are only approximate and thus, points falling near the limits should be reviewed in accordance with method (1).

Many plants prefer to use percent defective control charts since percentages seem to be more easily understood than proportions. Percent-defective and fraction-defective charts are identical, except for the ordinate-axis units. In the case of a percent-defective chart, 100 p-values are given on the ordinate axis.

Another feature of the p-chart, which should be mentioned, is the interpretation of a data point which occurs below the lower control limit (i.e., when the LCL is not zero). Out-of-control points, either above or below the limit lines, on an $\bar{x}$-chart indicate a need for corrective action on the process. However, points occurring below the lower control limit on either the R or p-charts reflect unusually good quality (i.e., unusual in the sense that causes may be other than random). Three interpretations are possible for points below the lower control limit: (1) a poor estimate of the average line of the chart, (2) inadequate inspection, and (3) existence of an unplanned assignable cause erratically contributing to good quality. In the latter case, it may be economic to attempt to identify this cause and formally incorporate it into the manufacturing procedure.

Control Chart for Defects per Unit

For many product items, defects-per-unit is an important indication of quality. In this case, a c-*control chart* is appropriate. A c-chart is based on a Poisson distribution function. This function applied to a c-control chart is

$$P(c) = \frac{e^{-\mu}\mu^c}{c!}$$

where $c =$ number of defects per inspection unit

$\mu =$ expected number of defects per unit

The Poisson distribution function describes a population wherein the opportunity for defects is large while the actual occurrence tends to be small. The latter condition means a small population fraction defective value π for each quality characteristic. The first condition restricts the use of a c-chart to assembly inspection (i.e., where there may be hundreds of quality characteristics per inspection unit which can be defective). A sample is usually one assembly unit.

The mean and variance of a Poisson distribution are equal, that is

$$\sigma_c = \sqrt{\mu}$$

Control limits for the c-chart are

$$\mu \pm 3 \, \sigma_c$$

Estimates of the control limits are

$$\bar{c} \pm 3 \sqrt{\bar{c}}$$

where

$$\bar{c} = \frac{1}{k} \sum_{j=1}^{k} c_j$$

Example

Ten assemblies are inspected and the defects per assembly are tallied as in Table 9.3. An estimate of μ is

$$\bar{c} = \frac{1}{k} \sum_{j=1}^{k} c_j$$

$$= \frac{1}{10} \, (36) = 3.6$$

A preliminary estimate of σ_c is

$$\sqrt{\bar{c}} = \sqrt{3.6} = 1.90$$

207

Table 9.3. **Defects-per-unit data.**

Sample	c_j
1	6
2	4
3	1
4	4
5	12
6	0
7	2
8	0
9	4
10	3
Total	36

Control limits are

$$\bar{c} \pm 3 \sqrt{\bar{c}}$$

$$= 3.6 \pm 3(1.90)$$

$$= 9.3 , 0$$

The resulting control chart is shown in Figure 9.14. As expected, the data point for sample 5 is out of control. Further data is required to give better estimates of μ and σ_c.

For specific control chart applications, quality-control departments develop special chart procedures that seem to suit their product and process conditions. Figure 9.15 shows a number of charts generated

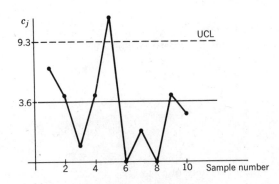

Figure 9.14. c-control chart.

from one composite data form — percent defective, percent effective, and defects-per-unit charts. Figure 9.16 indicates some examples of control charts being used as management tools. Other modifications in control-chart procedures are warning limits set at $\pm 2\sigma$ and control limits at $\pm 3\sigma$, procedure strategies for point trends, and so on. Tests[3] have been devised by which "runs" of data points (i.e., succession of points either above or below the central chart line, or steadily increasing or decreasing in magnitude) become signals for corrective action on the process. Also, there are occasions when moving-average and cumulative sum charts are preferred. These two control charts are briefly summarized here.

MOVING AVERAGE AND RANGE CHARTS

When production is such that it takes some time to produce a single item, moving-average and range charts may be appropriate. Computation of central and control-limit lines for these charts is identical to that for standard $\bar{x}$- and R-charts. However, plotting of new data points, for purposes of current control, is done differently. A brief example indicates the procedure.

Example

Ten successive observations are 4, 5, 9, 6, 3, 2, 3, 4, 4, 5. Instead of dividing the data into two samples of five each, the sample averages are computed

$$\bar{x}_1 = \frac{1}{5}(4 + 5 + 9 + 6 + 3)$$

$$\bar{x}_2 = \frac{1}{5}(5 + 9 + 6 + 3 + 2)$$

$$\bar{x}_3 = \frac{1}{5}(9 + 6 + 3 + 2 + 3)$$

. . .

That is, each new sample is constructed by dropping the first observation of the preceding sample and adding the most recent observation to the new sample data. Moving ranges are computed in the same manner.

[3]See Duncan, A. J. (1965), *Quality Control and Industrial Statistics*, Richard D. Irwin, Homewood, Ill., pp. 132-137.

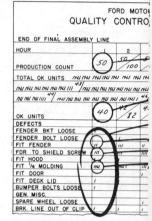

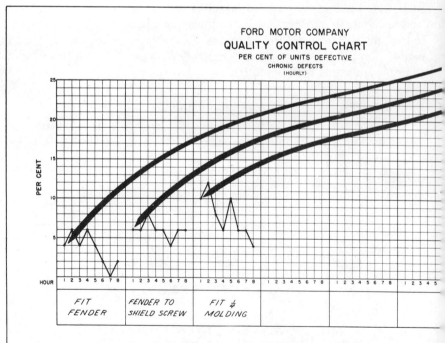

Figure 9.15.   Control charts used in industry.

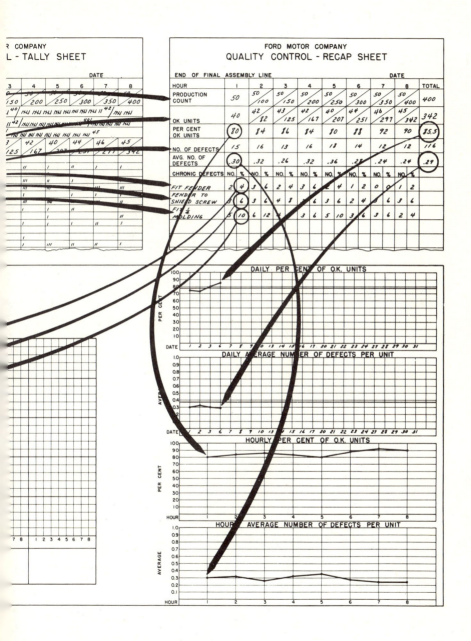

Figure 9-15 (Cont'd.)

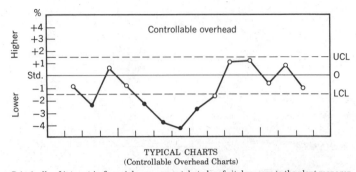

TYPICAL CHARTS
(Controllable Overhead Charts)

Principally of interest in financial management, but also of vital concern to the plant manager and his staff, controllable overhead represents non-fixed costs. For example, property taxes and depreciation are noncontrollable expenses. No matter what in-plant management does, these costs cannot be reduced. Costs of maintenance, inspection, quality assurance, warehouse operations and similar items are at least to some extent within managerial control.

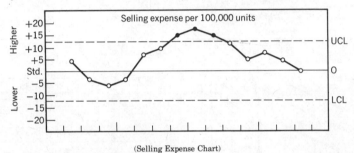

(Selling Expense Chart)

Of principal interest to sales administration, this chart shows the cost effort required to sell the plant's output. The plant manager should also be interested, since product design and quality have an important bearing on salability. Top management may use the chart on questions of promotional allocation, marketing channels, the effectiveness of product development, production, advertising, and proper coordination of these activities.

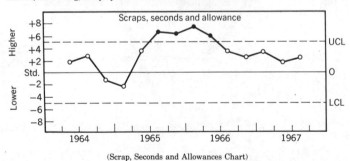

(Scrap, Seconds and Allowances Chart)

This familiar q.a. data should also be vital to top management, both from a financial aspect — the cost of poor quality — and from an administrative standpoint — is q.a. doing its job, is it receiving proper support, etc.

Figure 9.16. Control charts as a management tool. From N. L. Enrick (July, 1968), "The Control Chart as a Management Tool," *Quality Assurance*, Vol. 7, No. 7, pp. 38-40.

Cumulative Sum Chart

A small change in process average may not be detected by a standard $\bar{x}$-chart for a considerable number of samples. Such a small change may, however, be detected quickly if the effect of the change is cumulated over several samples. This is the argument in favor of a *cumulative sum chart* (or *cusum chart*).

For each new sample and corresponding mean $\bar{x}_j$, a sum is computed

$$x_c = \frac{1}{s_{\bar{x}}} \sum_{j=1}^{c} (\bar{x}_j - \bar{\bar{x}})$$

where x_c = cumulative sum of deviations

$\bar{x}_j$ = sample mean

$s_{\bar{x}}$ = standard deviation of means of samples of size n.

Each new data point x_c is plotted and evaluated by a V-mask as shown in Figure 9.17. The mask is placed such that its center P coincides with the data point x_c and the center-line P-O is horizontal. Lack of control is indicated by the existence of any previous data points in the shaded region.

The parameters of the V-mask are (θ, d). The values for (θ, d) may be approximated[4] by

$$\tan \theta = \frac{\delta}{2}$$

$$d \overset{\wedge}{=} -2\delta^{-2} \log_e \alpha$$

where δ = standard expected process change

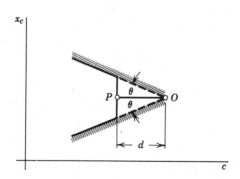

Figure 9.17. Cumulative sum control chart.

[4]Johnson, N. L. (1961), "A Simple Theoretical Approach to Cumulative Sum Charts," *American Statistical Association Journal,* Vol 56, pp. 835-840.

$$\alpha = P(\text{Type I decision error})$$

For example, if the process history suggests an expected change of 4 and the process operation has a standard deviation of 1.5, then $\delta = 4/1.5$.

Cumulative sum chart applications indicate that for

$$0.001 \leq \alpha \leq 0.005$$

the chart is much more effective in the detection of small process changes than the standard $\bar{x}$-chart. A disadvantage of this chart is its greater cost of design and application.

ECONOMICS OF CONTROL CHARTS

Production personnel are continually engaged in the technology of process control. This is one of the basic functions of a production job, and all production efforts in this connection constitute an unavoidable manufacturing cost.

Formal process-control assistance by quality-control staff and inspectors is frequently required to assure acceptable quality of production output. This extra effort involves expenses (avoidable costs) which must be weighed against the expected benefits from the expanded control activity. The extra control costs are mainly due to quality-control staff time, patrol-inspection time, and any other than normal setup and operator time for making extra measurements of process output, maintaining a control chart, and things of this kind. Also, if the formal control procedure restricts process yield, this cost should be considered (i.e., output per unit time being reduced because of more than normal machine downtime due to the operator being involved in the extra control effort).

The total of these extra control costs represents an investment in better quality. The expected return is a considerable reduction in quality losses for the particular process operation being controlled. Thus, a first economic question is whether to use formal control methods (e.g., control charts), or dispense with these procedures and use a rectifying inspection to bring the output to a satisfactory quality level. The principal cost factors in this situation are material and process costs of the product item. Clearly, if a product item involves many consecutive process operations in its manufacture and it becomes defective at one of the end operations, a considerable loss has been incurred.

Assuming it is economic to use control-chart procedures on a process operation, there are economic questions involved in the design of the control plan. A control-chart analysis is a statistical hypothesis test. The hypothesis is that the process is in a state of statistical control and, therefore, no assignable causes of variation are present. Two types of decision errors are possible — rejecting the hypothesis when it is true, and accepting the hypothesis when it is false. These decision errors lead to production expenses associated with looking for trouble that does not exist and failing to look for trouble that does exist. The design of a control plan must in some way balance these two kinds of costs. To do so, three factors must be determined: (1) control limits, (2) sample size, and (3) sampling interval.

Fetter[5] reports an interesting cost model and example involving these three elements. The example is abstracted here to stimulate interest in the economics of control charts.

Example

A process is to be aimed at a nominal specification value of 0.5250 in. The product specification is 0.5250 ± 0.0005 in. Historical data indicates σ_x to be 0.0002 in.

Process output is 1000 pieces per hour. The average frequency of process change is one in 10 hours. When the change occurs, the process shifts to a mean setting of 0.5254 in.

Assuming a normal output distribution, π is 0.0124 before the change and 0.3085 after the change. Unit inspection cost is $0.10, and a fixed inspection cost of $10 per sample is incurred. The average cost of an undetected defective is $5.

If a sample is taken once an hour, the extra loss due to defective output per inspection interval is

$$1000 \, (0.3085 - 0.0124) \, (\$5) = \$1480$$

The duration of this loss depends on how quickly the control plan detects the shift in process average. If sample size is 4 and control limits are set at ± $3\sigma_{\bar{x}}$, the probability of detecting a shift from 0.5250 to 0.5254 in. is 0.84 on any sample as indicated in Figure 9.18. Let P_{2j} denote the probability of failing to detect a process change to the

---

[5]The student is encouraged to review the original text of this example and to examine the computer simulation study of this problem. See Fetter, R. B. (1967), *The Quality Control System*, Richard D. Irwin, Homewood, Ill., pp. 67-70 and Appendix II.

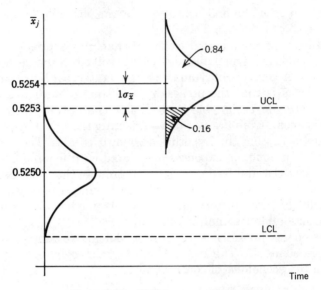

Figure 9.18. Shift in process average.

jth state. In this example, P_{2j} of a process shift to 0.5254 in. is $(1 - 0.84)$.

The expected value of the number of sample trials r until the change is detected is

$$\frac{1}{1 - P_{2j}} = \frac{1}{1 - 0.16} = 1.191$$

Assuming that the probability of a change is proportional to the interval between samples then, on the average, it is expected that approximately one half an interval is the duration of production in the new state until the first sample. Then the expected period of production in this state until the change is detected is (measured in sample intervals)

$$\frac{1}{1 - P_{2j}} - 0.5$$

The loss from defective production is

$$\text{(loss per interval) (duration)}$$

$$= \$1480 \ (1.191 - 0.5) = \$1020$$

Based on one change in 10 hours, the expected number of changes is 0.1 and thus the conditional loss is \$102.

Inspection cost is $10 plus ($0.10) (4) plus the expected cost of error. If a process correction incurs a cost of $10, the expected cost of an unnecessary correction (i.e., due to a Type I decision error) is approximately $0.03 for control limits of $\pm 3\sigma_{\bar{x}}$. Thus, the total inspection cost per interval is

$$\$10 + \$0.10(4) + \$0.03 = \$10.43$$

and the expected cost per hour for this plan is

$$\$102 + \$10.43 = \$112.43$$

Changing the sample interval, for example, from 60 to 30 minutes, the conditional loss is changed from $102 to $25.55. This illustrates the fact that an interval decrease has two effects: (1) the production period during which extra defectives are produced is reduced; and (2) the expected number of changes is reduced.

In general, the conditional loss per inspection period is

$$c_d \left(\frac{P}{N_S}\right) \sum_{j=2}^{j} \left(\frac{P_j}{N_S}\right) (P_j - P_1) \left(\frac{1}{1 - P_{2j}} - 0.5\right)$$

where c_d = cost of a defect

P = production rate per period

N_S = number of samples per period

j = states of system ($j = 1, 2, \ldots, J$), with state 1 the desired state.

P_j = expected number of changes to state j in period

p_j = fraction defective in state j

P_{2j} = probability that given plan will fail to detect a change to state j.

The cost of inspection per sample is

$$C = C_i + nc_i + c_e P_1$$

where C_i = fixed cost of inspection per sample

c_i = variable cost of inspection per unit

n = sample size

c_e = cost of inferring the process has changed when it has not

P_1 = probability of inferring the process has changed when it has not

The total expected cost per production period is

$$TC = \frac{1}{N_S} \left[c_d P \sum_{j=2}^{j} P_j \, (p_j - p_1) \left(\frac{1}{1 - P_{2j}} - 0.5 \right) \right] + N_S \, (C_i + nc_i + P_1 c_e)$$

The term in brackets is denoted by B. Control limits for the $\bar{x}$-chart are denoted $\pm Z\sigma_{\bar{x}}$ (i.e., usually the limits are $\pm 3\sigma_{\bar{x}}$ and $Z = 3.0$). For any set of values for n and Z, B is a constant. Thus, the minimum sampling interval can be established by

$$TC = \frac{B}{N_S} + N_S \, C$$

$$\frac{dTC}{dN_S} = -BN_S^{-2} + C$$

and equating this to zero gives

$$N_S \doteq \sqrt{\frac{B}{C}}$$

For the numerical values of this example,

$$B = \$5 \, (1000) \, (0.1) \, (0.3085 - 0.0124) \, (1.191 - 0.5)$$

$$= \$102$$

and

$$C = \$10.43$$

and

$$N_S = \sqrt{\frac{B}{C}}$$

$$= \sqrt{\frac{102}{10.43}}$$

$$= 3.13$$

or an inspection interval of about 19 minutes.
The expected cost per hour for this plan is

$$TC = \frac{\$102}{3.13} + 3.13 \, (\$10.43)$$

$$= \$65.21$$

218

If Z is reduced to 2.5 (i.e., control limits are set at $\pm 2.5\sigma_{\bar{x}}$), then P_{2j} becomes 0.067. Repeating the above computation yields $B = \$84.60$, $C = \$10.52$, $N_S = 2.84$, and $TC = \$59.70$.

Continuing in this manner, for $n = 4$, the minimum cost deviate is $Z = 2.0$ (i.e., control limits set at $\pm 2\sigma_{\bar{x}}$), for which $B = \$77.47$, $C = \$10.86$, and $TC = \$58$. The inspection interval is 22.5 minutes or 2.67 samples per period. Fetter[6] gives computer programs based on two basic modes of operation, a simulation mode and the expected cost mode. Various alternatives are studied by each operation mode.

SUMMARY

A basic production function is the control of process operations to assure output at an acceptable quality level. This control activity is mainly technological and involves the process engineer, first-line supervisor, setup man, process operator, and inspector. This production effort represents an unavoidable cost of manufacture.

Formal assistance by quality-control staff and inspectors is frequently required to obtain adequate process control. This extra control effort involves expenses (avoidable costs) that must be weighed against the expected benefits from the expanded control activity. The alternative, of course, is to dispense with formal control procedures and impose a rectifying inspection on the process to assure acceptable output quality. If formal control assistance is economic, statistical control charts can be used as quantitative measures of control.

A control chart tests the hypothesis that the process is in control at a satisfactory quality level. If the hypothesis is accepted, the process is considered to be in control. Process control is maintained by repeating the test at appropriate time intervals. Control chart methods minimize decision errors which lead to production expenses associated with looking for trouble that does not exist and failing to look for trouble that does exist.

Variables control charts commonly used are the $\bar{x}$-chart, R-chart, and cusum chart. Useful attributes control charts are the p-chart and c-chart. Computation of control-chart limits is simplified by using tabled coefficients given in Appendix B. The effectiveness of any control plan using statistical control charts depends on the ability of the chart to detect the presence of assignable causes of variation. The economic

---

[6]Fetter, op. cit., p. 215

design of a control plan balances the costs associated with Types I and II decision errors. This mainly involves consideration of three factors: (1) control limits, (2) sample size, and (3) sampling interval.

REFERENCES

ASTM Manual on Quality Control of Materials (1951), American Society for Testing Materials, Philadelphia, Pa.

Bowker, A. H. and Lieberman, G. J. (1959), *Engineering Statistics,* Prentice-Hall, Englewood Cliffs, N.J.

Burr, I. W. (1953), *Engineering Statistics and Quality Control,* McGraw Hill, New York.

Dixon, W. J. and Massey, F. J. (1957), *An Introduction to Statistical Analysis,* McGraw-Hill, New York.

Duncan, A. J. (1965), *Quality Control and Industrial Statistics,* Richard D. Irwin, Homewood, Ill.

Fetter, R. B. (1967), *The Quality Control System,* Richard D. Irwin, Homewood, Ill.

REVIEW QUESTIONS

1. Essentially, process control is a means of utilizing information regarding process instability to correct the process to its expected state. Identify two general situations where this information is not available.

2. Process control involves decisions as to whether or not the observed variation between output measurements and expected standards is acceptable. State the accepted definition or interpretation of (a) acceptable variation, and (b) nonacceptable variation.

3. A quantitative method of detecting assignable causes of variation is a statistical hypothesis test regarding the mean of the process-output population. Define a test of a hypothesis and identify the decision errors which are possible.

4. The $\bar{x}$-control chart is a tool for detecting shifts in the process average. Describe this chart in terms of a hypothesis test. What is the usual value of α?

5. Compare the $\bar{x}$ and R-control charts in terms of purpose. Why are they usually used together?

6. Use of control charts minimizes two kinds of decision errors: (1) looking for trouble that does not exist, and (2) failing to look for trouble which does exist. What are the usual physical consequences of these two decision errors?

7. Sample size for an $\bar{x}$-control chart is usually four or five. What two criteria operate to determine this sample size—one criterion operating to make the sample size small, the other to make it at least a minimum size?

8. Briefly, discuss the fact that process control is an important a-priori condition for process-capability determination, overlapping tolerance applications, and sampling inspection.

9. Give three possible interpretations for points occurring below the LCL on an R or p-control chart.

10. The c-control chart is based on a Poisson distribution function. Use of the Poisson model involves two conditions that restrict the c-chart to assembly inspection operations. State the two conditions.

11. Regarding the economics of process control, what is the first and basic economic question?

12. What are the principal cost factors involved in an economic analysis of control-chart methods?

13. State the three factors involved in economic control-chart design from the viewpoint of costs due to Type I and Type II decision errors.

PROBLEMS

1. A process operation generates output units characterized by measurements $x_1, x_2, \ldots, x_N$. Test the hypothesis that the mean x-measurement for the operation is 0.300 in. against the alternative that it is 0.309 in. The process variability is known and is measured by $\sigma_x = 0.009$ in. The probability of a Type I decision error is taken to be 0.05. A sample of 9 observations of the product output yields a mean x-measurement of 0.3066 in.

2. Using the OC curves of Figure 9.4, determine the probability of a Type II decision error.

3. Compute the exact probability of a Type II decision error for the conditions of problem 1.

4. Sample size was fixed for physical reasons in problem 1. Suppose, for the same problem conditions, the probability of a Type II decision error was taken to be 0.20 and sample size was to be determined. (a) Referring to the OC curves of Figure 9.4, determine sample size. (b) Compute the sample size exactly.

5. Ten samples of five measurements each are recorded in the following table. Compute the control limits for an $\bar{x}$-control chart and an R-control chart using $\bar{R}/d_2$ as an estimate of σ_x.

1	2	3	4	5	6	7	8	9	10
.577	.576	.576	.574	.580	.578	.575	.579	.576	.571
.580	.579	.577	.578	.573	.581	.577	.575	.575	.573
.578	.573	.572	.575	.575	.579	.575	.578	.574	.571
.572	.574	.576	.577	.576	.576	.576	.577	.575	.570
.578	.573	.574	.577	.574	.576	.577	.576	.575	.573

6. A process is in control at a quality level $\mu_0 = 0.5000$ in. The standard deviation σ_x is 0.0004 in. If sample size is four and control limits are based on an α-value of 0.003, what is the probability of detecting a process shift to $\mu = 0.5009$ in. by: (*a*) the next sample following the change, and (*b*) the next two samples?

7. The following hypothesis is to be tested: $H_0 : \pi = \frac{1}{4}$, $H_1 : \pi = \pi_1 > \pi_0$. For a sample size n = 10, determine the decision rule such that α is approximately equal to 0.01.

8. Twenty-five samples of 50 product items each are inspected and a total of 34 product items are found to be defective. Compute *p*-control chart limits for the following production period.

9. Twenty assemblies are inspected yielding the following number of defects per assembly: 10, 17, 16, 20, 10, 14, 7, 14, 19, 16, 21, 10, 13, 11, 25, 15, 11, 12, 8, 30. A *c*-control chart indicates assembly 20 (i.e., 30 defects) to be outside of the control limits. Subsequent investigation of this assembly discloses a number of assignable causes for the unusual number of defects. It is decided to delete this point from the data and prepare a new control chart. Compute the revised control limits.

The following problems and questions refer to the economic control-chart design model presented in the chapter (see Figure 9.18).

10. Paragraph 3 of the example states that the population fraction defective π is 0.0124 before the process change and 0.3085 after the change. Verify this by computation. (Note: π is also the probability of a defective.)

11. Explain the statement "the expected value of the number of sample trials *r* until the change is detected is

$$\frac{1}{1 - P_{2j}} = \frac{1}{1 - (1 - 0.84)} = 1.191.$$

12. Identify each term in the following equation. "The expected period of production in the new process state until the change is detected is (measured in sample intervals)

$$\frac{1}{1 - P_{2j}} - 0.5.$$

13. Explain the statement "the conditional loss is $102."

14. Identify each term in the following equation:

Total inspection cost/Interval = $10 + ($0.10)(4) + $0.03 = $10.43

15. What two effects follow from a decrease in the length of the sampling interval?

10

Sampling Inspection

In Chapter 2, inspection was classified by type into two main categories, and by purpose into several classes. Figure 10.1 reviews this inspection-activity structure. A *100% inspection* refers to the evaluation of all N items of a manufacturing lot composed of N product items. This is also called *sorting, detailing, screening,* or *rectifying inspection.* When a product lot undergoes a *sampling inspection,* the decision to accept or reject the lot is based on an examination of a random sample of n product items taken from the lot. Product lots rejected by sampling inspection are usually detailed.

Generally, the alternatives to 100% inspection are (1) control of the process at a satisfactory quality level, in which case formal inspection is not required, and (2) sampling inspection. In many cases, process control is the most economic means of achieving product quality.

224

However, when process identity of output cannot be preserved, control is not feasible. If the process is external to the manufacturing plant (e.g., a vendor supplier's process), control is not possible,[1] and a receiving inspection is required. Also, for many in-plant processes, technical and/or economic conditions preclude segregation of product by process machine and time (conditions necessary for control), and again inspection of product is necessary.

Assuming that process control is technically possible, the economics of inspection depends on various combinations of (1) control cost, (2) inspection cost, and (3) failure cost (i.e., costs generated by undetected defectives). All three costs are variable quantities in the sense that each depends on the expected fraction-defective level for the process.

Example

If a defective product unit is not detected by an inspection operation, a subsequent production loss of $10 is incurred. Unit cost of inspection is $0.15. The expected fraction-defective is 0.02.

Expected failure cost is (0.02) ($10) or $0.20. Thus, a 100% inspection of product is economic. That is, the unit gain from inspection is $0.20 minus $0.15 or $0.05.

Clearly, for this example, it is economic to screen process output when the fraction-defective level is greater than 0.015. However, the fraction-defective level is usually not known. It then becomes necessary to estimate output fraction-defective for each lot in order to decide

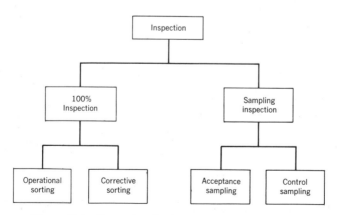

Figure 10.1. Inspection classification by type and purpose.

[1]An exception is vendor certification procedures. See Incoming Material Control, Chapter 2.

whether or not a rectifying inspection is required. A common technique for implementing this concept is sampling inspection.

SAMPLING FUNDAMENTALS

A sampling inspection plan, in its most simple form, is a systematic rule specifying lot size N, sample size n, and acceptance number c. Application of the rule involves the observed number of defectives d. That is, if d is less than or equal to c, the lot is accepted. If d is greater than c, the lot is rejected. Any development of criteria by which sampling plans are selected for specific process conditions depends on probability of acceptance computations. Briefly, interest is on the probability of acceptance for (1) different specified quality levels, and (2) different sampling plans. The probabilities are given by elementary combinatorial computations and certain distribution functions which are summarized here.

Combinations

If n is a positive integer, the symbol $n!$ (read n factorial) is defined by

$$n! = n(n - 1)(n - 2) \ldots (3)(2)(1)$$

and, for convenience, $0! = 1$

Consider n objects: $A_1, A_2, \ldots, A_n$. The number of different arrangements or permutations of the n objects is given by $n!$.

The number of permutations of the n objects taken k at a time is

$$P(n,k) = \frac{n!}{(n - k)!}$$

If the $k!$ permutations of the same k objects is called a combination, the number of combinations of n objects taken k at a time is

$$\binom{n}{k} = \frac{P(n,k)}{k!} = \frac{n!}{k!(n - k)!}$$

By definition,

$$\binom{n}{k} = 0 \qquad k > n$$

$$\binom{n}{k} = 1 \qquad k = n$$

$$\binom{n}{k} = 1 \qquad k = 0$$

Operations with Events and Probabilities

Given an experiment E having N exhaustive, mutually exclusive, and equally likely outcomes: $A_1, A_2, \ldots, A_N$. If m outcomes are associated with the occurrence of an event A and $n - m$ with the nonoccurrence of A, the probability of A, given the experiment E, is

$$P(A) = \frac{m}{n}$$

Example

E: toss of a pair of dice.
A: sum of the upturned faces to be 7.
Outcomes: $A_1 = (1,1)$, $A_2 = (1,2)$, $\ldots$, $A_N = (6,6)$.
There are $n = 36$ possible outcomes and $m = 6$ of these are associated with the occurrence of A, i.e., $(1,6)$, $(2,5)$, $\ldots$, $(6,1)$. The probability of A is given by

$$P(A) = \frac{m}{n} = \frac{6}{36}$$

Using the example as an illustration, note the $n = 36$ outcomes are *exhaustive*, that is, all possible outcomes are considered. The outcomes are *mutually exclusive*, that is, for any single trial of E, one and only one of the A_j outcomes can occur. The outcomes are *equally likely* if the dice and the tosses are unbiased. The problem of determining $P(A)$ under certain circumstances involves enumerating the equally likely cases favorable to the occurrence of A and those unfavorable to A. In a given application, it is really a matter of mutual agreement as to what constitutes the n exhaustive, mutually exclusive, and equally likely outcomes.

If A is certain to occur, then $P(A) = 1$. If A is certain not to occur, then $P(\text{not } A) = 1$, or $P(A) = 0$. Thus, $0 \le P(A) \le 1$.

Also, if $p = P(A)$ and $q = P(\text{not } A)$, then $p + q = 1$ and, of course, $p = 1 - q$.

The symbol $A + B$ denotes the event that either event A or event B occurs. The symbol A,B indicates the event that A and B occur jointly or simultaneously. If a outcomes of E are associated with the occurrence of A, b outcomes with the occurrence of B, and k outcomes with the joint occurrence of A and B, then

$$P(A + B) = \frac{a}{n} + \frac{b}{n} - \frac{k}{n}$$

or

$$P(A + B) = P(A) + P(B) - P(A,B)^2$$

If events A and B are mutually exclusive, then $P(A,B) = 0$ and the above equation reduces to

$$P(A + B) = P(A) + P(B)$$

Two events, A and B, are *independent* if the occurrence of A in no way affects the occurrence of B, and conversely. Thus,

$$P(A,B) = P(A) \cdot P(B) \qquad A \text{ and } B \text{ independent.}$$

$$P(A,B) = P(A) \cdot P\left(\frac{B}{A}\right) \qquad A \text{ and } B \text{ dependent.}$$

The term $P(B/A)$ is read "the probability of B, given that A has occurred." The implication, of course, is that the occurrence of A has altered the probability of B. This suggests an alternative definition of independence, namely: A and B are independent if

$$P\left(\frac{A}{B}\right) = P(A) \qquad \text{or} \qquad P\left(\frac{B}{A}\right) = P(B)$$

Bernoulli Distribution

An experiment E has exactly two outcomes, generally termed failure and success and denoted by the two values — zero and one, respectively. Designating the probability of success by p and the probability of failure by $q = 1 - p$, the frequency function is

$$f(x) = p^x q^{1-x}$$

---

[2] This may be extended to multiple events $A, B, C, \ldots$ as indicated in the following example (for three events): $P(A + B + C) = P(A) + P(B) + P(C) - P(A,B) - P(A,C) - P(B,C) + P(A,B,C)$

where the random variable x may assume values 0, 1. The mean and variance for this distribution function are given by

$$\mu = p \quad \text{and} \quad \sigma_x^2 = pq$$

Binomial Distribution

A binomial random variable x may be considered as the number of successes (or, the number of 1's) in n independent Bernoulli trials. The frequency function is

$$f(x) = \binom{n}{x} p^x q^{n-x} \quad x = 0, 1, 2, \ldots, n$$

The mean and variance for the binomial frequency function are given by

$$\mu = np \quad \text{and} \quad \sigma_x^2 = npq$$

If $n = 1$, the binomial distribution reduces to the Bernoulli distribution. The binomial distribution derives its name from the observation that the successive terms in the binomial expansion $(p + q)^n$ give the $f(x)$ values.

Poisson Distribution

The frequency function for this distribution is

$$f(x) = \frac{e^{-\mu} \mu^x}{x!} \quad x = 0, 1, 2, \ldots, n$$

The mean and variance for the Poisson frequency function are given by

$$\mu = np \quad \text{and} \quad \sigma_x^2 = np$$

Hypergeometric Distribution

Both the binomial and Poisson distribution functions describe the number of successes in n independent Bernoulli trials, where the probability p is constant from trial to trial. Thus, the binomial and Poisson distributions are appropriate models for (1) sampling from an infinite population, and (2) sampling with replacement from a finite population. In both cases, the probability p is unchanged from trial to

229

trial. If sampling is done without replacement from a finite population, the probability p changes from one trial to another. For this case, the hypergeometric distribution function gives the exact probability of x number of successes in n independent Bernoulli trials. The distribution function is

$$f(x) = \frac{\binom{Np}{x} \cdot \binom{Nq}{n-x}}{\binom{N}{n}} \qquad x = 1, 2, \ldots, n$$

The mean and variance for this distribution function are given by

$$\mu = np \quad \text{and} \quad \sigma_x^2 = (npq)\left(\frac{N-n}{N-1}\right)$$

The hypergeometric distribution function can be used to compute the probability of accepting a product lot of given fraction-defective quality for any specified sampling inspection plan. If lot size N is large relative to sample size n, the binomial distribution model can be used to compute the approximate probability of acceptance. If, in addition to the relative size condition for N and n, the probability p is small and n is sufficiently large, the Poisson distribution model can be used to compute the approximate probability of acceptance. Working rules for these conditions are

$$\frac{n}{N} < 0.1, \quad p < 0.1, \quad n > 16$$

The approximations greatly simplify probability of acceptance computations. Another possible simplification is to use the normal distribution function with standardized variable

$$Z = \frac{x - Np}{\sqrt{Npq}}$$

as an approximation to the binomial model. This is possible when N is large and neither p or q are close to zero.

OPERATING CHARACTERISTIC CURVE

Computing the probability of accepting a product lot of specified quality under a given sampling inspection plan is illustrated by the following example.

Example

A sampling inspection plan is described by $N = 50$, $n = 20$, and $c = 0$. Consider the problem of computing the probability of acceptance for a product lot, which is 4% defective.

The number of defectives in the lot is

$$Np = (50)(0.04) = 2$$

Thus, acceptance occurs when the sample contains 0 defectives from 2 available defectives and 20 effectives from 48 available effectives.

Using the hypergeometric frequency function, the probability of acceptance, denoted by P_a, is given by

$$P_a = \frac{\binom{48}{20} \cdot \binom{2}{0}}{\binom{50}{20}}$$

$$= \frac{\left(\frac{48!}{20!\,28!}\right)\left(\frac{2!}{0!\,2!}\right)}{\frac{50!}{20!\,30!}}$$

$$= 0.35$$

Tables of factorials can be used to facilitate the computation. Nevertheless, the arithmetic is laborious.

The preceding example was simplified by the acceptance number c being zero. If c is not zero, the probability of acceptance P_a is computed as shown in the following example.

Example

A sampling inspection plan is described by $N = 1000$, $n = 240$, and $c = 2$. The probability of acceptance for a 5% defective product lot is required. The number of defectives in the lot is

$$Np = (1000)(0.05) = 50$$

Acceptance occurs when the sample contains 0, 1, or 2 defectives.

The probabilities corresponding to these acceptance possibilities are denoted by P_0, P_1, and P_2 respectively. Thus,

$$P_a = P_0 + P_1 + P_2$$

$$= \frac{\binom{950}{240}\binom{50}{0}}{\binom{1000}{240}} + \frac{\binom{950}{239}\binom{50}{1}}{\binom{1000}{240}} + \frac{\binom{950}{238}\binom{50}{2}}{\binom{1000}{240}}$$

If N is large relative to n, the probability of acceptance P_a is essentially independent of N. That is, for a given fraction-defective quality level, P_a depends mainly on sample size n and the acceptance number c. With large N, the binomial distribution function can be used to compute an approximate P_a. Additionally, if p is small, the Poisson distribution function can be used to compute an approximate P_a. The following example illustrates the computational procedure.

Example

A sampling inspection plan is described by $n = 30$ and $c = 1$. The probability of acceptance for a 4% defective product lot is required.

Let d denote the observed number of defectives. Then, using the binomial distribution model

$$P_a = \sum_{d=0}^{c} \binom{n}{d} p^d q^{n-d}$$

$$= \sum_{d=0}^{1} \binom{30}{d} (0.04)^d (0.96)^{30-d}$$

$$= (0.96)^{30} + \frac{30!}{1!\,29!} (0.04)(0.96)^{29}$$

$$= 0.661$$

Using the Poisson distribution model

$$P_a = \sum_{d=0}^{c} \frac{e^{-np}(np)^d}{d!}$$

$$= \sum_{d=0}^{1} \frac{e^{-1.20}(1.20)^d}{d!}$$

$$= 0.663$$

The 0.663 value can be read from the table, Appendix C by entering the row for $\mu = 1.2$ and the column corresponding to $c = 1$.

Operating Characteristic Curve

A basic objective in selecting a sampling inspection plan is to obtain a plan that identifies product lots which should be accepted without further inspection and lots which should be 100% inspected for defectives. The manner in which this identification is effected is mainly an economic question. A basic decision-making aid in selecting a sampling plan is an *operating characteristic curve (OC curve)*.

An example of an OC curve is given in Figure 10.2. The curve indicates the probability of acceptance P_a for various fraction-defective quality levels under the given sampling plan. For example, if $p = 0.05$, this plan would accept such a lot 45% of the time. Constructing an OC curve involves probability of acceptance computations for various p-values. These computations were illustrated previously in this chapter.

A sampling plan should discriminate product lots around a break-even quality level. For example, if unit inspection cost is \$0.15 and unit failure cost due to an undetected defective is \$10, the break-even quality level is \$0.15/\$10 or 0.015. The theoretically ideal OC curve is shown in Figure 10.3. Product lots of quality better than $p = 0.015$ have a probability of acceptance equal to 1.0. Product lots of quality worse than $p = 0.015$ have zero probability of acceptance.

Any sampling plan involves possible decision errors. Thus, such an ideal OC curve does not exist. However, examination of this theoretical OC curve indicates that a sampling plan with good discrimination in the vicinity of the break-even quality level has an OC curve which is steep in this region (see Figure 10.4).

A sampling plan's discrimination can be increased by increasing the

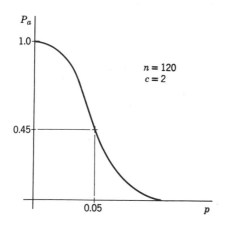

Figure 10.2.   Operating characteristic curve.

233

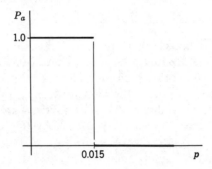

Figure 10.3.   Ideal OC curve.

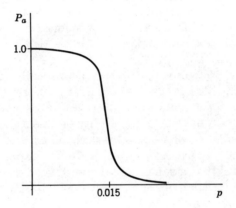

Figure 10.4.   Optimum OC curve.

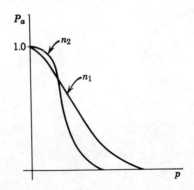

Figure 10.5.   Effect of increasing n from n_1 to n_2.

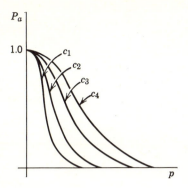

Figure 10.6.   Effect of increasing c from c_1 to c_4.

sample size n and the acceptance number c proportionately. Increasing n increases the steepness of the OC curve (see Figure 10.5). Changing the acceptance number moves the curve away from or towards the origin (see Figure 10.6).

CRITERIA FOR EVALUATING SAMPLING PLANS

Standard sampling inspection plans are indexed according to certain criteria. These criteria are summarized here. Sampling plans are selected by choosing an appropriate OC curve. The one chosen should reflect both the producer's and the consumer's[3] views as to the cost of making wrong decisions. A sampling plan is a test of a hypothesis that the product lot is acceptable. The hypothesis may be

$$H_0 : p \leq \frac{C_i}{C_d}$$

where

C_i = unit inspection cost

C_d = unit failure cost due to an undetected defective

[3]The meaning, in this context, is supplier and purchaser companies, or supplier and consumer departments within a manufacturing plant. See Inspection and Test, Chapter 2.

235

and thus,

$$\frac{C_i}{C_d} = \text{break-even quality level}$$

The decision rule is

$$\text{Accept } H_0 \text{ if } \frac{d}{n} \le \frac{C_i}{C_d}$$

$$\text{Reject } H_0 \text{ if } \frac{d}{n} > \frac{C_i}{C_d}$$

where

d = observed number of defectives

n = sample size

A more comprehensive hypothesis is possible, involving two distinct fraction-defective quality levels. One is an *acceptable quality level* (AQL); the other is a *lot tolerance fraction-defective level* (LTFD). AQL is a "good" quality level which, from the producer's viewpoint, should be accepted most of the time by the sampling plan. Usually, the probability of acceptance P_a for AQL quality lots is taken to be 0.95. LTFD quality is a "bad" quality level which, from the consumer's viewpoint, should be rejected most of the time by the sampling plan. Usually, P_a for LTFD quality lots is 0.10. The null and alternative hypotheses are

$$H_0 : p \le \text{AQL fraction defective}$$

$$H_1 : p \ge \text{LTFD fraction defective}$$

The probability that a sampling plan will reject AQL lots is called the *producer's risk* (α). The probability that the plan will accept LTFD lots is called *consumer's risk* (β). That is, if the lot quality is equal to or better than AQL quality, P_a is equal to or greater than $1 - \alpha$. Similarly, if the lot quality is equal to or worse than LTFD quality, P_a is equal to or less than β. Thus, α and β correspond to the probabilities of making Type I and Type II decision errors respectively.

Choice of a sampling inspection plan, under the preceding null and alternative hypotheses, involves selection of an OC curve passing through two points—(AQL, 1-α) and (LTFD, β). That is, n and c are such that the OC curve describing the sampling plan passes through

236

the two specified points. Practically, a sampling plan choice is made by referring to standard plans[4] and selecting an OC curve which best satisfies the two-point condition summarized in Figure 10.7.

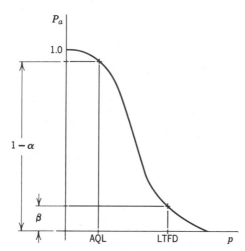

Figure 10.7. Producer's and consumer's risks.

Sampling Plan Design

Designing a sampling plan, which satisfies the α and β probability conditions for the hypothesized quality levels AQL and LTFD, involves considerable computation. The general procedure is summarized here.

Assuming lot size N is sufficiently large, a sampling plan is defined by n and c. Using the binomial distribution function as a model, the probability of acceptance $1 - \alpha$ is

$$1 - \alpha = \sum_{d=0}^{c} \binom{n}{d} p_1{}^{d} (1 - p_1)^{n-d}$$

where $\qquad\qquad p_1 =$ AQL fraction-defective quality

$\qquad\qquad\quad d\ =$ observed number of defectives

Similarly, the probability of acceptance β is

---

[4]For example, see Military Standard MIL-STD-105D (April, 1963), *Sampling Procedures and Tables for Inspection by Attributes*, Superintendent of Documents, U. S. Government Printing Office, Washington, D. C.

237

$$\beta = \sum_{d=0}^{c} \binom{n}{d} p_2{}^d (1 - p_2)^{n-d}$$

where $\qquad\qquad p_2 = \text{LTFD quality}$

The two equations for $1 - \alpha$ and β can be solved for integer values of n and c, which correspond as closely as possible to the values associated with the desired plan. For large n-values, the computation is very laborious. However, for intermediate p-values (i.e., p not near zero), the normal distribution function may be used to approximate binomial probabilities. For small p-values, the Poisson approximation may be used to reduce the computational burden. In this case,

$$1 - \alpha = \sum_{d=0}^{c} \frac{e^{-np_1} (np_1)^d}{d!}$$

$$\beta = \sum_{d=0}^{c} \frac{e^{-np_2} (np_2)^d}{d!}$$

These two equations can be solved for n and c. An approximate solution may be obtained by using cumulative probability values for the Poisson distribution function (see table, Appendix C).

Example

The specifications for a sampling plan are $p_1 = 0.02$, $\alpha = 0.05$, $p_2 = 0.08$, and $\beta = 0.10$. For various acceptance numbers c, values of $p_1 n$ and $p_2 n$ may be obtained from the table, Appendix C. For example, exploring the column corresponding to $c = 1$, the table value closest to $1 - \alpha = 0.95$ is 0.951. Thus, $p_1 n$ is 0.35. In like manner, exploring the $c = 1$ column, $\beta = 0.10$ is between 0.107 and 0.92. Interpolating, $p_2 n$ is 3.90. The pn values for various c-values are given in Table 10.1.

The ratio p_2/p_1 for the desired plan is 0.08/0.02 or 4, which is close to the p_2/p_1 ratio for $c = 4$. Taking c to be 4,

$$p_1 n = 1.96$$

$$(0.02)n = 1.96$$

$$n = 98$$

Then

$$p_2 n = (0.08) (98)$$

$$= 7.80$$

Table 10.1 **pn Values for Trial c-Values**

c	$p_1 n$	$p_2 n$	p_2 / p_1
0	–	2.30	–
1	0.35	3.90	11.2
2	0.80	5.33	6.7
3	1.36	6.70	4.9
4	1.96	8.00	4.1

From the table, Appendix C, for $np = 7.80$ and $c = 4$, β is equal to 0.112, which is sufficiently close to the specified value for β. Thus, the required sampling plan is: $n = 98$, $c = 4$.

The OC curve passes through the points (0, 1), (0.02, 0.95), (0.08, 0.10), and (1,0).

Average Outgoing Quality

A sampling plan criterion, important to the consumer, is *average outgoing quality* (AOQ). This measure gives the expected average quality of product shipped to the customer. Two fraction-defective quantities are averaged: (1) expected fraction-defective of product lots accepted by the sampling plan, and (2) expected fraction-defective of rejected lots. The latter fraction-defective is zero under the assumptions that rejected lots are screened and all defectives are replaced by effectives.

Example

Ten lots of 10,000 product items each are inspected under a sampling plan: $n = 300$, $c = 7$. The expected fraction-defective is 0.02.

The OC curve for this sampling plan indicates that 70% of the lots will be accepted (7 lots) and 30% rejected (3 lots). Thus, for the 10 outgoing lots, there are

$$(7) (10,000 - 300) (0.02) = 1358 \text{ defectives}$$

The average outgoing quality is given by

$$AOQ = \frac{(7) (10,000 - 300) (0.02)}{(10) (10,000)}$$

$$= \frac{1358}{100,000}$$

$$= 0.01358$$

239

Division of the numerator and denominator of the above expression for AOQ by 10, yields

$$AOQ = \frac{(0.7)\,(10{,}000 - 300)\,(0.02)}{10{,}000}$$

or,

$$AOQ = \frac{(P_a)\,(N - n)\,(p)}{N}$$

Thus, if N is large relative to n,

$$AOQ \stackrel{\wedge}{=} p\,P_a$$

Computation of AOQ for various p-values generates an AOQ curve as shown in Figure 10.8. The maximum value of AOQ represents the worst expected quality which will leave this plan. This is called *average outgoing quality limit* (AOQL).

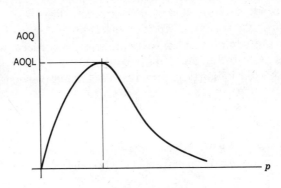

Figure 10.8.   AOQ curve.

Multiple Sampling Plans

A single sampling plan is given by (N, n, c). If N is large relative to n, the plan is defined essentially by (n,c). The decision rule is

$$d \le c, \text{accept the lot}$$
$$d > c, \text{reject the lot}$$

where d is the observed number of defectives.

240

A double sampling plan is defined by (n_1, n_2, c_1, c_2), where d_1 denotes the observed number of defectives in a first sample and d_2 the observed number of defectives in a second sample. One or two samples are required to reach a decision. The decision rule is as follows.

First sample of n_1 product items:

$$d_1 \leq c_1, \text{ accept the lot}$$

$$d_1 > c_2, \text{ reject the lot}$$

$$c_1 < d_1 \leq c_2, \text{ take a second sample}$$

Second sample of n_2 items:

$$d_1 + d_2 \leq c_2, \text{ accept the lot}$$

$$d_1 + d_2 > c_2, \text{ reject the lot}$$

Double sampling plans have the psychological advantage of giving a second chance to doubtful lots. The principal advantage of a double sampling plan is that, for a given quality protection, fewer total inspections are required (on the average) than for single sampling plans. Significant disadvantages are (1) more complex administration, (2) variable inspection loads, and (3) maximum amount of inspection can exceed that for single sampling plans (which is constant).

Double sampling plans are described by OC curves in the same manner as are single plans. Probability of acceptance computations are more complex for double sampling plans. Using the binomial distribution function as a model, the probability of acceptance P_a for a double sampling plan is given by

$$P_a = \sum_{d_1 = 0}^{c_1} \binom{n_1}{d_1} (p)^{d_1} (1 - p)^{n_1 - d_1}$$

$$+ \sum_{d_1 = c_1 + 1}^{c_2} \sum_{d_2 = 0}^{c_2 - d_1} \binom{n_1}{d_1} (p)^{d_1} (1 - p)^{n_1 - d_1} \binom{n_2}{d_2} (p)^{d_2} (1 - p)^{n_2 - d_2}$$

or, using the Poisson distribution model,

$$P_a = \sum_{d_1 = 0}^{c_1} \frac{e^{-n_1 p} (n_1 p)^{d_1}}{d_1!} + \sum_{d_1 = c_1 + 1}^{c_2} \sum_{d_2 = 0}^{c_2 - d_1} \frac{e^{-n_1 p} (n_1 p)^{d_1}}{d_1!} \cdot \frac{e^{-n_2 p} (n_2 p)^{d_2}}{d_2!}$$

Example

A sampling plan is defined by $n_1 = 20$, $c_1 = 0$, and $n_2 = 40$, $c_2 = 2$. The probability of acceptance for a 5% defective product lot is required.

There are four ways by which acceptance can occur as shown in Figure 10.9. The numbers in parentheses identify the separate computations which follow.

$d_1 \leq c_1$	$c_1 < d_1 \leq c_2$ $d_1 + d_2 \leq c_2$	
(1)	(2)	$d_2 = 0$
$d_1 = 0$	$d_1 = 1$	$d_2 = 1$
	(3)	
	$d_1 = 2$	$d_2 = 0$

Figure 10.9. Acceptance possibilities.

Using the Poisson distribution model, the probability of acceptance P_a is computed as follows:

$$n_1 p = (20)\,(0.05) = 1.0$$

$$n_2 p = (40)\,(0.05) = 2.0$$

(1) $\displaystyle\sum_{d_1 = 0}^{0} \frac{e^{-n_1 p}\,(n_1 p)^{d_1}}{d_1!} = 0.368$

(2) $\displaystyle\left[\sum_{d_1 = 0}^{1} \frac{e^{-n_1 p}\,(n_1 p)^{d_1}}{d_1!} - \sum_{d_1 = 0}^{0} \frac{e^{-n_1 p}\,(n_1 p)^{d_1}}{d_1!} \right] \left[\sum_{d_2 = 0}^{1} \frac{e^{-n_2 p}\,(n_2 p)^{d_2}}{d_2!} \right]$

$$= (0.736 - 0.368)\,(0.406)$$

$$= 0.149$$

(3) $\displaystyle\left[\sum_{d_1 = 0}^{2} \frac{e^{-n_1 p}\,(n_1 p)^{d_1}}{d_1!} - \sum_{d_1 = 0}^{1} \frac{e^{-n_1 p}\,(n_1 p)^{d_1}}{d_1!} \right] \left[\sum_{d_2 = 0}^{0} \frac{e^{-n_2 p}\,(n_2 p)^{d_2}}{d_2!} \right]$

$$= (0.920 - 0.736)\,(0.135)$$

$$= 0.025$$

$$P_a = 0.368 + 0.149 + 0.025$$

$$= 0.542$$

The probabilities corresponding to the Poisson expressions can be read directly from the table, Appendix C.

Sequential sampling plans have been developed to further reduce the average total inspections required. Sequential plans are defined by

Sample sizes: $n_1, n_2, \ldots, n_k$

Acceptance numbers: $c_1, c_2, \ldots, c_k$

Rejection numbers: $r_1, r_2, \ldots, r_k$

The decision rule is
First sample of n_1 product items:

$$d_1 \leq c_1, \text{ accept the lot}$$
$$d_1 \geq r_1, \text{ reject the lot}$$
$$c_1 < d_1 < r_1, \text{ take a second sample}$$

Second sample of n_2 items:

$$d_1 + d_2 \leq c_2, \text{ accept the lot}$$
$$d_1 + d_2 \geq r_2, \text{ reject the lot}$$
$$c_2 < d_1 + d_2 < r_2, \text{ take a third sample}$$

etc. to the kth sample specified by the plan, then

$$d_1 + d_2 + \ldots + d_k \leq c_k, \text{ accept the lot}$$
$$d_1 + d_2 + \ldots + d_k > c_k, \text{ reject the lot}$$

Variables Sampling Plans

The inspection plans discussed in previous sections of this chapter have been based on classifying product items as acceptable or non-acceptable (attributes plans). *Variables plans* are based on measurements of degree of conformance of output to specifications (see Inspection and Test, Chapter 2). The advantages of variables plans are (1) equivalent quality protection is obtained with a smaller sample size, and (2) additional diagnostic information is provided for process control purposes. The disadvantages of variables plans are mainly the higher cost of inspection (particularly instrumentation) and the more complex computations required. Variables plans are more economic than attributes plans when inspection is destructive.

There are many authoritative sources of variables sampling plans. A comprehensive source is *Sampling Procedures and Tables for Inspection by Variables for Per Cent Defective—MIL-STD 414*.[5] A sim-

[5]See Military Standard MIL-STD 414 (June, 1957), *Sampling Procedures and Tables for Inspection by Variables for Per Cent Defective*. Superintendent of Documents, U.S. Government Printing Office, Washington, D.C.

plified example is presented here to illustrate the variable sampling plan concept.

Example

A quality characteristic is defined by the specification 0.500 ± 0.004 in. Process capability data indicates σ_x to be equal to 0.0015 in. for the operation involved.

Distribution (A) of Figure 10.10 describes the best possible process condition. The process is centered at 0.500 in. and the resulting fraction-defective is 0.00758. The process setting may shift upward or downward resulting in a fraction-defective quality level greater than 0.00758.

A variables sampling plan is required for AQL quality of $p_1 = 0.01$ with a probability of acceptance P_a equal to 0.95 and LTFD quality of $p_2 = 0.03$ with P_a equal to 0.10.

Distributions (B) and (C) of Figure 10.10 indicate downward process shifts to AQL and LTFD quality levels, respectively. The quality characteristic is denoted by x_i and it is assumed that x is normally distributed. At the AQL level, the mean process setting is 0.499585 and p_1 is 0.01001. At the LTFD level, the mean process setting is 0.498825 and p_2 is 0.029685. Rounding off to four places

$$\mu_{\text{AQL}} = 0.4996 \qquad p_1 = 0.01$$

$$\mu_{\text{LTFD}} = 0.4988 \qquad p_2 = 0.03$$

Figure 10.11 indicates a solution for an acceptance mean $\bar{x}_c$ and sample size n. At the AQL level ($\mu = 0.4996$), the probability of acceptance P_a is $1 - \alpha/2$. At the LTFD level ($\mu = 0.4988$), P_a is $\beta/2$. Assuming the same protection against process shifts upward as that for downward shifts, α and β are split equally. Thus

$$Z_{\frac{\alpha}{2}} = -1.96 = \frac{\bar{x}_c = 0.4996}{0.0015/\sqrt{n}}$$

$$Z_{\frac{\beta}{2}} = +1.645 = \frac{\bar{x}_c - 0.4988}{0.0015/\sqrt{n}}$$

Subtracting the first equation from the second, $\bar{x}_c$ vanishes and

$$\sqrt{n} = \frac{(3.605)(0.0015)}{0.0008} = 6.75$$

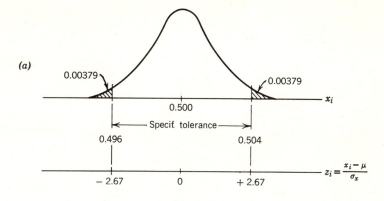

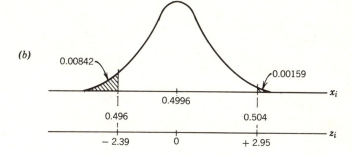

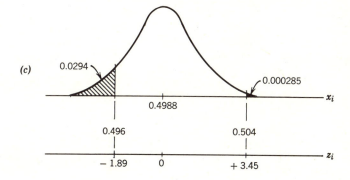

Figure 10.10.   Process shifts downward to AQL and LTFD quality levels.
(a) Process at optimum quality level ($\mu = 0.500$), $p = 2(0.00379) = 0.00758$.
(b) Process at AQL quality level ($\mu = 0.4996$), $p_1 = 0.00842 + 0.00159$
$$= 0.01001.$$
(c) Process at LTFD quality level ($\mu = 0.4988$), $p_2 = 0.0294 + 0.000285$
$$= 0.029685 \ (\text{or, } 0.03).$$

245

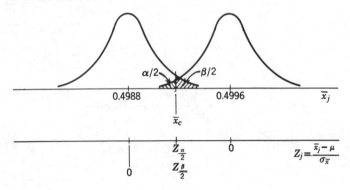

Figure 10.11.   Probability of acceptance for product at AQL and LTFD quality levels.

whence

$$n = 45.56$$

Taking n to be 46, a solution of either equation yields

$$\bar{x}_c = 0.4992$$

Symmetry considerations for the distribution of sample means yield an $\bar{x}_c$-value for upward process shifts equal to

$$0.5000 + 0.0008 = 0.5008$$

Thus, the required sampling plan is

one sample of $n = 46$ product items:

$$\bar{x}_{\text{sample}} \leq \bar{x}_c = 0.4992, \text{ reject the lot}$$

$$\bar{x}_{\text{sample}} \geq \bar{x}_c = 0.5008, \text{ reject the lot}$$

Otherwise, accept the lot.

The OC curve for this plan is given in Figure 10.12. P_a for AQL quality is

$$1 - \alpha = 0.95$$

That is, for each of the two AQL quality levels – 0.4996 in. and 0.5004 in. – the probability of rejection is $\alpha/2$.

Similarly, P_a for LTFD quality is

246

$$\beta = 0.10$$

where the probability of acceptance for each of the two LTFD quality levels — 0.4988 in. and 0.5012 in. — is $\beta/2$.

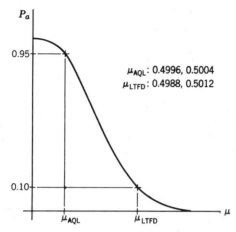

Figure 10.12. OC curve for variables plan.

To obtain the same degree of quality protection, using an attributes sampling plan, requires a considerably larger sample. A sampling plan can be derived from the table, Appendix C in the same manner as illustrated previously. The requirements for the plan are

$$p_1 = 0.01 \qquad \alpha = 0.05$$
$$p_2 = 0.03 \qquad \beta = 0.10$$

and

$$\frac{p_2 n}{p_1 n} = \frac{0.03}{0.01} = 3.0$$

For $c = 7$

$$p_1 n \overset{\wedge}{=} 4 \qquad p_2 n \overset{\wedge}{=} 12$$

and

$$\frac{p_2 n}{p_1 n} \overset{\wedge}{=} 3.0$$

247

Taking c to be 7

$$p_1 n = 4$$

$$(0.01)n = 4$$

$$n = 400$$

ECONOMICS OF SAMPLING INSPECTION

A Type I decision error occurs when the sample, through chance variation, indicates a larger proportion of defectives than that which is really present in the lot. Similarly, a Type II decision error occurs when the sample contains a smaller proportion of defectives than that actually present in the lot. The Type I error leads either to unnecessary 100% inspection or unjustified scrapping of material. The risk α of such an economic loss is called *producer's risk*. A Type II error causes the consumer to sustain certain kinds of economic loss. The risk β of such consumer losses is called *consumer's risk*.

Standard sampling plans and published tables develop minimum sample sizes for given degrees of quality protection. However, the minimization of sample size may reduce only a relatively small cost — small in relation to the costs generated by decision errors. The total real cost of sampling inspection includes (1) cost of taking and testing the sample, and (2) losses occasioned by the operation of producer's and consumer's risks. Two opposing sets of costs are involved. Clearly, the larger the sample, the more costly is inspection and test. On the other hand, risks and their attendant costs are reduced by large samples. An economic objective is to determine the relationship between size and cost of the sample so that total cost of sampling inspection can be minimized.

Producer's Risk

A Type I decision error is made whenever an acceptable lot is rejected by the sampling plan. If the inspection operation is nondestructive and if its cost is not prohibitively high, it is economical to 100% inspect product lots rejected by the sampling plan. In this manner, Type I decision errors are corrected. The cost of the 100% inspection is the cost of rejecting the acceptable lot.

If the inspection is costly or destructive, it is not feasible to 100% inspect a rejected lot. A rejection is, in effect, an order to scrap or rework the lot. In this case, the cost of rejecting acceptable product under a given sampling plan is

$$C_r = (N - n) \, (\alpha) \, (C_u - V_s)$$

where C_r = cost of rejection

C_u = unit cost of product item

V_s = unit salvage value of product item (or, its value as rework material)

N = lot size

n = sample size

α = producer's risk

Consumer's Risk

A Type II decision error is made whenever a nonacceptable lot is accepted by a sampling plan. Usually, the cost of accepting non-acceptable product under a given sampling plan cannot be accurately determined. There are two general cases: (1) the customer is a purchaser company, or a consumer using the product, and (2) the customer is another manufacturing department of the producer company. In the first case, the cost of accepting nonacceptable product is impossible to estimate beforehand. Almost always the loss due to the defective unit depends on the circumstances surrounding the malfunction. These are unpredictable. In the second case, if the product item involved is a component and the defect is one that will be discovered at assembly or test, then the nuisance loss of this type of defect can be determined. A method described by Smith[6] can then be used for determining sample size while minimizing the total cost of both risks and of sampling.

Total Cost of Sampling Inspection

Some work has been done in utilizing decision theory principles to incorporate the economic consequences of the decision into the choice of the sampling plan. It is possible, for specific applications, to obtain

[6]See Smith, B. E. (July, 1961), *Some Economic Aspects of Quality Control,* Technical Report No. 53, Applied Mathematics and Statistics Laboratories, Stanford University, Stanford, California.

optimal plans[7] to minimize the total cost of sampling inspection. However, models that have been developed usually apply to a relatively small portion of the total quality-control problem, and usually to comparatively simple process-control inspection situations. In order to use the models, it is necessary to acquire substantial information about the process and its output. Moreover, some of the resulting plans do not differ greatly from those that would be specified by an experienced quality-control man using less objective criteria.

Mandelson[8] describes a simplified approach to the problem of minimizing total sampling inspection cost. The cost associated with consumer's risk is omitted from the total cost equation. This cost is controlled by prescribing a suitable LTFD quality level corresponding to a consumer's risk β of 0.10. Since the sampling plan will reject a lot of LTFD quality nine times out of ten, the producer is under considerable economic pressure to avoid such wholesale rejection. Consequently, the producer's output must come from a process that is controlled at a fraction-defective level equal to roughly one third or one fourth of the LTFD. Mandelson sets LTFD equal to three or four times the process average fraction-defective.

The cost of inspection and test under destructive inspection is

$$n(C_u + C_i)$$

where C_u = unit cost of product item

C_i = unit inspection cost

Thus, total cost of sampling inspection TC is

$$TC = n(C_u + C_i) + (N - n)\,(\alpha)\,(C_u - V_s)$$

where the first term measures inspection and test cost per lot, and the second term the cost per lot of rejecting acceptable lots. This is called producer's risk cost. Clearly, $(N - n)\,(C_u - V_s)$ is the loss due to rejecting one lot and multiplying by α gives the average loss per lot for all

[7]See Fetter, R. B. (1967), *The Quality Control System,* Richard D. Irwin, Homewood, Ill., pp. 25-34; Mandelson, J. (November, 1946), "Estimation of Optimum Sample Size in Destructive Testing by Attributes," *Industrial Quality Control,* Vol. 3, pp. 24-26; Martin, C. A. (September, 1964), "The Cost Breakeven Point in Attribute Sampling," *Industrial Quality Control,* Vol. 21, No. 3, pp. 137-143; Smith, B. E. (March, 1965), "The Economics of Sampling Inspection," *Industrial Quality Control,* Vol. 21, No. 9, pp. 453-458.

[8]Mandelson, J. (March 1967), "Sampling Plans for Destructive or Expensive Testing," *Industrial Quality Control,* Vol. 23, No. 9, pp. 440-450.

lots inspected (i.e., $100(1 - \alpha)\%$ of the acceptable lots are accepted, and $100\alpha\%$ of the acceptable lots are rejected).

In practice, the producer desires to hold losses due to producer's risk to as low a value as practicable. This objective is shared by the consumer, but not at the price of using uneconomically large samples. Therefore, a sampling plan is developed which reduces producer's risk cost at the process average to such a figure that the total cost of sample and risk is a minimum. Obtaining this plan involves determining a number of plans (n,c) each having a $(1 - \beta) = 0.90$ protection against the acceptance of LTFD quality product. Trial solutions of the total cost equation for various n-values yields a minimum total cost for a certain n-value. This procedure involves considerable computation. A graphical method reported by Ellner and Savage[9] is illustrated by the following example.

Example

An n-value is required which minimizes total cost of sampling inspection for the following inspection and cost situation:

$$N = 5000 \qquad C_u = \$5$$

$$p_2 = 0.07 = \text{LTFD} \qquad C_i = \$10$$

$$\bar{p} = 0.02 \qquad V_s = \$3$$

The following required quantities are computed

$$A = C_u + C_i = \$15$$

$$B = C_u - V_s = \$2$$

$$\frac{B}{A} = \frac{\$2}{\$15} = 0.133$$

$$\frac{\bar{p}}{p_2} = \frac{0.02}{0.07} = 0.286$$

$$p_2 N = (0.07)(5000) = 350$$

$$p_2 N\left(\frac{B}{A}\right) = (350)(0.133) = 46.7$$

$$1 - \left(\frac{B}{A}\right) = 0.867$$

[9]Ellner, H. and Savage, I. R. (June 1957), *Sampling for Destructive or Expensive Testing by Attributes,* Army Science Conference, West Point, N.Y.

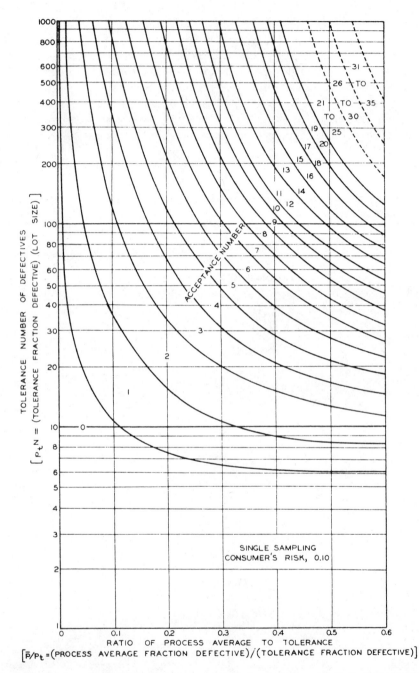

Figure 10.13. Chart for finding the acceptance number. From H. F. Dodge and H. G. Romig (1959), *Sampling Inspection Tables*, Wiley, New York, p. 14.

Enter Figure 10.13 with $\bar{p}/p_2$ (abscissa value) and $p_2N(B/A)$ (ordinate value and read $c = 4$. Enter Figure 10.14 with p_2N (abscissa value) and $c = 4$ (curve parameter) and read $p_2n = 8$ (ordinate value). Again, enter Figure 10.13 with $\bar{p}/p_2$ (abscissa value) and a modified ordinate value

$$p_2N\left(\frac{B}{A}\right) + \left(1 - \frac{B}{A}\right)(p_2n)$$

and read $c = 5$. Again, enter Figure 10.14 with p_2N (abscissa value) and $c = 5$ (curve parameter) and read $p_2n = 9.2$.

The required sample size is obtained from

$$p_2n = 9.2$$

$$n = \frac{9.2}{0.07}$$

$$n = 131$$

The solution is summarized in Figure 10.15.

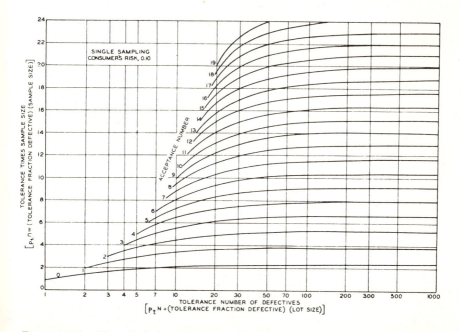

Figure 10.14.   Chart for finding sample size. From H. F. Dodge and H. G. Romig (1959), *Sampling Inspection Tables*, Wiley, New York, p. 15.

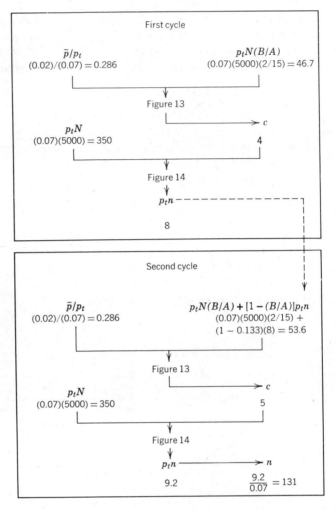

Figure 10.15. Flow chart for calculating optimum single-sampling plans.

STANDARD SAMPLING PLANS

A number of standard sampling inspection plans and tables have been published and made available to the industries. Also, many special purpose plans have been presented in the journals.[10] Two of the most widely used sets of plans are summarized here.

[10]For example, see *Industrial Quality Control,* Journal of the American Society for Quality Control, Milwaukee, Wisconsin.

Dodge-Romig Tables

In 1944, H. F. Dodge and H. G. Romig published a volume of attribute sampling tables and procedures called *Sampling Inspection Tables*; a revised second edition appeared in 1959.[11] Dodge and Romig sampling plans were prepared for use within the Bell Telephone System. The plans are designed primarily to minimize the total amount of inspection, assuming that rejected lots are screened. Single and double sampling tables are given for two acceptance criteria—lot tolerance fraction-defective (LTFD) and average outgoing quality limit (AOQL)—making a total of four types of plans available.

The single and double LTFD tables are indexed for eight values of LTFD (0.005, 0.01, 0.02, 0.03, 0.04, 0.05, 0.07, and 0.10) with β, the consumer's risk, set at 0.10. The tables specify different sample sizes and acceptance numbers for different lot sizes and quality averages. For any given lot size there is a choice of six plans, each for a different value of the process average. If the selected plan corresponds to the true process average fraction-defective, the plan guarantees that the average amount of inspection will be smaller than that for any of the five remaining plans.

The single and double AOQL tables are indexed for AOQL-values of 0.001, 0.0025, 0.005, 0.0075, 0.01, 0.015, 0.02, 0.025, 0.03, 0.04, 0.05, 0.07, and 0.10. The table gives LTFD-values for each plan. These plans also have the property that the average amount of inspection is smallest for that plan corresponding to the true process average fraction-defective. Typical single sampling AOQL plans are shown in Figure 10.16. Operating characteristic curves for these plans are given in Figure 10.17.

Military Standard 105D

A government standard for lot-by-lot sampling inspection by attributes, MIL-STD-105D,[12] (see Appendix D) has become an accepted standard for the industries. The specification of its use in most government contracts accounts, in part, for its widespread use. The sampling plans described by this document are relatively easy to select, apply, and interpret.

[11]Dodge, H. F. and Romig, H. G. (1959), *Sampling Inspection Tables,* Wiley, New York.

[12]Military Standard MIL-STD-105D (April, 1963), *Sampling Procedures and Tables for Inspection by Attributes,* Superintendent of Documents, U.S. Government Printing Office, Washington, D.C.

Single Sampling Table for Average Outgoing Quality Limit (AOQL) = 2.0%

Lot Size	Process Average 0 to 0.04%			Process Average 0.05 to 0.40%			Process Average 0.41 to 0.80%			Process Average 0.81 to 1.20%			Process Average 1.21 to 1.60%			Process Average 1.61 to 2.00%		
	n	c	$p_t\%$	n	c	$p_t\%$	n	c	$p_t\%$	n	c	$p_t\%$	n	c	$p_t\%$	n	c	$p_t\%$
1–15	All	0	–	All	0	–	All	0	–	All	0	–	All	0	–	All	0	–
16–50	14	0	13.6	14	0	13.6	14	0	13.6	14	0	13.6	14	0	13.6	14	0	13.6
51–100	16	0	12.4	16	0	12.4	16	0	12.4	16	0	12.4	16	0	12.4	16	0	12.4
101–200	17	0	12.2	17	0	12.2	17	0	12.2	17	0	12.2	35	1	10.5	35	1	10.5
201–300	17	0	12.3	17	0	12.3	17	0	12.3	37	1	10.2	37	1	10.2	37	1	10.2
301–400	18	0	11.8	18	0	11.8	38	1	10.0	38	1	10.0	38	1	10.0	60	2	8.5
401–500	18	0	11.9	18	0	11.9	39	1	9.8	39	1	9.8	60	2	8.6	60	2	8.6
501–600	18	0	11.9	18	0	11.9	39	1	9.8	39	1	9.8	60	2	8.6	60	2	8.6
601–800	18	0	11.9	40	1	9.6	40	1	9.6	65	2	8.0	65	2	8.0	85	3	7.5
801–1000	18	0	12.0	40	1	9.6	40	1	9.6	65	2	8.1	65	2	8.1	90	3	7.4
1001–2000	18	0	12.0	41	1	9.4	65	2	8.2	65	2	8.2	95	3	7.0	120	4	6.5
2001–3000	18	0	12.0	41	1	9.4	65	2	8.2	95	3	7.0	120	4	6.5	180	6	5.8
3001–4000	18	0	12.0	42	1	9.3	65	2	8.2	95	3	7.0	155	5	6.0	210	7	5.5
4001–5000	18	0	12.0	42	1	9.3	70	2	7.5	125	4	6.4	155	5	6.0	245	8	5.3
5001–7000	18	0	12.0	42	1	9.3	95	3	7.0	125	4	6.4	185	6	5.6	280	9	5.1
7001–10,000	42	1	9.3	70	2	7.5	95	3	7.0	155	5	6.0	220	7	5.4	350	11	4.8
10,001–20,000	42	1	9.3	70	2	7.6	95	3	7.0	190	6	5.6	290	9	4.9	460	14	4.4
20,001–50,000	42	1	9.3	70	2	7.6	125	4	6.4	220	7	5.4	395	12	4.5	720	21	3.9
50,001–100,000	42	1	9.3	95	3	7.0	160	5	5.9	290	9	4.9	505	15	4.2	955	27	3.7

Single Sampling Table for Average Outgoing Quality Limit (AOQL) = 2.5%

	Process Average 0 to 0.05%			Process Average 0.06 to 0.50%			Process Average 0.51 to 1.00%			Process Average 1.01 to 1.50%			Process Average 1.51 to 2.00%			Process Average 2.01 to 2.50%		
	n	c	$p_t\%$	n	c	$p_t\%$	n	c	$p_t\%$	n	c	$p_t\%$	n	c	$p_t\%$	n	c	$p_t\%$
1-10	All	0	—	All	0	—	All	0	—	All	0	—	All	0	—	All	0	—
11-50	11	0	17.6	11	0	17.6	11	0	17.6	11	0	17.6	11	0	17.6	11	0	17.6
51-100	13	0	15.3	13	0	15.3	13	0	15.3	13	0	15.3	13	0	15.3	13	0	15.3
101-200	14	0	14.7	14	0	14.7	14	0	14.7	29	1	12.9	29	1	12.9	29	1	12.9
201-300	14	0	14.9	14	0	14.9	30	1	12.7	30	1	12.7	30	1	12.7	30	1	12.7
301-400	14	0	15.0	14	0	15.0	31	1	12.3	31	1	12.3	31	1	12.3	48	2	10.7
401-500	14	0	15.0	14	0	15.0	32	1	12.0	32	1	12.0	49	2	10.6	49	2	10.6
501-600	14	0	15.1	32	1	12.0	32	1	12.0	50	2	10.4	50	2	10.4	70	3	9.3
601-800	14	0	15.1	32	1	12.0	32	1	12.0	50	2	10.5	50	2	10.5	70	3	9.4
801-1000	15	0	14.2	33	1	11.7	33	1	11.7	50	2	10.6	70	3	9.4	90	4	8.5
1001-2000	15	0	14.2	33	1	11.7	55	2	9.3	75	3	8.8	95	4	8.0	120	5	7.6
2001-3000	15	0	14.2	33	1	11.8	55	2	9.4	75	3	8.8	120	5	7.6	145	6	7.2
3001-4000	15	0	14.3	33	1	11.8	55	2	9.5	100	4	7.9	125	5	7.4	195	8	6.6
4001-5000	15	0	14.3	33	1	11.8	75	3	8.9	100	4	7.9	150	6	7.0	225	9	6.3
5001-7000	33	1	11.8	55	2	9.7	75	3	8.9	125	5	7.4	175	7	6.7	250	10	6.1
7001-10,000	34	1	11.4	55	2	9.7	75	3	8.9	125	5	7.4	200	8	6.4	310	12	5.8
10,000-20,000	34	1	11.4	55	2	9.7	100	4	8.0	150	6	7.0	260	10	6.0	425	16	5.3
20,001-50,000	34	1	11.4	55	2	9.7	100	4	8.0	180	7	6.7	345	13	5.5	640	23	4.8
50,001-100,000	34	1	11.4	80	3	8.4	125	5	7.4	235	9	6.1	435	16	5.2	800	28	4.5

n = sample size; c = acceptance number

"All" indicates that each piece in the lot is to be inspected

p_t = lot tolerance percent defective with a consumer's risk (P_c) of 0.10

Figure 10.16. Dodge-Romig AOQL sampling plans. From Dodge, H. F. and Romig, H. G. (1959), *Sampling Inspection Tables*, Wiley, New York.

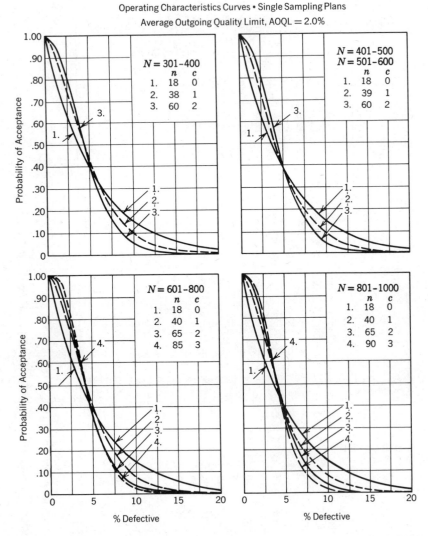

Operating Characteristics Curves • Single Sampling Plans
Average Outgoing Quality Limit, AOQL = 2.0%

Figure 10.17. OC curves for Dodge-Romig plans. From H. F. Dodge and H. G. Romig (1959), *Sampling Inspection Tables*, Wiley, New York.

MIL-STD-105D is a result of numerous revisions dating back to 1943, when the first Army Ordnance sampling tables were developed. Various sampling plans were subsequently constructed by the Navy and the Army Service Forces. After the unification of the armed services, a standard set of sampling plans (JAN-STD-105) was adopted by the Department of Defense. This standard was replaced by MIL-STD-105A in 1950. Two later revisions, 105B (1958) and 105C (1961), have now been supplanted by 105D (April, 1963). Military Standard MIL-STD-105D was developed by a working group representing the military services of Canada, the United Kingdom, and the United States of America with the assistance and cooperation of American and European organizations for quality control. The international designation for this document is ABC-STD-105.

The 105D standard consists of single, double and multiple sampling plans for various inspection levels and code letters. The *inspection level* identifies the lot size, the *code letter* the sample size. A sampling plan is obtained by using the average quality level (AQL) and the code letter to enter the tables. Thus, the plans are indexed by AQL. Tables and charts give average outgoing quality limit (AOQL), average sample size, and limiting quality (LQ) values for all plans. The LQ designation corresponds to the LTFD notation used previously in this chapter.

MIL-STD-105D is a sampling system that specifically links together three sets of sampling plans for accomplishing a balance between a protection against a run of unsatisfactory quality and savings of inspection effort during periods of satisfactory quality. That is, all plans are indexed according to *normal, tightened,* or *reduced* inspection provisions (together with rules for switching from one state to another). Normal sampling plans are used when the process average fraction-defective remains within satisfactory limits. Tightened plans are prescribed when the process average quality deteriorates. Under a switch to a tightened plan, sample size is unchanged but the acceptance number is reduced. This decreases the consumer's risk β at the expense of increasing producer's risk α (i.e., economic pressure is put on the producer). If the process average quality continues to be consistently good (or, in fact, improves), a switch can be made to a reduced sampling plan. This decreases sample size (reducing inspection costs) resulting in an increased β-value and a slight decrease of α.

The 105D standard is relative simple to apply. However, for those interested in a more thorough study of sampling inspection under this standard, a companion document is available—Department of Defense Handbook H 53.[13] A mathematical evaluation of the 105D standard is described by Larson and Stevens.[14] An excellent mathematical treatment of sampling inspection plan criteria is given by Dodge and Romig.[15]

[13] DoD Handbook H 53 (June, 1965), *Guide for Sampling Inspection,* Information Officer, Department of Defense, Pentagon Building, Washington, D.C.

[14] Larson, K. E. and Stephens, K. S. (January, 1967), "An Evaluation of the MIL-STD-105D System of Sampling Plans," *Industrial Quality Control,* Vol. 23, No. 7, pp. 310-319.

[15] Dodge and Ronnig, *op. cit.,* p. 000.

SUMMARY

There are two general types of inspection: (1) 100% inspection, and (2) sampling inspection. A *100% inspection* refers to the evaluation of all N items of a manufacturing lot composed of N product items. This inspection is also called *sorting, detailing, screening,* or *rectifying inspection*. When a product lot undergoes a *sampling inspection*, the lot is accepted or rejected, depending on the number of defectives found in a small sample of n product items randomly selected from the lot. Usually, lots rejected by sampling inspection are 100% inspected.

Sampling plans are constructed by computing probabilities of acceptance for various combinations of process average quality levels, sample sizes, and acceptance numbers. These probabilities are given by elementary combinatorial computations and certain distribution function models—mainly the binomial, Poisson, and normal distributions. A basic decision-making aid in selecting a sampling plan is an *operating characteristic curve* (*OC curve*), which gives the probability of acceptance for various fraction-defective quality levels of product submitted for inspection.

Various criteria are used to select appropriate sampling plans for given process and inspection conditions. One selection procedure is to choose a plan whose OC curve passes through two points corresponding to an *acceptable quality level* (AQL) and a *lot tolerance fraction-defective level* (LTFD). The probability of acceptance for AQL quality is $1 - \alpha$, where α is called *producer's risk*. The probability of acceptance of LTFD quality is β which is called *consumer's risk*. Other common criteria are *average outgoing quality* (AOQ) and *average outgoing quality limit* (AOQL).

Two basic sampling plan types are *attributes* plan and *variables* plans. Variables plans give equivalent quality protection with smaller samples than that required for attributes plans. Double and multiple plans possess the same advantage over single plans. A number of standard sampling inspection plans and tables are available. Two principle standards summarized in this chapter are the Dodge-Romig tables and Military Standard MIL-STD-105D.

REFERENCES

Bowker, A. H. and Lieberman, G. J. (1959), *Engineering Statistics,* Prentice-Hall, Engelwood Cliffs, N.J.

Burr, I. W. (1953), *Engineering Statistics and Quality Control,* McGraw-Hill, New York.

DoD Handbook H 53 (June, 1965), *Guide for Sampling Inspection,* Information Officer, Department of Defense, Pentagon Building, Washington, D.C.

Dodge, H. F., and Romig, H. G. (1959), *Sampling Inspection Tables,* Wiley, New York.

Ellner, H. and Savage, I. R. (June, 1957), *Sampling for Destructive or Expensive Testing by Attributes,* Army Science Conference, West Point, N.Y.

Fetter, R. B. (1967), *The Quality Control System,* Richard D. Irwin, Homewood, Ill.

Hansen, B. L. (1963), *Quality Control,* Prentice-Hall, Engelwood Cliffs, N.J.

Larson, K. E. and Stephens, K. S. (January, 1967), "An Evaluation of the MIL-STD-105D System of Sampling Plans," *Industrial Quality Control,* Vol. 23, No. 7, pp. 310-319.

Mandelson, J. (November, 1946), "Estimation of Optimum Sample Size in Destructive Testing by Attributes," *Industrial Quality Control,* Vol. 3, No. 3, pp. 24-26.

Mandelson, J. (March, 1967), "Sampling Plans for Destructive or Expensive Testing," *Industrial Quality Control,* Vol. 23, No. 9, pp. 440-450.

Martin, C. A. (September, 1964), "The Cost Breakeven Point in Attribute Sampling," *Industrial Quality Control,* Vol. 21, No. 3, pp. 137-143.

Military Standard MIL-STD-105D (April, 1963), *Sampling Procedures and Tables for Inspection by Attributes,* Superintendent of Documents, U.S. Government Printing Office, Washington, D.C.

Military Standard MIL-STD-414 (June, 1957), *Sampling Procedures and Tables for Inspection by Variables for Per Cent Defective,* Superintendent of Documents, U.S. Government Printing Office, Washington, D.C.

Smith, B. E. (July, 1961), *Some Economic Aspects of Quality Control,* Technical Report No. 53, Applied Mathematics and Statistics Laboratories, Stanford University, Stanford, Calif.

REVIEW QUESTIONS

1. State four common manufacturing names for a 100% inspection operation.

2. What are the two alternatives to a 100% inspection operation?

3. Define the term sampling inspection plan.

4. The hypergeometric distribution function is a function of the independent variable x and parameters N, n, p, and q. (a) What does this distribution function describe? (b) For what sampling situation is this distribution function appropriate?

5. Two important distribution function models for sampling inspection are the binomial and Poisson distribution functions. (a) What do these two distribution functions describe? (b) For what sampling situations are these distribution functions appropriate?

6. State the condition for using the binomial model to obtain the approximate probability of acceptance of a product lot of specified fraction-defective quality for a specified sampling inspection plan.

7. State two conditions for replacing the binomial model in question 6 with the Poisson model.

261

8. State two conditions for replacing the binomial model in question 6 with the normal distribution function model.

9. Two commonly used criteria for indexing sampling inspection plans are AQL and LTFD. Define each criterion.

10. Specifying α, β, AQL, and LTFD determines two points on the OC curve. Also, two other points corresponding to maximum and minimum P_a-values are always known. State the coordinates (p, P_a) of the four points.

11. What is the principal advantage of the double sampling inspection plan over a single plan? State three disadvantages of a double sampling plan.

12. Summarize the advantages and disadvantages of variables sampling inspection plans.

13. State the cost factors that contribute to the total real cost of sampling inspection.

14. A Type I decision error is the rejection of an acceptable lot by the sampling plan. How is the cost of a Type I error evaluated, if the inspection operation is nondestructive and its cost is reasonably low?

15. A Type II decision error is the acceptance of a non-acceptable lot by the sampling plan. State the two general cases for evaluating the cost of this decision error and discuss for each case the problem of evaluating the cost.

16. Identify what is being measured by each term of the following equation:

$$TC = n\ (C_u + C_i) + (N - n)\ (\alpha)\ (C_u - V_s)$$

Briefly describe how total sampling inspection cost is minimized under Mandelson's simplified model.

17. What is the primary objective of the Dodge and Romig Sampling Inspection Tables?

18. Briefly describe the purpose of the MIL-STD-105D sampling inspection system.

PROBLEMS

1. Set up (do not compute) the indicated combinatorial operations for computing the probability of acceptance P_a of a 5% defective product lot under the following sampling plans: (a) $N = 100$, $n = 10$, and $c = 0$, and (b) $N = 500$, $n = 75$, and $c = 1$.

2. Assume in problem 1b that N is very large. Using the binomial distribution function model, set up the indicated computation for P_a.

3. As an exercise only, replace the binomial model in problem 2 with the Poisson model and set up the indicated computation for P_a. Read the numerical value for P_a from the Table, Appendix C.

4. Unit inspection cost is \$0.30. Unit failure cost due to an undetected defective is \$40. Sketch the theoretically ideal OC curve for this quality situation.

5. As an exercise in relating α, β, AQL, and LTFD, assume that an OC curve is described by the simple function $P_a = -p + 1.0$. Compute producer's risk and consumers' risk corresponding to p-values of 0.10 and 0.60 respectively. Sketch the OC curve and identify the principal points of the curve.

6. Specifications for a sampling inspection plan are AQL quality, $p_1 = 0.01$, LTFD quality, $p_2 = 0.06$, $\alpha = 0.05$, and $\beta = 0.10$. (a) Using the Poisson Table, Appendix C, determine $p_1 n$, $p_2 n$, and p_2/p_1 values corresponding to $c = 1$, 2, 3, and 4. (b) Between what two c-values does the desired plan exist? (c) Holding $\beta = 0.10$ and $c = 2$, reading α and pn from the table, determine the corresponding sampling plan. (d) Also, try the following combinations holding $\beta = 0.10$ and $c = 3$, $\alpha = 0.05$ and $c = 2$, $\alpha = 0.05$ and $c = 3$.

7. Lot size N is 10,000, sample size n is 200, and acceptance number c is 3 for a given sampling inspection plan. The OC curve indicates a probability of acceptance $P_a = 0.86$ for an expected fraction defective $p = 0.01$. Compute the average outgoing quality (AOQ).

8. A double sampling inspection plan is defined by $n_1 = 35$, $c_1 = 0$ and $n_2 = 60$, $c_2 = 3$. Using the Poisson Table, Appendix C, compute the probability of acceptance for a 1% defective product lot. Assume lot size N to be very large.

9. Regarding problem 8, if lot size N is not very large, the respective probabilities of defectives on the second sample are not correct. If $N = 500$, what is the probability of 0, 1, or 2 defectives on the second sample, given that 1 defective occurs on the first sample?

10. A quality characteristic is defined by the specification 0.750 ± 0.005 in. Process capability indicates σ_x to be equal to 0.001 in. for the manufacturing operation. Design a variables sampling inspection plan for the following conditions. AQL quality is $p_1 = 0.01$ with a probability of acceptance $P_a = 0.95$. LTFD quality is $p_2 = 0.025$ with $P_a = 0.10$.

11. Using the Poisson Table, Appendix C, determine an attributes sampling plan corresponding to the variables plan of problem 10 and compare sample sizes for the two plans.

11

Inspection and Gaging

Cost is a prime criterion at every level of the quality system. Quality-planning operations are initiated by consumer quality requirements. A basic consumer consideration is cost. Quality-control operations are directed and implemented from a cost-criterion basis. Economic decisions underlie the development of specification tolerances, control procedures, and inspection plans.

Since economics is the core of the quality-decision process, serious consideration should be given to the accuracy of the input to cost models and cost computations. An important input factor is accuracy of measurement of quality characteristics. For example, consider a process-capability value, $6\sigma_x$ being equal to 0.005 in. What proportion of the 0.005 in. is attributable only to process variation, and what proportion to measurement error? A mean sample measurement is 0.507 in. and the corresponding point on the $\bar{x}$-chart indicates an out-of-control condition. Perhaps the sample mean is truly 0.504 in. and the process is in control. Measurement error has generated a decision error. In Chapter 7, overlapping specification tolerances are carefully computed from a λ-risk basis, where λ is dependent on certain production costs. However, the true λ-value can be considerably larger than the λ-value assumed in the tolerance computations, if a significant measurement error is involved in the inspection of component parts. In Chapter 10, sampling plans (n,c) are developed from an economic basis. Suppose, for example, that c is 3 and a sample contains 4 defectives. The lot should be rejected. Yet, the inspector may, because of measurement error, identify only 2 defectives and the lot is accepted.

In many production situations, specification requirements for modern products are so restrictive that measurement error becomes the most serious problem facing the quality-control and inspection staff. This is particularly true in many mechanical industries and especially true in the aerospace industry. In these cases, two elements of the quality subsystem S_2 (see Figure 2.4) become critical quality determinants. These elements are (1) tool and gage control, and (2) inspection and test.

In the following sections, measurement factors and gaging principles are abstracted by means of selected examples. The purpose is not to develop detailed knowledge in the field of metrology, but to expose measurement and control factors relevant to the quality problem and integrate these into the quality system. For the benefit of the student with a particular interest in the details of gaging hardware and inspection procedures, a selected list of textbooks is given in the references.

THE MEASUREMENT PROBLEM

Modern tolerancing systems recognize four basic product conditions to be controlled by tolerance specifications: (1) size, (2) form, (3) location, and (4) conditions of assembly, operation, or function (see Figure 4.1). In practice, these conditions interrelate to define quality characteristics and the problem of measuring quality characteristics to evaluate conformance to specifications becomes complex.

A physical factor, which makes it difficult to define and control product quality characteristics, is lack of true geometric perfection. Shapes into which material is to be fabricated are defined by geometric terms. The geometric definition assumes a perfect form. However, perfect forms cannot be produced. Thus, variations from perfect form

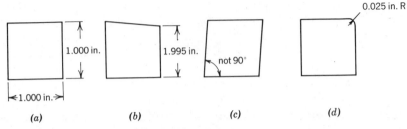

Figure 11.1. Macro errors.

must be defined and controlled if a specific quality is to be maintained. These geometric variations are called *macro* errors. Figure 11.1 indicates a simplified example. A perfect form is defined by the specified one-inch square in (a). Possible departures from perfect form are (b) nonparallelism, (c) not square, and (d) rounded corners.

When material is fabricated by a machining operation, certain surface texture variations are developed by the cutting tools used. That is, the surface is not perfectly flat. Surface texture variations are called *micro* errors. The basic definitional elements of surface texture variation are roughness, waviness, and lay. These elements are illustrated in Figure 11.2. The specification values are in microinch units (a microinch is 0.000001 in.). Figure 11.3 is an example of a surface profile reading using a common surface-texture measuring instrument.

Closely related to the problem of lack of true geometric form is lack of perfect rigidity. Production materials expand, stretch, spring,

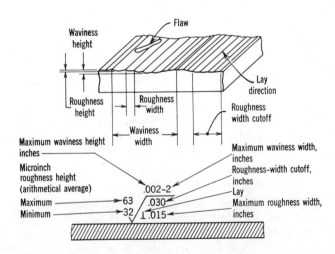

Figure 11.2. Surface texture elements and measures of variation. From ASA B46.1 (1962), *Surface Texture*, American Standards Association, 10 East 40 St., New York.

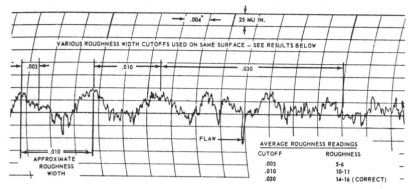

Figure 11.3. A surface texture reading. From P. W. Burrows (June, 1968), "Surface Texture Evaluation," *Quality Assurance*, Vol. 7, No. 6, p. 33.

warp, and bruise. Departures from perfect rigidity affect geometric form, size, and location conditions.

The interrelationships of size, form, and location conditions required to define quality characteristics, coupled with production variations due to geometric form and rigidity errors, lead to a variety of complex measurement problems involving sophisticated gaging methods. Figure 11.4 summarizes these product conditions and error factors.

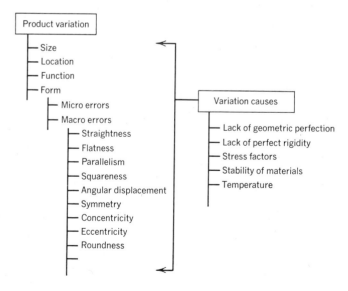

Figure 11.4. Product variation and variation sources.

267

A detailed discussion of this measurement-problem area is not given in this textbook. However, it should be clear that even for a simple size condition, the size may not be uniquely defined (e.g. what is the diameter size of a cylindrical part which is out-of-round?). In the following sections, some measurement principles are developed restricting examples to simple size conditions.

MEASUREMENT STANDARDS

In 1875, a length standard was established by the International Bureau of Weights and Measures at Sevres, France. The standard is a platinum-iridium bar with three microscopic lines engraved at each end. The distance between the central lines in each group of three lines defines the International Prototype Meter. Thirty-one meter-bar duplicates were constructed and distributed to the principal nations as standards. The United States received Meters No. 21 and 27, which have been retained as standards by the National Bureau of Standards.

A secondary definition of the meter was adopted in 1927. Under this definition, the meter is expressed in terms of the number of cadmium red light wavelengths (1,553,164.13) corresponding to the Prototype Meter, for specified conditions of temperature, humidity, and atmospheric pressure. In 1960, this standard was revised and is now expressed as 1,650,763.73 times the wavelength in vacuo of the orange-red radiation, corresponding to the transition between the energy levels $2p_{10}$ and $5d_5$ of the krypton 86 atom. Relative to this standard, the U.S.A. inch is 25.400051 millimeters.

Gage Blocks

Transfer of a length standard from the National Bureau of Standards to a manufacturing plant is accomplished by means of gage blocks. A *gage block* is a reference piece, either square or round in cross section, with two end faces which are the measurement surfaces. That is, the end faces are flat parallel surfaces whose separation has been established to light wave precision and accuracy. Figure 11.5 shows four gage blocks, whose reference sizes are 0.050, 0.350, 0.800, and 4.000 in., respectively.

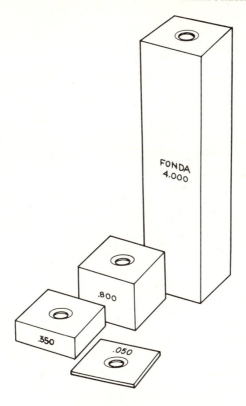

Figure 11.5.   Gage blocks.

Gage blocks are made from SAE 52100 alloy steel, tungsten carbide stainless steel, chrome-plated steel, and chromium carbide. A U.S. government accuracy standard for gage blocks lists the following grades:

AA-*Laboratory*, which are designed for use as laboratory working standards for calibrating other gage blocks or gages.
A-*Inspection*, assigned for the inspection of tool and shop projects.
B-*Work*, for laying out and setting up high-accuracy process operations.

Grade AA blocks must be accurate to ±2 μin. from nominal size, flatness, and parallelism. Grade A blocks must be accurate to +6, −2 μin., and Grade B blocks are limited to +10, −6 μin. The most important criteria for judging gage block integrity is its degree of flatness and parallelism since these factors bear directly on one's

269

ability to measure its length reliably. For every calibration there is some uncertainty in measurement. At the National Bureau of Standards, for AA certification, this uncertainty is estimated to be ± 2 μin. for sizes to 2 in., and ± 3 and ± 4 μin., respectively, for the 3 in. and 4 in. sizes.

Gage block sets are available in a wide variety of sizes, depending on measurement requirements. Figure 11.6 shows a standard 83-piece set of blocks. Accessories make it possible to use the blocks for production measurements and thus eliminate a possible source of error from an intermediate gage calibrated by the blocks. However, the primary purpose and use of gage blocks is to calibrate other gages used in the manufacturing plant. For example, the entire plant's production performance depends on the master set of gage blocks for that plant.

Figure 11.7 illustrates the assembly of gage blocks to calibrate another gage. A product specification is 2.4822 $\pm$ 0.0005 in. A gage-block stack is required to calibrate the gage at the lower product limit, 2.4817 in. Blocks are selected as shown, starting with the smallest

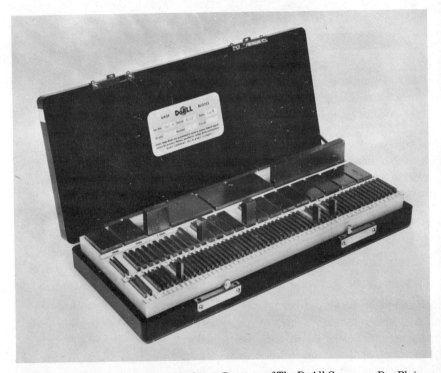

Figure 11.6. Example of a gage block set. Courtesy of The DoAll Company, Des Plaines, Ill.

COMBINING GAGE BLOCKS

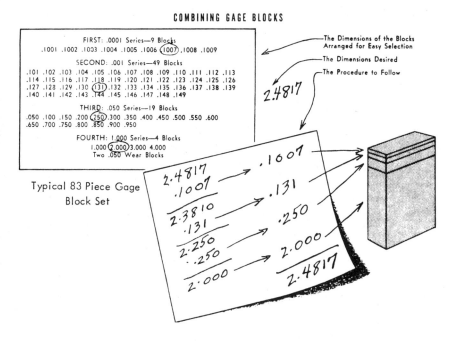

Typical 83 Piece Gage Block Set

Figure 11.7. Combining gage blocks. From T. Bush (1964), *Fundamentals of Dimensional Metrology*, Delman Publishers, Albany, N. Y., p. 163.

block first and proceeding in a manner which eliminates digits from the right.

A great deal of manual skill is involved in the assembly of gage blocks. Blocks must be very clean and they must be assembled in a way that eliminates air or grease space between adjacent blocks. Blocks with good geometry and surface finish usually have an interval space of $\frac{1}{3}$ to $\frac{1}{5}$ μin. Thus, in a stack of 4 blocks, which has 3 intervals, total interval length generates an error of approximately 1 μin.

Calibration of Gage Blocks

Gage blocks are calibrated by independent metrology laboratories, gage block manufacturers, and the National Bureau of Standards. Calibration is done at the international standard measuring temperature of 68°F. (20°C.). When gage blocks are used to calibrate other gages, temperature is critical. A 1-in. steel gage block expands or contracts 6 μin. for every degree above or below the standard calibration temperature. If gage blocks and parts being measured are

271

of dissimilar materials and at temperatures other than 68°F., a measurement correction is given by

$$E = N(\Delta C)\ (\Delta T)$$

where E = measurement error in microinches

N = nominal dimension in inches

ΔC = difference of expansion coefficients in inches

ΔT = deviation of temperature from 68°F.

Table 11.1 indicates typical coefficients of expansion in microinches per inch of length per degree F.

Table 11.1 **Typical coefficients of expansion in μin. units.**

Hardened tool steel	6.4
Stainless steel (410)	5.5
Chrome carbide	4.5
Tungsten carbide	3.6
Aluminum	12.8
Copper	9.4

Example

A 4-in. hardened tool-steel part is being compared with a 4-in. stack of tungsten carbide gage blocks. Assume the steel part and gage block stack to be identical within microinch accuracy. Ambient temperature is 85°F.

$$E = 4(6.4\text{-}3.6)(17)$$
$$= 190.4\ \mu\text{in.}$$

The steel part measures 190.4 μin. larger than the gage block stack. If the degree of required accuracy is of the order of ten-thousandths of an inch, the error is significant. The error is approximately 0.0002 in.

Calibration by means of a wavelength standard is called *interferometry*. Whereas master or laboratory-grade gage blocks are calibrated at metrology laboratories, inspection or working gage blocks may be calibrated by in-plant interferometry methods. Figure 11.8 shows a "poor man's interferometer," a shop-type device which is accurate, but relatively crude when compared to metrology-laboratory

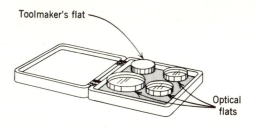

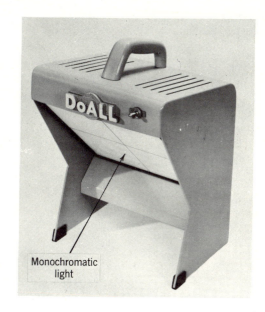

Figure 11.8. Shop interferometer set. Courtesy of The DoAll Company, Des Plaines, Ill.

techniques. This interferometer set consists of a helium monochromatic light source, a toolmaker's flat, and several optical flats. The toolmaker's flat is a steel piece that has two opposite polished reference surfaces. The optical flats are finely finished, distortion-free glass or quartz pieces.

Figure 11.9 illustrates a setup for checking a working gage block against a master gage block. Rays of monochromatic helium light passing through the optical flat are, in effect, split in two. One portion is reflected to the eye from the lower surface of the optical flat, the other passes on to the surface of the gage block and is reflected back toward the observer. When reflected portions cross each other, interference produces dark bands wherever the distance between the reflecting surfaces is one-half wavelength or a multiple thereof (see Figure 11.10). Since the wavelength of helium monochromatic light is 23.2 μin., each interference band corresponds to a difference in elevation of 11.6 μin. as shown in Figure 11.10.

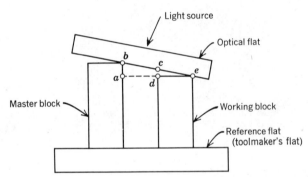

Figure 11.9.   Comparison of a working gage block with a master gage block.

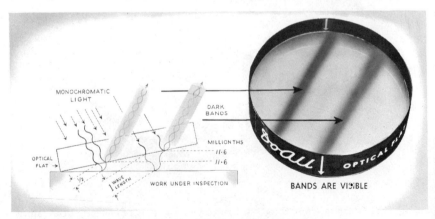

Figure 11.10.   Interferometry principle.

Example

Three interference bands appear above the working block (Figure 11.9). The distance cd is given by

$$cd = 3(11.6) = 34.8 \ \mu\text{in.}$$

Distance de is 1.000 in., and ae is 1.500 in. Similar triangles yield the proportion

$$\frac{ab}{cd} = \frac{ae}{de}$$

whence

$$ab = (ae)(cd)$$

$$= (2.5)(34.8)$$

$$= 87 \ \mu\text{in.}$$

The working block is 87 μin. smaller than the master block.

SOME COMMON GAGES

Most size-gaging devices operate by contacting the quality characteristic and translating the size of the characteristic to a calibrated scale for a measurement reading (principal exceptions are air and optical gages). The schematic diagram of Figure 11.11 illustrates this gaging method. The quality characteristic is the length q. Two gaging surfaces r and m contact the plane surfaces defining q and by some means translate q to a scale indicating the value of q. Gaging-surface r, called the *reference point*, is fixed. Gaging-surface m, called the *measuring point*, is movable. A basic gage-design problem is to (1) translate small displacements of m to indicator displacements along the scale, and (2) amplify displacements of m to much larger displacements along the scale.

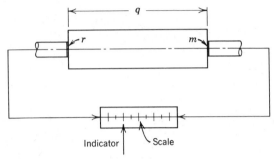

Figure 11.11. Gage elements.

Micrometer Gaging Devices

In 1638, William Gascoigne constructed a pair of vertical indicators on a microscope, demonstrating for the first time the micrometer principle. Many modern gaging devices are based on this principle. A simple micrometer is shown in Figure 11.12. The anvil face is the reference point, the spindle face the measuring point. An accurate screw (40 threads per inch) revolving in a fixed nut varies the distance between the anvil and spindle faces. One thimble revolution turns the screw one revolution, thus varying the distance between the reference and measuring points by 0.025 in. Dividing the thimble scale into 25 parts makes possible readings to 0.001 in. That is, $\frac{1}{25}$ revolution displaces the measuring point 0.001 in. A vernier scale on the barrel makes possible a division of 0.001 in. into 10 parts, each equal to 0.0001 in. Figure 11.13 illustrates the procedure for reading the micrometer scales.

Several measurement principles are illustrated by the micrometer. *Amplification* of gage measuring point displacement is obtained mechanically by means of the lead-screw mechanism. Various amplification methods are used in gage design—mechanical, electronic, optical, pneumatic, and fluid. A number of error sources exist relative to the use of a micrometer. For example, Figure 11.14 indicates a diameter measurement that is undersize from the true value. This is called a *geometry error*. Generally, the line joining the gage's reference and measuring points should be perpendicular to the product surfaces being contacted; the reference point is fixed and the measuring point explores for a maximum reading for exterior contours (minimum reading for interior contours).

Another error source is *gaging pressure*, which refers to how tight the measuring point (e.g., spindle face of the micrometer) is adjusted against the product surface when a measurement is being made. Gaging pressure is a source of error in all gages and various means

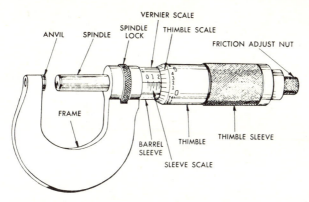

Figure 11.12. A common micrometer. From "Quality Assurance" (1963), *Tools of Metrology*, Hitchcock Publishing Co., Wheaton, Ill.

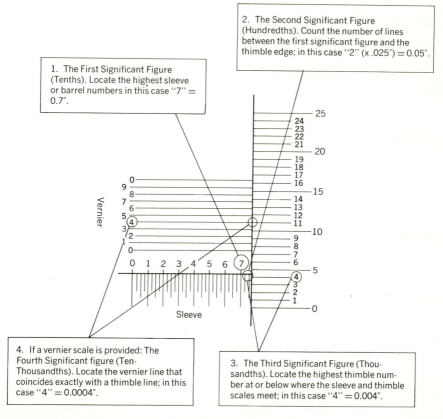

2. The Second Significant Figure (Hundredths). Count the number of lines between the first significant figure and the thimble edge; in this case "2" (x .025") = 0.05".

1. The First Significant Figure (Tenths). Locate the highest sleeve or barrel numbers in this case "7" = 0.7".

4. If a vernier scale is provided: The Fourth Significant figure (Ten-Thousandths). Locate the vernier line that coincides exactly with a thimble line; in this case "4" = 0.0004".

3. The Third Significant Figure (Thousandths). Locate the highest thimble number at or below where the sleeve and thimble scales meet; in this case "4" = 0.004".

Figure 11.13. Reading the micrometer scales. From "Quality Assurance" (1963), *Tools of Metrology*, Hitchcock Publishing Co., Wheaton, Ill.

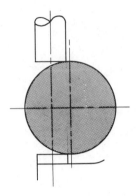

Figure 11.14.   Geometry error.

have been developed to equalize gaging pressure and minimize its error effect. Standard gaging pressure for a micrometer is 1 ounce/inch².[1] Many micrometers have spring-loaded ratchet devices for equalizing gaging pressure. The ratchet disengages at the standard pressure. These devices are helpful for apprentice process operators and inspectors but, in general, a good operator's sense of manual feel is more adequate for controlling gaging pressure. Torque momentum, friction of the micrometer screw, and mechanical variations in the ratchet generate error in the ratchet device itself.

All gages require periodic checks for accuracy. A micrometer calibration consists of (1) closing the spindle on the anvil and adjusting the zero scale reading, and (2) testing various micrometer readings against corresponding gage block standards.

Gage Operator Error

Gage operator error is a factor that becomes significant when (1) tolerances are small, and (2) the inspection operation is repetitive over a large volume of production parts. Human error seems to depend mainly on manual skill and fatigue. This error has been demonstrated experimentally many times. Figure 11.15 shows 100 micrometer readings of a steel strip thickness by the same inspector. The range of readings is 0.0012 in.

[1]*Torque* is the amount of "twist" on the thimble, generating *force* or "push" of the spindle face against the product surface. Force is in units of weight. *Pressure* is force acting on a specified area, such as pounds per square inch.

MICROMETER READINGS OF THICKNESS
SHOWING CHANCE VARIATION IN READING

Thickness in Inches	Number of Readings Secured
.0408	2
.0409	2
.0410	2
.0411	5
.0412	3
.0413	7
.0414	10
.0415	14
.0416	18
.0417	22
.0418	9
.0419	5
.0420	1
	100

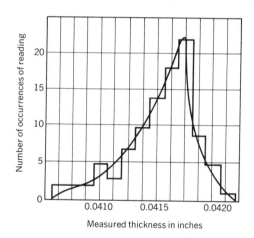

Figure 11.15. Distribution of micrometer readings of a test piece. From FG-4849, Bendix Automation and Measurement Division, Dayton, Ohio, p. 12.

Figure 11.16 gives the experimental results of Lawshe and Tiffin[2] for inspector accuracy, using a number of micrometer-type gages. The black percentage bars indicate the percent of inspectors whose measurements agreed with the expected accuracy of the gage, the white

[2]Lawshe, C. H. and Tiffin, J. (1945), "The Accuracy of Precision Instrument Measurement in Industrial Inspection," *Journal of Applied Psychology,* Vol. 29, pp. 413-419.

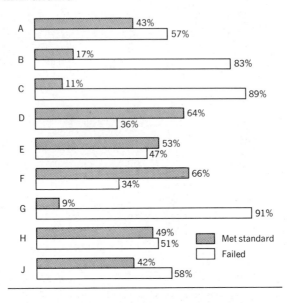

Figure 11.16. Inspector error using micrometer-type gages. From C. H. Lawshe and J. Tiffin (1945), "The Accuracy of Precision Instrument Measurement in Industrial Inspection, *Journal of Applied Psychology*, Vol. 29, pp. 413-419.

How inspectors fared on measuring tests in an aircraft propeller plant (From Lawshe and Tiffin):

Test	Task	Persons Tested
A	1-in. vernier micrometer, ±0.0001	172
B	2-in. vernier micrometer, ±0.0001	138
C	6-in. vernier micrometer, ±0.0001	131
D	3-in. regular micrometer, ±0.0001	146
E	Depth micrometer, ±0.001	142
F	Inside micrometer, ±0.001	117
G	Inside micrometer and 6-in. micrometer, ±0.002 in.	112
H	Outside caliper and 6-in. rule, $\pm\frac{1}{64}$	117
J	Inside vernier caliper, ±0.001 in.	113

bars the percent of inspectors who failed to attain this accuracy. For example, only 66% of the inspectors (see F) obtained readings within the expected discrimination of ±0.001 in. for an inside micrometer.

The solution of the problem of gage-operator error is, of course, to use a more sophisticated gage when small tolerances are involved. However, all gages are subject to some degree of gage-operator error. Table 11.2 gives an extensive classification of gage evaluations, using different criteria. The right two columns give expected gage discrimination taking into account expected gage-operator error. Column (a) refers to tool room and gage laboratory measurement, (b) to production measurement. Some of the precision-type gages listed here are briefly reviewed in the following sections.

Criteria for Selecting Gaging Equipment

Presentation of Table 11.2 requires a review, at this point, of certain terminology involved in inspection and gaging operations. To begin with, some distinction should be made between the terms accuracy, precision, and reliability—terms which are frequently misused.

Accuracy is a relative matter. It is a comparison of desired results with undesired results. Relative to gaging, accuracy refers to the ratio of correct to incorrect readings. It is frequently called the quality of conformity.

Precision is a measure of the variability of instrument readings. Precision can be expressed either in terms of the range or standard deviation of the distribution readings. The smaller the range or standard deviation, the higher is the precision of a gage. For example, in Figure 11.15 the precision can be expressed as 0.0012 in. The difference between accuracy and precision is illustrated by Figure 11.17.

Reliability means the probability of a reading occurring in a specified interval bisected by the true reading. The meaning of reliability corresponds to that of a confidence interval in statistics. Table 11.2 states the interval but not the probability, which is difficult to determine considering the varying gage-operator skills and environmental conditions under which the gage is used. It should be noted that the gage requirements implied by the three terms—accuracy, precision, and reliability—are not independent. For example, a change in a tolerance specification alters the accuracy requirement for the gage, and this in turn affects the precision and reliability requirements.

The term *designated precision* (see Table 11.2) is the gage manufacturer's identification. It should not be confused with accuracy and precision. For example, a one-ten-thousandth micrometer is not precise to 0.0001 in. *Discrimination* (see Table 11.2) is simply the value of the smallest graduation on the instrument scale. (The terms "linearity" and "sensitivity" used in Table 11.2 are defined in the following section.)

Some of the principal criteria for selecting gaging equipment are summarized here. *Amplification* (or magnification) is the ratio of the indicator displacement along the gage scale to the input dimensional displacement. If the scale indicator moves 2 in. to register a size

281

Table 11.2. Classification and comparison of measuring instruments

Instrument or Measurement	Type of Measurement	Normal Range	Designated Precision	Discrimination	Sensitivity	Linearity	Reliability* (a)	(b)
Rules, Tapes, Scaled Instruments								
Ordinary rulers	direct	12 in.	$\frac{1}{16}$ in.	$\frac{1}{16}$ in.	$\frac{1}{16}$ in.	$\frac{1}{16}$ in.	$\frac{1}{16}$ in.	never
Steel rules								
Decimal inch	direct	6,12,18,24 in.	0.02 in.	0.02 in.	0.02 in.	0.0003/in.	±0.02 in.	±0.04 in.
Fractional inch	direct	6,12,18,24 in.	$\frac{1}{64}$ in.	$\frac{1}{64}$ in.	$\frac{1}{64}$ in.	0.0003/in.	±$\frac{1}{64}$ in.	±$\frac{1}{32}$ in.
Steel tapes								
Decimal inch	direct	100 ft	0.10 in.	0.10 in.	0.10 in.	0.01 in.	±0.10 in.	±0.30 in.
Fractional inch	direct	100 ft	$\frac{1}{8}$ in.	$\frac{1}{8}$ in.	$\frac{1}{8}$ in.	0.01 in.	±$\frac{1}{8}$ in.	±$\frac{3}{8}$ in.
Depth gage								
Decimal inch	direct	5 in.	0.02 in.	0.02 in.	0.02 in.	0.0003/in.	±0.02 in.	±0.04 in.
Fractional inch	direct	5 in.	$\frac{1}{64}$ in.	$\frac{1}{64}$ in.	$\frac{1}{64}$ in.	0.0003/in.	±$\frac{1}{64}$ in.	±$\frac{1}{32}$ in.
Combination sets								
Decimal inch	direct	12 in.	0.02 in.	0.02 in.	0.02 in.	0.0003/in.	±0.02 in.	±0.04 in.
Fractional inch	direct	12 in.	$\frac{1}{64}$ in.	$\frac{1}{64}$ in.	$\frac{1}{64}$ in.	0.0003/in.	±$\frac{1}{64}$ in.	±$\frac{1}{32}$ in.
Calipers								
Decimal inch	transfer	6 in.	none	none	0.005 in.	none	±0.02 in.	±0.08 in.
Fractional inch	transfer	6 in.	none	none	0.005 in.	none	±$\frac{1}{64}$ in.	±$\frac{1}{16}$ in.
Slide calipers								
Decimal inch	direct	3 in.	0.02 in.	0.02 in.	0.02 in.	0.003/in.	±0.02 in.	±0.04 in.
Fractional inch	direct	3 in.	$\frac{1}{64}$ in.	$\frac{1}{64}$ in.	$\frac{1}{64}$ in.	0.003/in.	±$\frac{1}{64}$ in.	±$\frac{1}{32}$ in.
Vernier Instruments								
Vernier caliper	direct	24 in.	0.001 in.	0.001 in.	0.001 in.	0.0003/in.	±0.002 in.	±0.010 in.
Vernier depth gage	direct	12 in.	0.001 in.	0.001 in.	0.002 in.	0.0003/in.	±0.003 in.	±0.020 in.
Vernier height gage	direct	24 in.	0.001 in.	0.001 in.	0.001 in.	0.0003/in.	±0.002 in.	±0.008 in.
Micrometers								
Micrometer, bench	direct	1 in.	0.0001 in.	0.0001 in.	0.0001 in.	0.0001 in.	±0.0001 in.	±0.0005 in.
Micrometers, with verniers and ratchets 1 and 2 in.	direct	to size	0.0001 in.	0.0001 in.	0.0001 in.	0.0002 in.	±0.0001 in.	±0.001 in.
Micrometers, plain to 6 in.	direct	to size	0.001 in.	0.001 in.	0.0005 in.	0.0002 in.	±0.001 in.	±0.005 in.
6 to 12 in.	direct	to size	0.001 in.	0.001 in.	0.001 in.	0.0002 in.	±0.002 in.	±0.010 in.
over 12 in.	direct	to size	0.001 in.	0.001 in.	0.0001 in.	0.0002 in.	±0.005 in.	±0.015 in.

282

Instrument or Measurement	Type of Measurement	Normal Range	Designated Precision	Discrimination	Sensitivity	Linearity	Reliability* (a)	Reliability* (b)
Micrometers, inside	direct	to size	0.001 in.	0.001 in.	0.001 in.	0.0002 in.	±0.001 in.	±0.005 in.
Micrometers, depth	direct	to size	0.001 in.	0.001 in.	0.001 in.	0.0002 in.	±0.001 in.	±0.005 in.
Small hole gages	transfer	$\frac{1}{8}$ to $\frac{1}{2}$ in.	none	none	0.001 in.	none	±0.001 in.	±0.004 in.
Telescope gages	transfer	$\frac{1}{2}$ to 6 in.	none	none	0.002 in.	none	±0.002 in.	±0.005 in.
Gage Blocks								
Gage blocks, A grade								
0.0001 in. series	end stand.	0.1000 to 4.0000	+0.000006 −0.000002	0.0001	not applic.	0.000008/in.	0.000010	0.0001
0.000025 in. series	end stand.	0.1000 to 4.0000	+0.000006 −0.000002	0.000025	not applic.	0.000008/in.	0.000010	0.0001
long blocks	end stand.	4.0000 to 24.0000	+0.000006 −0.000002	0.0001	not applic.	0.000008/in.	0.00010	0.001
0.0001 in. series with holders	end stand.	0.1000 to 4.0000	+0.000006 −0.000002	0.0001	not applic.	0.000008/in.	0.000010	0.00005
long blocks with holders	end stand.	4.0000 to 24.0000	+0.000006 −0.000002	0.0001	not applic.	0.000008/in.	0.00005	0.0005
Precalibrated Indicators								
0.001 dial indicator	comparison	0.1000 to 6.0000	0.001	0.001	0.0001	limited by indicator	0.001	0.001
0.0001 dial indicator	comparison	0.1000 to 6.0000	0.0001	0.0001	0.00005	limited by indicator	0.0001	0.0002
0.00005 mech. dial indicator	comparison	0.1000 to 6.0000	0.00005	0.00005	0.00002	limited by indicator	0.00007	0.0001
Precalibrated Indicators (continued)								
0.00001 elect. dial indicator	comparison	0.1000 to 6.0000	0.00001	0.00001	0.000005	limited by indicator	0.00002	0.00008
0.000001 elect. dial indicator	comparison	0.1000 to 6.0000	0.000001	0.000001	0.000001	limited by indicator	0.00001	0.0001
Dial Indicators								
Test indicators	comparison	0.030 in.	0.001 in.	0.001 in.	0.0005 in.	2%	Not for measurement	

283

Table 11.2 (Continued)

Instrument or Measurement	Type of Measurement	Normal Range	Designated Precision	Discrimination	Sensitivity	Linearity	Reliability* (a)	Reliability* (b)
0.001 indicators								
on height gage stands	comparison	0.250 in.	0.001 in.	0.001 in.	0.0005 in.	2%	0.001 in.	0.010 in.
on comparator stands	comparison	0.250 in.	0.001 in.	0.001 in.	0.0005 in.	2%	0.0005 in.	0.005 in.
0.0001 indicators								
on height gage stands	comparison	0.050 in.	0.0001 in.	0.0001 in.	0.0001 in.	2%	0.0001 in.	0.001 in.
on comparator stands	comparison	0.050 in.	0.0001 in.	0.0001 in.	0.00005 in.	2%	0.00005 in.	0.0005 in.
0.00005 indicators								
on height gage stands	comparison	0.010 in.	0.00005 in.	0.00005 in.	0.0001 in.	2%	0.0001 in.	0.001 in.
on comparator stands	comparison	0.010 in.	0.00005 in.	0.00005 in.	0.00005 in.	2%	0.00003 in.	0.0003 in.
High Amplification Comparators								
Mechanical (5000X)	comparison	0.001 in.	0.000025 in.	0.000025 in.	0.00001 in.	2%	±0.00002 in.	±0.00025 in.
Electronic								
0.0001 scale	comparison	±0.0024 in.	0.0001 in.	0.0001 in.	0.00005 in.	2%	±0.00005 in.	±0.0001 in.
0.00005 scale	comparison	±0.0016 in.	0.00005 in.	0.00005 in.	0.00002 in.	2%	±0.00004 in.	±0.0005 in.
0.00001 scale	comparison	±0.00024 in.	0.00001 in.	0.00001 in.	0.000005 in.	2%	±0.000008 in.	±0.00001 in.
Pneumatic Comparators								
Back pressure, dial type air gages								
62½X Type 3†	comparison	0.060 in.	0.002 in.	0.002 in.	0.0004 in.	0.001 in.	0.005 in.	0.010 in.
7500X Type 2 or 3	comparison	0.005	0.0005	0.00002	0.00002	0.003 in.	0.0001	0.0003
Flow-rate, Type 2								
1000X	comparison	0.0075	0.0002	0.0002	0.00004	0.0001	0.001	0.003
40,000X	comparison	0.00022	0.000010	0.000005	0.000002	0.000005	0.00005	0.00015
100,000X	comparison	0.000090	0.000005	0.000002	0.000002	0.000002	0.00002	0.00005
Flow rate, Type 3								
62½X	comparison	0.080 in.	0.003	0.003	0.0005	0.0015	0.008	0.016
5000X	comparison	0.0018	0.0001	0.0001	0.00005	0.00005	0.0002	0.0006
Optical Flats								
Flatness	direct	0.0001 in.	1-10 mike	1-10 mike	1-10 mike	1-10 mike	1-3 mike	10 mike
Surface finish	direct	0.0001 in.	1-10 mike	1-10 mike	1-10 mike	1-10 mike	1-3 mike	10 mike
Length comparison	direct	0.0001 in.	1-10 mike	1-10 mike	1-10 mike	1-10 mike	3-5 mike	20 mike

Instrument or Measurement	Type of Measurement	Normal Range	Designated Precision	Discrimination	Sensitivity	Linearity	Reliability* (a)	Reliability* (b)
Squares†								
Combination square	comparison	none	none	not applic.	beyond accuracy	not applic.	30'	1°
Precision square	comparison	none	none	not applic.	beyond accuracy	not applic.	30"	1'
Surface plate square	comparison	none	none	not applic.	beyond accuracy	not applic.	10"	30"
Cylindrical square	comparison	none	none	not applic.	beyond accuracy	not applic.	5"	30"
Graduated cylindrical square	comparison	0 to 0.0012 in.	0.0001 in. in 6 in.	0.0002 in. in 6 in.	beyond accuracy	50 mike within 6 in.	0.0002 in. in 6 in.	0.0004 in. in 6 in.
Square and transfer stand		All factors limited by metrological data of transfer instruments.						
Mechanics' level	direct	6°	1°	1°	30'	30'	1°	2°
Precision level	direct	1'20"	10"	10"	5"	5"	10"	30"
Clinometer (average)	direct	0° to 360°	10"	10"	2"	2"	5"	15"

*(a) Practical tolerance for skilled measurement. (b) Practical manufacturing tolerance.
†Types 2 and 3 refer to gaging elements.
‡Angular measurements.

From Busch, T. (January 1965), "Classification of Measuring Instruments," *The Tool and Manufacturing Engineer*, Vol. 64, No. 1, pp. 53–55.

Measurements on One Unit of Product by Three Instruments

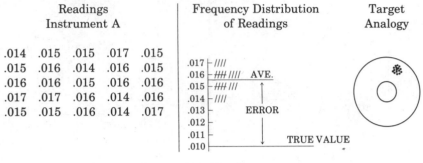

Readings Instrument A

.014	.015	.015	.017	.015
.015	.016	.014	.016	.015
.016	.016	.015	.016	.016
.017	.017	.016	.014	.016
.015	.015	.016	.014	.017

Frequency Distribution of Readings

Target Analogy

Precise, but Not Accurate

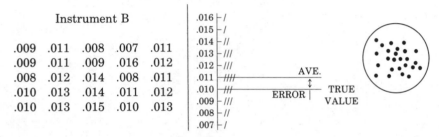

Instrument B

.009	.011	.008	.007	.011
.009	.011	.009	.016	.012
.008	.012	.014	.008	.011
.010	.013	.014	.011	.012
.010	.013	.015	.010	.013

Accurate, but Not Precise

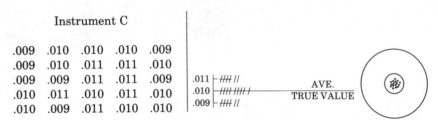

Instrument C

.009	.010	.010	.010	.009
.009	.010	.011	.011	.010
.009	.009	.011	.011	.009
.010	.011	.010	.011	.010
.010	.009	.011	.010	.010

Accurate and Precise

Figure 11.17. Distinction between accuracy and precision. From J. M. Juran (1962), *Quality Control Handbook*, McGraw-Hill, New York, p. 200.

change of 0.001 in., the gage's amplification is 2,000:1. *Discrimination* (or *resolution*) is the ability of the gage operator to visually separate scale divisions. Clearly, amplification facilitates discrimination and increases the precision of the gage. In selecting a gage for a given inspection job, a compromise is made between amplification and range of the indicator scale. For a fixed scale size, higher amplification decreases the range of the scale, and conversely.

286

Calibration accuracy (or *linearity*) describes how well readings at various points on the gage scale correspond to the true dimensions being measured. This refers to the full working range of the gage and is expressed either as a specific number or as percent of full scale.

Repeatability (repeat accuracy) refers to how closely the gage indicates the same reading over a series of trials using one or more test standards. One measure of a desirable degree of repeatability is that 99% of the readings (±3 standard deviations) in a large number of tests (100) should be within one-half a scale graduation. A negative measure is also used to describe repeatability. This is called *repeat error* (or *gage uncertainty*) and is expressed as a numerical quantity, such as "repeats within 20 millionths inch." To be meaningful, this figure should be specified at some level of assurance such as ± 3 standard deviations.

How well an instrument retains its calibration setting over a period of time is called stability (or drift). This is usually expressed as percent error in a given number of hours. This criterion is not absolute. That is, gage stability required to measure a large run of production parts would not be important when gaging just a few pieces.

Sensitivity is the smallest dimensional input to the gage that produces a readable change on the gage scale. This is usually expressed

Figure 11.18. Dial indicator gage. Courtesy of Federal Products Corporation, Providence, Rhode Island.

287

as a number, such as 20 millionths inch. Although high sensitivity is a desirable gage property, it can be wasted if the repeat accuracy is poor or if resolution is not adequate.

Amplification Methods

Mechanical gages amplify input dimensional displacement by some means of producing a mechanical advantage, such as a gear train or reed mechanism. Figure 11.18 shows a *dial-indicator* gage. Amplification is obtained by the ratio of the pinions and gears, and the length of the indicating pointer. Dial indicators are calibrated at zero indicator reading against a gage-block standard as shown in Figure 11.19. Product measurement is on a comparison basis, the indicator reading over- and undersize deviations from the gage-block standard. A typical dial indicator is usually not suitable for tolerances less than 0.0001 in. The gage repeatability is approximately 20% of this tolerance. Dial indicators are often mounted on a stand as shown in Figure 11.20. The principal advantage of a dial indicator is its versatility. Dial indicators can be mounted on fixtures to correspond to product geometries and thus simultaneously inspect many quality characteristics at one setting.

Another common mechanical means of obtaining amplification of dimensional input to the gage is the *reed mechanism* shown in Figure 11.21. A small displacement of the gage measuring-point causes the vertical reed structure r to flex, moving the indicator point in the path p. For a typical reed gage, a gage measuring-point displacement can be amplified into a movement along p equal to 20,000 times the

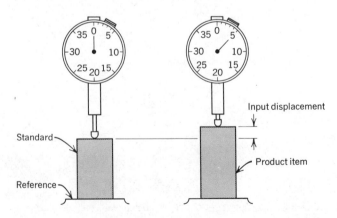

Figure 11.19.   Calibration and product measurement using a dial indicator gage.

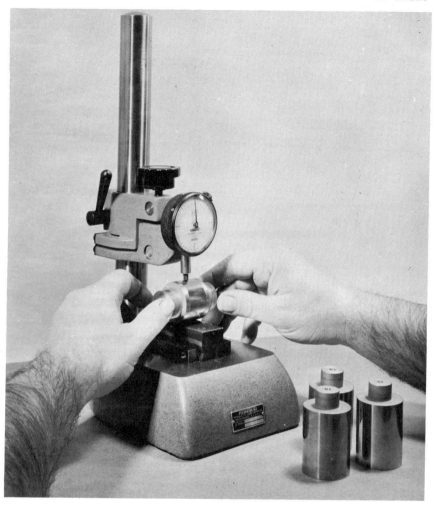

Figure 11.20.   Dial indicator mounted on a stand. Courtesy of Federal Products Corporation, Providence, Rhode Island.

input displacement. The indicating pointer can be used to indicate directly along a calibrated scale, or it can carry a bumper to close an electrical circuit to actuate colored signal lights (red for undersize, green for oversize). The pointer can also carry a target to incorporate an independent optical-amplification system. Like dial indicators, reed-type comparator gages are calibrated against gage block standards.

A reed-type comparator gage is shown in Figure 11.22. Gages of this type are sensitive, having very low internal friction and requiring

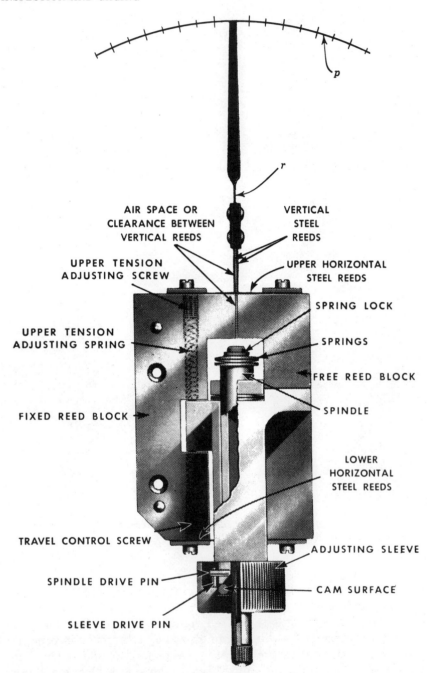

Figure 11.21. Courtesy of Bendix Automation and Measurement Division, Dayton, Ohio.

Figure 11.22. Courtesy of Bendix Automation and Measurement Division, Dayton, Ohio.

relatively low gaging force. Reed gages have a level of accuracy and repeatability appropriate to gage laboratory requirements. One design, which utilizes a twisted reed that rotates a pointer, achieves very high amplifications. At the 100,000:1 amplifications, the gage scale is graduated in $\frac{1}{2}$-millionth divisions. Precision is within $1\frac{1}{2}\%$ of full-scale range. Measuring range is small (40 millionths inch), but it increases proportionately at lower magnifications.

In electronic gaging systems, an input dimensional displacement at the gage measuring point produces an electrical output (e.g., voltage, current, resistance, reactance). Like reed-type gages, most electronic gages are comparators. The size of the electrical signal depends on the

291

size difference between the gage block standard used for the zero setting of the gage and the product-part size. The signal is amplified electronically to provide a scale reading. A simplified explanation of a typical electronic gage is given by Figure 11.23.

Advantages of electronic gaging systems are high amplification, variety of amplifications in a single instrument, and fast measurement speed. Amplifications of 40,000:1 are obtainable in standard gaging equipment, and 100,000 to 200,000:1 in laboratory gages. Total error is 1 to 2% of scale in most standard gages, and is as low as $\frac{1}{4}$% when special attention is given to circuit design and scale accuracy. Stability of electronic gages has improved greatly in the past few years, with the development of transistorized circuits and improved means of voltage regulation. Electronic gages produce a signal that is usable for a variety of applications. The amplifier's output can be fed to a number of display devices—scales, digital displays, oscilloscopes, signal lights, and to computers and print-out devices.

Air gaging systems measure size by monitoring the difference in flow or pressure of an air stream. The gage is first zeroed against a reference master of known size. Measurement is made by metering the pressure loss between the product-part surface and the master. Figure 11.24 shows several types of circuits used in air gages.[3] In the venturi-type circuit, compressed air at regulated pressure enters a large venturi chamber and then passes through the venturi throat into the smaller venturi chamber where velocity is higher and pres-

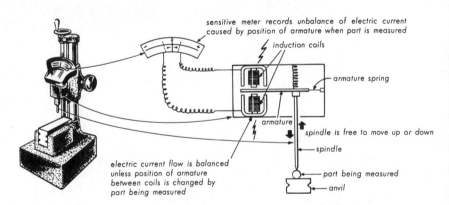

Figure 11.23.   Electronic gage.

[3]The figures and brief descriptions have been taken from Burden, W. W. (1960), *66 Centuries of Measurement,* Bendix Automation and Measurement Division, Dayton, Ohio, pp. 99–102. This is an excellent summary-type booklet prepared for nontechnical people as well as engineers.

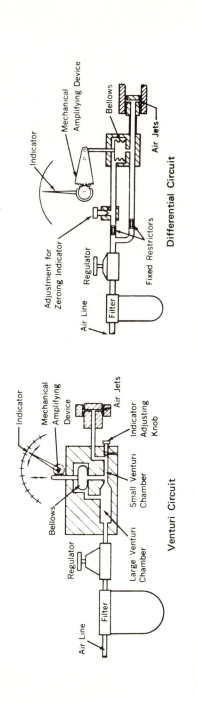

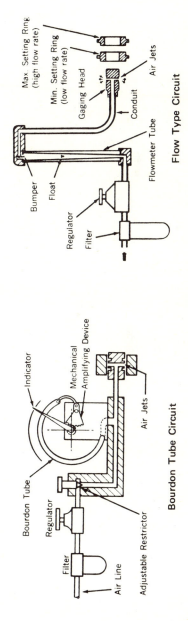

Figure 11.24. Typical circuits used in air gages.

293

sure lower than in the larger chamber. From the smaller chamber, the air passes out through the metering orifices in the gage tooling. A pressure tube from the large chamber allows the higher pressure of that chamber to act on the outside of the enclosed bellows. A similar tube from the smaller chamber is connected to the inside of the bellows to oppose the pressure in the bellows chamber. The spring action of the bellows, in conjunction with this pressure differential, causes the bellows to deflect until it reaches equilibrium. This bellows movement, amplified by a rack and a pinion, moves a pointer over a graduated dial.

The differential-type circuit also makes use of a bellows subject to pressure differential and a rack and pinion amplifier. Pressure-regulated air passes into two separate channels. One channel contains an atmospheric bleed for zeroing. The other channel terminates at the orifices of the gage tooling. The pressure differential in the two channels causes the bellows to deflect until equilibrium is reached. This movement registers the back pressure in the system, during the gaging operation, on a circular dial scale.

The Bourdon-type gage is another example of the back-pressure gage. Included in the circuit is a connection to a Bourdon tube which deflects with circuit pressure changes. These deflections are amplified by a rack and pinion mechanism. The flow-type circuit is the simplest of all air-gaging circuits. It is completely pneumatic. Filtered air at regulated pressure actuates a float whose movement depends on the amount of air flowing. The position of the float in the transparent tube indicates the amount of clearance between tooling and product part surface. The float position is read on a graduated scale next to the tube.

Air gages are especially useful in measuring small hole diameters, long holes, and various geometric conditions as out-of-roundness, taper, concentricity, and so forth. Amplifications of 20,000 to 40,000:1 with scale divisions of 5 μ in. are now standard on most air gages. Larger magnifications up to 400,000:1 are possible on laboratory gages. Precision of the order of 2 to 3% of scale range are standard, and down to 1% under laboratory conditions.

Optics is being increasingly used in modern gaging devices. Typical optical gages are simple hand-held magnifiers, microscopes with optical scales and micrometer stages, and optical comparators. The *optical comparator* is a widely used inspection method for checking linear and angular measurements, thread forms, gear teeth, and contours of all types. Figure 11.25 shows a typical optical comparator. Figure 11.26 indicates the elements of an optical comparator system. Measurements may be made directly by means of graduated scales

294

Figure 11.25. Optical comparator. Courtesy of Jones and Lamson Machine Company, Springfield, Vt.

on the screen, by linear displacement of the table, or by comparison with a template overlay on the screen. Standard comparators are available with calibrations of 0.0001 in. and 1 min. of arc.

Attributes Measurement

Gaging equipment described in the previous sections is appropriate for measuring the degree of product conformance to specifications (variables measurement). Instruments of this sort are called *indicating*-type gages. If product is inspected on an attributes-measurement basis, the gage merely classifies the product item as acceptable or non-

295

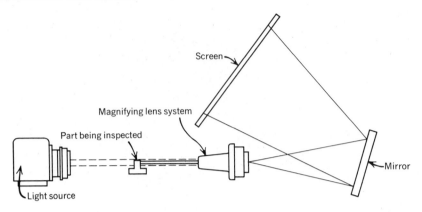

Figure 11.26. Elements of an optical comparator.

acceptable (or oversize, undersize, and acceptable). In this case, *fixed*-type gages are usually used.

Many specially designed fixed-type gages are used in the industries. Also, gage manufacturers produce a line of standard fixed-type gages — usually for inspecting cylindrical hole diameters and shaft diameters. Figure 11.27 shows a number of standard fixed-gage designs.

Each fixed gage has a *Go* member and a *No-Go* member (or there may be separate Go and No-Go gages). The Go gage checks removal of a minimum amount of stock necessary for the product item to meet specifications. The No-Go gage checks for possible removal of too much stock. Thus, the Go gage inspects maximum material limits, the No-Go gage minimum material limits. For example, consider a plug gage being used to inspect a 0.500/0.502 in. hole-diameter specification: the Go member inspects the 0.500 limit, the No-Go member the 0.502 limit. If the hole satisfies specifications, the Go plug should enter the hole freely and the No-Go plug should fail to enter. The use of Go gages assures that product parts will assemble. The use of No-Go gages controls the amount of clearance between matching product-part quality characteristics.

Fixed-type gages are the most economical means of inspecting product parts on a mass-production basis. A plug gage, for example, can check a hole specification in a matter of seconds. The cost savings from using a fixed gage, instead of an indicating gage, are due to (1) cost of the gage, and (2) speed of the gaging operation. One disadvantage, however, is that fixed gages can discriminate only to approximately 0.0001 to 0.0002 in.

In Chapter 1, the point was made that a technical specification is

296

valid only if it is translatable into a specific measurement method for checking product conformance. Translation may be difficult for functional or geometric reasons. The following discussion and example illustrate quantitative translation considerations related to measurement error.

In the manufacture of a fixed gage, a tolerance must be provided for gage fabrication. This is called gage maker's tolerance, or simply *gage tolerance* (GT). A tolerance provision is also made for *wear allowance* (WA). That is, the fitting of the gage into many product parts, for the inspection operation, involves gage wear. A typical Go, No-Go

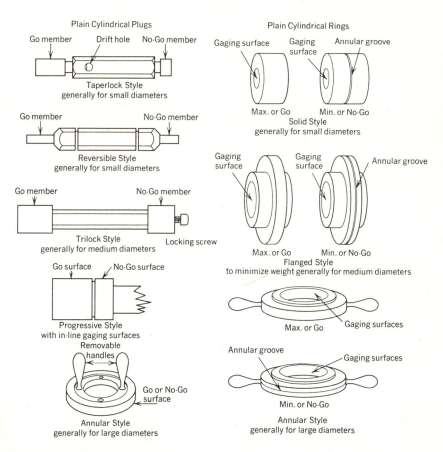

Fixed Gage Nomenclature

Figure 11.27.   Some standard fixed-type gages. From "Quality Assurance" (1963), *Tools of Metrology*, Hitchcock Publishing Co., Wheaton, Ill.

gage receives both GT and WA tolerances on the Go member and only a GT tolerance on the No-Go member. The controversial issue is whether the GT and WA tolerances should be derived entirely, or in part, or not at all from the product-specification tolerance.

Example

A product part has a square hole with specification size being 0.501 ± 0.001 × 0.501 ± 0.001 in. A Go, No-Go plug gage is required to check these two identical dimensional specifications. The tolerances GT and WA are to be derived entirely from the specification tolerance, and the magnitude of each is to be 10% of the specification tolerance.

The gage computations and resulting gage specifications are given by Figure 11.28.

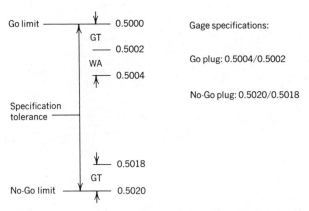

Figure 11.28.   Gage tolerance and wear allowance determine Go, No Go gage specifications.

In this example, GT and WA tolerances are derived entirely from the product-specification tolerance. Thus, effective production tolerance may be as small as

$$(\text{Specification tolerance}) - (2\text{ GT} + \text{WA})$$

Even if the gage maker produces a gage near the nominal gage specification sizes, production tolerance may be reduced to

$$(\text{Specification tolerance}) - (1.5\text{ GT} + 0.5\text{ WA})$$

298

The method of derivation of the GT and WA tolerances is called *gaging policy*. This example illustrates a gaging policy, the purpose of which is to minimize the probability of acceptance of defective product. This is accomplished at the expense of some rejection of marginally acceptable product. For safety and functional reasons, this type of gaging policy prevails in many production situations. In some cases, the GT and WA tolerances can either straddle or be entirely outside of the product specification limits. For either of these two practices, the purpose is to maximize the probability of acceptance of acceptable product, and this is accomplished at the expense of some acceptance of marginally defective product.

The type of gaging policy appropriate for a given set of product and manufacturing conditions is an economic matter. Clearly, a restrictive policy (as illustrated in the preceding example) reduces production tolerances and increases production costs. On the other hand, a more liberal policy resulting in the acceptance of a small percentage of marginally defective product may cause significant discovery-and-correction costs at assembly-work stations (or, field-service costs, if the defectives cause product malfunction).

The problem of gage-tolerance allocation is not limited strictly to fixed-type gages. For example, the reed-type mechanical gage discussed previously is frequently adapted to attributes-type gaging applications. The indicator pointer for each reed carries a bumper to close an electrical circuit to actuate red and green signal lights (red for oversize, green for undersize). In setting the gage against minimum and maximum gage-block standards, alternative procedures are to adjust the lights just barely on or just barely off. The decision is, in effect, a gaging policy choice. Adjusting the lights just barely on is called *rejecting the masters* and corresponds to a restrictive gaging policy which is reducing production tolerances. Adjusting the lights just barely off is called *accepting the masters* and this is a liberal gaging policy procedure.

TOOL AND GAGE CONTROL

In Chapter 2, the Tool and Gage Control element of the quality subsystem S_2 was discussed mainly from a document and record-keeping point of view. Description of this important quality-control function is now expanded to include the physical structure of dimensional control of gages. It should now be clear to the student that two major quality determinants are (1) ability to manufacture quality character-istics to restrictive tolerance specifications, and (2) ability to ac-curately and reliably measure conformance of these characteristics to the established specifications.

Gage Control Structure

There are three general classes of gages which span the entire conformance-evaluation function, from calibration of the reference standard to gaging of the production part. These are *working* gages used by process operators and setup men, *inspection* gages used by inspectors, and *master* gages used for calibrating working and in-spection gages. Also, tools frequently fix and control the dimensional elements of the product part and thus serve as a medium of inspection. In this sense, a tool can be a working gage and, thus, is subject to calibration by master gages.

Most precision gages are comparators, that is, the product part is measured after the gage is zeroed against a master of known size. A series of two or three transfer measurements may be required to cali-brate the working gage against the primary gage block standard. Two error factors are critical—transfer error and cumulative error. Every product measurement is subject to uncertainty. This uncertainty is the result of combined uncertainties in the size of the calibrating gage, errors intrinsic to each gage, and errors caused by operator technique and environment. This accumulated error must be kept to a practical

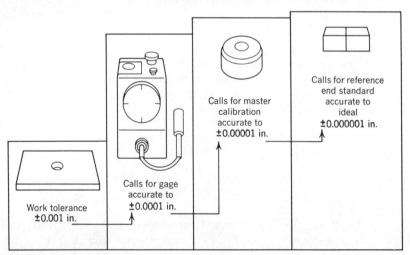

Calls for reference
end standard
accurate to
ideal
±0.000001 in.

Calls for master
calibration
accurate to
±0.00001 in.

Calls for gage
accurate to
±0.0001 in.

Work tolerance
±0.001 in.

Figure 11.29. For reliable measurement, each step in the gaging sequence, from work to gage-block calibration, should have ten times the accuracy of preceding step. From "Metalworking" (January, 1963), *Report on Precision Measurement*, Cahner's Publica-tion, Boston, Mass., p. A4.

300

Rule-of-Ten Catches More Bad Parts

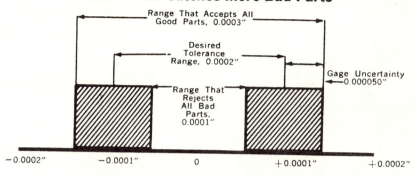

Gage Uncertainty = 50% Of Part Tolerance
50% Of In-Tolerance Range Could Pass Bad Parts

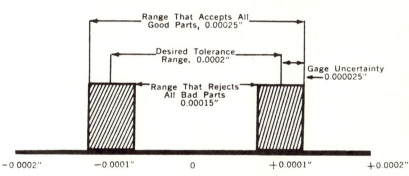

Gage Uncertainty = 25% Of Part Tolerance
25% Of In-Tolerance Range Could Pass Bad Parts

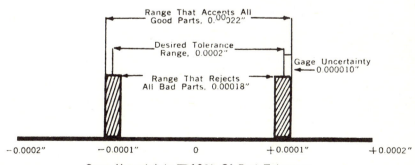

Gage Uncertainty = 10% Of Part Tolerance
10% Of In-Tolerance Range Could Pass Bad Parts

Figure 11.30. Gage uncertainty rules—50, 25, and 10%. From "Metalworking" (January, 1963), *Report on Precision Measurement*, Cahner's Publication, Boston, Mass., p. 45.

minimum to reduce the respective probabilities of accepting non-conforming product and rejecting product which conforms to the specifications. A common procedure for reducing these probabilities is the 10-to-1 rule followed in most industries. Figure 11.29 illustrates this practice. Application of the rule means that measurements at the calibration stage must be 100 and often 1000 times as accurate as the product specification tolerance. The argument for this rule is given in Figure 11.30. As calibration and other constant errors become a smaller fraction of the specification tolerance, the fractions of nonconforming product accepted and conforming product rejected decrease proportionately.

Gage uncertainty considerations imply, of course, that any manufacturing plant engaged in process operations requiring moderate accuracies of a few thousandths of an inch must have either within the plant, or through an external service, the facilities for calibrating its standards within a few millionths of an inch. These facilities consist of a temperature and humidity-controlled gage room, precision standards and laboratory gaging equipment, and personnel trained in the use of precision measuring instruments.

Measurement Error Analysis

Evaluation of measurement error involves both physical and statistical considerations. The engineer is interested in identifying error sources and designing better devices for restricting and controlling error effects. For example, Figure 11.31 gives the elements of an indicating gage. Measurement error sources are (1) the amplifying system, input errors from the gage point, and output errors to the indicating scale; (2) electrical or pneumatic input errors to the amplification system; (3) gaging pressure error; (4) geometry errors either in the product part being measured, or in the means of locating the part in the gage; (5) calibration error due to the standard used for setting the gage; (6) errors due to operator technique or environment.

Statistical methods are used to identify relative effects of error sources and to develop quantitative measures of error elements. Some statistical error-analysis techniques are summarized in the following sections.

Cumulative Effect of Calibration Errors

A quantitative method of evaluating cumulative calibration error has been suggested by Woods and Zehna.[4] The method is based on an

---

[4] Woods, W. M. and Zehna, P. W. (February, 1966), "Cumulative Effect of Measurement Errors," *Industrial Quality Control*, Vol. 22, No. 8, pp. 411-412.

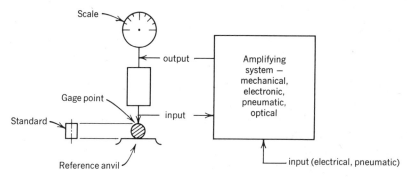

Figure 11.31. Elements of an indicating gage.

accuracy-ratio measure defined in terms of error standard deviations. The measure and resulting model are summarized here.

The example of Figure 11.29 involves three calibration levels, counting the metrology-laboratory calibration of the end standard as one level. Each level of calibration is a source of error in the final reading of the gage measuring the product quality characteristic. The gage reading of the product measurement is given by

$$Y = x + e$$

where x = true quality characteristic size

σ_x = standard deviation of x

e = total measurement error

and

$$e = e_1 + e_2 + \ldots + e_i + \ldots + e_n$$

Where e_i = error introduced at the ith calibration level

e_n = working gage error in measuring the product item

σ_i = standard deviation of e_i

An *accuracy ratio* (precision ratio is a more appropriate term) of the gage in relation to the quality characteristic being measured is given by

$$r = \frac{\sigma_x}{\sigma_n}$$

303

At each higher calibration level an analogous accuracy ratio is defined by

$$r_i = \frac{\sigma_{i+1}}{\sigma_i} \qquad i = 1, 2, \ldots, n \qquad \sigma_{n+1} = \sigma_x$$

Thus, r_i is the accuracy ratio at the ith calibration level, and is interpreted as the relative precision at that level in relation to the next highest level. (r_n now stands for σ_x/σ_n previously defined as the accuracy ratio for the working gage.)

Assuming the e_i are independent and applying the theorem for combination of independent random variables given in Chapter 7,

$$\sigma_e^2 = \sum_{i=1}^{n} \sigma_i^2$$

where

$$e = \sum_{i=1}^{n} e_i$$

Since σ_e is a measure of the total or resultant precision, a reasonable definition of resultant (or total) accuracy ratio is

$$r_t = \frac{\sigma_x}{\sigma_e}$$

which is a measure of the true precision for the final gage reading of the product measurement. Using this expression as the model, the following example is considered.

Example

An accuracy ratio of r_n is imposed on the gage measuring the product item. The true or resultant accuracy ratio is required — the ratio which accounts for all calibration errors.

$$r_t^2 = \frac{\sigma_x^2}{\sigma_e^2} = \frac{\sigma_x^2}{\displaystyle\sum_{i=1}^{n} \sigma_i^2}$$

Since r_i is usually specified at each calibration level, the above equation is better expressed in terms of the r_i. Using the definition of r_i recursively

$$r_t^2 = \frac{\prod\limits_{j=1}^{n} r_j^2}{1 + \sum\limits_{j=1}^{n-1} r_1^2 r_2^2 \dots r_j^2}$$

$$= \frac{r_1^2 r_2^2 \dots r_n^2}{1 + r_1^2 + r_1^2 r_2^2 + \dots + r_1^2 r_2^2 \cdots r_{n-1}^2}$$

This equation for r_t^2 may be simplified by letting $r_i = c$ for each i (e.g., in the 10-to-1 rule illustrated by Figure 11.29, each r_i is 10, here denoted by c). Then

$$r_t^2 = \frac{(c^2 - 1)\, c^{2n}}{c^{2n} - 1}$$

A lower bound on the resulting accuracy ratio may now be obtained. From the above equation for r_t^2, one observes that

$$r_t^2 \geq c^2 - 1$$

in fact

$$\lim_{n \to \infty} r_t^2 = c^2 - 1$$

Thus, if a 4-to-1 calibration rule is in effect at $n = 5$ calibration levels

$$r_t^2 \overset{\wedge}{=} 4^2 - 1$$

or

$$r_t \overset{\wedge}{=} \sqrt{15} = 3.873$$

Woods and Zehna[5] give accuracy ratios for five calibration rules (see Table 11.3). In comparing one calibration rule against another (e.g., a 10-to-1 versus a 4-to-1 rule), the relative gain in resultant accuracy must be weighed against the increased cost of maintaining the higher calibration accuracy ratio.

Gage Operator Error

For any quality characteristic, the distribution of production-output measurements reflects gage error, gage-operator error, and actual

[5]*Ibid*, p. 302.

Table 11.3. **Resultant accuracy ratio for five calibration levels.**

5 level	4 level	3 level	2 level	1 level	Resultant
10:1	10:1	10:1	10:1	10:1	9.95 to 1
10:1	4:1	4:1	4:1	4:1	9:68 to 1
4:1	10:1	10:1	10:1	10:1	3.98 to 1
4:1	4:1	4:1	4:1	4:1	3.87 to 1

production variation. Simple experiments can be performed to obtain rudimentary measures of the relative importance of gage and gage-operator errors.

A distribution of repeat measurements g can be obtained for one product unit by one gage operator using a specified gage. The product unit can also be measured using laboratory instrumentation to obtain an approximately true measurement p, or several independent laboratory measurements may be made, yielding a mean value $\bar{x}_p$. A measure of calibration error or gage bias is given by $|\bar{x}_p - \bar{x}_g|$. The range R_g (or σ_g) is a measure of repeat error or gage uncertainty. Some gage-operator error is certainly present and confounded with gage error. The gage-operator error influence can be practically minimized by using the very best operator for the experiment, or by using analysis-of-variance technique in a more sophisticated experiment.[6]

In similar fashion, a distribution of repeat measurements o can be obtained for one product unit by different gage operators using a specified gage. Gage error influence in the experiment is minimized by calibrating and maintaining the gage under controlled laboratory conditions. The range R_o (or σ_o) is a measure of gage-operator error.

Assuming independence, various error analyses can be made using

$$\sigma_m{}^2 = \sigma_x{}^2 + \sigma_g{}^2 + \sigma_0{}^2$$

where m = working gage reading

x = product quality characteristic size

g = gage error

o = gage operator error

---

[6]An example of a measurement-error experiment, using analysis-of-variance technique, is given later in this chapter.

Gage Repeatability

Various consequences of calibration error and repeat error can be evaluated by a comparison of a distribution of repeat measurements g (representing gage repeat error) with the specification tolerance range. Assuming no calibration error and considering only repeat error,

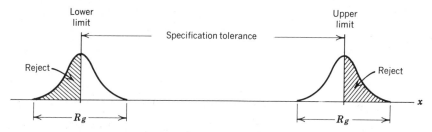

Figure 11.32.   Rejection due to gage repeat error — product at the specification limits.

Figure 11.32 shows the probability of rejection of conforming product at either specification limit to be 0.5. Furthermore, there are significant probabilities of rejecting conforming product, from the upper limit down to a point defined by (Upper limit $- R_g/2$), and from the lower limit up to a point given by (Lower limit $+ R_g/2$) as shown in Figure 11.33. A similar statement can be made regarding the probability of acceptance of marginally undersize and oversize product.

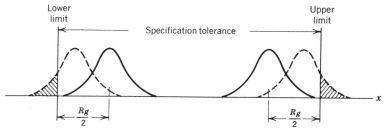

Figure 11.33.   Gage repeat error — product just inside the specification limits.

Clearly, it is important to minimize and control R_g. A common practice is to attempt to restrict gage repeat error to 10% of the specification tolerance. The operating characteristic curve shown in Figure 11.34 indicates that for repeat error of the order of 5 to 10% of the tolerance spread, gage uncertainty regions relative to product acceptance and rejection are comparatively small.

307

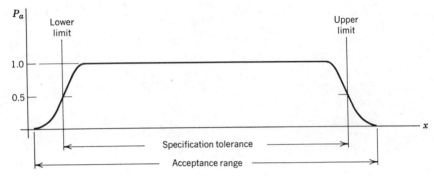

Figure 11.34. Operating characteristic curve.

Gantt[7] reports a General Electric Company practice of measuring gage repeat error to restrict it to 10% of the specification tolerance. The magnitude of the permissible repeat error is based on 99% of repeat gage readings of a single product part occurring within an interval equal to 10% of the specification tolerance. Figure 11.35 indicates the computation procedure which is summarized here.

Three operators A, B, and C measure 10 product parts twice each using the same gage. These readings are entered in columns 1 and 2 for each operator.

The differences between repeat readings of the same part by the same operator are denoted by R_A, R_B, and R_C. Average differences $\overline{R}_A$, $\overline{R}_B$, and $\overline{R}_C$ yield a grand average difference

$$\overline{R} = \frac{1}{3}(\overline{R}_A + \overline{R}_B + \overline{R}_C)$$
$$= 0.00016 \text{ in.}$$

An R-control chart is prepared, with the UCL being given by

$$\overline{R} + D_4\overline{R} = 0.00052 \text{ in.}$$

Out-of-control R-points are investigated. In this case, the three circled R-values are discarded and the mean range is re-computed, yielding

$$\overline{R} = 0.000097 \text{ in.}$$

[7]Gantt, J. S. (March 1959), "Let's Take the Guesswork out of Inspection," *American Machinist,* Vol. 103, No. 5, pp. 117–122.

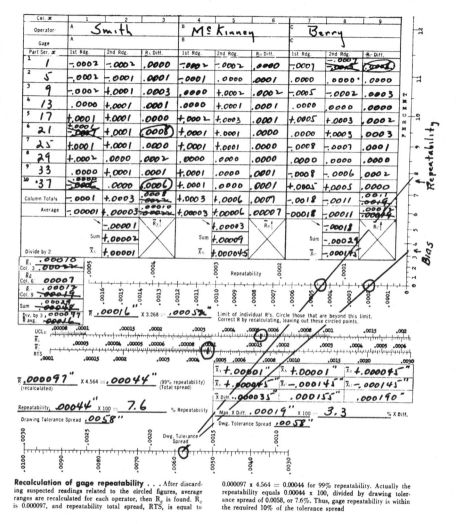

Figure 11.35. Gage repeatability test. From J. S. Gontt (March, 1959), "Let's Take the Guesswork Out of Inspection," *American Machinist*, Vol. 103, No. 5, pp. 117-122.

Using a nomograph, which is based on the coefficients given in the table in Appendix B, the $\bar{R}_c$ scale is entered with $\bar{R} = 0.000097$ in. giving a repeatability total spread (RTS) of 0.00044 in. This is based on 99% of the gage readings occurring in this interval.

Gage-repeat error is measured by 99% of the gage readings occurring within a percent of total specification tolerance. This percent is given by

$$\frac{(0.00044 \text{ in.}) (100)}{0.0058 \text{ in.}} = 7.6\%$$

where 0.0058 in. is the product-specification tolerance. Thus, the gage satisfies the repeat-error specification of 99% of gage readings occurring in an interval equal to 10% of specification tolerance.

Although the experiment is primarily directed at measuring gage-repeat error, a measure of operator bias (mean gage-operator error) is easily obtained. The average readings for the operators are denoted by $\bar{x}_A$, $\bar{x}_B$, and $\bar{x}_C$. Considering all combinations of these mean readings, the maximum difference is

$$\bar{x}_B - \bar{x}_C = 0.000190 \text{ in.}$$

Then

$$\frac{(0.000190 \text{ in.}) (100)}{0.0058 \text{ in.}} = 3.3\%$$

which is a measure of gage-operator bias in terms of percent of total specification tolerance.

Identification of Measurement Error Sources

When production parts are manufactured to specification tolerances of the order of 50-millionths inch, inspection procedures are complicated by conflict-of-measurement problems involving supplier and purchaser companies. If the measurement problem is a serious one, the time and expense of a more sophisticated experiment is justified. The following example[8] is of a gyro assembly whose parts would not assemble properly because of differences in measuring equipment and technique between the supplier and purchaser companies. Analysis of the problem involves (1) determining gage repeatability, and (2) identifying significant causes of measurement difference.

Table 11.4 records two measurements (coded), each of the same bearing, made by the same operator, using a specified gage (called "machine" in the tables and figures). The experiment involves four product parts (bearings), two sets of operators—one set for the purchaser company, one set for the supplier company—and two gages—the purchaser's and the supplier's.

[8]Hill, W. J. (June, 1959), "Measurement Error and Detection," *The Tool Engineer*, Vol. 42, No. 6, pp. 73-78.

Table 11.4. **Bearing inside diameter measurements (coded).**

Machine		Shop gage A			Supplier gage B		
Setting ring		Ford		Supplier		Ford		Supplier
Operator		F_1	F_2	F_1	F_2	S_1	S_2	S_1	S_2
B e a r i n g	A	5 0	0 10	10 0	10 5	30 15	20 40	20 35	20 30
	B	50 40	50 60	50 50	60 65	70 50	60 80	60 75	60 45
	C	100 95	95 100	100 110	100 90	115 95	110 95	95 115	115 100
	D	150 140	145 145	155 160	155 150	165 180	155 165	165 150	155 180

Figure 11.36 shows an R-control chart for differences between the repeat readings given in Table 11.4. All points are in control. However, the repeatability of the first 16 points is considerably better than that of the second 16 points. This observation is verified by a variance-ratio test, which indicates a significant difference between gages, but not between operators. It is concluded that the supplier's gage repeatability must be improved (or, the supplier should use the same type of gage used by the purchaser company).

Table 11.5 gives a nested factorial set of tables, showing all possible pairs of the variables – measuring machine (gage), bearing, and setting ring (gage standard). The table values are average measure-

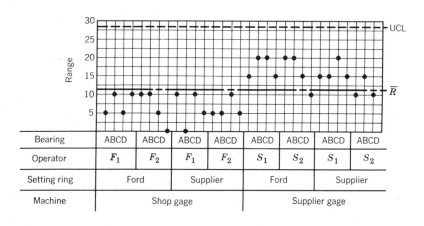

Figure 11.36. R-chart for differences in repeat readings.

311

ments. The extent of the random variation of average measurements from the grand average should be within the limits

$$U = \bar{\bar{x}} + \frac{t_\alpha \, \overline{R}}{1.128 \, \sqrt{n}}$$

$$L = \bar{\bar{x}} - \frac{t_\alpha \, \overline{R}}{1.128 \, \sqrt{n}}$$

Table 11.5.   Two-way tables of average measurements

Machine				Machine				Ring			
	Shop	Supplier	Avg.		Shop	Supplier	Avg.		Shop	Supplier	Avg.
B A	5.0	26.3	15.6					B A	15.0	16.3	15.6
e B	53.1	62.5	57.6		Shop	Supplier	Avg.	e B	57.5	58.1	57.8
a C	98.8	105.0	101.9	R F	74.1	90.3	82.2	a C	100.6	103.1	101.9
i D	150.0	164.4	157.2	i S	79.4	88.8	84.1	i D	155.6	158.8	157.2
n				n				n			
g Avg.	76.7	89.5	83.1	g Avg.	76.7	89.5	83.1	g Avg.	82.2	84.1	83.1

Figure 11.37 is a control chart for main effects. (No interactions are significant.) The effects of the measuring machine and bearing are significant. Since the supplier is required to grade bearings (A, B, C, and D classes with a 50-millionths inch spread for each class) for subsequent selective assembly at the purchaser company's plant, it is recommended that the supplier use the average of two measurements for those bearings whose initial measurement is within 20-millionths inch of the grading tolerance. This recommendation is in addition to that regarding gage repeatability. Further, the experiment indicates that gage-operator error is not a significant cause of the conflict-in-measurement trouble.

SUMMARY

In many production situations, specification requirements for modern products have become so restrictive that measurement error is the most serious problem facing the quality-control and inspection staff. In these cases, the Tool and Gage Control element of the quality subsystem S_2 (see Figure 2.4) becomes a major determinant of product quality.

Modern precision gages are designed to translate very small measurement differences to indicating scales and to amplify these differ-

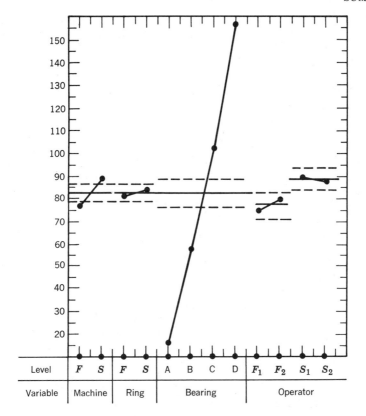

Figure 11.37. Control chart for main effects.

ences for easy discrimination by the gage operator. Various amplification methods are utilized—mechanical, electronic, pneumatic, and
optical. Most precision gages are comparators, that is, the product part
is measured after the gage is zeroed against a master of known size.
Calibrating a working or inspection gage may involve two, three, or
more transfer measurements corresponding to the calibration levels
required to assure manufacturing accuracy compatible with the
master gage blocks for the plant, and with length standards at the
National Bureau of Standards.

Every product measurement is subject to uncertainty. This uncertainty is the result of combined uncertainties in calibrating gage
standards, errors intrinsic to each gage, transfer and calibration
errors, and errors caused by gage-operator technique and environment. Various measures and criteria have been developed to evaluate
gaging procedure and measurement error. Common measures are
accuracy, precision, reliability, amplification, linearity, and repeat-

ability. Evaluation of measurement error involves both physical and statistical considerations. It is necessary to recognize physical sources of error, and engineer means of restricting and controlling error effects. Also, statistical methods are required to identify relative effects of error sources and develop quantitative methods of measuring error elements.

REFERENCES

American Standard ASA B46.1 (1962), American Standards Association, 10 East 40 St., New York.

Buckingham, E. (1954), *Dimensions and Tolerances for Mass Production,* Industrial Press, New York.

Burden, W. W. (1960), *66 Centuries of Measurement,* Bendix Automation and Measurement Division, Dayton, Ohio, pp. 99-102.

Burrows, P. W. (June, 1968), "Surface Texture Evaluation," *Quality Assurance,* Vol. 7, No. 6, p. 33.

Bush, T. (1964), *Fundamentals of Dimensional Metrology,* Delmar Publishers, Albany, New York.

Gantt, J. S. (March, 1959), "Let's Take the Guesswork out of Inspection," *American Machinist,* Vol. 103, No. 5, pp. 117-122.

Hill, W. J. (June, 1959), "Measurement Error and Detection," *The Tool Engineer,* Vol. 42, No. 6, pp. 73-78.

Hume, K. J. (1953), *Engineering Metrology,* MacDonald, London.

Juran, J. M. (1962), *Quality Control Handbook,* McGraw-Hill, New York.

Lawshe, C. H. and Tiffin, J. (1945), "The Accuracy of Precision Instrument Measurement in Industrial Inspection," *Journal of Applied Psychology,* Vol. 29, pp. 413-419.

"Metalworking" (January, 1963), *Precision Measurement,* Cahner's Publication, Boston, Mass.

"Quality Assurance" (1963), *The Tools of Metrology,* Hitchcock Publishing Company, Wheaton, Ill.

Woods, W. M. and Zehna, P. W. (February, 1966), "Cumulative Effect of Measurement Errors," *Industrial Quality Control,* Vol. 22, No. 8, pp. 411-412.

REVIEW QUESTIONS

1. Briefly outline (for linear measurement) the general system for transfer of accuracy from the metrology laboratory, to the manufacturing system, to the output product.

2. Explain the meaning of geometry error in Figure 11.14. What is the recommended gaging practice for measuring the size of this exterior product contour?

3. What is gaging pressure error?

4. When does gage operator error become a significant error factor?

5. What is the approximate standard deviation measure of gage operator error in Figure 11.15?

6. Define the term amplification of a gage.

7. State four general amplification means used in gages.

8. A product specification is 0.500 ± 0.002 in. outside diameter. Which specification limit is checked by the (a) Go gage, and (b) No-Go gage? Generally, what do the Go and No-Go gages inspect?

9. Define gage tolerance (GT) and wear allowance (WA).

10. Describe the 10-to-1 accuracy rule for gages.

11. What gain and loss must be considered when a decision is made to adopt a high calibration accuracy rule (e.g., changing from a 4-to-1 rule to a 10-to-1 rule)?

12. Briefly outline the steps of the Gantt method of measuring gage repeat error (see Figure 11.35).

PROBLEMS

1. Using the four series of blocks available in the gage block set shown in Figure 11.7, select the least number of blocks required for a 1.7529 in. stack.

2. Assuming the gage block set referred to in problem 1 is A-grade and the blocks to be of good geometry and surface finish, compute the maximum and minimum sizes of the 1.7529 in. stack. Consider variation due to individual gage block error and to air space or interval error between blocks. Assume ideal environmental conditions, standard gaging temperature, etc.

Answer: maximum: 1.7529246 in., minimum: 1.7528926 in.

3. Assume the maximum size condition for the 1.7529 in. stack of blocks in problem 2 and a temperature increase to 88°F. Compute the size of the gage block stack. Use the coefficient of expansion for hardened tool steel (see Table 11.1).

315

4. The following changes have been made on the micrometer shown in Figure 11.12: (a) the screw lead has been changed from $\frac{1}{40}$ to $\frac{1}{20}$ in. (i.e., one thimble revolution now advances the spindle $\frac{1}{20}$ in.), and (b) the number of divisions on the thimble has been changed from 25 to 30. What is the discrimination of the micrometer?

5. The true size of a quality characteristic is 0.500 in. Three measurements of this quality characteristic on a single product unit yield the values 0.497, 0.500, and 0.502 in. For this limited measurement data, what is the (a) accuracy of the measurement, and (b) precision of the measurement?

6. The specification for a slot width (i.e., interior dimension) is 0.750 ± 0.002 in. Deriving GT and WA tolerances entirely from the product specification tolerance, determine Go and No-Go gage specifications. Use 10% increments for GT and WA.

7. Suppose in problem 6 that the specification is for an exterior product dimension. Compute Go and No-Go gage specifications.

8. Using the Woods and Zehna model and imposing identical 2 to 1 accuracy ratios for 3 calibration levels, compute the resultant accuracy ratio r_t exactly using

$$r_t^2 = \frac{\displaystyle\prod_{j=1}^{n} r_j^2}{1 + \displaystyle\sum_{j=1}^{n-1} r_1^2 \, r_2^2 \ldots r_j^2}$$

9. Since identical accuracy ratios are used at all calibration levels in problem 8, r_t may be approximated by

$$r_t^2 = c^2 - 1$$

where $c = 2$ in problem 8. Compute r_t in this manner.

10. Twenty-five repeat measurements on one product unit by one gage operator using a specified working gage yield a mean measurement equal to 0.5001 in. and a standard deviation equal to 0.00015 in. Measuring the product unit using laboratory instrumentation, a mean of 0.50015 in. is obtained. Compute calibration error and repeat error of the working gage.

11. Specifications for a quality characteristic are $0.500 + 0.005 - 0.000$ in. An output unit of product from the manufacturing operation involved is 0.5005 in. (true size). If gage repeat error is 0.0006 in., what is the proba-

bility of rejection of this acceptable output unit? Assume that measurement error is normally distributed.

12. For Gantt's method of measuring gage repeat error (see Figure 11.35), a nomograph is used to determine total repeatability spread (RTS). Verify the 0.00044 in. value obtained for RTS by computation using the tabled coefficients in Appendix B.

13. A conflict-of-measurement problem has developed involving a supplier company's gage used on final inspection and a purchaser company's gage used in receiving inspection. An experiment is performed whereby three repeat measurements on the same product unit are made by each of three different inspectors using the supplier's gage B_1. The experiment is repeated using the purchaser's gage B_2. Inspectors A_1 and A_2 are from the supplier company and inspector A_3 is from the purchaser company. The results of the experiment are presented in the following table for a 3×2 Factorial Design experiment. Units are in 0.0001 in. deviations from the nominal specification size. Test for significant differences between gages and between inspectors. Use an $\alpha = 0.01$ level of significance.

Gages (B_j)	Inspectors (A_i)		
	1	2	3
1	0	− 1	0
	1	0	0
	2	− 1	1
2	0	0	1
	1	0	1
	1	1	2

12

Quality-Control Trends

The earliest recorded beginning of quality control dates back to 1924 when Dr. W. A. Shewhart of Bell Telephone Laboratories first applied a statistical quality-control chart to manufacturing operations. From 1931 (when Dr. Shewhart's book, *Economic Control of Manufactured Product*[1] appeared) to the early 1940's, interest centered on the development of statistical quality-control techniques. Sampling tables for acceptance inspection were published and their use was endorsed by the armed services. Military Standard 105 was initiated and now, after five general revisions, has become a standard accepted by most industries.

During World War II and the Korean War, emphasis was on the use of statistical methods by the inspection agencies of the Depart-

---

[1]Shewhart, W. A. (1931), *Economic Control of Manufactured Product*, D. Van Nostrand, New York.

ment of Defense. Following the Korean War, emphasis shifted to promotion of the use of quality-control techniques by the supplier, together with assurance methods used by the Department of Defense. Procurement activities of this department greatly influenced the quality-control practices in the industries.

The history of the quality-control function in many industries follows a pattern of a dramatic start with great potential for success, frequent mishandling due principally to an overemphasis on statistical methods, and a final maturing in the last ten years to a balanced and effective functional element of the production system. Significant progress has occurred both in the administrative and technical areas of quality control. The major administrative development has been the clarification and acceptance of the concept of total quality control, a philosophy first introduced by A. V. Feigenbaum[2] of the General Electric Company. The major technical development has been a blending of engineering and statistical approaches.

QUALITY-CONTROL TRENDS

A recent intensive study of quality control in the industries was made by the editors of *Quality Assurance* magazine.[3] The study is based on 25,000 copies of a survey form covering six categories of questions directed mainly at how management views quality control and what direction it expects quality control to take in the future. The essential results of the survey are summarized here. Liberal use is made of the survey questions and responses without the customary quotations.

Management's View on Quality Control

About 37% of industries' top executives report that their quality-control departments report at a higher management level than they did five years ago. The levels to which quality control presently reports are:

Vice President	27%
Plant Managers	20%
Manufacturing Managers	13%

[2] Feigenbaum, A. V. (1961), *Total Quality Control,* McGraw-Hill, New York.

[3] Special Report (August, 1968), "Who Cares about Quality" *Quality Assurance,* Vol. 7, No. 8, pp. 26-29.

General Managers	10%
Presidents	8%
Division Managers	7%
Operations Managers	4%
Executive Vice Presidents	3%
All Other Titles	8%

At least 85% of the quality departments have their own budgets. Nearly all quality managers are able to make budget proposals and administer the budget. Over 93% of the company executives encourage their quality department to assist purchasing in selecting quality suppliers and to participate, with design engineering, in reviewing designs and specifications. This is indicative of the modern trend of quality control, away from the inspection-of-quality concept and toward the philosophy of total quality control.

Company managers (96%) believe that the quality-control department will play an increasingly important role in their company. They prefer that the quality department become more active in the following areas (ranked in order of preference).

1. Design engineering
2. Purchasing and selection of suppliers
3. Manufacturing
4. Testing
5. Feedback of customer information

Nearly 100% of industries' top executives feel that today's increased emphasis on product warranties and product liability will make their quality department more important to their profit picture. Any manufacturer that backs up his product with a service and/or parts warranty has an economic stake in quality. For example, one automobile manufacturer reports that it costs 2c to put a part in an assembly, $8 to replace it while the car is on the production line, and approximately $100 to replace it under a dealer warranty.

Purchasing's Views on Quality Control

The average purchasing agent tends to rank price, delivery, and quality as being equally important. However, size of plant and product type has an effect on the importance of quality to purchasing. In plants of less than 250 employees (usually component-part manufacturers), purchasing agents rank quality of purchased supplies as being most important and delivery the least important. In plants of more than

1000 employees, purchasing agents prefer an equal balance of price, delivery, and quality. One exception is aerospace producers, where quality requirements dominate, and price and delivery are of secondary importance.

About 75% of the purchasing agents say they seek the advice of the quality department on the purchase of major components and materials. A few seek advice for all components and materials. The most frequently mentioned items for which purchasing relies on the quality department for advice are electrical components — switches, relays, transformers, capacitors, etc. — precision machine parts, and fabricated parts such as forgings, castings, and stampings.

Design Engineering and Quality-Control Viewpoints

A most revealing response is the fact that 76% of the design engineers report that they consult the quality department on materials and components. Some producers of military-type products say that their quality departments review and approve all engineering designs, drawings, and specifications for all components and materials. The implication of this, of course, is that quality control is becoming an increasingly technical function in many companies.

A quality-control staff cannot, as in the past, be composed only of inspectors and statisticians. Cocca[4] reports that a major transition, underway for a number of years, has been the acquisition of professional engineering skills in the quality-control field. The highly technical, more complex nature of present-day industrial output antiquates many of the quality practices that were commonplace only a decade ago. Increased demands in accuracies, stresses and stress measurements, and exotic performance requirements in general have presented many new problems. The increasing complexity of inspection and testing, defect identification, causal analysis, and defect prevention is resulting, generally, in a more cooperative and supporting relationship between design engineering and quality control. Thus, out of necessity, quality control is turning to the engineering profession for ever-increasing numbers of its people.

This reported trend is also implied by the *Quality Assurance* survey. One question, directed at the quality-control personnel, requested the type of basic instructional materials of primary interest to them. Their responses (weighted and ranked in order of preference) were as follows:

[4]Cocca, O. A. (November, 1967), *The Emerging Role of the Engineer in Quality Control*, Winter Annual Meeting and Energy Systems Exposition, Pittsburgh, Pa., The American Society of Mechanical Engineers.

1. Dimensional metrology
2. Electric/electronic measurement
3. Economics of quality
4. Quality assurance administration
5. Testing methods
6. Vendor and product evaluation
7. Statistical quality control

COMPUTER APPLICATIONS TO QUALITY CONTROL

Quality-control operations are based on evaluation of quality through various stages of the production system-design, purchasing, manufacturing, and use of the product by the customer. A large number of control procedures rely on mathematical techniques for identifying quality problems at the earliest and least costly point in the production system. Mathematically based control procedures are complicated by (1) the large mass of data that must be handled and analyzed, (2) the wide area over which the data originates, and (3) the number of people originating the data. Automatic data processing methods can be used to reduce the data information to meaningful and useful form. These methods are already common in large manufacturing plants. All indications are that the quality-control function of the future will be based on integrated information flow systems tied to the computer. Selected examples of computer applications to quality control are summarized in the following sections. The examples are chosen to illustrate how data from each of the principal functions—design, purchasing, manufacturing, and performance—can be fed to the computer for analysis to improve product quality.

Designing Quality

A study of products in the design and development stage permits anticipation of problems that may occur in manufacturing. Statistical analysis of laboratory and test data can be used to design quality into the product prior to actual production. A simple example is that of simulating the assembly quality-characteristic distribution to study overlapping tolerance situations (see Table 7.2). A summary example[5]

---

[5] From *General Information Manual* (1962), IBM Management Operating System Quality Assurance for Manufacturing Industries, International Business Machines Corporation, Data Processing Division, White Plains, New York.

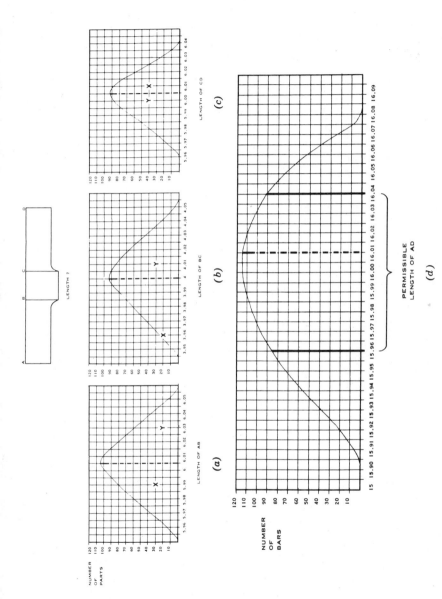

Figure 12.1. Computer simulation in design of quality.

is given in Figure 12.1. The assembly quality characteristic is the length *AD* made up of component lengths *AB, BC,* and *CD,* whose probable values are obtainable from distributions (*a*), (*b*), and (*c*). Monte Carlo techniques are utilized by the computer to simulate the assembly quality-characteristic distribution shown in (*d*). This facilitates the development of realistic production specifications as described in Chapter 7.

Many quality problems can be analyzed by the computer at the design and development stage of the production system. Regression analysis and analysis-of-variance procedures can be used to study quality cost estimates, test and gaging requirements, and critical quality standards.

Purchasing Quality

An example of computer assistance to purchasing is that of prompt evaluation of vendor shipments of parts and materials to a purchaser company. Data processing equipment helps improve the quality of purchases by rapidly preparing a report to show both management and the supplier how closely product conforms to specifications. These reports are used by quality control to determine those suppliers requiring technical assistance, and by purchasing to help select future suppliers. An example[6] of a specific IBM procedure for generating reports of this type is given here.

When parts or materials are received from a supplier, receiving inspection uses a pre-punched supplier-conformance card (Figure 12.2) for recording inspection information. Data recorded on this card are lot type, inspection code, quantity inspected, quantity rejected, shipment disposal (accepted or returned), and inspection time. The conformance cards are sent to the data processing section, where they are punched, duplicated, and recorded on magnetic tape.

A duplicate card goes to reclamation for disposition of the material and to purchasing for preparation of a rejected-parts report. At the end of a given time period, the tape containing data for each inspected lot is run with a master name and address tape to prepare a supplier quality-conformance report (Figure 12.3). The evaluations shown on this report are derived from comparisons of actual inspection costs with predetermined allowable dollar amounts for each supplier. The computer-costing operation is based only on an inspection-time input and considers rework costs and a quality control burden rate.

---

[6]*Ibid.*, p. 322.

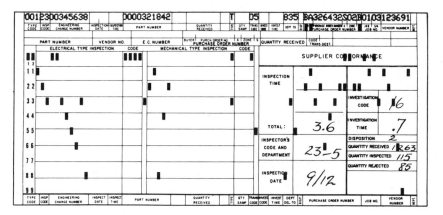

Figure 12.2. Supplier conformance card.

Manufacturing Quality

During the production cycle, manufacturing performance and quality-control procedures must be measured. Automatic data processing facilitates statistical and cost analyses which enable management to identify significant quality trouble areas and evaluate quality costs. A typical IBM procedure[7] is described by Figures 12.4 through 12.7.

For each inspection operation, the inspector records on a troubles-found card (Figure 12.4) the machine type, model, serial number, major unit, parts code, audit station, actual repair time, and trouble code in accordance with a prepared code listing. These cards are sent daily to the card punching section and are recorded on magnetic tape (detail tape shown in Figure 12.4). The detail tape is sorted and matched against the master tape. Rework time is multiplied by a burden rate carried on the master tape.

A summary tape is written containing the input data plus number of defects, number of hours, and repair costs per hour. This tape is used to prepare a variety of reports as indicated by Figures 12.5 and 12.6.

The procedures summarized above refer strictly to the preparation of quality reports. An automatic data processing application having the greatest potential for quality assurance is computer-assisted corrective quality action. Many major industries[8] have already

[7]*Ibid.*, p. 322.

[8]For a mechanical industry's application, see Geschelin, J. (June, 1964), "Chrysler's Assembly Line Computers Provide Instant Quality Control," *Automotive Industries,* Vol. 131, No. 9, pp. 37-39.

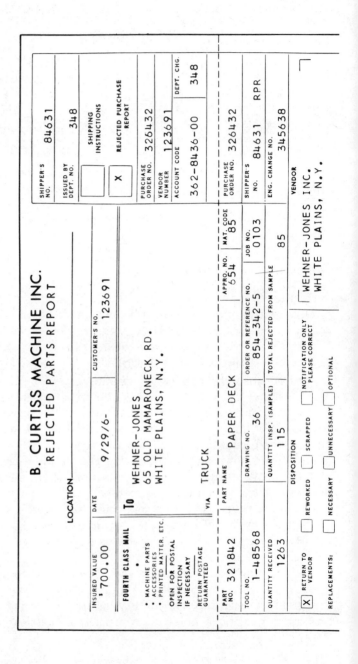

Detail Tape

SAMPLE ☐ ENCLOSED ☐ FORWARDED ON S.I. NO. _____

TOTAL REJECTED OR TOTAL SHIPPED	QTY. REJECTED (SAMPLE) OR QTY. TO B.O.	REASON FOR REJECTION — DESCRIPTION OF SHIPMENT	UNIT COST	TOTAL COST
1263	1263	PARTS NOT PLATED TO PROPER THICKNESS	.50	631.50

NO. OF BOXES	CLASSIFICATION OR DESCRIPTION OF MATERIAL	WEIGHT	INCOMING CHARGES
14	3 SKIDS	5,000	95.00

SHIPPING DEPT. TIME STAMP

9/29/6 3:30

PREPAID _____ COLLECT ✓ SHIPPED VIA JOHNS VANS INC.

PACKED BY: 45

OUT GOING CHARGES: 63.00

TOTAL: 158.00

SIGNATURE _____ S.I. ☐ (LABEL)

348 DEPT. 1

1 REJ. ☐ (LABEL AND PACKING LIST) SHIPPING DEPT.

Figure 12.3. Supplier conformance report.

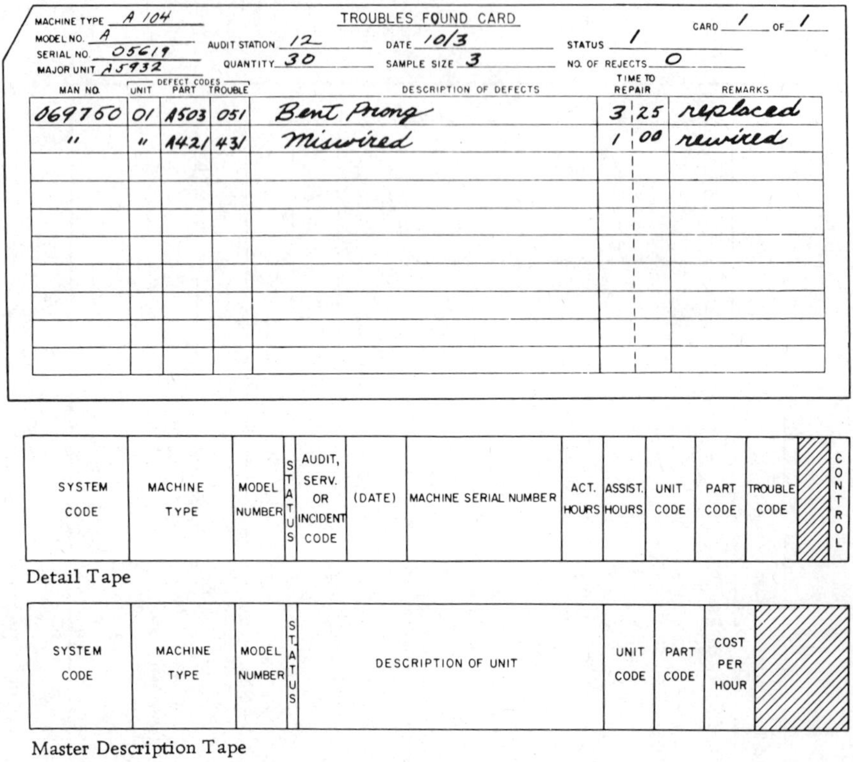

MACHINE TYPE _A 104_				TROUBLES FOUND CARD			CARD _1_ OF _1_

MODEL NO. _A_ SERIAL NO. _05619_ MAJOR UNIT _A5932_   AUDIT STATION _12_ QUANTITY _30_   DATE _10/3_ SAMPLE SIZE _3_   STATUS _1_ NO. OF REJECTS _0_

MAN NO.	UNIT	DEFECT CODES PART	TROUBLE	DESCRIPTION OF DEFECTS	TIME TO REPAIR		REMARKS
069760	01	A503	051	*Bent Prong*	3	25	*replaced*
"	"	A421	431	*Miswired*	1	00	*rewired*

SYSTEM CODE	MACHINE TYPE	MODEL NUMBER	S T A T U S	AUDIT, SERV. OR INCIDENT CODE	(DATE)	MACHINE SERIAL NUMBER	ACT. HOURS	ASSIST. HOURS	UNIT CODE	PART CODE	TROUBLE CODE	C O N T R O L

Detail Tape

SYSTEM CODE	MACHINE TYPE	MODEL NUMBER	S T A T U S	DESCRIPTION OF UNIT	UNIT CODE	PART CODE	COST PER HOUR	

Master Description Tape

Figure 12.4.   Troubles Found card.

adapted the computer to this control purpose. In the application reported by Geschelin, inspectors encircle defect numbers on quality-control defect coding cards (Figure 12.7). The data system is designed to collect and transmit defect data as it is detected. A computer with random access storage counts the defects being transmitted, stores the totals generated and controls remote typing stations, thus providing the means of quickly notifying production superintendents of defect trends.

As the computer system accumulates defect totals, each new total is compared against a trend indicator point. When the defect total exceeds this point value, a message is transmitted to the remote typing station in the office of the superintendent of the responsible department, alerting him to the significant defect trend. This control method is called off-line computer processing and is essentially a conversion of measurement data into a transfer or storage medium

MANUFACTURING PERFORMANCE ANALYSIS

SYSTEM	MACHINE TYPE	MODEL NUMBER	STATUS	AUDIT STATION	NUMBER OF MACHINES	NUMBER OF DEFECTS	DEFECTS PER MACHINE	OVER HIGH LIMIT	REPORTING PERIOD FROM	TO	DATE OF REPORT
X2056	EJV421	2	NEW	104	49	100	2.1	NONE	9/30	10/30	NOV 5,6-

PAGE 1

NUMBER OF DEFECTS	% FALLING IN EACH CATEGORY
NO DEFECTS	/////////////////////
01-02 DEFECTS	//////////////////////////////
03-04 DEFECTS	//////////////////////////
05-06 DEFECTS	/////////////////
07-08 DEFECTS	
09-10 DEFECTS	
11-12 DEFECTS	
13-14 DEFECTS	
15-16 DEFECTS	
17-18 DEFECTS	
19-20 DEFECTS	
21-22 DEFECTS	
23-24 DEFECTS	
25-26 DEFECTS	
27-28 DEFECTS	

% OF MACHINES — PERFORMANCE CURVE

100
95
90
85
80
75
70
65
60
55
50
45
40
35
30
25
20
15
10
5
0

.0   .8   .9   l.l   1.2   1.3   1.6   1.9   2.l   2.5   3.2   4.4   6.8   16.0

DEFECT FREE DAYS

MANUFACTURING PERFORMANCE REPORT

SYSTEM	MACHINE TYPE	MODEL NUMBER	STATUS	AUDIT STATION	NUMBER OF MACHINES	NUMBER OF DEFECTS	DEFECTS PER MACHINE	OVER HIGH LIMIT	REPORTING PERIOD FROM	TO	DATE OF REPORT
X2056	EJV421	2	NEW	104	49	100	2.1	NONE	9/30	10/30	NOV5,6-

PAGE 2

DESCRIPTION OF MAJOR UNIT	COST OF REPAIR	ACTUAL NO. OF DEFECTS	% DEFECTIVE	% LISTING IN ORDER OF NUMBER OF DEFECTS
SYNC UNIT	11.00	50	50	OVER 40%
PRINTER	17.00	26	26	////////////////////////
READER	14.00	12	12	////////////
MAIN FRAME	8.00	8	8	////////
POWER SUPPLY	10.00	4	4	////

Figure 12.5.   Manufacturing performance reports.

329

MANUFACTURING PERFORMANCE REPORT

SYSTEM	MACHINE TYPE	MODEL NUMBER	STATUS	AUDIT STATION	NUMBER OF MACHINES	NUMBER OF DEFECTS	DEFECTS PER MACHINE	OVER HIGH LIMIT	REPORTING PERIOD FROM	TO	DATE OF REPORT
X2056	EJV421	2	NEW	104	49	100	2.1	NONE	9/30	10/30	NOV5,6-

PAGE 3

DESCRIPTION OF MAJOR UNIT	COST OF REPAIR	HOURS TO REPAIR	EXTENDED COST	% LISTING IN ORDER OF EXTENDED COST
POWER SUPPLY	10.00	25.0	250	/////////////////////////
MAIN FRAME	8.00	30.0	240	////////////////////////
SYNC UNIT	11.00	10.0	110	///////////
PRINTER	17.00	5.0	85	/////////
READER	14.00	5.0	70	/////// EACH SLASH=$10.00

MANUFACTURING PERFORMANCE REPORT

SYSTEM	MACHINE TYPE	MODEL NUMBER	STATUS	AUDIT STATION	NUMBER OF MACHINES	NUMBER OF HOURS	DEFECTS PER MACHINES	OVER HIGH LIMIT	REPORTING PERIOD FROM	TO	DATE OF REPORT
X2056	EJV421	2	NEW	104	49	75	2.1	NONE	9/30	10/30	NOV5,6-

PAGE 4

DESCRIPTION OF MAJOR UNIT	COST OF REPAIR	HOURS TO REPAIR	% TOTAL HOURS	% LISTING IN ORDER OF NUMBER OF HOURS
MAIN FRAME	8.00	30	40	/////////////////////////////////////
POWER SUPPLY	10.00	25	33	///////////////////////////////
SYNC UNIT	11.00	10	13	/////////////
PRINTER	17.00	5	7	////////
READER	14.00	5	7	////////

Figure 12.6. Manufacturing performance reports.

(punched cards or magnetic tape), which digests the data and performs the decision-making functions.

Another basic control-method type is to employ the measurement information directly and immediately with decision-making devices to indicate action to be performed or to actuate directly and automatically the mechanism to complete demanded action. This is called on-line computer processing. This method has been applied to direct in-process control of some metal-removal type process operations involving pneumatic and electronic gaging equipment to control the process.

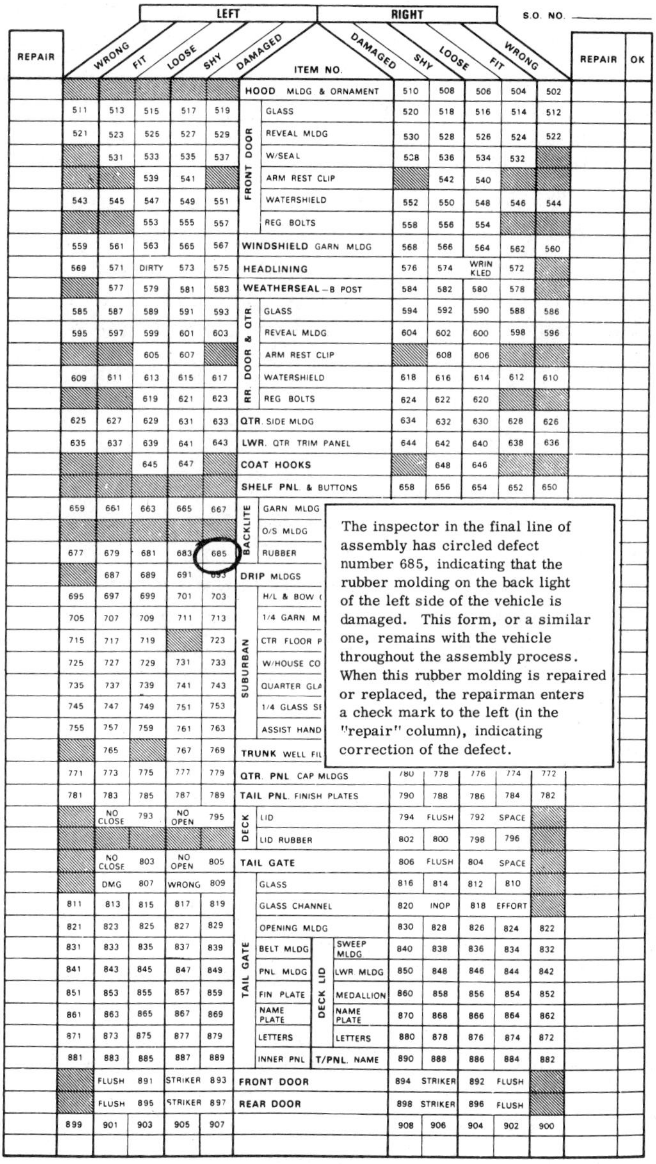

	LEFT					RIGHT					S.O. NO.	
REPAIR	WRONG	FIT	LOOSE	SHY	DAMAGED	ITEM NO. / DAMAGED	SHY	LOOSE	FIT	WRONG	REPAIR	OK
						HOOD MLDG & ORNAMENT 510	508	506	504	502		
	511	513	515	517	519	GLASS 520	518	516	514	512		
	521	523	525	527	529	REVEAL MLDG (FRONT DOOR) 530	528	526	524	522		
		531	533	535	537	W/SEAL 538	536	534	532			
			539	541		ARM REST CLIP 542	540					
	543	545	547	549	551	WATERSHIELD 552	550	548	546	544		
		553	555	557		REG BOLTS 558	556	554				
	559	561	563	565	567	WINDSHIELD GARN MLDG 568	566	564	562	560		
	569	571	DIRTY	573	575	HEADLINING 576	574	WRIN KLED	572			
		577	579	581	583	WEATHERSEAL —B POST 584	582	580	578			
	585	587	589	591	593	GLASS (QTR) 594	592	590	588	586		
	595	597	599	601	603	REVEAL MLDG 604	602	600	598	596		
			605	607		ARM REST CLIP 608	606					
	609	611	613	615	617	WATERSHIELD 618	616	614	612	610		
			619	621	623	REG BOLTS 624	622	620				
	625	627	629	631	633	QTR. SIDE MLDG 634	632	630	628	626		
	635	637	639	641	643	LWR. QTR TRIM PANEL 644	642	640	638	636		
			645	647		COAT HOOKS 648	646					
						SHELF PNL & BUTTONS 658	656	654	652	650		
	659	661	663	665	667	GARN MLDG						
						O/S MLDG						
	677	679	681	683	685	RUBBER						
		687	689	691	693	DRIP MLDGS						
	695	697	699	701	703	H/L & BOW						
	705	707	709	711	713	1/4 GARN M						
	715	717	719		723	CTR FLOOR P						
	725	727	729	731	733	W/HOUSE CO						
	735	737	739	741	743	QUARTER GLA						
	745	747	749	751	753	1/4 GLASS SI						
	755	757	759	761	763	ASSIST HAND						
		765		767	769	TRUNK WELL FIL						
	771	773	775	777	779	QTR. PNL CAP MLDGS 780	778	776	774	772		
	781	783	785	787	789	TAIL PNL. FINISH PLATES 790	788	786	784	782		
		NO CLOSE	793	NO OPEN	795	LID 794	FLUSH	792	SPACE			
						LID RUBBER 802	800	798	796			
		NO CLOSE	803	NO OPEN	805	TAIL GATE 806	FLUSH	804	SPACE			
		DMG	807	WRONG	809	GLASS 816	814	812	810			
	811	813	815	817	819	GLASS CHANNEL 820	INOP	818	EFFORT			
	821	823	825	827	829	OPENING MLDG 830	828	826	824	822		
	831	833	835	837	839	BELT MLDG / SWEEP MLDG 840	838	836	834	832		
	841	843	845	847	849	PNL MLDG / LWR MLDG 850	848	846	844	842		
	851	853	855	857	859	FIN PLATE / MEDALLION 860	858	856	854	852		
	861	863	865	867	869	NAME PLATE / NAME PLATE 870	868	866	864	862		
	871	873	875	877	879	LETTERS / LETTERS 880	878	876	874	872		
	881	883	885	887	889	INNER PNL / T/PNL. NAME 890	888	886	884	882		
		FLUSH	891	STRIKER	893	FRONT DOOR 894	STRIKER	892	FLUSH			
		FLUSH	895	STRIKER	897	REAR DOOR 898	STRIKER	896	FLUSH			
	899	901	903	905	907	908	906	904	902	900		

The inspector in the final line of assembly has circled defect number 685, indicating that the rubber molding on the back light of the left side of the vehicle is damaged. This form, or a similar one, remains with the vehicle throughout the assembly process. When this rubber molding is repaired or replaced, the repairman enters a check mark to the left (in the "repair" column), indicating correction of the defect.

FINAL ASSEMBLY - SOUTH

Figure 12.7.   Quality-control defect coding sheet.

331

An example is given in Figure 12.8, which summarizes the equipment required, as specified by one gaging-hardware manufacturer.[9] The Electrojet gaging sensor generates the signals for product-part deviation measurements. The signals are amplified as analog signals by the Accutron amplifier. A prepared tape of the specification measurements is injected into the computer process and the computer determines absolute product part dimensions during the process operation. Signals are also converted into appropriate code for printout and tape or card punch. This permits subsequent computations which review and summarize product part results. In expanding this type of system, several Electrojet sensors (2, 3, . . . , n as shown) can be incorporated by a programmed switching means to control other locational dimensions such as positions of process machine slides, product part, or sensor from established datums.

Quality Performance

An important element of the quality system is the feedback of information regarding the performance of the product in the field. Evaluation of product performance and consumer reaction to the product is done in a number of ways — customer surveys, determining the amounts of and reasons for returned goods, analyzing the number and type of complaints, and establishing the cost of repair and replacement.

A general procedure is to compute a dollar value or cost for each service call. Analysis of these costs indicates areas where concentrated quality actions are economically justifiable. The same data subsequently analyzed in the light of engineering change effects on the time and cost of field services provides an indication of the continued effectiveness of the quality program.

Figure 12.9 shows an incident report card used by IBM for installation test and servicing information regarding their data processing products. Pertinent defects and costs information is entered on the card and later translated to tape for the preparation of various reports. The procedure is similar to that for the troubles-found card method of reporting in-plant quality failures (see Figure 12.4). The reports generated by the incident report card are used for a number of analyses: (1) diagnosis of component failures, (3) need for engineering changes, (3) comparisons of product models, etc. An interesting IBM analysis involves the use of statistical linear regression to relate each new machine to a performance factor category. Various performance factors are considered, such as functional operations performed by

[9] Courtesy of Bendix Automation and Measurement Division, Dayton, Ohio.

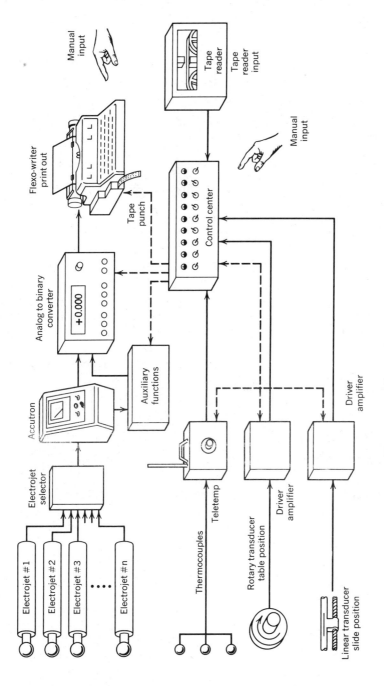

Figure 12.8. On-line computer control of quality.

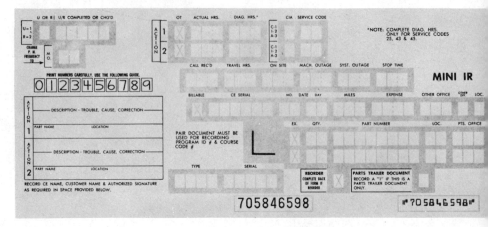

Figure 12.9.   Incident report card.

the equipment, number and complexity of components, and the number of manufacturing operations. The relationship of the observed number of defects to the performance factors of comparable equipment yields a base against which future observed data can be measured. Differences between observed results and base values result in index numbers used for rating product-equipment performance. This procedure is an effective tool for the identification of production problems and determination of quality of new models.

RELIABILITY AND QUALITY CONTROL

Some quality-control textbooks give extensive consideration to the topic of reliability. The appropriateness of this emphasis is debatable. At the student level, an erroneous impression is easily created, namely that reliability is a unique element of the quality system. Reliability involves the quality function, as it does other key areas of the production system. Reliability also makes use of some of the same techniques of statistical inference used by quality control. However, reliability is strictly a design concept and, from a pedagogical point of view, should be treated within the engineering context of design courses, principally electrical and mechanical. Some reference is made to reliability in the following sections, to place its relationship to the quality system in proper perspective and to relate it to trends in quality control.

Definition of Reliability

Reliability is the probability of a device performing its purpose adequately for the period of time intended under the operating conditions encountered. The period of time during which the device performs satisfactorily is of primary interest in reliability measurements because it is a measure of the reliability of the device. In making life tests, a measurement is usually made of the time to failure of each unit of a sample, and from this, the average life of the population from which the sample was taken is inferred. This type of procedure is called working in the time domain. Based on time domain estimates, attempts are made to infer the probability of failure to time x (or, mean time to failure, MTTF). This is called working in the probability domain. Most of the mathematical theory of reliability deals with the time and probability domains.

Essentially, reliability is concerned with two main areas of analysis. The first is the design of a system such that its reliability is higher than that of its separate components (i.e., systems reliability). This analysis deals with the study of the physical behavior of elements which are functionally related in different ways (i.e., systems design). The second analysis area involved is evaluation of the separate reliabilities of the individual components which comprise the system. Evaluations involve the quality function, but not necessarily the quality-control department. The quality-control department is involved only to the extent that it is responsible for laboratory-type inspection and test (and this depends greatly on the degree of technical and engineering training of the quality-control staff).

Reliability Parameters

Three types of failures may occur when components or systems built from components are in operation. These failure types are (1) early failure, (2) chance failure, and (3) wearout failure. The first type of failure is of lesser importance in reliability calculations. Once early failure cause is identified and corrected, and good repair policies adopted, this kind of failure should not occur in the later life of the equipment. Thus, the reliability of mature equipment is governed by the probability of chance and wearout failure. Chance failures are exponentially distributed, with constant failure and replacement rates. Wearout failures are distributed normally or log normally, with a steep increase of failure rate in the wearout period and a constant replacement rate after a stabilization period.

The frequency of both chance and wearout failure of the equipment

335

jointly determines the equipment's reliability. To perform reliability calculations or determine optimum replacement schedules for preventive maintenance, the separate distributions of chance and wearout failure must be known.

Parameters of interest are the population mean time to failure λ, population mean wearout life δ, and the standard deviation σ_δ of the wearout failures. The parameters δ and σ_δ are used to determine suitable replacement or overhaul schedules. The parameter λ is used to compute the probability that no chance failures will occur in the periods between replacements or overhauls.

Clearly, all three parameters $-\lambda$, δ, and σ_δ $-$ of a component population change with the stress level at which the components are operated. The exact laws governing changes of reliability parameters with changing stress levels are not known. Thus, when high precision of reliability measurement is required, it is necessary to laboratory test the components at identical stress levels as that at which they will operate in service. This is called laboratory reliability measurements at simulated stress conditions.

Life Distributions

The exponential probability function is commonly used in life tests. This function is given by

$$f(x) = \frac{1}{\lambda} e^{-\frac{x}{\lambda}}$$

where x denotes time and λ the MTTF. Since λ is greater than zero and x is greater than or equal to zero, this function is a decreasing exponential with

$$f(x) = \frac{1}{\lambda} \quad \text{for } x = 0$$

The probability of failure in the interval (o,t) is expressed by

$$\int_0^t \frac{1}{\lambda} e^{-\frac{x}{\lambda}} \, dx = 1 - e^{-\frac{t}{\lambda}}$$

The probability of no failure to time t, also called the reliability function, $R(t)$ is

$$R(t) = 1 - \left[1 - e^{-\frac{t}{\lambda}} \right] = e^{-\frac{t}{\lambda}}$$

Thus, reliability testing of exponential equipment is comparatively simple since all that is needed is to determine the value of λ by a test.

The failure rate $G(t, \Delta t)$ is defined as the probability of failure in the interval t to $(t + \Delta t)$ divided by the probability of survival to time t and multiplied by $1/\Delta t$, or

$$G(t, \Delta t) = \frac{1}{\Delta t \, R(t)} \int_t^{t + \Delta t} \frac{1}{\lambda} e^{-\frac{x}{\lambda}} \, dx$$

$$= \frac{1}{\Delta t} \left[1 - e^{-\frac{\Delta t}{\lambda}} \right]$$

The hazard rate $Z(t)$, or instantaneous failure rate, is defined as the limit of the failure rate as Δt approaches zero, or

$$Z(t) = \lim_{\Delta t \to 0} G(t, \Delta t)$$

$$= \frac{f(t)}{R(t)}$$

$$= \frac{\frac{1}{\lambda} e^{-\frac{t}{\lambda}}}{e^{-\frac{t}{\lambda}}} = \frac{1}{\lambda}$$

Thus, for the exponential distribution, the failure rate is a constant and is equal to the reciprocal of the MTTF.

In reliability work, the distribution type (exponential or otherwise) is discovered by experiment, and then data from the test samples is used to verify if the hypothesized life distribution is reasonable. Both the chi-square method and the Kolmogorov-Smirnov test for goodness of fit are used for this purpose.

Decision Making

When working with an exponential distribution in life tests, interest is generally on whether λ, the MTTF of the population, is greater or less than some specified value λ_0. That is,

$$H_0 : \lambda \geq \lambda_0$$

$$H_1 : \lambda < \lambda_0$$

The hypothesis test is based on r number of observed failures in the test sample.

Hypothesis testing, in the case of wearout failure, involves the normal distribution and concern is with the possibility of mean wearout life δ being greater or less than a specified δ_0. That is,

$$H_0 : \delta = \delta_0$$
$$H_1 : \delta = \delta_1 > \delta_0$$

The hypothesis test is based on the t-distribution, in the usual manner.

Also, of concern in reliability tests is the determination of estimates of population parameters. For example, in the exponential distribution case, n items are life-tested and testing is discontinued after a predetermined rth failure has occurred. The maximum-likelihood estimate of the MTTF is

$$\hat{\lambda} = \frac{\displaystyle\sum_{i=1}^{r} x_{i,n} + (n - r)\, x_{r,n}}{r}$$

where the observed $x_{i,n}$ are arranged in the order of failure. A $(1-\alpha)$ confidence interval estimate of the MTTF is

$$\frac{2r\hat{\lambda}}{X^2_{\alpha/2,\, 2r}},\ \frac{2r\hat{\lambda}}{X^2_{1 - \frac{\alpha}{2},\, 2r}}$$

The decision-making procedures for the exponential distribution case involve relatively simple calculations. For other distributions, complex computations are necessary. There are digital-computer routines for much of this work. For example, a program called Distat, written for the IBM 1620, computes the mean, variance, and range, and also provides a test of normality and a histogram plot for a set of life-test observations.

Reliability and Quality Control

The role of quality assurance in the achievement of product reliability depends on the nature of the product and the organization of the manufacturing system for creating it. One point of view is that reliability is simply concerned with another set of quality characteristics—those dealing with quality in relation to time—whereas the conventional quality characteristics pertain to quality at one specific time point, namely, the time of manufacture. Thus, reliability is naturally an element of the quality assurance system. Another argument is that, except by pure chance, a product will not have a greater reliability than the designer has engineered into it. Design engineering is mainly responsible for a product's reliability and it follows that reliability is naturally a component of the product design function.

Actually, there are five areas of the production system involved in the effort to achieve reliability. These are design, production, inspection and test, maintenance, and field operations. Design is, of course, the key area. However, the designer does not know what degree of reliability he has obtained until the stages of production and substantial usage have passed. Models are constructed and subjected to test (usually very limited tests in terms of actual service requirements). However, many of the causes of unreliability, especially those like stress-cracking which require time for their development, are disclosed only by product usage. No test, no simulation can equivalently substitute for actual service in the hands of the user.

It is in the area of field service information that the quality-control department can perhaps make the greatest contribution to product reliability. In most companies, the organizational means for obtaining field service data and translating it into corrective action already resides with the quality assurance function. The quality-control department is independent of responsibility for design, production, or use of the product. Its analysis of customer complaints is likely to be an accurate barometer of product performance. Customer complaints have an important bearing on design, particularly reliability design. Expanding the means of obtaining customer complaints to include performance troubles, which may not be considered cause for complaint, is also important. In many cases of initially unreported trouble, a careful analysis of the conditions involved would disclose potentially serious causes of failure. Thus, specific arrangements seem to be needed to acquire, on a continuing basis, performance results in addition to those furnished through complaint channels.

An important factor, which bears directly on the quality-control department's ability to make a useful contribution to the company's reliability effort, is the technical competence of the quality department's staff. Many modern products are most complex with technically arduous functions never dreamed of five and ten years ago. The usual quality tasks of defect identification and causal analysis are such that only trained and experienced engineers can perform them. For many products (particularly aerospace and military), the volume and complexity of reliability specifications involved create a formidable challenge even to a competent engineer. Figure 12.10 indicates the extent of major and support documents required in defense contract administration. Thus, as reported previously in this chapter, it seems very likely that the quality assurance function of the future will rely

Major Reliability Documents

Mil-Std-785 (DOD) Reliability Program Requirements	NPC250-1 (NASA) Reliability Program Provisions for Space Contractors	NAV WEPS OD29304 Guide Manual for Reliability Measurement Program	MICOM Regulation 702-1 Reliability, Quality Assurance and Maintainability
AFCR 80-1 Reliability Program for Systems, Subsystems & Equipments	SP6002 (NASA) Reliability Program Evaluation Procedures	AFSCM/AFLCM 320-1 Management of Contractor's Data and Reports	AFSCM 375 (USAF) -1 Configuration Mg't -4 Program Management -5 System Engineering

Reliability in Design, Development and Production of Equipments and Subsystems Specifications

Mil-R-19610 (WEPS) Production Electronic Equipment	Mil-R-22732 (Ships) Shipboard and Ground Electronic Equipment	Mil-R-27173 (USAF) Ground Checkout Equipment	Mil-R-26484 (USAF) Development-Systems and Subsystems

Other Reliability Documents

USAF Spec Bltn 506 Monitoring	Mil-R-26667 (USAF) Demonstration Requirements	Mil-Std-721 (NAVY) Definitions	Mil-Std-756 (WEP) Prediction Techniques
Mil-R-38100 (USAF) Reliability Assurance Program for Established Reliable Parts	Mil-A-8866 (USAF) Airplane Strength and Rigidity Reliability Requirements, Repeated Loads and Fatigue	Mil-Std-790 (DOD) Reliability Assurance Program for Electronic Parts Specifications	M-REL-131-62 (NASA) Reliability Engineering Program Provisions for Space Systems Contractors
Mil-R-22973 (WEP) Index Determination for Avionic Equipment	Mil-R-23094 Assurance for Production Avionic Equipment	Mil-Std-280 (DOD) Definition of Terms for Equipment Divisions	Mil-Std-757 (DOD) Reliability Evaluation from Demonstration Area
WR-41 (NAVY) Reliability Evaluation			

Support Documents

Maintainability	Quality Control	Provisioning	Design
Mil-M-23313 (NAVY)	Mil-I-45206 (DOD)	Mil-B-5005 (DOD)	Mil-E-4158 (USAF)
Mil-M-23603 (NAVY)	Mil-Q-9858 (DOD)	Mil-E-17362 (Ships)	Mil-E-5400 (ASG)
Mil-M-26512 (USAF)	Mil-Q-21549 (WEPS)	Mil-Std-726 (DOD)	Mil-E-8189 (ASG)
Mil-M-45764 (ORD)	Mil-Std-109	DOD Installation 4151.7	Mil-E-16400 (Ships)
Mil-M-45764 (ARMY)	DCAS EX62-10 (USAF)	MCP-71-650	Mil-E-19600 (WEPS)
Mil-M-55214 (EL)	DOD-Hdbk-50 (DOD)	MCP-71-673	Mil-Std-439
Mil-S-26303	H 110	PP-SIG-SE-1	AD 114274 (ASTIA)
Mil-Std-778 (DOD)	NAV-P-1034 Appendix	SAR-398	AD 148556 (ASTIA)
SCL-4301 (ARMY)	"A"	SAR-400	AD 418907 (ASTIA)
WR-30 (NAVY)	NPC 200-1 (NASA)	WR-1	ANA Bulletin 444
WR-3099-1 (NAVY)	NPC 200-2 (NASA)	WR-2	
	NPC 200-3 (NASA)		
	SP 6003 (NASA)		

Figure 12.10. Department of Defense reliability documents. From Reynolds, L. G. (January 1966), "Defogging Reliability Specs," *Quality Assurance*, Vol. 5, No. 1, pp. 33–36. Stratification of government documents establishing and supporting reliability requirements. For copies, contact your local Defense Contract Administration Services Office.

Sampling	Human Factors	Environmental Factors	Test Methods
Mil-Hdbk-107 (ARMY)	Mil-H-22174 (BU WEPS)	Mil-Std-210	Mil-E-5272
Mil-Hdbk-109 (ARMY)	Mil-H-27894	Mil-Std-446 (DOD)	Mil-T-4807 (USAF)
Mil-Std-105	Mil-H-46819 (ARMY)	Mil-T-152 (DOD)	Mil-T-5422 (ASG)
Mil-Std-414	Mil-Std-803 (USAF)	ANC Bulletin 22	Mil-T-18303 (NAVY)
Mil-Std-690 (DOD)	Mil-Std-1248 (MI)	ASD-TR-61-363	Mil-Std-202
DOD-Hdbk-106	Hel-Std-5-4-65 (ARMY)	USAF Spec Bltn 106	Mil-Std-210
DOD-Hdbk-108	OD-27070 (WEPS)	USAF Spec Bltn 115	Mil-Std-446
H-105	SCL-1787	USAF Spec Bltn 523	Mil-Std-690
H-108			Mil-Std-750
H-109			Mil-Std-810

Parts	Wiring	Interference	Preservation & Packaging
Mil- -38000 Series High	Mil-E-45782	Mil-E-6051 (USAF)	Mil-P-116 (DOD)
Reliability Parts from	Mil-T-713 (DOD)	Mil-I-6181 (USAF)	Mil-P-9024 (USAF)
Minute Man Project	Mil-W-5088 (ASG)	Mil-I-26600 (USAF)	MCP-71-163
Mil- -39000 Series High	Mil-W-8160 (USAF)	PD-R-186 (ABMA)	USAF Spec Bltn 56 AF
Reliability Parts from			
AGREE Report PSME-1			

Training	Data	Enclosures	Test Equipment
Mil-T-4860 (USAF)	Mil-D-9412 (USAF)	Mil-C-172 (DOD)	Mil-T-945 (DOD)
Mil-T-26137 (USAF)	Mil-D-26239 (USAF)	Mil-E-2036 (NAVY)	Mil-T-18306 (WEPS)
Mil-T-27382 (USAF)	Mil-D-70327	Mil-Std-108	Mil-T-21200 (ASG)

Test Levels	Equipment Types	Installation	Preparation for Delivery
Mil-Std-781	Mil-D-3098	Mil-E-25366 (USAF)	Mil-P-38105 (USAF)
Test Levels and Accept	Mil-Std-243	Mil-I-8700 (ASG)	
or Reject Levels			

Vibration	Reports
Mil-Std-167	Mil-R-18136 (WEPS)

REFERENCE DOCUMENTS:

AD 148868 (ASTIA)	RADC Reliability Notebook TR-58-111	PB 181-080	Department of Commerce, Reliability Analysis Data
PB 121839	NAVY Reliability Design Handbook		for Systems and Components Design Engineers
NAV-AER-16-1-519	Handbook of Preferred Circuits	USAF Spec Bltn 128	Data for Aerospace Ground Equipment Analysis
NAVSHIPS 900-193	Rel Stress Analysis for Electronic Equipment	USAF Spec Bltn 519	Bibliography, Reliability Documents
NAVSHIPS 93820	Handbook for Prediction — Shipboard and Shore Elec-	IDEP-1	Interservice Data Exchange Program
	tronic Equipment Reliability	IDEP-2	Interservice Data Exchange
AFSC-TR-65-1	Requirements Methodology		Program
-65-2	Prediction Measurement	Mil-Hdbk-217	Reliability Stress and Fail-
-65-3	Data Collection and		ure Rate Data for
	Management Reports		Electronic Equipment
-65-4	Cost Effectiveness	NEL Suggestions for Designers of Electronic	
	Optimization	Equipment	
-65-5	Management Systems	AGREE Report, Reliability of Military Electronic	
-65-6	Chairman's Final Report	Equipment	
PSMR-1	Parts Spec Management	Reliability Engineering Notes, Diamond	
	for Reliability	Ordnance Fuze Laboratory	

heavily on professional engineering skills, particularly if this function is extensively involved also with the reliability effort.

Organization for reliability is presently a somewhat controversial topic. In many companies, separate quality and reliability empires have been created, with much duplication of effort, competition, and even friction being reported. Freedberg[10] describes a recent survey made among major companies in the electronics industry. The survey is based on a questionnaire developed to obtain information concerning the organizational arrangements, operations, and significant problems of reliability departments in the electronics industry. Some of the questions and responses are summarized here.

In response to the question of separate quality and reliability groups, 70% of the reporting companies indicate they have separate quality and reliability departments. Without exception, the companies reporting that both functions are combined within one department are organizations employing less than 500 people. In many of these companies, the quality and reliability department includes other assurative activities such as value engineering, maintainability, and so forth.

Regarding the reliability personnel qualifications, most of the responses indicate (1) the head of the reliability section is a graduate engineer with 10 to 25 years of industrial experience, and (2) the reliability staff consists mainly of graduate engineers with 3 to 10 years industrial experience (and 70% of this group are continuing in education toward advanced degrees).

One survey question is directed at causes for not attaining reliability goals. Topping the list of reported causes is lack of field usage data. Most of the companies expressed a need for an improved field failure reporting system for the industry, with manufacturers cooperating to make report information available to each other.

SUMMARY

In the past ten years, significant progress has occurred in both the administrative and technical areas of quality control. The major administrative development has been the clarification and acceptance of the concept of total quality control. A significant technical development has been a blending of engineering and statistical approaches

[10] Freedberg, M. (November, 1966), "Reliability Management—A Survey," *Industrial Quality Control*, Vol. 23, No. 5, pp. 224-226.

to quality problems. A recent survey of the industries indicates (1) an increasing participation of the quality-control department in purchasing and design engineering activities to design quality into the product, and (2) a developing need for professional engineering skills in the quality assurance function.

Many quality-control procedures are based on mathematical techniques for identifying quality problems at the earliest and least costly point in the production system. These procedures are complicated by (1) the large mass of data that must be handled and analyzed, (2) the wide area over which the data originates, and (3) the number of people generating the data. Automatic data processing methods are being increasingly used to reduce data information to meaningful and useful forms. All indications are that the quality-control function of the future will be based on integrated information flow systems tied to the computer.

Reliability design and evaluation concerns five areas of the production system – design, production, inspection and test, maintenance, and field operation. Design is the key area; it is responsible for systems and system reliability design. The quality-control department is involved with reliability evaluation, principally in the inspection and test area and also in the collection, handling, and analysis of field service data. Organization for reliability varies from one industry to another. However, a recent survey in the electronics industry reveals that most companies in this industry have separate reliability and quality departments, with the reliability section being staffed, for the most part, by graduate engineers with considerable industrial experience.

REFERENCES

Cocca, O. A. (November, 1967), *The Emerging Role of the Engineer in Quality Control,* Winter Annual Meeting and Energy Systems Exposition, Pittsburgh, Pa., The American Society of Mechanical Engineers.

Feigenbaum, A. V. (1961), *Total Quality Control,* McGraw-Hill, New York.

Freedberg, M. (November, 1966), "Reliability Management – A Survey," *Industrial Quality Control,* Vol. 23, No. 5, pp. 224-226.

General Informations Manual (1962), IBM Management Operating System Quality Assurance for Manufacturing Industries, International Business Machines Corporation, Data Processing Division, White Plains, New York.

Geschelin, J. (June, 1964), "Chrysler Assembly Line Computers Provide Instant Quality Control," *Automotive Industries,* Vol. 131, No. 9, pp. 37-39.

Hansen, B. L. (1963), *Quality Control,* Prentice-Hall, Engelwood Cliffs, New Jersey.

Shewhart, W. A. (1931), *Economic Control of Manufactured Product,* D. Van Nostrand, New York.

Special Report (August, 1968), "Who Cares About Quality," *Quality Assurance,* Vol. 7, No. 8, pp. 26-29.

REVIEW QUESTIONS

1. Briefly explain the trend toward the acquisition of professional engineering skills in the quality-control field.

2. State three constraints in connection with mathematically based control procedures which operate to favor the use of automatic data processing methods in quality control.

3. A routine computer application to quality control is the preparation of quality reports. What computer application has the greatest potential for quality assurance?

4. With reference to the answer to question 3, distinguish between off-line and on-line computer processing.

5. Reliability is not a unique element of the quality system. Reliability only involves the quality function. What element of the production system is responsible for the major reliability decisions?

6. Define the term reliability.

7. What are the two main areas of analysis in reliability considerations?

8. State three types of failures which may occur when components or systems built from components are in operation. Which failure types are important in reliability evaluations?

9. Identify the principal parameters of interest in reliability evaluations.

10. In what activity area can the quality-control department make the greatest contribution to product reliability? Briefly summarize the argument for this observation.

Appendixes

Areas under the Normal Curve from Z_α to $+\infty$

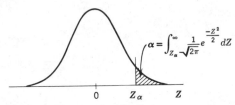

$$\alpha = \int_{Z_\alpha}^{\infty} \frac{1}{\sqrt{2\pi}} e^{\frac{-Z^2}{2}} dZ$$

Z_α	.00	.01	.02	.03	.04	.05	.06	.07	.08	.09
0.0	.5000	.4960	.4920	.4880	.4840	.4801	.4761	.4721	.4681	.4641
0.1	.4602	.4562	.4522	.4483	.4443	.4404	.4364	.4325	.4286	.4247
0.2	.4207	.4168	.4129	.4090	.4052	.4013	.3974	.3936	.3897	.3859
0.3	.3821	.3783	.3745	.3707	.3669	.3632	.3594	.3557	.3520	.3483
0.4	.3446	.3409	.3372	.3336	.3300	.3264	.3228	.3192	.3156	.3121
0.5	.3085	.3050	.3015	.2981	.2946	.2912	.2877	.2843	.2810	.2776
0.6	.2743	.2709	.2676	.2643	.2611	.2578	.2546	.2514	.2483	.2451
0.7	.2420	.2389	.2358	.2327	.2296	.2266	.2236	.2206	.2177	.2148
0.8	.2119	.2090	.2061	.2033	.2005	.1977	.1949	.1922	.1894	.1867
0.9	.1841	.1814	.1788	.1762	.1736	.1711	.1685	.1660	.1635	.1611
1.0	.1587	.1562	.1539	.1515	.1492	.1469	.1446	.1423	.1401	.1379
1.1	.1357	.1335	.1314	.1292	.1271	.1251	.1230	.1210	.1190	.1170
1.2	.1151	.1131	.1112	.1093	.1075	.1056	.1038	.1020	.1003	.0985
1.3	.0968	.0951	.0934	.0918	.0901	.0885	.0869	.0853	.0838	.0823
1.4	.0808	.0793	.0778	.0764	.0749	.0735	.0721	.0708	.0694	.0681
1.5	.0668	.0655	.0643	.0630	.0618	.0606	.0594	.0582	.0571	.0559
1.6	.0548	.0537	.0526	.0516	.0505	.0495	.0485	.0475	.0465	.0455
1.7	.0446	.0436	.0427	.0418	.0409	.0401	.0392	.0384	.0375	.0367
1.8	.0359	.0351	.0344	.0336	.0329	.0322	.0314	.0307	.0301	.0294
1.9	.0287	.0281	.0274	.0268	.0262	.0256	.0250	.0244	.0239	.0233
2.0	.0228	.0222	.0217	.0212	.0207	.0202	.0197	.0192	.0188	.0183
2.1	.0179	.0174	.0170	.0166	.0162	.0158	.0154	.0150	.0146	.0143
2.2	.0139	.0136	.0132	.0129	.0125	.0122	.0119	.0116	.0113	.0110
2.3	.0107	.0104	.0102	.00990	.00964	.00939	.00914	.00889	.00866	.00842
2.4	.00820	.00798	.00776	.00755	.00734	.00714	.00695	.00676	.00657	.00639
2.5	.00621	.00604	.00587	.00570	.00554	.00539	.00523	.00508	.00494	.00480
2.6	.00466	.00453	.00440	.00427	.00415	.00402	.00391	.00379	.00368	.00357
2.7	.00347	.00336	.00326	.00317	.00307	.00298	.00289	.00280	.00272	.00264
2.8	.00256	.00248	.00240	.00233	.00226	.00219	.00212	.00205	.00199	.00193
2.9	.00187	.00181	.00175	.00169	.00164	.00159	.00154	.00149	.00144	.00139

Z_α	.0	.1	.2	.3	.4	.5	.6	.7	.8	.9
3	.00135	$.0^3968$	$.0^3687$	$.0^3483$	$.0^3337$	$.0^3233$	$.0^3159$	$.0^3108$	$.0^4723$	$.0^4481$
4	$.0^4317$	$.0^4207$	$.0^4133$	$.0^5854$	$.0^5541$	$.0^5340$	$.0^5211$	$.0^5130$	$.0^6793$	$.0^6479$
5	$.0^6287$	$.0^6170$	$.0^7996$	$.0^7579$	$.0^7333$	$.0^7190$	$.0^7107$	$.0^8599$	$.0^8332$	$.0^8182$
6	$.0^8987$	$.0^9530$	$.0^9282$	$.0^9149$	$.0^{10}777$	$.0^{10}402$	$.0^{10}206$	$.0^{10}104$	$.0^{11}523$	$.0^{11}260$

Reprinted by permission from Frederick E. Croxton, *Elementary Statistics with Applications in Medicine*, Prentice-Hall, Englewood Cliffs, N. J., 1953, p. 323.

Factors for Computing Control Chart Lines[1]

Number of Observations in Sample, n	Chart for Averages — Factors for Control Limits			Chart for Standard Deviations — Factors for Central Line		Chart for Standard Deviations — Factors for Control Limits				Chart for Ranges — Factors for Central Line			Chart for Ranges — Factors for Control Limits			
	A	A_1	A_2	c_2	$1/c_2$	B_1	B_2	B_3	B_4	d_2	$1/d_2$	d_3	D_1	D_2	D_3	D_4
2	2.121	3.760	1.880	0.5642	1.7725	0	1.843	0	3.267	1.128	0.8865	0.853	0	3.686	0	3.267
3	1.732	2.394	1.023	0.7236	1.3820	0	1.858	0	2.568	1.693	0.5907	0.888	0	4.358	0	2.575
4	1.500	1.880	0.729	0.7979	1.2533	0	1.808	0	2.266	2.059	0.4857	0.880	0	4.698	0	2.282
5	1.342	1.596	0.577	0.8407	1.1894	0	1.756	0	2.089	2.326	0.4299	0.864	0	4.918	0	2.115
6	1.225	1.410	0.483	0.8686	1.1512	0.026	1.711	0.030	1.970	2.534	0.3946	0.848	0	5.078	0	2.004
7	1.134	1.277	0.419	0.8882	1.1259	0.105	1.672	0.118	1.882	2.704	0.3698	0.833	0.205	5.203	0.076	1.924
8	1.061	1.175	0.373	0.9027	1.1078	0.167	1.638	0.185	1.815	2.847	0.3512	0.820	0.387	5.307	0.136	1.864
9	1.000	1.094	0.337	0.9139	1.0942	0.219	1.609	0.239	1.761	2.970	0.3367	0.808	0.546	5.394	0.184	1.816
10	0.949	1.028	0.308	0.9227	1.0837	0.262	1.584	0.284	1.716	3.078	0.3249	0.797	0.687	5.469	0.223	1.777
11	0.905	0.973	0.285	0.9300	1.0753	0.299	1.561	0.321	1.679	3.173	0.3152	0.787	0.812	5.534	0.256	1.744
12	0.866	0.925	0.266	0.9359	1.0684	0.331	1.541	0.354	1.646	3.258	0.3069	0.778	0.924	5.592	0.284	1.716
13	0.832	0.884	0.249	0.9410	1.0627	0.359	1.523	0.382	1.618	3.336	0.2998	0.770	1.026	5.646	0.308	1.692
14	0.802	0.848	0.235	0.9453	1.0579	0.384	1.507	0.406	1.594	3.407	0.2935	0.762	1.121	5.693	0.329	1.671
15	0.775	0.816	0.223	0.9490	1.0537	0.406	1.492	0.428	1.572	3.472	0.2880	0.755	1.207	5.737	0.348	1.652
16	0.750	0.788	0.212	0.9523	1.0501	0.427	1.478	0.448	1.552	3.532	0.2831	0.749	1.285	5.779	0.364	1.636
17	0.728	0.762	0.203	0.9551	1.0470	0.445	1.465	0.466	1.534	3.588	0.2787	0.743	1.359	5.817	0.379	1.621
18	0.707	0.738	0.194	0.9576	1.0442	0.461	1.454	0.482	1.518	3.640	0.2747	0.738	1.426	5.854	0.392	1.608
19	0.688	0.717	0.187	0.9599	1.0418	0.477	1.443	0.497	1.503	3.689	0.2711	0.733	1.490	5.888	0.404	1.596
20	0.671	0.697	0.180	0.9619	1.0396	0.491	1.433	0.510	1.490	3.735	0.2677	0.729	1.548	5.922	0.414	1.586
21	0.655	0.679	0.173	0.9638	1.0376	0.504	1.424	0.523	1.477	3.778	0.2647	0.724	1.606	5.950	0.425	1.575
22	0.640	0.662	0.167	0.9655	1.0358	0.516	1.415	0.534	1.466	3.819	0.2618	0.720	1.659	5.979	0.434	1.566
23	0.626	0.647	0.162	0.9670	1.0342	0.527	1.407	0.545	1.455	3.858	0.2592	0.716	1.710	6.006	0.443	1.557
24	0.612	0.632	0.157	0.9684	1.0327	0.538	1.399	0.555	1.445	3.895	0.2567	0.712	1.759	6.031	0.452	1.548
25	0.600	0.619	0.153	0.9696	1.0313	0.548	1.392	0.565	1.435	3.931	0.2544	0.709	1.804	6.058	0.459	1.541
Over 25	$\dfrac{3}{\sqrt{n}}$	$\dfrac{3}{\sqrt{n}}$	.....	.....	.....	*	**	*	**	.....	.....	.....	.....	.....	.....	.....

$$*1 - \frac{3}{\sqrt{2n}} \qquad **1 + \frac{3}{\sqrt{2n}}$$

[1] Reproduced by permission from *ASTM Manual on Quality Control of Materials*, American Society for Testing Materials, Philadelphia, Pa., 1951.

From A. H. Bowker and G. J. Lieberman, *Engineering Statistics*, Prentice-Hall, Englewood Cliffs, N. J.

Summation of Terms of Poisson's Exponential Binomial Limit*

(1,000 × probability of c or less occurrences of event that has an average number of occurrences equal to c' or np')

c' or np' \\ c	0	1	2	3	4	5	6	7	8	9
0.02	980	1,000								
0.04	961	999	1,000							
0.06	942	998	1,000							
0.08	923	997	1,000							
0.10	905	995	1,000							
0.15	861	990	999	1,000						
0.20	819	982	999	1,000						
0.25	779	974	998	1,000						
0.30	741	963	996	1,000						
0.35	705	951	994	1,000						
0.40	670	938	992	999	1,000					
0.45	638	925	989	999	1,000					
0.50	607	910	986	998	1,000					
0.55	577	894	982	998	1,000					
0.60	549	878	977	997	1,000					
0.65	522	861	972	996	999	1,000				
0.70	497	844	966	994	999	1,000				
0.75	472	827	959	993	999	1,000				
0.80	449	809	953	991	999	1,000				
0.85	427	791	945	989	998	1,000				
0.90	407	772	937	987	998	1,000				
0.95	387	754	929	984	997	1,000				
1.00	368	736	920	981	996	999	1,000			
1.1	333	699	900	974	995	999	1,000			
→ 1.2	301	663	879	966	992	998	1,000			

*Reprinted by permission from E. L. Grant, *Statistical Quality Control*, 2nd ed., McGraw-Hill, New York, 1952.

Summation of Terms of Poisson's
Exponential Binomial Limit (continued)

c'or np' \ c	0	1	2	3	4	5	6	7	8	9
1.3	273	627	857	957	989	998	1,000			
1.4	247	592	833	946	986	997	999	1,000		
1.5	223	558	809	934	981	996	999	1,000		
1.6	202	525	783	921	976	994	999	1,000		
1.7	183	493	757	907	970	992	998	1,000		
1.8	165	463	731	891	964	990	997	999	1,000	
1.9	150	434	704	875	956	987	997	999	1,000	
2.0	135	406	677	857	947	983	995	999	1,000	
2.2	111	355	623	819	928	975	993	998	1,000	
2.4	091	308	570	779	904	964	988	997	999	1,000
2.6	074	267	518	736	877	951	983	995	999	1,000
2.8	061	231	469	692	848	935	976	992	998	999
3.0	050	199	423	647	815	916	966	988	996	999
3.2	041	171	380	603	781	895	955	983	994	998
3.4	033	147	340	558	744	871	942	977	992	997
3.6	027	126	303	515	706	844	927	969	988	996
3.8	022	107	269	473	668	816	909	960	984	994
4.0	018	092	238	433	629	785	889	949	979	992
4.2	015	078	210	395	590	753	867	936	972	989
4.4	012	066	185	359	551	720	844	921	964	985
4.6	010	056	163	326	513	686	818	905	955	980
4.8	008	048	143	294	476	651	791	887	944	975
5.0	007	040	125	265	440	616	762	867	932	968
5.2	006	034	109	238	406	581	732	845	918	960
5.4	005	029	095	213	373	546	702	822	903	951
5.6	004	024	082	191	342	512	670	797	886	941
5.8	003	021	072	170	313	478	638	771	867	929
6.0	002	017	062	151	285	446	606	744	847	916

c'or np'	10	11	12	13	14	15	16
2.8	1,000						
3.0	1,000						
3.2	1,000						
3.4	999	1,000					
3.6	999	1,000					
3.8	998	999	1,000				
4.0	997	999	1,000				

c c' or np'	0	1	2	3	4	5	6	7	8	9
4.2	996	999	1,000							
4.4	994	998	999	1,000						
4.6	992	997	999	1,000						
4.8	990	996	999	1,000						
5.0	986	995	998	999	1,000					
5.2	982	993	997	999	1,000					
5.4	977	990	996	999	1,000					
5.6	972	988	995	998	999	1,000				
5.8	965	984	993	997	999	1,000				
6.0	957	980	991	996	999	999	1,000			
6.2	002	015	054	134	259	414	574	716	826	902
6.4	002	012	046	119	235	384	542	687	803	886
6.6	001	010	040	105	213	355	511	658	780	869
6.8	001	009	034	093	192	327	480	628	755	850
7.0	001	007	030	082	173	301	450	599	729	830
7.2	001	006	025	072	156	276	420	569	703	810
7.4	001	005	022	063	140	253	392	539	676	788
7.6	001	004	019	055	125	231	365	510	648	765
7.8	000	004	016	048	112	210	338	481	620	741
8.0	000	003	014	042	100	191	313	453	593	717
8.5	000	002	009	030	074	150	256	386	523	653
9.0	000	001	006	021	055	116	207	324	456	587
9.5	000	001	004	015	040	089	165	269	392	522
10.0	000	000	003	010	029	067	130	220	333	458

	10	11	12	13	14	15	16	17	18	19
6.2	949	975	989	995	998	999	1,000			
6.4	939	969	986	994	997	999	1,000			
6.6	927	963	982	992	997	999	999	1,000		
6.8	915	955	978	990	996	998	999	1,000		
7.0	901	947	973	987	994	998	999	1,000		
7.2	887	937	967	984	993	997	999	999	1,000	
7.4	871	926	961	980	991	996	998	999	1,000	
7.6	854	915	954	976	989	995	998	999	1,000	
7.8	835	902	945	971	986	993	997	999	1,000	
8.0	816	888	936	966	983	992	996	998	999	1,000
8.5	763	849	909	949	973	986	993	997	999	999
9.0	706	803	876	926	959	978	989	995	998	999
9.5	645	752	836	898	940	967	982	991	996	998
10.0	583	697	792	864	917	951	973	986	993	997

	20	21	22

Summation of Terms of Poisson's Exponential Binomial Limit (continued)

c' or np' \ c	0	1	2	3	4	5	6	7	8	9
8.5	1,000									
9.0	1,000									
9.5	999	1,000								
10.0	998	999	1,000							
10.5	000	000	002	007	021	050	102	179	279	397
11.0	000	000	001	005	015	038	079	143	232	341
11.5	000	000	001	003	011	028	060	114	191	289
12.0	000	000	001	002	008	020	046	090	155	242
12.5	000	000	000	002	005	015	035	070	125	201
13.0	000	000	000	001	004	011	026	054	100	166
13.5	000	000	000	001	003	008	019	041	079	135
14.0	000	000	000	000	002	006	014	032	062	109
14.5	000	000	000	000	001	004	010	024	048	088
15.0	000	000	000	000	001	003	008	018	037	070

	10	11	12	13	14	15	16	17	18	19
10.5	521	639	742	825	888	932	960	978	988	994
11.0	460	579	689	781	854	907	944	968	982	991
11.5	402	520	633	733	815	878	924	954	974	986
12.0	347	462	576	682	772	844	899	937	963	979
12.5	297	406	519	628	725	806	869	916	948	969
13.0	252	353	463	573	675	764	835	890	930	957
13.5	211	304	409	518	623	718	798	861	908	942
14.0	176	260	358	464	570	669	756	827	883	923
14.5	145	220	311	413	518	619	711	790	853	901
15.0	118	185	268	363	466	568	664	749	819	875

	20	21	22	23	24	25	26	27	28	29
10.5	997	999	999	1,000						
11.0	995	998	999	1,000						
11.5	992	996	998	999	1,000					
12.0	988	994	997	999	999	1,000				
12.5	983	991	995	998	999	999	1,000			
13.0	975	986	992	996	998	999	1,000			
13.5	965	980	989	994	997	998	999	1,000		
14.0	952	971	983	991	995	997	999	999	1,000	
14.5	936	960	976	986	992	996	998	999	999	1,000
15.0	917	947	967	981	989	994	997	998	999	1,000

c' or np' \ c	4	5	6	7	8	9	10	11	12	13
16	000	001	004	010	022	043	077	127	193	275
17	000	001	002	005	013	026	049	085	135	201
18	000	000	001	003	007	015	030	055	092	143
19	000	000	001	002	004	009	018	035	061	098
20	000	000	000	001	002	005	011	021	039	066
21	000	000	000	000	001	003	006	013	025	043
22	000	000	000	000	001	002	004	008	015	028
23	000	000	000	000	000	001	002	004	009	017
24	000	000	000	000	000	000	001	003	005	011
25	000	000	000	000	000	000	001	001	003	006

	14	15	16	17	18	19	20	21	22	23
16	368	467	566	659	742	812	868	911	942	963
17	281	371	468	564	655	736	805	861	905	937
18	208	287	375	469	562	651	731	799	855	899
19	150	215	292	378	469	561	647	725	793	849
20	105	157	221	297	381	470	559	644	721	787
21	072	111	163	227	302	384	471	558	640	716
22	048	077	117	169	232	306	387	472	556	637
23	031	052	082	123	175	238	310	389	472	555
24	020	034	056	087	128	180	243	314	392	473
25	012	022	038	060	092	134	185	247	318	394

	24	25	26	27	28	29	30	31	32	33
16	978	987	993	996	998	999	999	1,000		
17	959	975	985	991	995	997	999	999	1,000	
18	932	955	972	983	990	994	997	998	999	1,000
19	893	927	951	969	980	988	993	996	998	999
20	843	888	922	948	966	978	987	992	995	997
21	782	838	883	917	944	963	976	985	991	994
22	712	777	832	877	913	940	959	973	983	989
23	635	708	772	827	873	908	936	956	971	981
24	554	632	704	768	823	868	904	932	953	969
25	473	553	629	700	763	818	863	900	929	950

	34	35	36	37	38	39	40	41	42	43
19	999	1,000								
20	999	999	1,000							
21	997	998	999	999	1,000					
22	994	996	998	999	999	1,000				
23	988	993	996	997	999	999	1,000			
24	979	987	992	995	997	998	999	999	1,000	
25	966	978	985	991	994	997	998	999	999	1,000

Appendix D
Military Standard MIL-STD-105D

SAMPLING PROCEDURES AND TABLES

FOR INSPECTION BY ATTRIBUTES

April, 1963

1. SCOPE

1.1 PURPOSE. This publication establishes sampling plans and procedures for inspection by attributes. When specified by the responsible authority, this publication shall be referenced in the specification, contract, inspection instructions, or other documents and the provisions set forth herein shall govern. The "responsible authority" shall be designated in one of the above documents.

1.2 APPLICATION. Sampling plans designated in this publication are applicable, but not limited, to inspection of the following:

a. End items.

b. Components and raw materials.

c. Operations.

d. Materials in process.

e. Supplies in storage.

f. Maintenance operations.

g. Data or records.

h. Administrative procedures.

These plans are intended primarily to be used for a continuing series of lots or batches.

The plans may also be used for the inspection of isolated lots or batches, but, in this latter case, the user is cautioned to consult the operating characteristic curves to find a plan which will yield the desired protection (see 11.6).

1.3 INSPECTION. Inspection is the process of measuring, examining, testing, or otherwise comparing the unit of product (see 1.5) with the requirements.

1.4 INSPECTION BY ATTRIBUTES. Inspection by attributes is inspection whereby either the unit of product is classified simply as defective or nondefective, or the number of defects in the unit of product is counted, with respect to a given requirement or set of requirements.

1.5 UNIT OF PRODUCT. The unit of product is the thing inspected in order to determine its classification as defective or nondefective or to count the number of defects. It may be a single article, a pair, a set, a length, an area, an operation, a volume, a component of an end product, or the end product itself. The unit of product may or may not be the same as the unit of purchase, supply, production, or shipment.

2. CLASSIFICATION OF DEFECTS AND DEFECTIVES

2.1 METHOD OF CLASSIFYING DEFECTS.
A classification of defects is the enumeration of possible defects of the unit of product classified according to their seriousness. A defect is any nonconformance of the unit of product with specified requirements. Defects will normally be grouped into one or more of the following classes; however, defects may be grouped into other classes, or into subclasses within these classes.

2.1.1 CRITICAL DEFECT.
A critical defect is a defect that judgment and experience indicate is likely to result in hazardous or unsafe conditions f o r individuals using, maintaining, or depending upon the product; or a defect that judgment and experience indicate is likely to prevent performance of the tactical function of a major end item such as a ship, aircraft, tank, missile or space vehicle. NOTE: For a special provision relating to critical defects, see 6.3.

2.1.2 MAJOR DEFECT.
A major defect is a defect, other than critical, that is likely to result in failure, or to reduce materially the usability of the unit of product for its intended purpose.

2.1.3 MINOR DEFECT.
A minor defect is a defect that is not likely to reduce materially the usability of the unit of product for its intended purpose, or is a departure from established standards having little bearing on the effective use or operation of the unit.

2.2 METHOD OF CLASSIFYING DEFECTIVES.
A defective is a unit of product which contains one or more defects. Defectives will usually be classified as follows:

2.2.1 CRITICAL DEFECTIVE.
A critical defective contains one or more critical defects and may also contain major and or minor defects. NOTE: For a special provision relating to critical defectives, see 6.3.

2.2.2 MAJOR DEFECTIVE.
A major defective contains one or more major defects, and may also contain minor defects but contains no critical defect.

2.2.3 MINOR DEFECTIVE.
A minor defective contains one or more minor defects but contains no critical or major defect.

3. PERCENT DEFECTIVE AND DEFECTS PER HUNDRED UNITS

3.1 EXPRESSION OF NONCONFORMANCE.
The extent of nonconformance of product shall be expressed either in terms of percent defective or in terms of defects per hundred units.

3.2 PERCENT DEFECTIVE.
The percent defective of any given quantity of units of product is one hunderd times the number of defective units of product contained therein divided by the total number of product, i.e.:

$$\text{Percent defective} = \frac{\text{Number of defectives}}{\text{Number of units inspected}} \times 100$$

3.3 DEFECTS PER HUNDRED UNITS.
The number of defects per hundred units of any given quantity of units of product is one hundred times the number of defects contained therein (one or more defects being possible in any unit of product) divided by the total number of units of product, i.e.:

$$\frac{\text{Defects per}}{\text{hundred units}} = \frac{\text{Number of defects}}{\text{Number of units inspected}} \times 100$$

4. ACCEPTABLE QUALITY LEVEL (AQL)

4.1 USE. The AQL, together with the Sample Size Code Letter, is used for indexing the sampling plans provided herein.

4.2 DEFINITION. The AQL is the maximum percent defective (or the maximum number of defects per hundred units) that, for purposes of sampling inspection, can be considered satisfactory as a process average (see 11.2).

4.3 NOTE ON THE MEANING OF AQL. When a consumer designates some specific value of AQL for a certain defect or group of defects, he indicates to the supplier that his (the consumer's) acceptance sampling plan will accept the great majority of the lots or batches that the supplier submits, provided the process average level of percent defective (or defects per hundred units) in these lots or batches be no greater than the designated value of AQL. Thus, the AQL is a designated value of percent defective (or defects per hundred units) that the consumer indicates will be accepted most of the time by the acceptance sampling procedure to be used. The sampling plans provided herein are so arranged that the probability of acceptance at the designated AQL value depends upon the sample size, being generally higher for large samples than for small ones, for a given AQL. The AQL alone does not describe the protection to the consumer for individual lots or batches but more directly relates to what might be expected from a series of lots or batches, provided the steps indicated in this publication are taken. It is necessary to refer to the operating characteristic curve of the plan, to determine what protection the consumer will have.

4.4 LIMITATION. The designation of an AQL shall not imply that the supplier has the right to supply knowingly any defective unit of product.

4.5 SPECIFYING AQLs. The AQL to be used will be designated in the contract or by the responsible authority. Different AQLs may be designated for groups of defects considered collectively, or for individual defects. An AQL for a group of defects may be designated in addition to AQLs for individual defects, or subgroups, within that group. AQL values of 10.0 or less may be expressed either in percent defective or in defects per hundred units; those over 10.0 shall be expressed in defects per hundred units only.

4.6 PREFERRED AQLs. The values of AQLs given in these tables are known as preferred AQLs. If, for any product, an AQL be designated other than a preferred AQL, these tables are not applicable.

5. SUBMISSION OF PRODUCT

5.1 LOT OR BATCH. The term lot or batch shall mean "inspection lot" or "inspection batch," i.e., a collection of units of product from which a sample is to be drawn and inspected to determine conformance with the acceptability criteria, and may differ from a collection of units designated as a lot or batch for other purposes (e.g., production, shipment, etc.).

5.2 FORMATION OF LOTS OR BATCHES. The product shall be assembled into identifiable lots, sublots, batches, or in such other manner as may be prescribed (see 5.4). Each lot or batch shall, as far as is practicable,

356

5. SUBMISSION OF PRODUCT (Continued)

consist of units of product of a single type, grade, class, size, and composition, manufactured under essentially the same conditions, and at essentially the same time.

5.3 LOT OR BATCH SIZE. The lot or batch size is the number of units of product in a lot or batch.

5.4 PRESENTATION OF LOTS OR BATCHES. The formation of the lots or batches, lot or batch size, and the manner in which each lot or batch is to be presented and identified by the supplier shall be designated or approved by the responsible authority. As necessary, the supplier shall provide adequate and suitable storage space for each lot or batch, equipment needed for proper identification and presentation, and personnel for all handling of product required for drawing of samples.

6. ACCEPTANCE AND REJECTION

6.1 ACCEPTABILITY OF LOTS OR BATCHES. Acceptability of a lot or batch will be determined by the use of a sampling plan or plans associated with the designated AQL or AQLs.

6.2 DEFECTIVE UNITS. The right is reserved to reject any unit of product found defective during inspection whether that unit of product forms part of a sample or not, and whether the lot or batch as a whole is accepted or rejected. Rejected units may be repaired or corrected and resubmitted for inspection with the approval of, and in the manner specified by, the responsible authority.

6.3 SPECIAL RESERVATION FOR CRITICAL DEFECTS. The supplier may be required at the discretion of the responsible authority to inspect every unit of the lot or batch for critical defects. The right is reserved to inspect every unit submitted by the supplier for critical defects, and to reject the lot or batch immediately, when a critical defect is found. The right is reserved also to sample, for critical defects, every lot or batch submitted by the supplier and to reject any lot or batch if a sample drawn therefrom is found to contain one or more critical defects.

6.4 RESUBMITTED LOTS OR BATCHES. Lots or batches found unacceptable shall be resubmitted for reinspection only after all units are re-examined or retested and all defective units are removed or defects corrected. The responsible authority shall determine whether normal or tightened inspection shall be used, and whether reinspection shall include all types or classes of defects or for the particular types or classes of defects which caused initial rejection.

7. DRAWING OF SAMPLES

7.1 SAMPLE. A sample consists of one or more units of product drawn from a lot or batch, the units of the sample being selected at random without regard to their quality. The number of units of product in the sample is the sample size.

7.2 REPRESENTATIVE SAMPLING. When appropriate, the number of units in the sample shall be selected in proportion to the size of sublots or subbatches, or parts of the lot or batch, identified by some rational criterion.

7. DRAWING OF SAMPLES (Continued)

When representative sampling is used, the units from each part of the lot or batch shall be selected at random.

7.3 TIME OF SAMPLING. Samples may be drawn after all the units comprising the lot or batch have been assembled, or sam-ples may be drawn during assembly of the lot or batch.

7.4 DOUBLE OR MULTIPLE SAMPLING. When double or multiple sampling is to be used, each sample shall be selected over the entire lot or batch.

8. NORMAL, TIGHTENED AND REDUCED INSPECTION

8.1 INITIATION OF INSPECTION. Normal inspection will be used at the start of inspection unless otherwise directed by the responsible authority.

8.2 CONTINUATION OF INSPECTION. Normal, tightened or reduced inspection shall continue unchanged for each class of defects or defectives on successive lots or batchs except where the switching procedures given below require change. The switching procedures given below require a change. The switching procedures shall be applied to each class of defects or defectives independently.

8.3 SWITCHING PROCEDURES.

8.3.1 NORMAL TO TIGHTENED. When normal inspection is in effect, tightened inspection shall be instituted when 2 out of 5 consecutive lots or batches have been rejected on original inspection (i.e., ignoring resubmitted lots or batches for this procedure).

8.3.2 TIGHTENED TO NORMAL. When tightened inspection is in effect, normal inspection shall be instituted when 5 consecutive lots or batches have been considered acceptable on original inspection.

8.3.3 NORMAL TO REDUCED. When normal inspection is in effect, reduced inspection shall be instituted providing that all of the following conditions are satisfied:

a. The preceding 10 lots or batches (or more, as indicated by the note to Table VIII) have been on normal inspection and none has been rejected on original inspection; and

b. The total number of defectives (or defects) in the samples from the preceding 10 lots or batches (or such other number as was used for condition "a" above) is equal to or less than the applicable number given in Table VIII. If double or multiple sampling is in use, all samples inspected should be included, not "first" samples only; and

c. Production is at a steady rate; and

d. Reduced inspection is considered desirable by the responsible authority.

8.3.4 REDUCED TO NORMAL. When reduced inspection is in effect, normal inspection shall be instituted if any of the following occur on original inspection:

a. A lot or batch is rejected; or

b. A lot or batch is considered acceptable under the procedures of 10.1.4; or

c. Production becomes irregular or delayed; or

d. Other conditions warrant that normal inspection shall be instituted.

8.4 DISCONTINUATION OF INSPECTION. In the event that 10 consecutive lots or batches remain on tightened inspection (or such other number as may be designated by the responsible authority), inspection under the provisions of this document should be discontinued pending action to improve the quality of submitted material.

358

9. SAMPLING PLANS

9.1 SAMPLING PLAN. A sampling plan indicates the number of units of product from each lot or batch which are to be inspected (sample size or series of sample sizes) and the criteria for determining the acceptability of the lot or batch (acceptance and rejection numbers).

9.2 INSPECTION LEVEL. The inspection level determines the relationship between the lot or batch size and the sample size. The inspection level to be used for any particular requirement will be prescribed by the responsible authority. Three inspection levels: I, II, and III, are given in Table I for general use. Unless otherwise specified, Inspection Level II will be used. However, Inspection Level I may be specified when less discrimination is needed, or Level III may be specified for greater discrimination. Four additional special levels: S–1, S–2, S–3 and S–4, are given in the same table and may be used where relatively small sample sizes are necessary and large sampling risks can or must be tolerated.

NOTE: In the designation of inspection levels S–1 to S–4, care must be exercised to avoid AQLs inconsistent with these inspection levels.

9.3 CODE LETTERS. Sample sizes are designated by code letters. Table I shall be used to find the applicable code letter for the particular lot or batch size and the prescribed inspection level.

9.4 OBTAINING SAMPLING PLAN. The AQL and the code letter shall be used to obtain the sampling plan from Tables II, III or IV. When no sampling plan is available for a given combination of AQL and code letter, the tables direct the user to a different letter. The sample size to be used is given by the new code letter not by the original letter. If this procedure leads to different sample sizes for different classes of defects, the code letter corresponding to the largest sample size derived may be used for all classes of defects when designated or approved by the responsible authority. As an alternative to a single sampling plan with an acceptance number of 0, the plan with an acceptance number of 1 with its correspondingly larger sample size for a designated AQL (where available), may be used when designated or approved by the responsible authority.

9.5 TYPES OF SAMPLING PLANS. Three types of sampling plans: Single, Double and Multiple, are given in Tables II, III and IV, respectively. When several types of plans are available for a given AQL and code letter, any one may be used. A decision as to type of plan, either single, double, or multiple, when available for a given AQL and code letter, will usually be based upon the comparison between the administrative difficulty and the average sample sizes of the available plans. The average sample size of multiple plans is less than for double (except in the case corresponding to single acceptance number 1) and both of these are always less than a single sample size. Usually the administrative difficulty for single sampling and the cost per unit of the sample are less than for double or multiple.

359

10. DETERMINATION OF ACCEPTABILITY

10.1 PERCENT DEFECTIVE INSPECTION. To determine acceptability of a lot or batch under percent defective inspection, the applicable sampling plan shall be used in accordance with 10.1.1, 10.1.2, 10.1.3, 10.1.4, and 10.1.5.

10.1.1 SINGLE SAMPLING PLAN. The number of sample units inspected shall be equal to the sample size given by the plan. If the number of defectives found in the sample is equal to or less than the acceptance number, the lot or batch shall be considered acceptable. If the number of defectives is equal to or greater than the rejection number, the lot or batch shall be rejected.

10.1.2 DOUBLE SAMPLING PLAN. The number of sample units inspected shall be equal to the first sample size given by the plan. If the number of defectives found in the first sample is equal to or less than the first acceptance number, the lot or batch shall be considered acceptable. If the number of defectives found in the first sample is equal to or greater than the first rejection number, the lot or batch shall be rejected. If the number of defectives found in the first sample is between the first acceptance and rejection numbers, a second sample of the size given by the plan shall be inspected. The

number of defectives found in the first and second samples shall be accumulated. If the cumulative number of defectives is equal to or less than the second acceptance number, the lot or batch shall be considered acceptable. If the cumulative number of defectives is equal to or greater than the second rejection number, the lot or batch shall be rejected.

10.1.3 MULTIPLE SAMPLE PLAN. Under multiple sampling, the procedure shall be similar to that specified in 10.1.2, except that the number of successive samples required to reach a decision may be more than two.

10.1.4 SPECIAL PROCEDURE FOR REDUCED INSPECTION. Under reduced inspection, the sampling procedure may terminate without either acceptance or rejection criteria having been met. In these circumstances, the lot or batch will be considered acceptable, but normal inspection will be reinstated starting with the next lot or batch (see 8.3.4 (b)).

10.2 DEFECTS PER HUNDRED UNITS INSPECTION. To determine the acceptability of a lot or batch under Defects per Hundred Units inspection, the procedure specified for Percent Defective inspection above shall be used, except that the word "defects" shall be substituted for "defectives."

11. SUPPLEMENTARY INFORMATION

11.1 OPERATING CHARACTERISTIC CURVES. The operating characteristic curves for normal inspection, shown in Table X (pages 30–62), indicate the percentage of lots or batches which may be expected to be accepted under the various sampling plans for a given process quality. The curves shown are for single sampling; curves for double

and multiple sampling are matched as closely as practicable. The O. C. curves shown for AQLs greater than 10.0 are based on the Poisson distribution and are applicable for defects per hundred units inspection; those for AQLs of 10.0 or less and sample sizes of 80 or less are based on the binomial distribution and are applicable for percent defec-

11. SUPPLEMENTARY INFORMATION (Continued)

tive inspection; those for AQLs of 10.0 or less and sample sizes larger then 80 are based on the Poisson distribution and are applicable either for defects per hundred units inspection, or for percent defective inspection (the Poisson distribution being an adequate approximation to the binomial distribution under these conditions). Tabulated values, corresponding to selected values of probabilities of acceptance (P_a, in percent) are given for each of the curves shown, and, in addition, for tightened inspection, and for defects per hundred units for AQLs of 10.0 or less and sample sizes of 80 or less.

11.2 PROCESS AVERAGE. The process average is the average percent defective or average number of defects per hundred units (whichever is applicable) of product submitted by the supplier for original inspection. Original inspection is the first inspection of a particular quantity of product as distinguished from the inspection of product which has been resubmitted after prior rejection.

11.3 AVERAGE OUTGOING QUALITY (AOQ). The AOQ is the average quality of outgoing product including all accepted lots or batches, plus all rejected lots or batches after the rejected lots or batches have been effectively 100 percent inspected and all defectives replaced by nondefectives.

11.4 AVERAGE OUTGOING QUALITY LIMIT (AOQL). The AOQL is the maximum of the AOQs for all possible incoming qualities for a given acceptance sampling plan. AOQL values are given in Table V–A for each of the single sampling plans for normal inspection and in Table V–B for each of the single sampling plans for tightened inspection.

11.5 AVERAGE SAMPLE SIZE CURVES. Average sample size curves for double and multiple sampling are in Table IX. These show the average sample sizes which may be expected to occur under the various sampling plans for a given process quality. The curves assume no curtailment of inspection and are approximate to the extent that they are based upon the Poisson distribution, and that the sample sizes for double and multiple sampling are assumed to be 0.631n and 0.25n respectively, where n is the equivalent single sample size.

11.6 LIMITING QUALITY PROTECTION. The sampling plans and associated procedures given in this publication were designed for use where the units of product are produced in a continuing series of lots or batches over a period of time. However, if the lot or batch is of an isolated nature, it is desirable to limit the selection of sampling plans to those, associated with a designated AQL value, that provide not less than a specified limiting quality protection. Sampling plans for this purpose can be selected by choosing a Limiting Quality (LQ) and a consumer's risk to be associated with it. Tables VI and VII give values of LQ for the commonly used consumer's risks of 10 percent and 5 percent respectively. If a different value of consumer's risk is required, the O.C. curves and their tabulated values may be used. The concept of LQ may also be useful in specifying the AQL and Inspection Levels for a series of lots or batches, thus fixing minimum sample size where there is some reason for avoiding (with more than a given consumer's risk) more than a limiting proportion of defectives (or defects) in any single lot or batch.

361

TABLE 1 — Sample size code letters

(See 9.2 and 9.3)

Lot or batch size			Special inspection levels				General inspection levels		
			S-1	S-2	S-3	S-4	I	II	III
2	to	8	A	A	A	A	A	A	B
9	to	15	A	A	A	A	A	B	C
16	to	25	A	A	B	B	B	C	D
26	to	50	A	B	B	C	C	D	E
51	to	90	B	B	C	C	C	E	F
91	to	150	B	B	C	D	D	F	G
151	to	280	B	C	D	E	E	G	H
281	to	500	B	C	D	E	F	H	J
501	to	1200	C	C	E	F	G	J	K
1201	to	3200	C	D	E	G	H	K	L
3201	to	10000	C	D	F	G	J	L	M
10001	to	35000	C	D	F	H	K	M	N
35001	to	150000	D	E	G	J	L	N	P
150001	to	500000	D	E	G	J	M	P	Q
500001	and	over	D	E	H	K	N	Q	R

CODE LETTERS

362

TABLE II-A—Single sampling plans for normal inspection (Master table)

(See 9.4 and 9.5)

Acceptable Quality Levels (normal inspection)

Values shown as **Ac Re** (Ac = Acceptance number, Re = Rejection number). ↓ = use first sampling plan below arrow; ↑ = use first sampling plan above arrow.

Sample size code letter	Sample size	0.010	0.015	0.025	0.040	0.065	0.10	0.15	0.25	0.40	0.65	1.0	1.5	2.5	4.0	6.5	10	15	25	40	65	100	150	250	400	650	1000
A	2															↓	0 1	1 2	2 3	3 4	5 6	7 8	10 11	14 15	21 22	30 31
B	3														↓	0 1	1 2	2 3	3 4	5 6	7 8	10 11	14 15	21 22	30 31	44 45
C	5													↓	0 1	1 2	2 3	3 4	5 6	7 8	10 11	14 15	21 22	30 31	44 45	↑
D	8												↓	0 1	1 2	2 3	3 4	5 6	7 8	10 11	14 15	21 22	30 31	44 45	↑	
E	13											↓	0 1	1 2	2 3	3 4	5 6	7 8	10 11	14 15	21 22	30 31	44 45	↑		
F	20										↓	0 1	1 2	2 3	3 4	5 6	7 8	10 11	14 15	21 22	30 31	44 45	↑			
G	32									↓	0 1	1 2	2 3	3 4	5 6	7 8	10 11	14 15	21 22	30 31	44 45	↑				
H	50								↓	0 1	1 2	2 3	3 4	5 6	7 8	10 11	14 15	21 22	30 31	44 45	↑					
J	80							↓	0 1	1 2	2 3	3 4	5 6	7 8	10 11	14 15	21 22	30 31	44 45	↑						
K	125						↓	0 1	1 2	2 3	3 4	5 6	7 8	10 11	14 15	21 22	30 31	44 45	↑							
L	200					↓	0 1	1 2	2 3	3 4	5 6	7 8	10 11	14 15	21 22	30 31	44 45	↑								
M	315				↓	0 1	1 2	2 3	3 4	5 6	7 8	10 11	14 15	21 22	30 31	44 45	↑									
N	500			↓	0 1	1 2	2 3	3 4	5 6	7 8	10 11	14 15	21 22	30 31	44 45	↑										
P	800		↓	0 1	1 2	2 3	3 4	5 6	7 8	10 11	14 15	21 22	30 31	44 45	↑											
Q	1250	↓	0 1	1 2	2 3	3 4	5 6	7 8	10 11	14 15	21 22	30 31	44 45	↑												
R	2000	0 1	1 2	2 3	3 4	5 6	7 8	10 11	14 15	21 22	30 31	44 45	↑													

↓ = Use first sampling plan below arrow. If sample size equals, or exceeds, lot or batch size, do 100 percent inspection.

↑ = Use first sampling plan above arrow.

Ac = Acceptance number.

Re = Rejection number.

SINGLE NORMAL

TABLE II-B—Single sampling plans for tightened inspection (Master table)

(See 9.4 and 9.5)

Acceptable Quality Levels (tightened inspection)

Each cell below lists **Ac Re** (Acceptance number, Rejection number). ↓ = use first sampling plan below arrow; ↑ = use first sampling plan above arrow.

Sample size code letter	Sample size	0.010	0.015	0.025	0.040	0.065	0.10	0.15	0.25	0.40	0.65	1.0	1.5	2.5	4.0	6.5	10	15	25	40	65	100	150	250	400	650	1000
A	2	↓	↓	↓	↓	↓	↓	↓	↓	↓	↓	↓	↓	↓	↓	↓	↓	0 1	1 2	2 3	3 4	5 6	8 9	12 13	18 19	27 28	41 42
B	3	↓	↓	↓	↓	↓	↓	↓	↓	↓	↓	↓	↓	↓	↓	↓	0 1	1 2	2 3	3 4	5 6	8 9	12 13	18 19	27 28	41 42	↑
C	5	↓	↓	↓	↓	↓	↓	↓	↓	↓	↓	↓	↓	↓	↓	0 1	1 2	2 3	3 4	5 6	8 9	12 13	18 19	27 28	41 42	↑	↑
D	8	↓	↓	↓	↓	↓	↓	↓	↓	↓	↓	↓	↓	↓	0 1	1 2	2 3	3 4	5 6	8 9	12 13	18 19	27 28	41 42	↑	↑	↑
E	13	↓	↓	↓	↓	↓	↓	↓	↓	↓	↓	↓	↓	0 1	1 2	2 3	3 4	5 6	8 9	12 13	18 19	27 28	41 42	↑	↑	↑	↑
F	20	↓	↓	↓	↓	↓	↓	↓	↓	↓	↓	↓	0 1	1 2	2 3	3 4	5 6	8 9	12 13	18 19	27 28	41 42	↑	↑	↑	↑	↑
G	32	↓	↓	↓	↓	↓	↓	↓	↓	↓	↓	0 1	1 2	2 3	3 4	5 6	8 9	12 13	18 19	27 28	41 42	↑	↑	↑	↑	↑	↑
H	50	↓	↓	↓	↓	↓	↓	↓	↓	↓	0 1	1 2	2 3	3 4	5 6	8 9	12 13	18 19	27 28	41 42	↑	↑	↑	↑	↑	↑	↑
J	80	↓	↓	↓	↓	↓	↓	↓	↓	0 1	1 2	2 3	3 4	5 6	8 9	12 13	18 19	27 28	41 42	↑	↑	↑	↑	↑	↑	↑	↑
K	125	↓	↓	↓	↓	↓	↓	↓	0 1	1 2	2 3	3 4	5 6	8 9	12 13	18 19	27 28	41 42	↑	↑	↑	↑	↑	↑	↑	↑	↑
L	200	↓	↓	↓	↓	↓	↓	0 1	1 2	2 3	3 4	5 6	8 9	12 13	18 19	27 28	41 42	↑	↑	↑	↑	↑	↑	↑	↑	↑	↑
M	315	↓	↓	↓	↓	↓	0 1	1 2	2 3	3 4	5 6	8 9	12 13	18 19	27 28	41 42	↑	↑	↑	↑	↑	↑	↑	↑	↑	↑	↑
N	500	↓	↓	↓	↓	0 1	1 2	2 3	3 4	5 6	8 9	12 13	18 19	27 28	41 42	↑	↑	↑	↑	↑	↑	↑	↑	↑	↑	↑	↑
P	800	↓	↓	↓	0 1	1 2	2 3	3 4	5 6	8 9	12 13	18 19	27 28	41 42	↑	↑	↑	↑	↑	↑	↑	↑	↑	↑	↑	↑	↑
Q	1250	↓	↓	0 1	1 2	2 3	3 4	5 6	8 9	12 13	18 19	27 28	41 42	↑	↑	↑	↑	↑	↑	↑	↑	↑	↑	↑	↑	↑	↑
R	2000	↓	0 1	1 2	2 3	3 4	5 6	8 9	12 13	18 19	27 28	41 42	↑	↑	↑	↑	↑	↑	↑	↑	↑	↑	↑	↑	↑	↑	↑
S	3150	0 1	1 2	2 3	3 4	5 6	8 9	12 13	18 19	27 28	41 42	↑	↑	↑	↑	↑	↑	↑	↑	↑	↑	↑	↑	↑	↑	↑	↑

↓ = Use first sampling plan below arrow. If sample size equals or exceeds lot or batch size, do 100 percent inspection.
↑ = Use first sampling plan above arrow.
Ac = Acceptance number.
Re = Rejection number.

SINGLE TIGHTENED

TABLE II-C—Single sampling plans for reduced inspection (Master table)

(See 9.4 and 9.5)

SINGLE REDUCED

Acceptable Quality Levels (reduced inspection)†

Sample size code letter	Sample size	0.010	0.015	0.025	0.040	0.065	0.10	0.15	0.25	0.40	0.65	1.0	1.5	2.5	4.0	6.5	10	15	25	40	65	100	150	250	400	650	1000
		Ac Re	Ac Re	Ac Re	Ac Re	Ac Re	Ac Re	Ac Re	Ac Re	Ac Re	Ac Re	Ac Re	Ac Re	Ac Re	Ac Re	Ac Re	Ac Re	Ac Re	Ac Re	Ac Re	Ac Re	Ac Re	Ac Re	Ac Re	Ac Re	Ac Re	Ac Re
A	2	↓	↓	↓	↓	↓	↓	↓	↓	↓	↓	↓	↓	↓	↓	↓	⇩⇧	0 1	1 2	2 3	3 4	5 6	7 8	10 11	14 15	21 22	30 31
B	2	↓	↓	↓	↓	↓	↓	↓	↓	↓	↓	↓	↓	↓	↓	↓	⇩⇧	0 1	1 2	2 3	3 4	5 6	7 8	10 11	14 15	21 22	30 31
C	2	↓	↓	↓	↓	↓	↓	↓	↓	↓	↓	↓	↓	↓	⇩⇧	0 1	0 2	1 3	1 4	2 5	3 6	5 8	7 10	10 13	14 17	21 24	↑
D	3	↓	↓	↓	↓	↓	↓	↓	↓	↓	↓	↓	↓	⇩⇧	0 1	0 2	1 3	1 4	2 5	3 6	5 8	7 10	10 13	14 17	21 24	↑	↑
E	5	↓	↓	↓	↓	↓	↓	↓	↓	↓	↓	↓	⇩⇧	0 1	0 2	1 3	1 4	2 5	3 6	5 8	7 10	10 13	14 17	21 24	↑	↑	↑
F	8	↓	↓	↓	↓	↓	↓	↓	↓	↓	↓	⇩⇧	0 1	0 2	1 3	1 4	2 5	3 6	5 8	7 10	10 13	14 17	21 24	↑	↑	↑	↑
G	13	↓	↓	↓	↓	↓	↓	↓	↓	↓	⇩⇧	0 1	0 2	1 3	1 4	2 5	3 6	5 8	7 10	10 13	14 17	21 24	↑	↑	↑	↑	↑
H	20	↓	↓	↓	↓	↓	↓	↓	↓	⇩⇧	0 1	0 2	1 3	1 4	2 5	3 6	5 8	7 10	10 13	14 17	21 24	↑	↑	↑	↑	↑	↑
J	32	↓	↓	↓	↓	↓	↓	↓	⇩⇧	0 1	0 2	1 3	1 4	2 5	3 6	5 8	7 10	10 13	14 17	21 24	↑	↑	↑	↑	↑	↑	↑
K	50	↓	↓	↓	↓	↓	↓	⇩⇧	0 1	0 2	1 3	1 4	2 5	3 6	5 8	7 10	10 13	14 17	21 24	↑	↑	↑	↑	↑	↑	↑	↑
L	80	↓	↓	↓	↓	↓	⇩⇧	0 1	0 2	1 3	1 4	2 5	3 6	5 8	7 10	10 13	14 17	21 24	↑	↑	↑	↑	↑	↑	↑	↑	↑
M	125	↓	↓	↓	↓	⇩⇧	0 1	0 2	1 3	1 4	2 5	3 6	5 8	7 10	10 13	14 17	21 24	↑	↑	↑	↑	↑	↑	↑	↑	↑	↑
N	200	↓	↓	↓	⇩⇧	0 1	0 2	1 3	1 4	2 5	3 6	5 8	7 10	10 13	14 17	21 24	↑	↑	↑	↑	↑	↑	↑	↑	↑	↑	↑
P	315	↓	↓	⇩⇧	0 1	0 2	1 3	1 4	2 5	3 6	5 8	7 10	10 13	14 17	21 24	↑	↑	↑	↑	↑	↑	↑	↑	↑	↑	↑	↑
Q	500	↓	⇩⇧	0 1	0 2	1 3	1 4	2 5	3 6	5 8	7 10	10 13	14 17	21 24	↑	↑	↑	↑	↑	↑	↑	↑	↑	↑	↑	↑	↑
R	800	⇩⇧	0 1	0 2	1 3	1 4	2 5	3 6	5 8	7 10	10 13	14 17	21 24	↑	↑	↑	↑	↑	↑	↑	↑	↑	↑	↑	↑	↑	↑

⇩⇧ = Use first sampling plan below arrow. If sample size equals or exceeds lot or batch size, do 100 percent inspection.
⇧ = Use first sampling plan above arrow.
Ac = Acceptance number.
Re = Rejection number.
† = If the acceptance number has been exceeded, but the rejection number has not been reached, accept the lot, but reinstate normal inspection (see 10.1.4).

TABLE III-A — Double sampling plans for normal inspection (Master table)

(See 9.4 and 9.5)

Acceptable Quality Levels (normal inspection). Each AQL cell gives the values **Ac Re** (Acceptance number, Rejection number). ↓ = use first sampling plan below arrow; ↑ = use first sampling plan above arrow; * = use corresponding single sampling plan.

Code	Sample	Sample size	Cumulative sample size	0.010	0.015	0.025	0.040	0.065	0.10	0.15	0.25	0.40	0.65	1.0	1.5	2.5	4.0	6.5	10	15	25	40	65	100	150	250	400	650	1000
A	—	—	—	↓	↓	↓	↓	↓	↓	↓	↓	↓	↓	↓	↓	↓	↓	↓	↓	*	↑	↑	↑	↑	↑	↑	↑	↑	↑
B	First	2	2	↓	↓	↓	↓	↓	↓	↓	↓	↓	↓	↓	↓	↓	↓	↓	*	0 2	0 3	1 4	2 5	3 7	5 9	7 11	11 16	17 22	25 31
	Second	2	4																	1 2	3 4	4 5	6 7	8 9	12 13	18 19	26 27	37 38	56 57
C	First	3	3	↓	↓	↓	↓	↓	↓	↓	↓	↓	↓	↓	↓	↓	↓	*	0 2	0 3	1 4	2 5	3 7	5 9	7 11	11 16	17 22	25 31	↑
	Second	3	6																1 2	3 4	4 5	6 7	8 9	12 13	18 19	26 27	37 38	56 57	
D	First	5	5	↓	↓	↓	↓	↓	↓	↓	↓	↓	↓	↓	↓	↓	*	0 2	0 3	1 4	2 5	3 7	5 9	7 11	11 16	17 22	25 31	↑	↑
	Second	5	10															1 2	3 4	4 5	6 7	8 9	12 13	18 19	26 27	37 38	56 57		
E	First	8	8	↓	↓	↓	↓	↓	↓	↓	↓	↓	↓	↓	↓	*	0 2	0 3	1 4	2 5	3 7	5 9	7 11	11 16	17 22	25 31	↑	↑	↑
	Second	8	16														1 2	3 4	4 5	6 7	8 9	12 13	18 19	26 27	37 38	56 57			
F	First	13	13	↓	↓	↓	↓	↓	↓	↓	↓	↓	↓	↓	*	0 2	0 3	1 4	2 5	3 7	5 9	7 11	11 16	17 22	25 31	↑	↑	↑	↑
	Second	13	26													1 2	3 4	4 5	6 7	8 9	12 13	18 19	26 27	37 38	56 57				
G	First	20	20	↓	↓	↓	↓	↓	↓	↓	↓	↓	↓	*	0 2	0 3	1 4	2 5	3 7	5 9	7 11	11 16	17 22	25 31	↑	↑	↑	↑	↑
	Second	20	40												1 2	3 4	4 5	6 7	8 9	12 13	18 19	26 27	37 38	56 57					
H	First	32	32	↓	↓	↓	↓	↓	↓	↓	↓	↓	*	0 2	0 3	1 4	2 5	3 7	5 9	7 11	11 16	17 22	25 31	↑	↑	↑	↑	↑	↑
	Second	32	64											1 2	3 4	4 5	6 7	8 9	12 13	18 19	26 27	37 38	56 57						
J	First	50	50	↓	↓	↓	↓	↓	↓	↓	↓	*	0 2	0 3	1 4	2 5	3 7	5 9	7 11	11 16	17 22	25 31	↑	↑	↑	↑	↑	↑	↑
	Second	50	100										1 2	3 4	4 5	6 7	8 9	12 13	18 19	26 27	37 38	56 57							
K	First	80	80	↓	↓	↓	↓	↓	↓	↓	*	0 2	0 3	1 4	2 5	3 7	5 9	7 11	11 16	17 22	25 31	↑	↑	↑	↑	↑	↑	↑	↑
	Second	80	160									1 2	3 4	4 5	6 7	8 9	12 13	18 19	26 27	37 38	56 57								
L	First	125	125	↓	↓	↓	↓	↓	↓	*	0 2	0 3	1 4	2 5	3 7	5 9	7 11	11 16	17 22	25 31	↑	↑	↑	↑	↑	↑	↑	↑	↑
	Second	125	250								1 2	3 4	4 5	6 7	8 9	12 13	18 19	26 27	37 38	56 57									
M	First	200	200	↓	↓	↓	↓	↓	*	0 2	0 3	1 4	2 5	3 7	5 9	7 11	11 16	17 22	25 31	↑	↑	↑	↑	↑	↑	↑	↑	↑	↑
	Second	200	400							1 2	3 4	4 5	6 7	8 9	12 13	18 19	26 27	37 38	56 57										
N	First	315	315	↓	↓	↓	↓	*	0 2	0 3	1 4	2 5	3 7	5 9	7 11	11 16	17 22	25 31	↑	↑	↑	↑	↑	↑	↑	↑	↑	↑	↑
	Second	315	630						1 2	3 4	4 5	6 7	8 9	12 13	18 19	26 27	37 38	56 57											
P	First	500	500	↓	↓	↓	*	0 2	0 3	1 4	2 5	3 7	5 9	7 11	11 16	17 22	25 31	↑	↑	↑	↑	↑	↑	↑	↑	↑	↑	↑	↑
	Second	500	1000					1 2	3 4	4 5	6 7	8 9	12 13	18 19	26 27	37 38	56 57												
Q	First	800	800	↓	↓	*	0 2	0 3	1 4	2 5	3 7	5 9	7 11	11 16	17 22	25 31	↑	↑	↑	↑	↑	↑	↑	↑	↑	↑	↑	↑	↑
	Second	800	1600				1 2	3 4	4 5	6 7	8 9	12 13	18 19	26 27	37 38	56 57													
R	First	1250	1250	↓	*	0 2	0 3	1 4	2 5	3 7	5 9	7 11	11 16	17 22	25 31	↑	↑	↑	↑	↑	↑	↑	↑	↑	↑	↑	↑	↑	↑
	Second	1250	2500			1 2	3 4	4 5	6 7	8 9	12 13	18 19	26 27	37 38	56 57														

↓ = Use first sampling plan below arrow. If sample size equals or exceeds lot or batch size, do 100 percent inspection.
↑ = Use first sampling plan above arrow.
Ac = Acceptance number
Re = Rejection number
* = Use corresponding single sampling plan (or alternatively, use double sampling plan below, where available).

DOUBLE NORMAL

DOUBLE
TIGHTENED

TABLE III-B—Double sampling plans for tightened inspection (Master table)

(See 9.4 and 9.5)

Acceptable Quality Levels (tightened inspection)

↓ = Use first sampling plan below arrow. If sample size equals or exceeds lot or batch size, do 100 percent inspection.

↑ = Use first sampling plan above arrow.

Ac = Acceptance number

Re = Rejection number

• = Use corresponding single sampling plan (or, alternatively, use double sampling plan below, where available)

367

TABLE III-C — Double sampling plans for reduced inspection (Master table)

(See 9.4 and 9.5.)

Sample size code letter	Sample	Sample size	Cumulative sample size	\multicolumn{Acceptable Quality Levels (reduced inspection)†}

Acceptable Quality Levels (reduced inspection)† — columns: 0.010, 0.015, 0.025, 0.040, 0.065, 0.10, 0.15, 0.25, 0.40, 0.65, 1.0, 1.5, 2.5, 4.0, 6.5, 10, 15, 25, 40, 65, 100, 150, 250, 400, 650, 1000 (each with Ac / Re sub-columns)

Code	Sample	Sample size	Cumulative
A			
B			
C			
D	First	2	2
	Second	2	4
E	First	3	3
	Second	3	6
F	First	5	5
	Second	5	10
G	First	8	8
	Second	8	16
H	First	13	13
	Second	13	26
J	First	20	20
	Second	20	40
K	First	32	32
	Second	32	64
L	First	50	50
	Second	50	100
M	First	80	80
	Second	80	160
N	First	125	125
	Second	125	250
P	First	200	200
	Second	200	400
Q	First	315	315
	Second	315	630
R	First	500	500
	Second	500	1000

= Use first sampling plan below arrow. If sample size equals or exceeds lot or batch size, do 100 percent inspection.

= Use first sampling plan above arrow.

Ac = Acceptance number.

Re = Rejection number.

= Use corresponding single sampling plan (or alternatively, use double sampling plan below, when available.)

† = If, after the second sample, the acceptance number has been exceeded, but the rejection number has not been reached, accept the lot, but reinstate normal inspection (see 10.14).

DOUBLE
REDUCED

TABLE IV-A—Multiple sampling plans for normal inspection (Master table)

(See 9.4 and 9.5)

MULTIPLE NORMAL

Acceptable Quality Levels (normal inspection)

The table presents, across the top, the Acceptable Quality Levels (AQL) columns, each with Ac (Acceptance number) and Re (Rejection number):

0.010, 0.015, 0.025, 0.040, 0.065, 0.10, 0.15, 0.25, 0.40, 0.65, 1.0, 1.5, 2.5, 4.0, 6.5, 10, 15, 25, 40, 65, 100, 150, 250, 400, 650, 1000

Left-hand columns: Sample size code letter | Sample | Sample size | Cumulative sample size

Code letter	Sample	Sample size	Cumulative sample size
A			
B			
C			
D	First / Second / Third / Fourth / Fifth / Sixth / Seventh	2 / 2 / 2 / 2 / 2 / 2 / 2	2 / 4 / 6 / 8 / 10 / 12 / 14
E	First / Second / Third / Fourth / Fifth / Sixth / Seventh	3 / 3 / 3 / 3 / 3 / 3 / 3	3 / 6 / 9 / 12 / 15 / 18 / 21
F	First / Second / Third / Fourth / Fifth / Sixth / Seventh	5 / 5 / 5 / 5 / 5 / 5 / 5	5 / 10 / 15 / 20 / 25 / 30 / 35
G	First / Second / Third / Fourth / Fifth / Sixth / Seventh	8 / 8 / 8 / 8 / 8 / 8 / 8	8 / 16 / 24 / 32 / 40 / 48 / 56
H	First / Second / Third / Fourth / Fifth / Sixth / Seventh	13 / 13 / 13 / 13 / 13 / 13 / 13	13 / 26 / 39 / 52 / 65 / 78 / 91
J	First / Second / Third / Fourth / Fifth / Sixth / Seventh	20 / 20 / 20 / 20 / 20 / 20 / 20	20 / 40 / 60 / 80 / 100 / 120 / 140

Legend:

↓ = Use first sampling plan below arrow (refer to continuation of table on following page, when necessary). If sample size equals or exceeds lot or batch size, do 100 percent inspection.

↑ = Use first sampling plan above arrow.

Ac = Acceptance number.

Re = Rejection number.

⇨ = Use corresponding single sampling plan (or alternatively, use multiple sampling plan below, where available).

⟨⟩ = Use corresponding double sampling plan (or alternatively, use multiple sampling plan below, where available).

* = Acceptance not permitted at this sample size.

369

TABLE IV-A — Multiple sampling plans for normal inspection (Master table)
(Continued)

(See 9.4 and 9.5)

Acceptable Quality Levels (normal inspection). Each AQL cell gives the pair **Ac Re** (Acceptance number / Rejection number). "#" = Acceptance not permitted at this sample size; "↓" = use first sampling plan below arrow.

Code	Sample	Cum. sample size	0.010	0.015	0.025	0.040	0.065	0.10	0.15	0.25	0.40	0.65	1.0	1.5	2.5	4.0	6.5	10	15	25	40	65	100	150	250	400	650	1000
K	First	32										# 2	# 3	# 4	0 4	0 5	1 7	↓										
	Second	64										0 2	0 3	1 5	1 6	3 8	4 10											
	Third	96										0 2	0 4	2 6	3 8	6 10	8 13											
	Fourth	128										0 3	1 5	3 7	5 10	8 13	12 17											
	Fifth	160										1 3	2 5	5 8	7 11	11 15	17 20											
	Sixth	192										1 3	3 5	7 9	10 12	14 17	21 23											
	Seventh	224										2 3	4 6	9 10	13 14	18 19	25 26											
L	First	50									# 2	# 3	# 4	0 4	0 5	1 7	2 9	↓										
	Second	100									0 2	0 3	1 5	1 6	3 8	4 10	7 14											
	Third	150									0 2	0 4	2 6	3 8	6 10	8 13	13 19											
	Fourth	200									0 3	1 5	3 7	5 10	8 13	12 17	19 25											
	Fifth	250									1 3	2 5	5 8	7 11	11 15	17 20	25 29											
	Sixth	300									1 3	3 5	7 9	10 12	14 17	21 23	31 33											
	Seventh	350									2 3	4 6	9 10	13 14	18 19	25 26	37 38											
M	First	80								# 2	# 3	# 4	0 4	0 5	1 7	2 9	↓											
	Second	160								0 2	0 3	1 5	1 6	3 8	4 10	7 14												
	Third	240								0 2	0 4	2 6	3 8	6 10	8 13	13 19												
	Fourth	320								0 3	1 5	3 7	5 10	8 13	12 17	19 25												
	Fifth	400								1 3	2 5	5 8	7 11	11 15	17 20	25 29												
	Sixth	480								1 3	3 5	7 9	10 12	14 17	21 23	31 33												
	Seventh	560								2 3	4 6	9 10	13 14	18 19	25 26	37 38												
N	First	125							# 2	# 3	# 4	0 4	0 5	1 7	2 9	↓												
	Second	250							0 2	0 3	1 5	1 6	3 8	4 10	7 14													
	Third	375							0 2	0 4	2 6	3 8	6 10	8 13	13 19													
	Fourth	500							0 3	1 5	3 7	5 10	8 13	12 17	19 25													
	Fifth	625							1 3	2 5	5 8	7 11	11 15	17 20	25 29													
	Sixth	750							1 3	3 5	7 9	10 12	14 17	21 23	31 33													
	Seventh	875							2 3	4 6	9 10	13 14	18 19	25 26	37 38													
P	First	200						# 2	# 3	# 4	0 4	0 5	1 7	2 9	↓													
	Second	400						0 2	0 3	1 5	1 6	3 8	4 10	7 14														
	Third	600						0 2	0 4	2 6	3 8	6 10	8 13	13 19														
	Fourth	800						0 3	1 5	3 7	5 10	8 13	12 17	19 25														
	Fifth	1000						1 3	2 5	5 8	7 11	11 15	17 20	25 29														
	Sixth	1200						1 3	3 5	7 9	10 12	14 17	21 23	31 33														
	Seventh	1400						2 3	4 6	9 10	13 14	18 19	25 26	37 38														
Q	First	315					# 2	# 3	# 4	0 4	0 5	1 7	2 9	↓														
	Second	630					0 2	0 3	1 5	1 6	3 8	4 10	7 14															
	Third	945					0 2	0 4	2 6	3 8	6 10	8 13	13 19															
	Fourth	1260					0 3	1 5	3 7	5 10	8 13	12 17	19 25															
	Fifth	1575					1 3	2 5	5 8	7 11	11 15	17 20	25 29															
	Sixth	1890					1 3	3 5	7 9	10 12	14 17	21 23	31 33															
	Seventh	2205					2 3	4 6	9 10	13 14	18 19	25 26	37 38															
R	First	500				# 2	# 3	# 4	0 4	0 5	1 7	2 9	↓															
	Second	1000				0 2	0 3	1 5	1 6	3 8	4 10	7 14																
	Third	1500				0 2	0 4	2 6	3 8	6 10	8 13	13 19																
	Fourth	2000				0 3	1 5	3 7	5 10	8 13	12 17	19 25																
	Fifth	2500				1 3	2 5	5 8	7 11	11 15	17 20	25 29																
	Sixth	3000				1 3	3 5	7 9	10 12	14 17	21 23	31 33																
	Seventh	3500				2 3	4 6	9 10	13 14	18 19	25 26	37 38																

↓ = Use first sampling plan below arrow. If sample size equals or exceeds lot or batch size, do 100 percent inspection.
↑ = Use first sampling plan above arrow.
Ac = Acceptance number.
Re = Rejection number.
∗ = Use corresponding single sampling plan (or alternatively, use multiple plan below, where available).
= Acceptance not permitted at this sample size.

MULTIPLE NORMAL

TABLE IV-B — Multiple sampling plans for tightened inspection (Master table)

(See 9.4 and 9.5)

Acceptable Quality Levels (tightened inspection)

↑ = Use first sampling plan below arrow (refer to continuation of table on following page, when necessary). If sample size equals or exceeds lot or batch size, do 100 percent inspection.

↓ = Use first sampling plan above arrow.

Ac = Acceptance number

Re = Rejection number

= Use corresponding single sampling plan (or alternatively, use multiple sampling plan below, where available)

= Use corresponding double sampling plan (or alternatively, use multiple sampling plan below, where available)

* = Acceptance not permitted at this sample size.

TABLE IV-B — Multiple sampling plans for tightened inspection (Master table) (Continued)

(See 9.4 and 9.5)

Acceptable Quality Levels (tightened inspection)

Sample size code letter	Sample	Sample size	Cumulative sample size
K	First	32	32
	Second	32	64
	Third	32	96
	Fourth	32	128
	Fifth	32	160
	Sixth	32	192
	Seventh	32	224
L	First	50	50
	Second	50	100
	Third	50	150
	Fourth	50	200
	Fifth	50	250
	Sixth	50	300
	Seventh	50	350
M	First	80	80
	Second	80	160
	Third	80	240
	Fourth	80	320
	Fifth	80	400
	Sixth	80	480
	Seventh	80	560
N	First	125	125
	Second	125	250
	Third	125	375
	Fourth	125	500
	Fifth	125	625
	Sixth	125	750
	Seventh	125	875
P	First	200	200
	Second	200	400
	Third	200	600
	Fourth	200	800
	Fifth	200	1000
	Sixth	200	1200
	Seventh	200	1400
Q	First	315	315
	Second	315	630
	Third	315	945
	Fourth	315	1260
	Fifth	315	1575
	Sixth	315	1890
	Seventh	315	2205
R	First	500	500
	Second	500	1000
	Third	500	1500
	Fourth	500	2000
	Fifth	500	2500
	Sixth	500	3000
	Seventh	500	3500
S	First	800	800
	Second	800	1600
	Third	800	2400
	Fourth	800	3200
	Fifth	800	4000
	Sixth	800	4800
	Seventh	800	5600

Acceptable Quality Levels (tightened inspection) column headings: 0.010, 0.015, 0.025, 0.040, 0.065, 0.10, 0.15, 0.25, 0.40, 0.65, 1.0, 1.5, 2.5, 4.0, 6.5, 10, 15, 25, 40, 65, 100, 150, 250, 400, 650, 1000 — each with Ac and Re sub-columns.

↓ = Use first sampling plan below arrow. If sample size equals or exceeds lot or batch size, do 100 percent inspection.
↑ = Use first sampling plan above arrow (refer to preceding page, when necessary).
Ac = Acceptance number
Re = Rejection number
∎ = Use corresponding single sampling plan (or alternatively, use multiple sampling plan below, where available).
✱ = Acceptance not permitted at this sample size.

MULTIPLE
TIGHTENED

MULTIPLE
REDUCED

TABLE IV-C—Multiple sampling plans for reduced inspection (Master table)

(See 9.4 and 9.5)

Sample size code letter	Sample	Sample size	Cumulative sample size
A			
B			
C			
D			
E			
F	First	2	2
	Second	2	4
	Third	2	6
	Fourth	2	8
	Fifth	2	10
	Sixth	2	12
	Seventh	2	14
G	First	3	3
	Second	3	6
	Third	3	9
	Fourth	3	12
	Fifth	3	15
	Sixth	3	18
	Seventh	3	21
H	First	5	5
	Second	5	10
	Third	5	15
	Fourth	5	20
	Fifth	5	25
	Sixth	5	30
	Seventh	5	35
J	First	8	8
	Second	8	16
	Third	8	24
	Fourth	8	32
	Fifth	8	40
	Sixth	8	48
	Seventh	8	56
K	First	13	13
	Second	13	26
	Third	13	39
	Fourth	13	52
	Fifth	13	65
	Sixth	13	78
	Seventh	13	91

Acceptable Quality Levels (reduced inspection) † — columns (each with Ac and Re): 0.010, 0.015, 0.025, 0.040, 0.065, 0.10, 0.15, 0.25, 0.40, 0.65, 1.0, 1.5, 2.5, 4.0, 6.5, 10, 15, 25, 40, 65, 100, 150, 250, 400, 650, 1000

⇩ = Use first sampling plan below arrow (refer to continuation of table on following page, when necessary). If sample size equals, or exceeds lot or batch size, do 100 percent inspection.

⇧ = Use first sampling plan above arrow.

Ac = Acceptance number

Re = Rejection number

⇩⇩ = Use corresponding single sampling plan (or alternatively, use multiple sampling plan below, where available).

• = Use corresponding double sampling plan (or alternatively, use multiple sampling plan below, where available).

‡ = Acceptance not permitted at this sample size.

† = If, after the final sample, the acceptance number has been exceeded, but the rejection number has not been reached, accept the lot but reinstate normal inspection (see 10.1.4).

373

TABLE IV-C—Multiple sampling plans for reduced inspection (Master table) (Continued)

(See 9.4 and 9.5)

Acceptable Quality Levels (reduced inspection) †

Sample size code letter	Sample	Sample size	Cumulative sample size	6.5 Ac Re	4.0 Ac Re	2.5 Ac Re	1.5 Ac Re	1.0 Ac Re	0.65 Ac Re
L	First	20	20	0 6	↑				
	Second	20	40	3 9					
	Third	20	60	6 12					
	Fourth	20	80	8 15					
	Fifth	20	100	11 17					
	Sixth	20	120	14 20					
	Seventh	20	140	18 22					
M	First	32	32	↓	0 6	↑			
	Second	32	64		3 9				
	Third	32	96		6 12				
	Fourth	32	128		8 15				
	Fifth	32	160		11 17				
	Sixth	32	192		14 20				
	Seventh	32	224		18 22				
N	First	50	50		↓	0 6	↑		
	Second	50	100			3 9			
	Third	50	150			6 12			
	Fourth	50	200			8 15			
	Fifth	50	250			11 17			
	Sixth	50	300			14 20			
	Seventh	50	350			18 22			
P	First	80	80			↓	0 6	↑	
	Second	80	160				3 9		
	Third	80	240				6 12		
	Fourth	80	320				8 15		
	Fifth	80	400				11 17		
	Sixth	80	480				14 20		
	Seventh	80	560				18 22		
Q	First	125	125				↓	0 6	↑
	Second	125	250					3 9	
	Third	125	375					6 12	
	Fourth	125	500					8 15	
	Fifth	125	625					11 17	
	Sixth	125	750					14 20	
	Seventh	125	875					18 22	
R	First	200	200					↓	0 6
	Second	200	400						3 9
	Third	200	600						6 12
	Fourth	200	800						8 15
	Fifth	200	1000						11 17
	Sixth	200	1200						14 20
	Seventh	200	1400						18 22

(Columns for Acceptable Quality Levels 0.010, 0.015, 0.025, 0.040, 0.065, 0.10, 0.15, 0.25, 0.40, 1.0, and 10 through 1000 contain progressively smaller acceptance/rejection plans for code letters M–R and directional arrows; see master table. Columns 10, 15, 25, 40, 65, 100, 150, 250, 400, 650, 1000 carry left-pointing arrows for all code letters.)

↓ = Use first sampling plan below arrow. If sample size equals, or exceeds, lot or batch size, do 100 percent inspection.
↑ = Use first sampling plan above arrow (refer to preceding page when necessary).
Ac = Acceptance number
Re = Rejection number
* = Acceptance not permitted at this sample size.
+ = If, after the final sample, the acceptance number has been exceeded, but the rejection number has not been reached, accept the lot, but reinstate normal inspection (see 10.1.4).

MULTIPLE REDUCED

374

TABLE V-A — Average Outgoing Quality Limit Factors for Normal Inspection (Single sampling)

(See 11.4)

Code Letter	Sample Size	Acceptable Quality Level																									
		0.010	0.015	0.025	0.040	0.065	0.10	0.15	0.25	0.40	0.65	1.0	1.5	2.5	4.0	6.5	10	15	25	40	65	100	150	250	400	650	1000
A	2																		42	69	97	160	220	330	470	730	1000
B	3																	28	46	65	110	150	220	310	490	720	1100
C	5																17	27	39	63	90	130	190	290	430	660	1100
D	8															18	17	24	40	56	82	120	180	270	410		
E	13														12	11	15	24	34	50	72	110	170	250			
F	20													7.4	6.5	11	16	22	33	47	73						
G	32												4.6	4.2	6.9	9.7	14	21	29	46							
H	50											2.8	2.6	4.3	6.1	9.9	13	19	29								
J	80									1.2	1.1	1.7	2.7	3.9	6.3	9.0	12	18									
K	125								0.74	0.67	1.1	1.7	2.4	4.0	5.6	8.2	12										
L	200							0.46	0.42	0.69	0.97	1.6	2.5	3.6	5.2	7.5											
M	315						0.17	0.27	0.44	0.62	1.00	1.6	2.2	3.3	4.7	7.3											
N	500					0.18	0.17	0.27	0.39	0.63	0.90	1.4	2.1	3.0	4.7												
P	800				0.12	0.11	0.17	0.24	0.40	0.56	0.82	1.3	1.9	2.9													
Q	1250		0.046	0.074	0.067	0.11	0.16	0.25	0.36	0.52	0.75	1.2	1.8														
R	2000	0.029		0.042	0.069	0.097	0.16	0.22	0.33	0.47	0.73	1.2															

Note: For the exact AOQL, the above values must be multiplied by $\left(1 - \dfrac{\text{Sample size}}{\text{Lot or Batch size}}\right)$ (see 11.4)

TABLE V-B—Average Outgoing Quality Limit Factors for Tightened Inspection (Single sampling)

(See 11.4)

Acceptable Quality Level

Code letter	Sample size	0.010	0.015	0.025	0.040	0.065	0.10	0.15	0.25	0.40	0.65	1.0	1.5	2.5	4.0	6.5	10	15	25	40	65	100	150	250	400	650	1000
A	2																		28	42	69	97	160	260	400	620	970
B	3																		27	46	65	110	170	270	410	550	1100
C	5																	17	24	39	63	100	160	250	390	610	
D	8															12	11	17	24	40	64	99	160	240	380		
E	13														7.4	6.5	11	15	24	40	61	95	150	240			
F	20													4.6	4.2	6.9	9.7	16	26	40	62						
G	32												2.8	2.6	4.3	6.1	9.9	16	25	39							
H	50											1.8	1.7	2.7	3.9	6.3	10	16	25								
J	80										1.2	1.1	1.7	2.4	4.0	6.4	9.9	16									
K	125									0.74	0.67	1.1	1.6	2.5	4.1	6.4	9.9										
L	200								0.46	0.42	0.69	0.97	1.6	2.6	4.0	6.2											
M	315							0.29	0.27	0.44	0.62	1.0	1.6	2.5	3.9												
N	500						0.18	0.17	0.24	0.39	0.63	1.0	1.6	2.5													
P	800					0.12	0.11	0.17	0.25	0.40	0.64	0.99	1.6														
Q	1250				0.074	0.067	0.11	0.16	0.26	0.41	0.64	0.99															
R	2000			0.046	0.042	0.069	0.097	0.16		0.40	0.62																
S	3150	0.018	0.029	0.027																							

Note: For the exact AOQL, the above values must be multiplied by $\left(1 - \dfrac{\text{Sample size}}{\text{Lot or Batch size}}\right)$ (see 11.4)

AOQL
TIGHTENED

TABLE VI-A—Limiting Quality (in percent defective) for which P_a = 10 Percent
(for Normal Inspection, Single sampling)

(See 11.6)

Code letter	Sample size	Acceptable Quality Level															
		0.010	0.015	0.025	0.040	0.065	0.10	0.15	0.25	0.40	0.65	1.0	1.5	2.5	4.0	6.5	10
A	2															68	
B	3														54		
C	5													37			58
D	8												25			41	54
E	13											16		27		36	44
F	20										11			18	25	30	42
G	32									6.9			12	16	20	27	34
H	50								4.5			7.6	10	13	18	22	29
J	80							2.8			4.8	6.5	8.2	11	14	19	24
K	125						1.8			3.1	4.3	5.4	7.4	9.4	12	16	23
L	200					1.2			2.0	2.7	3.3	4.6	5.9	7.7	10	14	
M	315				0.73			1.2	1.7	2.1	2.9	3.7	4.9	6.4	9.0		
N	500			0.46			0.78	1.1	1.3	1.9	2.4	3.1	4.0	5.6			
P	800		0.29			0.49	0.67	0.84	1.2	1.5	1.9	2.5	3.5				
Q	1250	0.18			0.31	0.43	0.53	0.74	0.94	1.2	1.6	2.3					
R	2000			0.20	0.27	0.33	0.46	0.59	0.77	1.0	1.4						

LQ (DEFECTIVES) 10.0%

377

TABLE VI-B—Limiting Quality (in defects per hundred units) for which P_a = 10 Percent
(for Normal Inspection, Single sampling)

(See 11.6)

Code letter	Sample size	0.010	0.015	0.025	0.040	0.065	0.10	0.15	0.25	0.40	0.65	1.0	1.5	2.5	4.0	6.5	10	15	25	40	65	100	150	250	400	650	1000
																Acceptable Quality Level											
A	2															120			200	270	330	460	590	770	1000	1400	1900
B	3														77			130	180	220	310	390	510	670	940	1300	1800
C	5													46			78	110	130	190	240	310	400	560	770	1100	
D	8												29			49	67	84	120	150	190	250	350	480	670		
E	13											18			30	41	51	71	91	120	160	220	300	410			
F	20										12			20	27	33	46	59	77	100	140						
G	32									7.2			12	17	21	29	37	48	63	88							
H	50								4.6			7.8	11	13	19	24	31	40	56								
J	80							2.9			4.9	6.7	8.4	12	15	19	25	35									
K	125						1.8			3.1	4.3	5.4	7.4	9.4	12	16	23										
L	200					1.2			2.0	2.7	3.3	4.6	5.9	7.7	10	14											
M	315				0.73			1.2	1.7	2.1	2.9	3.7	4.9	6.4	9.0												
N	500			0.46			0.78	1.1	1.3	1.9	2.4	3.1	4.0	5.6													
P	800		0.29			0.49	0.67	0.84	1.2	1.5	1.9	2.5	3.5														
Q	1250	0.18			0.31	0.43	0.53	0.74	0.94	1.2	1.6	2.3															
R	2000			0.20	0.27	0.33	0.46	0.59	0.77	1.0	1.4																

LQ (DEFECTS)
10%

378

TABLE VII-A — Limiting Quality (in percent defective) for which $P_a = 5$ Percent (for Normal Inspection, Single sampling)

(See 11.6)

Code letter	Sample size	Acceptable Quality Level															
		0.010	0.015	0.025	0.040	0.065	0.10	0.15	0.25	0.40	0.65	1.0	1.5	2.5	4.0	6.5	10
A	2															78	
B	3														63		
C	5													45			66
D	8												31			47	60
E	13											21			32	41	50
F	20										14			22	28	34	46
G	32									8.9			14	18	23	30	37
H	50								5.8			9.1	12	15	20	25	32
J	80							3.7			5.8	7.7	9.4	13	16	20	26
K	125						2.4			3.8	5.0	6.2	8.4	11	14	18	24
L	200					1.5			2.4	3.2	3.9	5.3	6.6	8.5	11	15	
M	315				0.95			1.5	2.0	2.5	3.3	4.2	5.4	7.0	9.6		
N	500			0.60			0.95	1.3	1.6	2.1	2.6	3.4	4.4	6.1			
P	800		0.38			0.59	0.79	0.97	1.3	1.6	2.1	2.7	3.8				
Q	1250	0.24			0.38	0.50	0.62	0.84	1.1	1.4	1.8	2.4					
R	2000			0.24	0.32	0.39	0.53	0.66	0.85	1.1	1.5						

LQ (DEFECTIVES)
5.0%

379

TABLE VII-B—Limiting Quality (in defects per hundred units) for which P_a = 5 Percent (for Normal Inspection, Single sampling)

(See 11.6)

Column values under the heading *Acceptable Quality Level*.

Code letter	Sample size	0.010	0.015	0.025	0.040	0.065	0.10	0.15	0.25	0.40	0.65	1.0	1.5	2.5	4.0	6.5	10	15	25	40	65	100	150	250	400	650	1000
A	2															150			240	320	390	530	660	850	1100	1500	2000
B	3														100			160	210	260	350	440	570	730	1000	1400	1900
C	5													60			95	130	160	210	260	340	440	610	810	1100	
D	8												38			59	79	97	130	160	210	270	380	510	710		
E	13											23			37	48	60	81	100	130	170	230	310	440			
F	20										15			24	32	39	53	66	85	110	150						
G	32									9.4			15	20	24	33	41	53	68	95							
H	50								6.0			9.5	13	16	21	26	34	44	61								
J	80							3.8			5.9	7.9	9.7	13	16	21	27	38									
K	125						2.4			3.8	5.0	6.2	8.4	11	14	18	24										
L	200					1.5			2.4	3.2	3.9	5.3	6.6	8.5	11	15											
M	315				0.95			1.5	2.0	2.5	3.3	4.2	5.4	7.0	9.6												
N	500			0.60			0.95	1.3	1.6	2.1	2.6	3.4	4.4	6.1													
P	800		0.38			0.59	0.79	0.97	1.3	1.6	2.1	2.7	3.8														
Q	1250	0.24			0.38	0.50	0.62	0.84	1.1	1.4	1.8	2.4															
R	2000			0.24	0.32	0.39	0.53	0.66	0.85	1.1	1.5																

LQ (DEFECTS)
5%

TABLE VIII — Limit Numbers for Reduced Inspection

(See 8.3.3)

Acceptable Quality Level

Number of sample units from last 10 lots or batches	0.010	0.015	0.025	0.040	0.065	0.10	0.15	0.25	0.40	0.65	1.0	1.5	2.5	4.0	6.5	10	15	25	40	65	100	150	250	400	650	1000
20 - 29	•	•	•	•	•	•	•	•	•	•	•	•	•	•	•	0	0	2	4	8	14	22	40	68	115	181
30 - 49	•	•	•	•	•	•	•	•	•	•	•	•	•	•	0	0	1	3	7	13	22	36	63	105	178	277
50 - 79	•	•	•	•	•	•	•	•	•	•	•	•	•	0	0	2	3	7	14	25	40	63	110	181	301	
80 - 129	•	•	•	•	•	•	•	•	•	•	•	•	0	0	2	4	7	14	24	42	68	105	181	297		
130 - 199	•	•	•	•	•	•	•	•	•	•	0	0	0	2	4	7	13	25	42	72	115	177	301	490		
200 - 319	•	•	•	•	•	•	•	•	•	•	0	0	2	4	8	14	22	40	68	115	181	277	471			
320 - 499	•	•	•	•	•	•	•	•	•	0	2	1	4	8	14	24	39	68	113	189						
500 - 799	•	•	•	•	•	•	•	•	0	0	4	3	7	14	25	40	63	110	181							
800 - 1249	•	•	•	•	•	•	•	0	0	2	7	7	14	24	42	68	105	181								
1250 - 1999	•	•	•	•	•	•	0	0	2	4	14	13	24	40	69	110	169									
2000 - 3149	•	•	•	•	•	0	0	2	4	8	24	22	40	68	115	181										
3150 - 4999	•	•	•	•	0	0	1	4	8	14	40	39	67	111	186											
5000 - 7999	•	•	•	0	0	2	3	7	14	25	68	63	110	181												
8000 - 12499	•	•	0	0	2	4	7	14	24	42	110	105	181													
12500 - 19999	•	0	0	2	4	7	13	24	40	69	181	169														
20000 - 31499	0	0	2	4	8	14	22	40	68	115																
31500 - 49999	0	1	4	8	14	24	38	67	111	186																
50000 & Over	2	3	7	14	25	40	63	110	181	301																

• Denotes that the number of sample units from the last ten lots or batches is not sufficient for reduced inspection for this AQL. In this instance more than ten lots or batches may be used for the calculation, provided that the lots or batches used are the most recent ones in sequence, that they have all been on normal inspection, and that none has been rejected while on original inspection.

TABLE IX—*Average sample size curves for double and multiple sampling*
(normal and tightened inspection)

(See 11.5)

n = Equivalent single sample size
c = Single sample acceptance number
← = AQL for normal inspection

AVERAGE
SAMPLE SIZE

382

TABLE X-A—Tables for sample size code letter: A

CHART A - OPERATING CHARACTERISTIC CURVES FOR SINGLE SAMPLING PLANS
(Curves for double and multiple sampling are matched as closely as practicable)

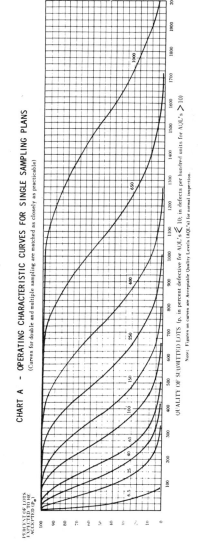

PER CENT OF LOTS EXPECTED TO BE ACCEPTED (P_a)

QUALITY OF SUBMITTED LOTS (p, in percent defective for AQL's $\leq$ 10; in defects per hundred units for AQL's $>$ 10)

Note: Figures on curves are Acceptable Quality Levels (AQL's) for normal inspection.

TABLE X-A-1 - TABULATED VALUES FOR OPERATING CHARACTERISTIC CURVES FOR SINGLE SAMPLING PLANS

P_a	6.5	6.5	25	40	65	100	150	250	X	400	X	650	X	1000
	p (in percent defective)	p (in defects per hundred units)												
99.0	0.501	7.45	21.8	41.2	89.2	145	175	239		305		374		517
95.0	2.53	17.8	40.9	68.3	131	199	235	308		385		462		622
90.0	5.13	26.6	55.1	87.3	158	233	272	351		432		515		684
75.0	13.4	48.1	86.8	127	211	298	342	431		521		612		795
50.0	29.3	83.9	134	184	284	383	433	533		633		733		933
25.0	50.0	135	196	256	371	484	540	651		761		870		1087
10.0	68.4	195	266	334	464	589	650	770		889		1006		1238
5.0	77.6	237	315	388	526	657	722	848		972		1094		1334
1.0	90.0	332	420	502	655	800	870	1007		1141		1272		1529
	X	X	40	65	100	150	250	X	400	X	650	X	1000	X

(continued columns)

P_a	650	X	1000
99.0	629	859	977
95.0	745	995	1122
90.0	812	1073	1206
75.0	934	1314	1354
50.0	1083	1383	1533
25.0	1248	1568	1728
10.0	1409	1748	1916
5.0	1512	1862	2035
1.0	1718	2088	2270

Acceptable Quality Levels (normal inspection) — across top.
Acceptable Quality Levels (tightened inspection) — across bottom.

Note: Binomial distribution used for percent defective computations; Poisson for defects per hundred units.

TABLE X-A-2 – SAMPLING PLANS FOR SAMPLE SIZE CODE LETTER: A

Type of sampling plan	Cumulative sample size	Acceptable Quality Levels (normal inspection)																									
		Less than 6.5		6.5		10		15		25		40		65		100		150		250		400		650		1000	
		Ac	Re	Ac	Re	Ac	Re	Ac	Re	Ac	Re	Ac	Re	Ac	Re	Ac	Re	Ac	Re	Ac	Re	Ac	Re	Ac	Re	Ac	Re
Single	2	▽		0	1	Use		Use		1	2	2	3	3	4	5	6	7	8	9	10	13	14	21	22	30	31
Double	2	▽		•		Use Letter D		Use Letter C		(•)		(•)		(•)		(•)		(•)		(•)		(•)		(•)		(•)	
								Letter B																			
Multiple		▽		•						•		•		•		•		•		•		•		•		•	

	Less than 10	10	15	25	40	65	100	150	250	400	650	1000
Acceptable Quality Levels (tightened inspection)	▽	✕	✕	✕	✕	✕	✕	✕	✕	✕	✕	✕

▽ = Use next subsequent sample size code letter for which acceptance and rejection numbers are available.

Ac = Acceptance number

Re = Rejection number

• = Use single sampling plan above (or alternatively use letter D).

(•) = Use single sampling plan (or alternatively use letter B).

A

B

TABLE X-B—Tables for sample size code letter: B

(Curves for double and multiple sampling are matched as closely as practicable)

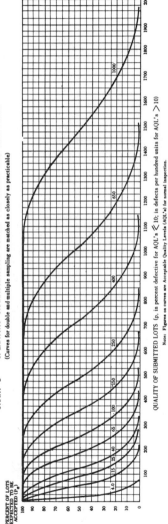

PERCENT OF LOTS
EXPECTED TO BE
ACCEPTED (P_a)

QUALITY OF SUBMITTED LOTS (p, in percent defective for AOL's ≤ 10; in defects per hundred units for AOL's > 10)

Note: Figures on curves are Acceptable Quality Levels (AQL's) for normal inspection.

TABLE X-B-1 - TABULATED VALUES FOR OPERATING CHARACTERISTIC CURVES FOR SINGLE SAMPLING PLANS

P_a	Acceptable Quality Levels (normal inspection)																
	4.0	4.0	15	25	40	65	100	150.	250	400	650	1000
		p (in defects per hundred units)										
99.0	0.33	0.34	4.97	14.5	27.4	59.5	96.9	117	159	203	249	345	419	573	651	947	1029
95.0	1.70	1.71	11.8	27.3	45.5	87.1	133	157	206	256	308	415	496	663	748	1065	1152
90.0	3.45	3.50	17.7	36.7	58.2	105	155	181	234	288	343	456	541	716	804	1131	1222
75.0	9.14	9.60	32.0	57.6	84.5	141	199	228	287	347	408	530	623	809	903	1249	1344
50.0	20.6	23.1	55.9	89.1	122	189	256	289	356	422	489	622	722	922	1022	1389	1489
25.0	37.0	46.2	89.8	131	170	247	323	360	434	507	580	724	832	1046	1152	1539	1644
10.0	53.6	76.8	130	177	223	309	392	433	514	593	671	825	939	1165	1277	1683	1793
5.0	63.2	99.9	158	210	258	350	438	481	565	648	730	890	1008	1241	1356	1773	1886
1.0	78.4	154	221	280	335	437	533	580	672	761	848	1019	1145	1392	1513	1951	2069
	6.5	6.5	25	40	65	100	150	250	400	650	1000	
		Acceptable Quality Levels (tightened inspection)										

Note: Binomial distribution used for percent defective computations; Poisson for defects per hundred units.

385

TABLE X-B-2 — SAMPLING PLANS FOR SAMPLE SIZE CODE LETTER: B

Acceptable Quality Levels (normal inspection)

Type of sampling plan	Cumulative sample size	Less than 4.0	4.0 (Ac Re)	6.5	10	15 (Ac Re)	25 (Ac Re)	40 (Ac Re)	65 (Ac Re)	100 (Ac Re)	150 (Ac Re)	250 (Ac Re)	400 (Ac Re)	650 (Ac Re)	1000 (Ac Re)
Single	3	▽	0 1	Use Letter ↓	Use Letter ↓	1 2	2 3	3 4	5 6	7 8	10 11	14 15	21 22	30 31	44 45
Double	2	▽	•	Use Letter A	Use Letter C	0 2	0 3	1 4	2 5	3 7	5 9	7 11	9 14	11 16	16 20
Double	4					1 2	3 4	4 5	6 7	8 9	12 13	18 19	26 27	37 38	56 57
Multiple		▽	• (D)			‡	‡	‡	‡	‡	‡	‡	‡	‡	‡

Acceptable Quality Levels (tightened inspection)

Less than 6.5	6.5	10	15	25	40	65	100	150	250	400	650	1000
✕	✕	✕	✕	✕	✕	✕	✕	✕	✕	✕	✕	✕

▽ = Use next subsequent sample size code letter for which acceptance and rejection numbers are available.

Ac = Acceptance number

Re = Rejection number

• = Use single sampling plan above (or alternatively use letter E).

‡ = Use double sampling plan above (or alternatively use letter D).

B

TABLE X-C—Tables for sample size code letter: C

CHART C - OPERATING CHARACTERISTIC CURVES FOR SINGLE SAMPLING PLANS
(Curves for double and multiple sampling are matched as closely as practicable)

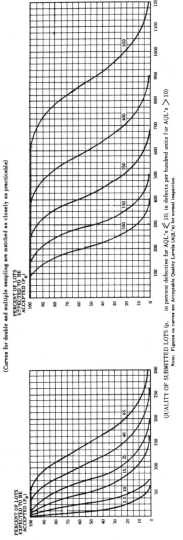

PERCENT OF LOTS EXPECTED TO BE ACCEPTED (P_a)

QUALITY OF SUBMITTED LOTS (p. in percent defective for AQL's ≤ 10; in defects per hundred units for AQL's > 10)

Note: Figures on curves are Acceptable Quality Levels (AQL's) for normal inspection.

TABLE X-C-1 - TABULATED VALUES FOR OPERATING CHARACTERISTIC CURVES FOR SINGLE SAMPLING PLANS

P_a	Acceptable Quality Levels (normal inspection)																	
	p (in percent defective)		p (in defects per hundred units)															
	2.5	10	2.5	10	15	25	40	65	100	X	150	X	250	X	400	X	650	X
99.0	0.20	3.28	0.20	2.89	8.72	16.5	35.7	58.1	70.1	95.4	122	150	207	251	344	391	568	618
95.0	1.02	7.63	1.03	7.10	16.4	27.3	52.3	79.6	93.9	123	154	185	249	298	398	449	639	691
90.0	2.09	11.2	2.10	10.6	22.0	34.9	63.0	93.1	109	140	173	206	273	325	429	482	679	733
75.0	5.59	19.4	5.76	19.2	34.5	50.7	84.4	119	137	172	208	245	318	374	485	542	749	806
50.0	12.9	31.4	13.9	33.6	53.5	73.4	113	153	173	213	253	293	373	433	553	613	833	893
25.0	24.2	45.4	27.7	53.9	78.4	102	148	194	216	260	304	348	435	499	627	691	923	987
10.0	36.9	58.4	46.1	77.8	106	134	186	235	260	308	356	403	495	564	699	766	1010	1076
5.0	45.1	65.8	59.9	94.9	126	155	210	263	289	339	389	438	534	605	745	814	1064	1131
1.0	60.2	77.8	92.1	133	168	201	262	320	348	403	456	509	612	687	835	908	1171	1241
	4.0	X	4.0	15	25	40	65	100	150	X	250	X	400	X	650	X	X	X
	Acceptable Quality Levels (tightened inspection)																	

Note: Binomial distribution used for percent defective computations; Poisson for defects per hundred units.

C

387

TABLE X-C-2 - SAMPLING PLANS FOR SAMPLE SIZE CODE LETTER: C

Type of sampling plan	Cumulative sample size	Less than 2.5		2.5		4.0		6.5		10		15		25		40		65		100		150		250		400		650		1000	
		Ac	Re	Ac	Re	Ac	Re	Ac	Re	Ac	Re	Ac	Re	Ac	Re	Ac	Re	Ac	Re	Ac	Re	Ac	Re	Ac	Re	Ac	Re	Ac	Re	Ac	Re
Single	5	▽		0	1	Use Letter B		Use Letter D		1	2	2	3	3	4	5	6	6	7	8	9	10	11	13	14	18	19	21	22	27	28	⊠	
																											30	31	41	42	44	45
Double	3	▽		*		Use Letter B		Use Letter E		0	2	0	3	1	4	2	5	3	7	5	9	7	11	9	14	11	16	15	20	17	22	⊠	
	6									1	2	1	3	3	4	4	5	6	7	8	9	11	12	15	16	18	19	23	24	26	27		
						Letter B		Letter D																		20	17	35	37	22	23	29	25	31
																									34	35	37	38	52	53	56	57
Multiple		▽		*		Use Letter B		Use Letter E		‡		‡		‡		‡		‡		‡		‡		‡		‡		‡		‡		‡	

Acceptable Quality Levels (tightened inspection)

	Less than 4.0	4.0	6.5	10	15	25	40	65	100	150	250	400	650	1000
	⊠			⊠	⊠	⊠	⊠	⊠	⊠	⊠	⊠	⊠	⊠	⊠

▽ = Use next subsequent sample size code letter for which acceptance and rejection numbers are available.

Ac = Acceptance number.

Re = Rejection number.

* = Use single sampling plan above (or alternatively use letter F).

‡ = Use double sampling plan above (or alternatively use letter D).

C

TABLE X-D—Tables for sample size code letter: D

CHART D - OPERATING CHARACTERISTIC CURVES FOR SINGLE SAMPLING PLANS

(Curves for double and multiple sampling are matched as closely as practicable)

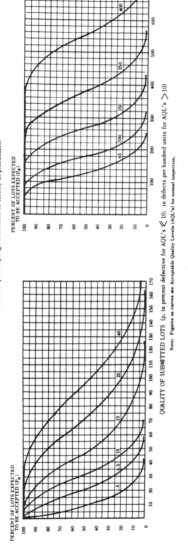

PERCENT OF LOTS EXPECTED TO BE ACCEPTED (Pₐ)

QUALITY OF SUBMITTED LOTS (p, in percent defective for AQL's ≤ 10; in defects per hundred units for AQL's > 10)

Note: Figures on curves are Acceptable Quality Levels (AQL's) for normal inspection.

TABLE X-D-1 - TABULATED VALUES FOR OPERATING CHARACTERISTIC CURVES FOR SINGLE SAMPLING PLANS

Pₐ	\multicolumn{17}{c	}{Acceptable Quality Levels (normal inspection)}
	1.5	6.5	10	1.5	6.5	10	15	25	40	65	100	150	250	400
	p (in percent defective)			\multicolumn{14}{c	}{p (in defects per hundred units)}
99.0	0.13	2.00	6.00	0.13	1.86	5.45	10.3	22.3	36.3	43.8	59.6	76.2	93.5	129	157	215	244	355	386
95.0	0.64	2.64	11.1	0.64	4.44	10.2	17.1	32.7	49.8	58.7	77.1	96.1	116	156	186	249	281	399	432
90.0	1.31	6.88	14.7	1.31	6.65	13.8	21.8	39.4	58.2	67.9	87.8	108	129	171	203	268	301	424	458
75.0	3.53	12.1	22.1	3.60	12.0	21.6	31.7	52.7	74.5	85.5	108	130	153	199	234	303	339	468	504
50.0	8.30	20.1	32.1	8.66	21.0	33.4	45.9	70.9	95.9	108	133	158	183	233	271	346	383	521	558
25.0	15.9	30.3	43.3	17.3	33.7	49.0	63.9	92.8	121	135	163	190	218	272	312	392	432	577	617
10.0	25.0	40.6	53.9	28.8	48.6	66.5	83.5	116	147	162	193	222	252	309	352	437	478	631	672
5.0	31.2	47.1	59.9	37.5	59.3	78.7	96.9	131	164	180	212	243	274	334	378	465	509	665	707
1.0	43.8	58.8	70.7	57.6	83.0	105	126	164	200	218	252	285	318	382	429	522	568	732	776
	2.5	10		2.5	10	15	25	40	65		100	150	250		150	250	400		400
	\multicolumn{19}{c	}{Acceptable Quality Levels (tightened inspection)}

D

389

TABLE X-D-2 — SAMPLING PLANS FOR SAMPLE SIZE CODE LETTER: D

Acceptable Quality Levels (normal inspection) — values shown as Ac Re for each AQL

Type of sampling plan	Cumulative sample size	Less than 1.5	1.5	2.5	4.0	6.5	10	15	25	40	65	100	150	250	400	Higher than 400	Cumulative sample size
Single	8	▽	0 1	Use Letter C	Use Letter E	1 2	2 3	3 4	5 6	7 8	10 11	14 15	21 22	30 31	44 45	△	8
Double	5	▽	•	Use Letter C	Use Letter E	0 2	0 3	1 4	2 5	3 7	5 9	7 11	11 16	17 22	25 31	△	5
Double	10					1 2	3 4	4 5	6 7	8 9	12 13	18 19	26 27	37 38	56 57		10
Multiple	2	▽	•	Use Letter F		# 2	# 2	# 3	# 4	0 4	0 5	1 7	1 8	4 12	6 16	△	2
Multiple	4					# 2	0 3	0 3	1 5	1 6	3 8	4 10	7 14	11 19	17 27		4
Multiple	6					0 2	0 3	1 4	2 6	3 8	6 10	8 13	13 19	19 27	29 39		6
Multiple	8					0 3	1 4	2 5	3 7	5 10	8 13	12 17	19 25	27 34	40 49		8
Multiple	10					1 3	2 4	3 6	5 8	7 11	11 15	17 20	25 29	36 43	53 58		10
Multiple	12					1 3	3 5	4 6	7 9	10 12	14 17	20 22	31 33	45 47	65 68		12
Multiple	14					2 4	4 5	6 7	9 10	13 14	18 19	25 26	37 38	53 54	77 78		14

Acceptable Quality Levels (tightened inspection)

		Less than 2.5	2.5	4.0	6.5	10	15	25	40	65	100	150	250	400	Higher than 400	

△ = Use next preceding sample size code letter for which acceptance and rejection numbers are available.

▽ = Use next subsequent sample size code letter for which acceptance and rejection numbers are available.

Ac = Acceptance number

Re = Rejection number

• = Use single sampling plan above (or alternatively use letter G).

= Acceptance not permitted at this sample size.

D

390

E

TABLE X-E—Tables for sample size code letter: E

CHART E - OPERATING CHARACTERISTIC CURVES FOR SINGLE SAMPLING PLANS

(Curves for double and multiple sampling are matched as closely as practicable)

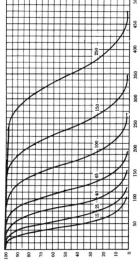

Left axis: PERCENT OF LOTS EXPECTED TO BE ACCEPTED (P_a)

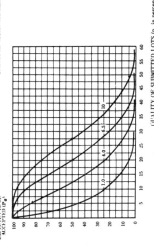

QUALITY OF SUBMITTED LOTS (p, in percent defective for AQL's ≤ 10; in defects per hundred units for AQL's > 10)

Note: Figures on curves are Acceptable Quality Levels (AQL's) for normal inspection.

TABLE X-E-1 - TABULATED VALUES FOR OPERATING CHARACTERISTIC CURVES FOR SINGLE SAMPLING PLANS

p (in percent defective)

P_a	1.0	4.0	6.5	10
99.0	0.077	1.19	3.63	7.00
95.0	0.394	2.81	6.63	11.3
90.0	0.807	4.16	8.80	14.2
75.0	2.19	7.41	13.4	19.9
50.0	5.19	12.6	20.0	27.5
25.0	10.1	19.4	28.0	36.2
10.0	16.2	26.8	36.0	44.4
5.0	20.6	31.6	41.0	49.5
1.0	29.8	41.5	50.6	58.7
	1.5	6.5	10	✕

Acceptable Quality Levels (normal inspection) — p (in percent defective) for AQL ≤ 10; p (in defects per hundred units) for AQL > 10

P_a	1.0	4.0	6.5	10	15	25	40	65	100	150	250
99.0	0.078	1.15	3.35	6.33	13.7	22.4	27.0	36.7	46.9	57.5	79.6
95.0	0.395	2.73	6.29	10.5	20.1	30.6	36.1	47.5	59.2	71.1	95.7
90.0	0.808	4.09	8.48	13.4	24.2	35.8	41.8	54.0	66.5	79.2	105
75.0	2.22	7.39	13.3	19.5	32.5	45.8	52.6	66.3	80.2	94.1	122
50.0	5.33	12.9	20.6	28.2	43.6	59.0	66.7	82.1	97.5	113	144
25.0	10.7	20.7	30.2	39.3	57.1	74.5	83.1	100	117	134	167
10.0	17.7	29.9	40.9	51.4	71.3	90.5	100	119	137	155	190
5.0	23.0	36.5	48.4	59.6	80.9	101	111	130	150	168	205
1.0	35.4	51.1	64.7	77.3	101	123	134	155	176	196	235
	96.7	115	125	144	168	192	217	233	264	✕	✕
	132	153	165	187	213	241	269	286	321		
	150	173	185	208	236	266	295	313	349		
	219	246	261	288	321	355	388	409	450		
	238	266	282	310	344	379	414	435	477		

Acceptable Quality Levels (tightened inspection)

	1.5	6.5	10	15	25	40	65	100	150	250	✕

Note: Binomial distribution used for percent defective computations; Poisson for defects per hundred units.

391

TABLE X-E-2 – SAMPLING PLANS FOR SAMPLE SIZE CODE LETTER: E

Acceptable Quality Levels (normal inspection)

Type of sampling plan	Cumulative sample size	Less than 1.0 (Ac)	1.0 (Ac Re)	1.5	2.5	4.0 (Ac Re)	6.5 (Ac Re)	10 (Ac Re)	15 (Ac Re)	25 (Ac Re)	40 (Ac Re)	65 (Ac Re)	100 (Ac Re)	150 (Ac Re)	250 (Ac Re)	Higher than 250 (Re)
Single	13	▽	0 1	Use	Use	1 2	2 3	3 4	4 5	6 7	8 9	11 12	13 14 15	19 21 22	28 30 31	41 42 44 45	△
Double	8	▽	*	Use	Use (Letter G)	0 2	0 3	1 4	2 5	3 7	5 9	7 10 11	9 14	16 18	22 23	25	31	△
	16			(Letter D)	(Letter F)	1 3	2 3	3 4	5 6	7 8	9 11 12	13 15	16 18 19	24 26	34 35	38	52 53 56 57	
Multiple	3	▽	*			#	#	#	3 #	4 #	5 0	6 1	7 1	8 2	9 3	10	6 16	△
	6					#	2 0	3 0	3 1	5 1	6 2	7 3	9 4	10 7	14 10	17 11	15 25 17 27	
	9					0 2	2 0	4 1	4 2	6 3	8 4	10 6	13 8	17 13	19 17	24 19	26 36 29 39	
	12					0 3	3 1	5 2	5 3	7 5	10 6	13 8	15 12	17 16	22 19	25 24	31 27 34 37 40 46 49	
	15					1 3	3 2	6 3	7 4	8 7	11 9	14 11	17 15	20 22	25 25	29 31	32 36 40 45 53 55 58	
	18					1 5	4 3	6 4	7 5	9 10	12 11	15 13	17 17	20 22	23 27	29 31 33	40 43 47 61 64 65 68	
	21					2 5	4 5	6 6	9 7	10 13	14 15	18 18	21 23	25 27	26 32	33 37 38 48 49 53 54	72 73 77 78	

Acceptable Quality Levels (tightened inspection)

Less than 1.5	1.5	2.5	4.0	6.5	10	15	25	40	65	100	150	Higher than 250
X	1.5	2.5	4.0	6.5	10	15	25	40	65	100	150	X

△ = Use next preceding sample size-code letter for which acceptance and rejection numbers are available.

▽ = Use next subsequent sample size code letter for which acceptance and rejection numbers are available.

Ac = Acceptance number.

Re = Rejection number.

* = Use single sampling plan above (or alternatively use letter H).

= Acceptance not permitted at this sample size.

E

392

TABLE X-F—Tables for sample size code letter: F

CHART F - OPERATING CHARACTERISTIC CURVES FOR SINGLE SAMPLING PLANS

(Curves for double and multiple sampling are matched as closely as practicable)

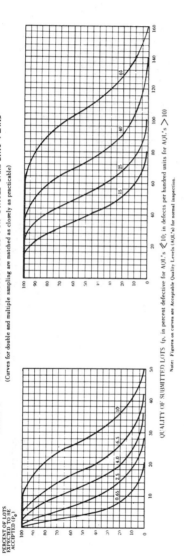

QUALITY OF SUBMITTED LOTS (p, in percent defective for AQL's $\leqslant$ 10; in defects per hundred units for AQL's $>$ 10)

Note: Figures on curves are Acceptable Quality Levels (AQL's) for normal inspection.

TABLE X-F-1 - TABULATED VALUES FOR OPERATING CHARACTERISTIC CURVES FOR SINGLE SAMPLING PLANS

P_a	0.65	2.5	4.0	6.5	10	0.65	2.5	4.0	6.5	10	15	25	40	65
	p (in percent defective)					p (in defects per hundred units)								
99.0	0.050	0.75	2.25	4.31	9.75	0.051	0.75	2.18	4.12	8.92	14.5	23.9	37.4	62.9
95.0	0.256	1.80	4.22	7.13	14.0	0.257	1.78	4.09	6.83	13.1	19.9	30.8	46.2	74.5
90.0	0.525	2.69	5.64	9.03	16.6	0.527	2.66	5.51	8.73	15.8	23.3	35.1	51.5	81.2
75.0	1.43	4.81	8.70	12.8	21.6	1.44	4.81	8.68	12.7	21.1	29.8	43.1	61.2	93.4
50.0	3.41	8.25	13.1	18.1	27.9	3.47	8.39	13.4	18.4	28.4	38.3	53.3	73.3	108
25.0	6.70	12.9	18.7	24.2	34.8	6.93	13.5	19.6	25.5	37.1	48.4	65.1	87.0	125
10.0	10.9	18.1	24.5	30.4	41.5	11.5	19.5	26.6	33.4	46.4	58.9	77.0	101	141
5.0	13.9	21.6	28.3	34.4	45.6	15.0	23.7	31.5	38.8	52.6	65.7	84.8	109	151
1.0	20.6	28.9	35.6	42.0	53.4	23.0	33.2	42.0	50.2	65.5	80.0	101	127	172
	1.0	4.0	6.5	10	X	1.0	4.0	6.5	10	15	25	40	65	X
	Acceptable Quality Levels (tightened inspection)													

Note: Binomial distribution used for percent defective computations; Poisson for defects per hundred units.

TABLE X-F-2 — SAMPLING PLANS FOR SAMPLE SIZE CODE LETTER: F

Acceptable Quality Levels (normal inspection) — each cell shows Ac / Re

Type of sampling plan	Cumulative sample size	Less than 0.65	0.65	1.0	1.5	2.5	4.0	6.5	10	15	25	40	65	Higher than 65
Single	20	▽	▽	▽	0 / 1	1 / 2	2 / 3	3 / 4	5 / 6	7 / 8	10 / 11	14 / 15	21 / 22	△
Double	13	▽	▽	▽	•	0 / 2	0 / 3	1 / 4	2 / 5	3 / 7	5 / 9	7 / 11	11 / 16	△
Double	26					1 / 2	3 / 4	4 / 5	6 / 7	8 / 9	12 / 13	18 / 19	26 / 27	
Multiple	5	▽	▽	▽	•	* / 2	* / 3	* / 4	0 / 4	0 / 5	0 / 6	1 / 7	2 / 9	△
Multiple	10					0 / 3	0 / 3	0 / 5	1 / 6	2 / 7	3 / 8	4 / 10	7 / 14	
Multiple	15					0 / 3	1 / 4	1 / 6	3 / 8	4 / 9	6 / 10	8 / 13	13 / 19	
Multiple	20					1 / 4	2 / 5	2 / 7	5 / 10	6 / 11	8 / 13	12 / 17	19 / 25	
Multiple	25					2 / 4	3 / 6	3 / 8	7 / 11	9 / 12	11 / 15	17 / 20	25 / 29	
Multiple	30					3 / 5	4 / 6	5 / 9	10 / 12	12 / 14	14 / 17	21 / 23	31 / 33	
Multiple	35					4 / 5	6 / 7	8 / 9	13 / 14	14 / 15	18 / 19	25 / 26	37 / 38	

Acceptable Quality Levels (tightened inspection): Less than 1.0 | 1.0 | 1.5 | 2.5 | 4.0 | 6.5 | 10 | 15 | 25 | 40 | 65 | Higher than 65

△ = Use next preceding sample size code letter for which acceptance and rejection numbers are available.

▽ = Use next subsequent sample size code letter for which acceptance and rejection numbers are available.

Ac = Acceptance number

Re = Rejection number

• = Use single sampling plan above (or alternatively use letter J).

* = Acceptance not permitted at this sample size.

F

TABLE X-G—Tables for sample size code letter: G

CHART G - OPERATING CHARACTERISTIC CURVES FOR SINGLE SAMPLING PLANS

(Curves for double and multiple sampling are matched as closely as practicable)

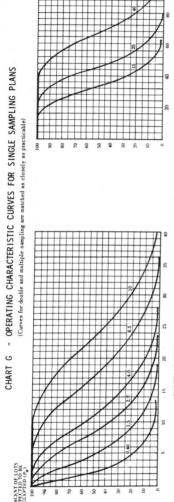

QUALITY OF SUBMITTED LOTS (p, in percent defective for AQL's ≤ 10; in defects per hundred units for AQL's > 10)

Note: Figures on curves are Acceptable Quality Levels (AQL's) for normal inspection.

TABLE X-G-1 - TABULATED VALUES FOR OPERATING CHARACTERISTIC CURVES FOR SINGLE SAMPLING PLANS

P_a	Acceptable Quality Levels (normal inspection)														
	p (in percent defective)						p (in defects per hundred units)								
	0.40	1.5	2.5	4.0	6.5	10	0.40	1.5	2.5	4.0	6.5	10	15	25	40
99.0	0.032	0.475	1.38	2.63	5.94	9.75	0.032	0.466	1.36	2.57	5.57	9.08	14.9	23.4	39.3
95.0	0.161	1.13	2.59	4.39	8.50	13.1	0.160	1.10	2.55	4.26	8.16	12.4	19.3	28.9	46.5
90.0	0.329	1.67	3.50	5.56	10.2	15.1	0.328	1.66	3.44	5.45	9.85	14.6	21.9	32.2	50.8
75.0	0.895	3.01	5.42	7.98	13.4	19.0	0.900	3.00	5.39	7.92	13.2	18.6	26.9	38.2	58.4
50.0	2.14	5.19	8.27	11.4	17.5	23.7	2.16	5.24	8.35	11.5	17.7	24.0	33.3	45.8	67.7
25.0	4.23	8.19	11.9	15.4	22.3	29.0	4.33	8.41	12.3	16.0	23.2	30.3	40.7	54.4	78.0
10.0	6.94	11.6	15.8	19.7	27.1	34.1	7.19	12.2	16.6	20.9	29.0	36.8	48.1	62.9	88.1
5.0	8.94	14.0	18.4	22.5	30.1	37.2	9.36	14.8	19.7	24.2	32.9	41.1	53.0	68.4	94.5
1.0	13.5	19.0	23.7	28.0	35.9	43.3	14.4	20.7	26.3	31.4	41.0	50.0	63.0	79.5	107
	0.65	2.5	4.0	6.5	10	✕	0.65	2.5	4.0	6.5	10	15	✕	25	✕
	Acceptable Quality Levels (tightened inspection)														

Note: Binomial distribution used for percent defective computations; Poisson for defects per hundred units.

TABLE X-G-2 - SAMPLING PLANS FOR SAMPLE SIZE CODE LETTER: G

Acceptable Quality Levels (normal inspection)

Type of sampling plan	Cumulative sample size	Less than 0.40	0.40 Ac	0.40 Re	0.65	1.0	1.5 Ac	1.5 Re	2.5 Ac	2.5 Re	4.0 Ac	4.0 Re	6.5 Ac	6.5 Re	10 Ac	10 Re	15 Ac	15 Re	25 Ac	25 Re	40 Ac	40 Re	Higher than 40	Cumulative sample size
Single	32	▽	0	1	Use Letter F	Use Letter J	1	2	2	3	3	4	5	6	7	8	10	11	14	15	21	22	△	32
Double	20	▽	*		Use Letter F	Use Letter J	0	2	0	3	1	4	2	5	3	7	5	9	7	11	11	16	△	20
	40						1	2	3	4	4	5	6	7	8	9	12	13	18	19	26	27		40
Multiple	8	▽	*			Use Letter H	#	2	#	2	#	3	#	4	0	4	0	5	1	7	2	9	△	8
	16						#	3	0	3	0	3	1	5	1	6	3	8	4	10	7	14		16
	24						0	3	0	3	1	4	2	6	3	8	6	10	8	13	13	19		24
	32						0	4	1	4	2	5	3	7	5	10	8	13	12	17	19	25		32
	40						1	5	2	4	3	6	5	8	7	11	11	15	17	20	25	29		40
	48						1	6	3	5	4	6	7	9	10	12	14	17	21	23	31	33		48
	56						2	7	4	5	6	7	9	10	13	14	18	19	25	26	37	38		56

	Less than 0.65	0.65	1.0	1.5	2.5	4.0	6.5	10	15	25	40	Higher than 40

Acceptable Quality Levels (tightened inspection)

△ = Use next preceding sample size code letter for which acceptance and rejection numbers are available.
▽ = Use next subsequent sample size code letter for which acceptance and rejection numbers are available.
Ac = Acceptance number.
Re = Rejection number.
• = Use single sampling plan above (or alternatively use letter K).
= Acceptance not permitted at this sample size.

G

TABLE X-H—Tables for sample size code letter: H

CHART H - OPERATING CHARACTERISTIC CURVES FOR SINGLE SAMPLING PLANS
(Curves for double and multiple sampling are matched as closely as practicable)

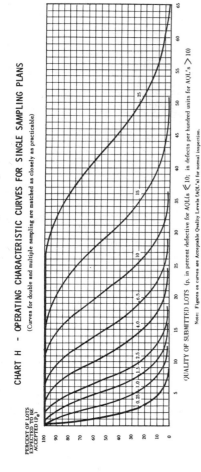

PERCENT OF LOTS EXPECTED TO BE ACCEPTED (P_a)

QUALITY OF SUBMITTED LOTS (p, in percent defective for AQL's ≤ 10; in defects per hundred units for AQL's > 10)

Note: Figures on curves are Acceptable Quality Levels (AQL's) for normal inspection.

TABLE X-H-1 - TABULATED VALUES FOR OPERATING CHARACTERISTIC CURVES FOR SINGLE SAMPLING PLANS

Acceptable Quality Levels (normal inspection)

p (in percent defective)

P_a	0.25	1.0	1.5	2.5	4.0	6.5	✕
99.0	0.020	0.306	0.888	1.69	3.66	6.06	7.41
95.0	0.103	0.712	1.66	2.77	5.34	8.20	9.74
90.0	0.210	1.07	2.23	3.54	6.42	9.53	11.2
75.0	0.574	1.92	3.46	5.09	8.51	12.0	13.8
50.0	1.38	3.33	5.31	7.30	11.3	15.2	17.2
25.0	2.74	5.30	7.70	10.0	14.5	18.8	21.0
10.0	4.50	7.56	10.3	12.9	17.8	22.4	24.7
5.0	5.82	9.13	12.1	14.8	19.9	24.7	27.0
1.0	8.80	12.5	15.9	18.8	24.3	29.2	31.7
(tightened AQL)	0.40	1.5	2.5	4.0	6.5	✕	10

p (in defects per hundred units)

P_a	0.25	1.0	1.5	2.5	4.0	6.5	✕	10	✕	15	✕	25
99.0	0.020	0.298	0.872	1.65	3.57	5.81	7.01	9.54	12.2	15.0	20.7	25.1
95.0	0.103	0.710	1.64	2.73	5.23	7.96	9.39	12.3	15.4	18.5	24.9	29.8
90.0	0.210	1.06	2.20	3.49	6.30	9.31	10.9	14.0	17.3	20.6	27.3	32.5
75.0	0.576	1.92	3.45	5.07	8.44	11.9	13.7	17.2	20.8	24.5	31.8	37.4
50.0	1.39	3.36	5.35	7.34	11.3	15.3	17.3	21.6	25.3	29.3	37.3	43.3
25.0	2.77	5.39	7.84	10.2	14.8	19.4	21.6	26.0	30.4	34.8	43.5	49.9
10.0	4.61	7.78	10.6	13.4	18.6	23.5	26.0	30.8	35.6	40.3	49.5	56.4
5.0	5.99	9.49	12.6	15.5	21.0	26.3	28.9	33.9	38.9	43.8	53.4	60.5
1.0	9.21	13.3	16.8	20.1	26.2	32.0	34.8	40.3	45.6	50.9	61.1	68.7
(tightened AQL)	0.40	1.5	2.5	4.0	6.5	✕	10	✕	15	✕	25	✕

Acceptable Quality Levels (tightened inspection)

Note: Binomial distribution used for percent defective computations; Poisson for defects per hundred units.

TABLE X-H-2 — SAMPLING PLANS FOR SAMPLE SIZE CODE LETTER: H

Acceptable Quality Levels (normal inspection) — (Ac, Re)

Type of sampling plan	Cumulative sample size	Less than 0.25	0.25	0.40	0.65	1.0	1.5	2.5	4.0	6.5	10	15	25	Higher than 25
Single	50	▽	0 1	Use Letter G	Use Letter K	1 2	2 3	3 4	5 6	7 8	10 11	14 15	21 22	△
Double	32	▽		Use Letter G	Use Letter J	0 2	0 3	1 4	2 5	3 7	5 9	7 11	11 16	△
	64					1 2	3 4	4 5	6 7	8 9	12 13	18 19	26 27	
Multiple	13	▽				# 2	# 2	# 3	# 4	0 4	0 5	0 6	2 9	△
	26					# 2	0 3	0 3	1 5	1 6	3 8	3 9	7 14	
	39					0 2	0 3	1 4	2 6	3 8	6 10	8 13	13 19	
	52					0 3	1 4	2 5	3 7	5 10	8 13	12 17	19 25	
	65					1 3	2 4	3 6	5 8	7 11	11 15	17 20	25 29	
	78					1 3	3 5	4 6	7 9	10 12	14 17	21 23	31 33	
	91					2 3	4 5	6 7	9 10	13 14	18 19	25 26	37 38	

Acceptable Quality Levels (tightened inspection)

Less than 0.40	0.40	0.65	1.0	1.5	2.5	4.0	6.5	10	15	25	Higher than 25

△ = Use next preceding sample size code letter for which acceptance and rejection numbers are available.

▽ = Use next subsequent sample size code letter for which acceptance and rejection numbers are available.

Ac = Acceptance number

Re = Rejection number

• = Use single sampling plan above (or alternatively use letter L).

= Acceptance not permitted at this sample size.

H

TABLE X-J—Tables for sample size code letter: J

CHART J - OPERATING CHARACTERISTIC CURVES FOR SINGLE SAMPLING PLANS

(Curves for double and multiple sampling are matched as closely as practicable)

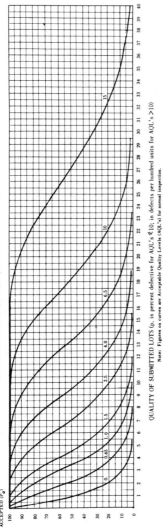

PERCENT OF LOTS EXPECTED TO BE ACCEPTED (Pₐ)

QUALITY OF SUBMITTED LOTS (p, in percent defective for AQL's ≤ 10; in defects per hundred units for AQL's > 10)

Note: Figures on curves are Acceptable Quality Levels (AQL's) for normal inspection.

TABLE X-J-1 - TABULATED VALUES FOR OPERATING CHARACTERISTIC CURVES FOR SINGLE SAMPLING PLANS

Acceptable Quality Levels (normal inspection)

p (in percent defective)

Pₐ	0.15	0.25	0.40	0.65	1.0	1.5	2.5	4.0	6.5	10
99.0	0.013	0.188	0.550	1.05	2.30	3.72	4.50	6.13	7.88	9.75
95.0	0.064	0.444	1.03	1.73	3.32	5.06	5.98	7.91	9.89	11.9
90.0	0.132	0.666	1.38	2.20	3.98	5.91	6.91	8.95	11.0	13.2
75.0	0.359	1.202	2.16	3.18	5.30	7.50	8.62	10.9	13.2	15.5
50.0	0.863	2.09	3.33	4.57	7.06	9.55	10.8	13.3	15.8	18.3
25.0	1.72	3.33	4.84	6.31	9.14	11.9	13.3	16.0	18.6	21.3
10.0	2.84	4.78	6.52	8.16	11.3	14.2	15.7	18.6	21.4	24.2
5.0	3.68	5.80	7.66	9.39	12.7	15.8	17.3	20.3	23.2	26.0
1.0	5.59	8.00	10.1	12.0	15.6	18.9	20.5	23.6	26.5	29.5

p (in defects per hundred units)

Pₐ	0.15	0.25	0.40	0.65	1.0	1.5	2.5	4.0	6.5	10	15	25
99.0	0.013	0.186	0.545	1.03	2.23	3.63	4.38	5.96	7.62	9.35	12.9	15.7
95.0	0.064	0.444	1.02	1.71	3.27	4.98	5.87	7.71	9.61	11.6	15.6	18.6
90.0	0.131	0.665	1.38	2.18	3.94	5.82	6.79	8.78	10.8	12.9	17.1	20.3
75.0	0.360	1.20	2.16	3.17	5.27	7.45	8.55	10.8	13.0	15.3	19.9	23.4
50.0	0.866	2.10	3.34	4.59	7.09	9.59	10.8	13.3	15.8	18.3	23.3	27.1
25.0	1.73	3.37	4.90	6.39	9.28	12.1	13.5	16.3	19.0	21.8	27.2	31.2
10.0	2.88	4.86	6.65	8.35	11.6	14.7	16.2	19.3	22.2	25.2	30.9	35.2
5.0	3.75	5.93	7.87	9.69	13.1	16.4	18.0	21.2	24.3	27.4	33.4	37.8
1.0	5.76	8.30	10.5	12.6	16.4	20.0	21.8	25.2	28.5	31.8	38.2	42.9

Acceptable Quality Levels (tightened inspection)

p (in percent defective): 0.25 | 0.40 | 0.65 | 1.0 | 1.5 | 2.5 | 4.0 | 6.5 | 10 | 15

p (in defects per hundred units): 0.25 | 0.40 | 0.65 | 1.0 | 1.5 | 2.5 | 4.0 | 6.5 | 10 | 15 | 25 | 40

Note: All values given in above table based on Poisson distribution as an approximation to the Binomial.

J

399

TABLE X-J-2 — SAMPLING PLANS FOR SAMPLE SIZE CODE LETTER: J

Type of sampling plan	Cumulative sample size		Less than 0.15	0.15		0.25	0.40	0.65		1.0		1.5		2.5		4.0		6.5		10		15		Higher than 15
				Ac	Re			Ac	Re	Ac	Re	Ac	Re	Ac	Re	Ac	Re	Ac	Re	Ac	Re	Ac	Re	
Single	80		▽	0	1			1	2	2	3	3	4	5	6	7	8	10	11	14	15	21	22	△
Double	50		▽	•		Use Letter	Use Letter	0	2	0	3	1	4	2	5	3	7	5	9	7	11	11	16	△
	100					Letter	Letter	1	2	3	4	4	5	6	7	8	9	12	13	18	19	26	27	
Multiple	20		▽	•		H	L	K																	△
	20							"	2	"	2	"	3	"	4	0	4	0	5	1	7	2	9	
	40							0	2	0	3	1	4	1	5	1	6	3	8	4	10	7	14	
	60							0	2	1	3	2	4	2	6	3	8	6	10	6	13	13	19	
	80							0	3	2	4	3	5	3	7	5	10	8	13	12	17	19	25	
	100							1	3	3	4	4	6	5	8	7	11	11	15	17	20	25	29	
	120							1	3	4	5	6	6	7	9	10	12	14	17	20	23	31	33	
	140							2	3	5	6	7	7	9	10	13	14	18	19	25	26	37	38	

Acceptable Quality Levels (normal inspection)

		Less than 0.25	0.25			0.40	0.65	1.0	1.5	2.5	4.0	6.5		15	Higher than 15

Acceptable Quality Levels (tightened inspection)

△ = Use next preceding sample size code letter for which acceptance and rejection numbers are available.

▽ = Use next subsequent sample size code letter for which acceptance and rejection numbers are available.

Ac = Acceptance number

Re = Rejection number

• = Use single sampling plan above (or alternatively use letter M)

" = Acceptance not permitted at this sample size.

J

400

K

TABLE X-K—Tables for sample size code letter: K

CHART K - OPERATING CHARACTERISTIC CURVES FOR SINGLE SAMPLING PLANS

(Curves for double and multiple sampling are matched as closely as practicable)

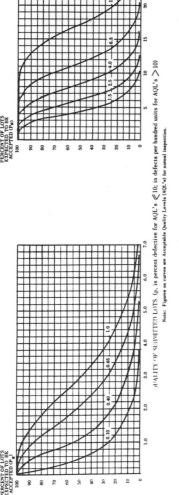

Note: Figures on curves are Acceptable Quality Levels (AQL's) for normal inspection.

TABLE X-K-1 - TABULATED VALUES FOR OPERATING CHARACTERISTIC CURVES FOR SINGLE SAMPLING PLANS

P_a	Acceptable Quality Levels (normal inspection)										
	0.10	0.40	0.65	1.0	1.5	2.5	4.0	6.5	10
	p (in percent defective or defects per hundred units)								
99.0	0.0081	0.119	0.349	0.658	1.43	2.33	3.82	5.98	8.28		10.1
95.0	0.0410	0.284	0.654	1.09	2.09	3.19	4.94	7.40	9.95		11.9
90.0	0.0840	0.426	0.882	1.40	2.52	3.73	5.62	8.24	10.9		13.0
75.0	0.230	0.769	1.34	2.03	3.38	4.77	6.90	9.79	12.7		14.9
50.0	0.554	1.34	2.14	2.94	4.54	6.14	8.53	11.7	14.9		17.3
25.0	1.11	2.15	3.14	4.09	5.94	7.75	10.4	13.9	17.4		20.0
10.0	1.84	3.11	4.26	5.35	7.42	9.42	12.3	16.1	19.8		22.5
5.0	2.40	3.80	5.04	6.20	8.41	10.5	13.6	17.5	21.4		24.2
1.0	3.68	5.31	6.73	8.04	10.5	12.8	16.1	20.4	24.5		27.5
	0.15	0.65	1.0	1.5	2.5		4.0	6.5	10	
	Acceptable Quality Levels (tightened inspection)								

Note: All values given in above table based on Poisson distribution as an approximation to the Binomial.

401

TABLE X-K-2 – SAMPLING PLANS FOR SAMPLE SIZE CODE LETTER: K

Single and Double plans — Acceptable Quality Levels (normal inspection)
(each cell gives Ac Re)

Type of sampling plan	Cumulative sample size	Less than 0.10	0.10	0.15	0.25	0.40	0.65	1.0	1.5	2.5	4.0	6.5	10	Higher than 10
Single	125	▽	0 1	Use Letter J	Use Letter L	1 2	2 3	3 4	5 6	7 8	10 11	14 15	21 22	△
Double	80	▽	•	Use Letter J	Use Letter M	0 2	0 3	1 4	2 5	3 7	5 9	7 11	11 16	△
Double	160					1 2	3 4	4 5	6 7	8 9	12 13	18 19	26 27	

Multiple plans — Acceptable Quality Levels (normal inspection)
(each cell gives Ac Re)

Cumulative sample size	Less than 0.10	0.10	0.15	0.25	0.40	0.65	1.0	1.5	2.5	4.0	6.5	10	Higher than 10
32	▽	•		Use Letter L	∗ 2	∗ 2	∗ 3	∗ 4	0 4	0 5	1 7	2 9	△
64					∗ 2	0 3	0 3	1 5	1 6	3 8	4 10	7 14	
96					0 2	0 3	1 4	2 6	3 8	6 10	8 13	13 19	
128					0 3	1 4	2 5	3 7	5 10	8 13	12 17	19 25	
160					1 3	2 4	3 6	5 8	7 11	11 15	17 20	25 29	
192					1 3	3 5	4 6	7 9	10 12	14 17	21 23	31 33	
224					2 3	4 5	6 7	9 10	13 14	18 19	25 26	37 38	

Acceptable Quality Levels (tightened inspection) — column headings shift one step:

Less than 0.15	0.15	0.25	0.40	0.65	1.0	1.5	2.5	4.0	6.5	Higher than 10

Legend:

△ = Use next preceding sample size code letter for which acceptance and rejection numbers are available.

▽ = Use next subsequent sample size code letter for which acceptance and rejection numbers are available.

Ac = Acceptance number

Re = Rejection number

• = Use single sampling plan above (or alternatively use letter N).

∗ = Acceptance not permitted at this sample size.

K

L

TABLE X-L—Tables for sample size code letter: L

CHART L - OPERATING CHARACTERISTIC CURVES FOR SINGLE SAMPLING PLANS
(Curves for double and multiple sampling are matched as closely as practicable)

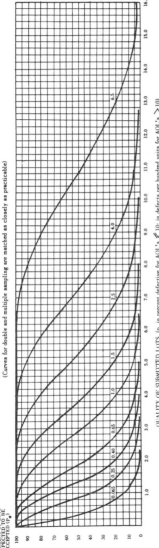

PERCENT OF LOTS EXPECTED TO BE ACCEPTED (P_a)

QUALITY OF SUBMITTED LOTS (p, in percent defective for AQL's $\leqslant$ 10; in defects per hundred units for AQL's $>$ 10)

Note: Figures on curves are Acceptable Quality Levels (AQL's) for normal inspection.

TABLE X-L-1 - TABULATED VALUES FOR OPERATING CHARACTERISTIC CURVES FOR SINGLE SAMPLING PLANS

P_a	0.065	0.25	0.40	0.65	1.0	1.5	X	2.5	X	4.0	X	6.5
	p (in percent defective or defects per hundred units)											
99.0	0.0051	0.075	0.218	0.412	0.893	1.45	1.75	2.39	3.05	3.74	5.17	6.29
95.0	0.0256	0.178	0.409	0.683	1.31	1.99	2.35	3.09	3.85	4.62	6.22	7.45
90.0	0.0525	0.266	0.551	0.873	1.58	2.33	2.72	3.51	4.32	5.15	6.84	8.12
75.0	0.144	0.481	0.864	1.27	2.11	2.98	3.42	4.31	5.21	6.12	7.95	9.34
50.0	0.347	0.839	1.34	1.84	2.84	3.84	4.33	5.33	6.33	7.33	9.33	10.8
25.0	0.693	1.35	1.96	2.56	3.71	4.84	5.40	6.51	7.61	8.70	10.9	12.5
10.0	1.15	1.95	2.66	3.34	4.64	5.89	6.50	7.70	8.89	10.1	12.4	14.1
5.0	1.50	2.37	3.15	3.88	5.26	6.57	7.22	8.48	9.72	10.9	13.3	15.1
1.0	2.30	3.32	4.20	5.02	6.55	8.00	8.70	10.1	11.4	12.7	15.3	17.2
	0.10	X	0.40	0.65	1.0	X	1.5	X	2.5	X	4.0	6.5

Acceptable Quality Levels (tightened inspection)

Note: All values given in above table based on Poisson distribution as an approximation to the Binomial.

403

TABLE X-L-2 - SAMPLING PLANS FOR SAMPLE SIZE CODE LETTER: L

Type of sampling plan	Cumulative sample size	Acceptable Quality Levels (normal inspection)																																		Cumulative sample size
		Less than 0.065		0.065		0.10		X		0.15		0.25		0.40		0.65		1.0		1.5		X		2.5		X		4.0		X		6.5		Higher than 6.5		
		Ac	Re	Ac	Re	Ac	Re	Ac	Re	Ac	Re	Ac	Re	Ac	Re	Ac	Re	Ac	Re	Ac	Re	Ac	Re	Ac	Re	Ac	Re	Ac	Re	Ac	Re	Ac	Re	Ac	Re	
Single	200	▽		0	1	Use Letter K		Use Letter N		Use Letter M		1	2	2	3	3	4	5	6	7	8	8	9	10	11	12	13	14	15	18	19	21	22	△		200
Double	125	▽		*								0	2	0	3	1	4	2	5	3	7	3	7	5	9	6	10	7	11	9	14	11	16	△		125
	250											1	2	3	4	4	5	6	7	8	9	11	12	12	13	15	16	18	19	23	24	26	27			250
Multiple	50	▽		*								#	2	#	2	#	3	#	4	0	4	0	4	0	5	0	6	1	7	1	8	2	9	△		50
	100											#	2	0	3	0	3	1	5	1	6	2	7	3	8	3	9	4	10	6	12	7	14			100
	150											0	2	0	3	1	4	2	6	3	8	4	9	6	10	7	12	8	13	11	17	13	19			150
	200											0	3	1	4	2	5	3	7	5	10	6	11	8	13	10	15	12	17	16	22	19	25			200
	250											1	3	2	4	3	6	5	8	7	11	9	12	11	15	14	17	17	20	22	25	25	29			250
	300											1	3	3	5	4	6	7	9	10	12	12	14	14	17	18	20	21	23	27	29	31	33			300
	350											2	3	4	5	6	7	9	10	13	14	14	15	18	19	21	22	25	26	32	33	37	38			350
		Less than 0.10		0.10		X		0.15		0.25		0.40		0.65		1.0		1.5		X		2.5		X		4.0		X		6.5		X		Higher than 6.5		
		Acceptable Quality Levels (tightened inspection)																																		

△ = Use next preceding sample size code letter for which acceptance and rejection numbers are available.

▽ = Use next subsequent sample size code letter for which acceptance and rejection numbers are available.

Ac = Acceptance number

Re = Rejection number

* = Use single sampling plan above (or alternatively use letter P).

\# = Acceptance not permitted at this sample size.

L

TABLE X-M—Tables for sample size code letter: M

CHART M - OPERATING CHARACTERISTIC CURVES FOR SINGLE SAMPLING PLANS

(Curves for double and multiple sampling are matched as closely as practicable)

PERCENT OF LOTS EXPECTED TO BE ACCEPTED (P_a)

(Chart with vertical axis 100, 90, 80, 70, 60, 50, 40, 30, 20, 10, 0 and horizontal axis 1.0 to 10.0; curves labeled 0.040, 0.15, 0.25, 0.40, 0.65, 1.0, 1.5, 2.5, 4.0)

QUALITY OF SUBMITTED LOTS (p, in percent defective for AQL's $\leqslant 10$; in defects per hundred units for AQL's > 10)

Note: Figures on curves are Acceptable Quality Levels (AQL's) for normal inspection.

TABLE X-M-1 - TABULATED VALUES FOR OPERATING CHARACTERSTIC CURVES FOR SINGLE SAMPLING PLANS

P_a	Acceptable Quality Levels (normal inspection)											
	0.040	0.15	0.25	0.40	0.65	1.0	✕	1.5	✕	2.5	✕	4.0
	p (in percent defective or in defects per hundred units)											
99.0	0.0032	0.047	0.138	0.261	0.566	0.922	1.11	1.51	1.94	2.38	3.28	3.99
95.0	0.0163	0.112	0.259	0.433	0.829	1.26	1.49	1.96	2.44	2.94	3.95	4.73
90.0	0.0333	0.168	0.349	0.533	1.00	1.48	1.72	2.23	2.75	3.27	4.34	5.16
75.0	0.0914	0.305	0.580	0.804	1.34	1.89	2.17	2.74	3.31	3.89	5.05	5.93
50.0	0.220	0.532	0.848	1.17	1.80	2.43	2.75	3.39	4.02	4.66	5.93	6.88
25.0	0.440	0.854	1.24	1.62	2.36	3.07	3.43	4.13	4.83	5.52	6.90	7.92
10.0	0.731	1.23	1.69	2.12	2.94	3.74	4.13	4.89	5.65	6.39	7.86	8.95
5.0	0.951	1.51	2.00	2.46	3.34	4.17	4.58	5.38	6.17	6.95	8.47	9.60
1.0	1.46	2.11	2.67	3.19	4.16	5.08	5.53	6.40	7.25	8.08	9.71	10.9
	0.065	0.25	0.40	0.65	1.0	1.5	✕	2.5	✕	4.0	✕	
	Acceptable Quality Levels (tightened inspection)											

Note: All values given in above table based on Poisson distribution as an approximation to the Binomial.

M

405

TABLE X-M-2 – SAMPLING PLANS FOR SAMPLE SIZE CODE LETTER: M

Acceptable Quality Levels (normal inspection). Each cell shows **Ac Re** (acceptance number / rejection number).

Type of sampling plan	Cum. sample size	Less than 0.040	0.040	0.065	0.10	0.15	0.25	0.40	0.65	1.0	1.5	2.5	4.0	Higher than 4.0
Single	315	▽	0 1	Use Letter L	Use Letter P	1 2	2 3	3 4	5 6	7 8	10 11	14 15	21 22	△
Double	200	▽	•	(Use Letter L)	(Use Letter P)	0 2	0 3	1 4	2 5	3 7	5 9	7 11	11 16	△
	400					1 2	3 4	4 5	6 7	8 9	12 13	18 19	26 27	
Multiple	80	▽	•	(Use Letter L)	(Use Letter P)	# 2	# 2	# 3	# 4	0 4	0 5	1 7	2 9	△
	160					# 2	0 3	1 4	1 5	2 6	3 8	4 10	7 14	
	240					0 2	0 3	2 4	3 6	4 8	6 10	8 13	13 19	
	320					0 3	1 4	3 5	5 7	6 11	8 13	12 17	19 25	
	400					1 3	2 4	4 6	7 8	9 11	11 15	17 20	25 29	
	480					1 3	3 5	5 6	9 10	12 12	14 17	21 23	31 33	
	560					2 3	4 5	6 7	9 13	14 14	18 19	25 26	37 38	

Acceptable Quality Levels (tightened inspection): Less than 0.065 | 0.065 | 0.10 | 0.15 | 0.25 | 0.40 | 0.65 | 1.0 | 1.5 | 2.5 | 4.0 | Higher than 4.0 (columns shifted one position; extreme cells marked ⤬).

△ = Use next preceding sample size code letter for which acceptance and rejection numbers are available.

▽ = Use next subsequent sample size code letter for which acceptance and rejection numbers are available.

Ac = Acceptance number.

Re = Rejection number.

• = Use single sampling plan above (or alternatively use letter O).

= Acceptance not permitted at this sample size.

M

TABLE X-N—Tables for sample size code letter: N

CHART N - OPERATING CHARACTERISTIC CURVES FOR SINGLE SAMPLING PLANS
(Curves for double and multiple sampling are matched as closely as practicable)

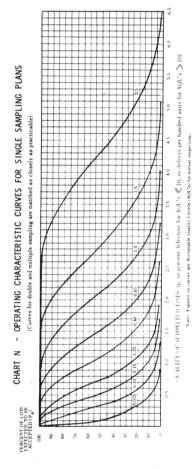

PERCENT OF LOTS EXPECTED TO BE ACCEPTED (P_a)

QUALITY OF SUBMITTED LOTS (p, in percent defective for AQL's ≤ 10; in defects per hundred units for AQL's > 10)

Note: Figures on curves are Acceptable Quality Levels (AQL's) for normal inspection.

TABLE X-N-1 - TABULATED VALUES FOR OPERATING CHARACTERISTIC CURVES FOR SINGLE SAMPLING PLANS

P_a	Acceptable Quality Levels (normal inspection)											
	0.025	0.10	0.15	0.25	0.40	0.65	1.0	X	1.5	X	2.5	2.5
	p (in percent defective or in defects per hundred units)											
99.0	0.0020	0.030	0.087	0.165	0.357	0.581	0.701	0.954	1.22	1.50	2.07	2.51
95.0	0.0103	0.071	0.164	0.273	0.523	0.796	0.919	1.23	1.54	1.85	2.49	2.98
90.0	0.0210	0.106	0.220	0.349	0.630	0.931	1.09	1.40	1.73	2.06	2.73	3.25
75.0	0.0576	0.192	0.345	0.507	0.844	1.19	1.37	1.72	2.08	2.45	3.18	3.74
50.0	0.139	0.336	0.535	0.734	1.13	1.53	1.73	2.13	2.53	2.93	3.73	4.33
25.0	0.277	0.539	0.784	1.02	1.48	1.94	2.16	2.60	3.04	3.48	4.35	4.99
10.0	0.461	0.778	1.06	1.34	1.86	2.35	2.60	3.08	3.56	4.03	4.95	5.64
5.0	0.599	0.949	1.26	1.55	2.10	2.63	2.89	3.39	3.89	4.38	5.34	6.05
1.0	0.921	1.328	1.68	2.01	2.62	3.20	3.48	4.03	4.56	5.09	6.12	6.87
		0.040	0.15	0.25	0.40	0.65	1.0	X	1.5	X	2.5	X
	Acceptable Quality Levels (tightened inspection)											

Note: All values given in above table based on Poisson distribution as an approximation to the Binomial

N

407

TABLE X-N-2 – SAMPLING PLANS FOR SAMPLE SIZE CODE LETTER: N

Acceptable Quality Levels (normal inspection) — values given as Ac|Re

Type of sampling plan	Cumulative sample size	Less than 0.025	0.025	0.040	0.065	0.10	0.15	0.25	0.40	0.65	1.0	1.5	2.5	Higher than 2.5
Single	500	▽	0|1	Use Letter M	Use Letter P	1|2	2|3	3|4	5|6	7|8	10|11	14|15	21|22	△
Double	315	▽	•			0|2	0|3	1|4	2|5	3|7	5|9	7|11	11|16	△
Double	630					1|2	3|4	4|5	6|7	8|9	12|13	18|19	26|27	
Multiple	125	▽	•		Q	#|2	#|2	#|3	0|4	0|4	0|5	1|7	2|9	△
Multiple	250					#|2	0|2	0|3	1|5	1|6	3|8	4|10	7|14	
Multiple	375					0|2	0|3	1|4	2|6	3|8	6|10	8|13	13|19	
Multiple	500					0|3	1|3	2|5	3|7	5|10	8|13	12|17	19|25	
Multiple	625					1|3	2|4	3|6	5|8	7|11	11|15	17|20	25|29	
Multiple	750					1|3	3|5	4|6	7|9	10|12	14|17	21|25	31|33	
Multiple	875					2|3	4|5	6|7	9|10	13|14	18|21	25|26	37|38	

Acceptable Quality Levels (tightened inspection):

0.040	0.065	0.10	0.15	0.25	0.40	0.65	1.0	1.5	2.5	Higher than 2.5

△ = Use next preceding sample size code letter for which acceptance and rejection numbers are available.

▽ = Use next subsequent sample size code letter for which acceptance and rejection numbers are available.

Ac = Acceptance number

Re = Rejection number

• = Use single sampling plan above (or alternatively use letter R).

= Acceptance not permitted at this sample size.

N

408

TABLE X-P—Tables for sample size code letter: P

CHART P - OPERATING CHARACTERISTIC CURVES FOR SINGLE SAMPLING PLANS

(Curves for double and multiple sampling are matched as closely as practicable)

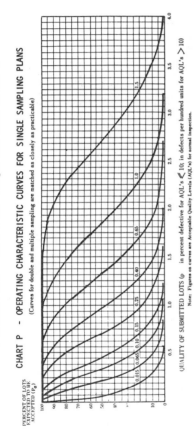

PERCENT OF LOTS EXPECTED TO BE ACCEPTED (P_a)

QUALITY OF SUBMITTED LOTS (p, in percent defective for AQL's $\leq$ 10; in defects per hundred units for AQL's $>$ 10)

Note: Figures on curves are Acceptable Quality Levels (AQL's) for normal inspection.

TABLE X-P-1 - TABULATED VALUES FOR OPERATING CHARACTERISTIC CURVES FOR SINGLE SAMPLING PLANS

P_a	0.015	0.065	0.10	0.15	0.25	0.40	0.65	X	1.0	X	1.5
	p (in percent defective or defects per hundred units)										
99.0	0.0013	0.0186	0.055	0.103	0.223	0.363	0.596	0.762	0.935	1.29	1.57
95.0	0.0064	0.0444	0.102	0.171	0.327	0.498	0.771	0.961	1.16	1.56	1.86
90.0	0.0131	0.0665	0.138	0.218	0.394	0.582	0.878	1.08	1.29	1.71	2.03
75.0	0.0360	0.120	0.216	0.317	0.527	0.745	1.08	1.30	1.53	1.99	2.34
50.0	0.0866	0.210	0.334	0.459	0.709	0.959	1.33	1.58	1.83	2.33	2.71
25.0	0.173	0.337	0.490	0.639	0.928	1.21	1.63	1.90	2.18	2.72	3.12
10.0	0.288	0.486	0.665	0.835	1.16	1.47	1.93	2.22	2.52	3.09	3.52
5.0	0.375	0.593	0.787	0.969	1.31	1.64	2.12	2.43	2.74	3.34	3.78
1.0	0.576	0.830	1.05	1.26	1.64	2.00	2.52	2.85	3.18	3.82	4.29
	0.025	0.10	0.15	0.25	0.40	0.65	X	1.0	X	1.5	X

Acceptable Quality Levels (normal inspection) — top header row

Acceptable Quality Levels (tightened inspection) — bottom header row

Note: All values given in above table based on Poisson distribution as an approximation to the Binomial.

P

409

TABLE X-P-2 – SAMPLING PLANS FOR SAMPLE SIZE CODE LETTER: P

Acceptable Quality Levels (normal inspection)

Type of sampling plan	Cumulative sample size	0.010	0.015 (Ac Re)	0.025	0.040	0.065 (Ac Re)	0.10 (Ac Re)	0.15 (Ac Re)	0.25 (Ac Re)	0.40 (Ac Re)	0.65 (Ac Re)	1.0 (Ac Re)	1.5 (Ac Re)	Higher than 1.5
Single	800	▽	0 1	Use Letter N	Use Letter Q	1 2	2 3	3 4	5 6	7 8	11 12	14 15	21 22	△
Double	500	▽	•	Use Letter R	Use Letter Q	0 2	0 3	1 4	2 5	3 7	5 9	7 11	11 16	△
	1000					1 2	3 4	4 5	6 7	8 9	12 13	18 19	26 27	
Multiple	200	▽	•			* 2	* 2	* 3	* 4	0 4	0 5	1 7	2 9	△
	400					* 2	0 3	0 3	1 5	1 6	3 8	4 10	7 14	
	600					0 2	0 3	1 4	2 6	3 8	7 12	8 13	13 19	
	800					0 3	1 4	2 5	3 7	5 10	10 15	12 17	19 25	
	1000					1 3	2 4	3 6	5 8	7 11	14 17	17 20	25 29	
	1200					1 3	3 5	4 6	7 9	10 12	18 20	21 23	31 33	
	1400					2 3	4 5	6 7	9 10	13 14	21 22	25 26	37 38	

Acceptable Quality Levels (tightened inspection)

	Less than 0.025	0.025	0.040	0.065	0.10	0.15	0.25	0.40	0.65	1.0	1.5	Higher than 1.5

△ = Use next preceding sample size code letter for which acceptance and rejection numbers are available.

▽ = Use next subsequent sample size code letter for which acceptance and rejection numbers are available.

Ac = Acceptance number.

Re = Rejection number.

• = Use single sampling plan above.

* = Acceptance not permitted at this sample size.

P

TABLE X-Q—Tables for sample size code letter: Q

CHART Q - OPERATING CHARACTERISTIC CURVES FOR SINGLE SAMPLING PLANS

(Curves for double and multiple sampling are matched as closely as practicable)

QUALITY OF SUBMITTED LOTS (p, in percent defective for AQL's ≤ 10; in defects per hundred units for AQL's > 10)

Note: Figures on curves are Acceptable Quality Levels (AQL's) for normal inspection)

TABLE X-Q-1 - TABULATED VALUES FOR OPERATING CHARACTERISTIC CURVES FOR SINGLE SAMPLING PLANS

P_a	Acceptable Quality Levels (normal inspection)													
	0.010	0.040	0.065	0.10	0.15	0.25	0.40	0.65		1.0
	p (in percent defective or defects per hundred units)									
99.0	0.00081	0.0119	0.0349	0.0656	0.143	0.232	0.382	0.598	X	1.01
95.0	0.00410	0.0284	0.0654	0.109	0.209	0.318	0.494	0.740	0.828	1.19
90.0	0.00840	0.0426	0.0882	0.140	0.252	0.372	0.562	0.824	0.995	1.30
75.0	0.0230	0.0769	0.138	0.203	0.338	0.476	0.690	0.979	1.09	1.49
50.0	0.0554	0.134	0.214	0.294	0.454	0.614	0.853	1.17	1.27	1.73
25.0	0.111	0.215	0.314	0.409	0.594	0.775	1.04	1.39	1.49	2.00
10.0	0.184	0.310	0.426	0.534	0.742	0.942	1.23	1.61	1.74	2.25
5.0	0.240	0.380	0.504	0.620	0.841	1.05	1.36	1.75	1.98	2.42
1.0	0.368	0.531	0.672	0.804	1.05	1.28	1.61	1.83	2.14	2.75
	0.015	0.065	0.10	0.15	0.25	X	0.40	0.65	X	2.45
	Acceptable Quality Levels (tightened inspection)								1.0	X

Note: All values given in above table based on Poisson distribution as an approximation to the Binomial

411

TABLE X-Q-2 — SAMPLING PLANS FOR SAMPLE SIZE CODE LETTER: Q

Acceptable Quality Levels (normal inspection)

Type of sampling plan	Cumulative sample size	0.010 Ac	0.010 Re	0.015	0.025	0.040 Ac	0.040 Re	0.065 Ac	0.065 Re	0.10 Ac	0.10 Re	0.15 Ac	0.15 Re	0.25 Ac	0.25 Re	0.40 Ac	0.40 Re	0.65 Ac	0.65 Re	1.0 Ac	1.0 Re	Higher than 1.0 Ac	Higher than 1.0 Re
Single	1250	0	1	Use Letter R	Use Letter R	1	2	2	3	3	4	5	6	7	8	10	11	14	15	21	22	Δ	
Double	800	•		Use Letter P	Use Letter S	0	2	0	3	1	4	2	5	3	7	5	9	7	11	11	16	Δ	
Double	1600					1	2	3	4	4	5	6	7	8	9	12	13	18	19	26	27		
Multiple	315	•		Use Letter P	Use Letter S	*	2	*	2	*	3	*	4	0	4	0	5	1	7	2	9	Δ	
Multiple	630					*	2	0	3	0	3	1	5	1	6	3	8	4	10	7	14		
Multiple	945					0	2	0	3	1	4	2	6	3	8	6	10	8	13	13	19		
Multiple	1260					0	3	1	4	2	5	3	7	5	10	8	13	12	17	19	25		
Multiple	1575					1	3	2	4	3	6	5	8	7	11	11	15	17	20	25	29		
Multiple	1890					1	3	3	5	4	6	7	9	10	12	14	17	21	23	31	33		
Multiple	2205					2	3	4	5	6	7	9	10	13	14	18	19	25	26	37	38		

Tightened inspection AQLs (read across the same columns): 0.010 | 0.015 | 0.025 | 0.040 | 0.065 | 0.10 | 0.15 | 0.25 | 0.40 | 0.65 | Higher than 1.0

Acceptable Quality Levels (tightened inspection)

Δ = Use next preceding sample size code letter for which acceptance and rejection numbers are available.
Ac = Acceptance number
Re = Rejection number
• = Use single sampling plan above.
* = Acceptance not permitted at this sample size.

Q

TABLE X-R—Tables for sample size code letter: R

CHART R - OPERATING CHARACTERISTIC CURVES FOR SINGLE SAMPLING PLANS

(Curves for double and multiple sampling are matched as closely as practicable)

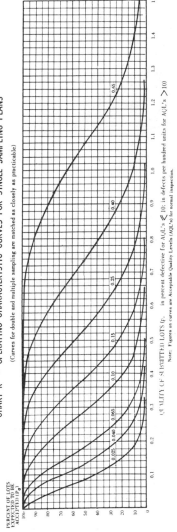

PERCENT OF LOTS EXPECTED TO BE ACCEPTED (Pₐ)

QUALITY OF SUBMITTED LOTS (p, in percent defective for AQL's ≤ 10; in defects per hundred units for AQL's > 10)

Note: Figures on curves are Acceptable Quality Levels (AQL's) for normal inspection.

TABLE X-R-1 - TABULATED VALUES FOR OPERATING CHARACTERISTIC CURVES FOR SINGLE SAMPLING PLANS

P_a	Acceptable Quality Levels (normal inspection)												
	0.025	0.040	0.065	0.10	0.15	0.25	0.40	0.65	1.0				0.65
	p (in percent defective or defects per hundred units)												
99.0	0.0074	0.0218	0.0412	0.0892	0.145	0.175	0.239	0.305	0.374	0.517	X		0.629
95.0	0.0178	0.0409	0.0683	0.131	0.199	0.235	0.309	0.385	0.462	0.622			0.745
90.0	0.0266	0.0551	0.0873	0.158	0.233	0.272	0.351	0.432	0.515	0.684			0.812
75.0	0.0481	0.0868	0.127	0.211	0.298	0.342	0.431	0.521	0.612	0.795			0.934
50.0	0.0839	0.134	0.184	0.284	0.384	0.433	0.533	0.633	0.733	0.933			1.08
25.0	0.115	0.196	0.256	0.371	0.484	0.540	0.651	0.761	0.870	1.09			1.25
10.0	0.195	0.266	0.334	0.464	0.589	0.650	0.770	0.889	1.01	1.24			1.41
5.0	0.237	0.315	0.388	0.526	0.657	0.722	0.848	0.972	1.09	1.33			1.51
1.0	0.332	0.420	0.502	0.655	0.800	0.870	1.02	1.14	1.27	1.53			1.72
	0.040	0.065	0.10	0.15	0.25	0.40	0.65	1.0		0.40	0.65	X	
	Acceptable Quality Levels (tightened inspection)												

Note: All values given in above table based on Poisson distribution as an approximation to the Binomial

TABLE X-R-2 – SAMPLING PLANS FOR SAMPLE SIZE CODE LETTER: R

Each data cell below shows the pair **Ac Re** (acceptance number, rejection number).

Type of sampling plan	Cumulative sample size	\<— Acceptable Quality Levels (normal inspection) —\>										
		0.010	0.015	0.025	0.040	0.065	0.10	0.15	0.25	0.40	0.65	Higher than 0.65
Single	2000	0 1		1 2	2 3	3 4	5 6	7 8	10 11	14 15	21 22	△
Double	1250	Use Letter Q	Use Letter P	Use Letter S	0 3	1 4	2 5	3 7	5 9	7 11	11 16	△
	2500	Q	P	S	3 4	4 5	6 7	8 9	12 13	18 19	26 27	
Multiple	500				* 2	* 3	* 4	0 4	0 5	1 7	2 9	△
	1000				* 2	0 3	1 5	1 6	3 8	4 10	7 14	
	1500				0 2	1 4	2 6	3 8	6 10	8 13	13 19	
	2000				0 3	2 5	3 7	5 10	8 13	12 17	19 25	
	2500				1 3	3 6	5 8	7 11	11 15	17 20	25 29	
	3000				1 3	4 6	7 9	10 12	14 17	21 23	31 33	
	3500				2 3	6 7	9 10	13 14	18 19	25 26	37 38	

Acceptable Quality Levels (tightened inspection) — read one column to the left of the corresponding normal‑inspection heading:

0.010	0.015	0.025	0.040	0.065	0.10	0.15	0.25	0.40	0.65	Higher than 0.65

Legend:

△ = Use next preceding sample size code letter for which acceptance and rejection numbers are available.

Ac = Acceptance number.

Re = Rejection number.

● = Use single sampling plan above.

✱ = Acceptance not permitted at this sample size.

R

414

TABLE X-S—Tables for sample size code letter: S

Type of sampling plan	Cumulative sample size	Acceptable Quality Level (normal inspection)	
		Ac	Re
Single	3150	1	2
Double	2000	0	2
	4000	1	2
Multiple	800	#	2
	1600	#	2
	2400	0	2
	3200	0	3
	4000	1	3
	4800	1	3
	5600	2	3
		Acceptable Quality Level (tightened inspection)	0.025

Ac = Acceptance number

Re = Rejection number

= Acceptance not permitted at this sample size.

Copies of this standard may be obtained by directing requests to:

Commanding Officer
U.S. Naval Supply Depot
ATTN: Code DMD
5801 Tabor Avenue
Philadelphia 20, Pennsylvania

Copies of this Military Standard may be obtained for other than official use by individuals, firms, and contractors from the Superintendent of Documents, U.S. Government Printing Office, Washington 25, D. C.

Both the title and identifying symbol number should be stipulated when requesting copies of Military Standards.

Custodians:

Army - Munitions Command
Navy - Bureau of Weapons
Air Force - Air Force Logistics Command
Defense Supply Agency

Preparing Activity:

Army - Munitions Command

417

Index

419